THE
AMIENS
RAID

SECRETS REVEALED

Dr Jean-Pierre Ducellier

Edited and with additional
research and text
by
Simon W Parry

First published 2011.
Red Kite
PO Box 223, Walton-on-Thames,
Surrey, KT12 3YQ
England

Purchase this and other Red Kite books directly from the Red Kite website;

www.redkitebooks.co.uk

Based on the book
Les secrets du bombardment
de la prison d'Amiens.
© Jean-Pierre Ducellier 2002

© English text Simon W Parry 2011

Cover design by Mark Postlethwaite GAvA

Printed by
Dimograf, Sp. Z o. o. Poland

ISBN   9780955473524

This book is dedicated to the memory of all the victims of the 'Amiens Raid' and associated incidents that took place on Friday 18th February 1944.

THE AMIENS LEGEND

Eighteen Mosquitos racing over the
snow-covered French countryside...
their target... Amiens prison.
Their task... to break down the prison walls
and give 120 resistance fighters a chance
to escape before they face execution
the next day.
Heading the desperate rescue attempt;
war-time film star Group Captain Pickard.
Operation Jericho is under way...

Or so the legend goes...

CONTENTS

EDITOR'S NOTE

The work of Jean-Pierre Ducellier first came to my attention when researching air combat in the Somme region of France. He is the author of several comprehensive monographs covering specific days during which air raids and air combats took place in the Somme and specifically the Doullens and Amiens area. Later, while making a television documentary with M. Ducellier, he showed me his files on the Amiens Prison raid and I was instantly taken with the detail of his work. Having interviewed many of the inhabitants of Amiens and the surrounding area, as well as some members of the Resistance he had been able to create a minute-by-minute account of the attack itself, something that not even the RAF had been able to do.

Over dinner he explained to me that there was far more to the attack than a simple, if noble, attempt to free condemned prisoners. The story he told was wildly at variance to the one I had always believed to be historical fact and I expressed my belief that an English version of his book on the raid should be published. To my surprise M. Ducellier was sceptical, 'The English do not want to know the real story,' he said, 'You like the heroic legend.'

I agreed that an English edition would look very different to the French book, but that the findings and spirit of his work would remain unchanged, whether it showed the Allies in a good light - or not. The time for the true story to be told had surely arrived after so many years.

As part of the editing process, I scoured the National Archives to double check the translations and document sources. During this research, I discovered a lot of new material that had not been available to Dr Ducellier at the time of his investigation. I have therefore included all of this new information and modified some of the chapters accordingly.

Production Team

Editor - Simon W Parry

Design - Mark Postlethwaite

Translation - Julian Even-Hart, Martine Gourlain, Nicola, Ann and David Iles.

Additional assistance - Pierre Ben, Robert Lyon, Frank Philipson, Adam Robinson, Chris Lethbridge, Barry York, Christine Hamill, Tom Willis, E B 'Ted' Sismore - Air Commodore (Rtd).

Foreword

In 1944, the air war raged above northern France. As I was less than one year old at the time, I have no recollection of these events myself. I had been living with my grandparents in the village of Lucheux, about 40 kilometres north of Amiens, since the latter part of 1943. The cataclysmic events of the war and the devastation of lives and cities around me totally escaped my perception at the time. However, a few years later, the environment created by these times and the memories passed down to me by people who remembered these experiences would make a distinct and deep impression upon me. I will always remember their accounts of the aerial combats that took place above our villages. Many aircraft crashed in the vicinity and pieces of aircraft fell all around Lucheux, including the occasional drop tank shed by Allied fighter planes. These wartime artefacts were eagerly collected by my brothers and I can still picture them today. I recall accounts of Allied fighters literally hedgehopping at low level up the slopes, and banking sharply to avoid the tall trees. On one Sunday in 1944, the Allied aircraft were not so lucky: I was told about two Flying Fortresses that had been hit by German anti-aircraft fire and disintegrated in the air; debris whirled down and was smashed upon impact. One bomber had a wing torn off and this floated down like a flapping sheet in the wind, falling eventually to the ground near the village of Bouquemaison. Such accounts will remain with me forever.

Another account was one given by my aunt, Germaine Daussin, who was then living at 4 rue Louis Braille in the St-Pierre district of Amiens. This was of my brother Henri gathering up his 'valuables' on 18th February 1944, just as the first bomb explosions could be heard. Such recollections have become firmly implanted in my memory and were responsible for stimulating my original desire to find out just what had happened on this date.

Some years ago, during one of my first visits to The National Archives in London, I managed to gather together a small amount of documentation relating to the raid that my brother and aunt witnessed. However, on this occasion I was rather more preoccupied with the search for records relating to the town of Doullens and its surroundings in the spring and summer of 1944. I therefore decided to return on another day to dedicate more time to research the Amiens Prison Raid.

Whilst looking for information on this mission with my colleague Pierre Ben, I realized that there were still some very large gaps in my research. Moreover, certain details did not correspond with the documentary evidence that I knew of, and bore little similarity to what has been accepted as historic 'fact'. It was then that I decided to concentrate on the raid of 18th February 1944 in far more detail; in fact, I would now invest all my spare time in this research. This would involve a return visit to London and trips to just about anywhere else that information could be found.

I had no illusions as to the difficulties of getting the information I needed to investigate in depth and often refute, or at least challenge, the officially accepted version. I was determined that, whatever the details discovered, they would not be presented in the accepted form that has so often been published before. It was therefore hardly a surprise to discover that the official history of the raid published in 1944 seemed to have no bearing on the actions that took place that day according to other sources. What was a surprise though, was that, as I dug deeper, more and more discrepancies from the standard and accepted portrayal of this mission came to light. It seemed that even Group Captain Pickard's actions and the associated records had been modified to fit in with what was then deemed to be acceptable. Therefore RAF records, whilst helpful, did not give the accuracy I desired. However, the conclusions drawn from my research seemed to leave little margin for error or alternative theories. The scale of revelations seemed to grow throughout the research as it became clear just how critical this attack had been to the war effort and it became increasingly difficult to believe that Group Captain Pickard himself had actually attacked the prison; this alone is some considerable departure from the 'officially' accepted version of events. Such revelations did not stop there; incredibly that much-used code name for the raid 'Operation Jericho' did not exist prior to, or even at the time of, the raid; it was conjured up for a post-war film.

I believe the meticulous research methods used for this book, and therefore the depth of detail, finally reveal the truth about the legendary Amiens Prison Raid.

Many of the wartime documents studied do not actually mention the prison at Amiens but, as explained by several wartime operations staff who were interviewed, the Allies regularly used 'Special Means' to disguise potential targets. Diffusion of rumours, messages and general distortion of information all helped create what is now called 'misinformation'. Such actions make it all the more difficult for the modern-day investigator. Throughout the research, all events and actions have been closely analysed; it seems that the attack on Amiens Prison was as exposed to wartime distortion as other operations of the time. However, one can find many subtleties that simply lead to a suspicion about factors that can never be verified. Some conclusions must be left to the reader to interpret. I kindly ask the reader to forgive the complex nature of some chapters; however, this level of complexity is essential to the understanding of this astonishing attack.

Jean-Pierre Ducellier, Lucheux, France

AIR ACTIVITY AROUND AMIENS 1940-1944

After the occupation, there followed the expansion and development of airfields such as Barly, Remaisnil, Amiens, Glisy, Rosieres-Ensanterre, Poix-de Picardie, Abbeville and Drucat. These airfields, along with many others in the Pas-de-Calais and northern France, gave the Luftwaffe forward bases from which to attack England. The oncoming battle would be fought largely over the Channel and the English mainland, but preparations led to a massive increase in aerial activity for northern France. Many new types of aircraft appeared in the skies: Heinkel He111s, Junkers Ju88s, Messerschmitt Bf110s and the strangely crank-winged Stuka. To the French, it seemed the huge formations of aircraft were invincible as they began gathering to attack England. Sometimes however, impressions of supposed invincibility were shattered.

Even though the Luftwaffe's attempt to defeat the RAF and gain aerial superiority eventually failed, numerous German aircraft flew over at night in 'The Blitz'. On 27th December 1940, a German bomber in difficulty dropped its bomb load over Lucheaux. Approximately fifty incendiary bombs scattered over the village: fortunately, the only damage caused was by one bomb that penetrated the roof of a house and started a fire. The fire was fought by a neighbour and the author's parents, who doused it with water. The explosion caused by water hitting the phosphorous only served to fuel the blaze. Fortunately, under the protective cloches in my grandmother's vegetable garden lay some soft, unfrozen, soil and this was used to smother the flames.

From here on restrictions imposed on civilians began to increase, coinciding with a reduction in Luftwaffe activity in this area. In Lucheaux and the surrounding districts the German soldiers began to repaint their vehicles before departing in huge numbers; they were heading for Russia and the horrors of the Eastern Front.

By late 1942, the American 8th Air Force began to make an appearance in the skies, firstly the famous B-17 shortly followed by the B-24 Liberator. Soon they became involved in the increasingly heavy aerial bombing, the local Luftwaffe aerodromes of Amiens, Glisy, Poix-de-Picardie, Abbeville and Drucat and the aviation factories at Méaulte all came in for serious attention. On 6th September 1942, a B-17 Flying Fortress, one of the first to be shot down over France, crashed returning from a raid on Méaulte. The disintegrating wreckage fell in fields close to the village of Saint-vast-en-Chausseé, just north of Amiens.

The raids continued into 1943, with a noticeable increase in American bombers during the day and RAF bombers passing over the Somme region at night. The Allies'

Towards the end of 1943, the Amiens area saw a marked increase in German activity as they began constructing launch sites for the new V-1 flying bombs.

attention seemed to be mainly directed at the German industrial heartland. Combats between the Luftwaffe and USAAF / RAF in the skies above the Somme and Pas-de-Calais became commonplace as the Allied fighters attempted to protect the bombers. People frequently stopped work to watch the vicious dog fighting.

At the end of 1943, the Germans began to build mysterious and massive concrete structures at Watten, Wizernes and Éperlecques, with smaller ones all over the Pas-de-Calais and lower Seine districts. These were to be the so-called 'ski sites' for the launching of Germany's latest technical innovation, the V-1 flying bomb. Numerous faulty launches and the strange shape of the buildings began to attract attention from Allied photographic reconnaissance aircraft that were often spotted. During November and December 1943 there seemed to be a massive increase in attacks on such bases. In the Amiens area, several ski sites appeared and necessitated the arrival of many technical staff as well as prisoners who were used, amongst other things, as labourers. The sites near Amiens were at: Beauvoir, Bonnières, le Meillard, Agenvillers, Domart/Flixecourt, Gorenflos, Ailly-le-haut-Clocher, Béhen, Longuemort, Marquenneville, Moyenneville, Croisette, Vacquerie-Le-Bouc, Vacqueriette, St-Josse, Campagne-lès-Hesdin, Raye-sur-Authie, Montorgueil, Ligescourt, Petite-Bois-de-Tillencourt, Maison-Ponthieu, Yvrench/Bois Carré and Yvrencheux.

Some of the first raids by B-17s were at V-1 sites in Beauvoir and Bonnières. These attacks greatly impressed the residents of Doullens. One of the heaviest raids took place on 24th December 1943, destroying several V-1 launch sites in the Pas-de-Calais. This involved 670 four engined bombers escorted by 541 fighters.

In late 1943, local residents spotted a new type of American aircraft, the B-26 Marauder operating with the 9th Air Force. On 31st December 1943, bombs dropped on the adjacent V-1 site shook the small village of Lucheaux. At 2pm, a formation of 18 of these twin-engined aircraft approached the site, at first just specks in the sky, then a distant drum of engines followed by colossal bomb bursts. Bombs fell away from the bellies of the approaching planes, visible for all to see. The name 'Marauder' appeared to both the locals and Germans to be a very appropriate name for this aeroplane. On this occasion, many bombs fell to the north of the village and exploded in the north-eastern edge of a wood. Another group of Marauders from the 387th Bomb Group then raided a V-1 site at Montorgueil, some 24 kilometers north-west of Lucheaux; however, again many bombs fell harmlessly in woodland.

The first real aerial drama that the population of Doullens experienced came on 1st January 1944. Local workmen were forced to undertake construction and repair work on the V-1 site at Beauvoir when, unfortunately, the site was chosen as a target for that day. Many workmen were killed during the raid.

On 6th January 1944, a 'Rhubarb' operation using Typhoon 1bs of No.1 Squadron on the V-1 site at Vacquerie-Le-Bouc caused extensive damage. A large hangar near the hamlet of Ransart-Les-Doullens, that had been used by the Germans to store and assemble V-1s, was also targeted on this mission. Four 500lb bombs were dropped, three exploded beside the building and a fourth dropped straight through the roof but failed to explode. Residents of the town of Doullens and its outskirts were now getting very used to such lightning-fast attacks being delivered on V-1 sites in their area.

On the following night, two 500lb bombs fell and exploded on the Thievet and Tempez Farms along the road to Arras. This was not the intended target, as only arable fields were located there. It would seem that a Mosquito from 418 Squadron was returning from an intruder mission to Rambouillet and was caught in German searchlights. In order to take evasive action, it had been necessary to jettison the two under-slung bombs to gain speed. Fortunately, the Mosquito, now much lightened, belted away at high speed across the area and vanished into the darkness.

7th January 1944 saw the return of American bombers passing overhead and droning on into Germany. Locals witnessed the Luftwaffe fighters attacking the massed formations, one combat resulting in a Luftwaffe fighter being shot down overhead. With its fuselage disintegrating and in flames, the unidentified fighter spiralled down and smashed into the farm of Alfred Laigle. M. Laigle, who was Mayor of Outrebois at the time, watched as the resulting fire consumed several of his farm buildings.

A continued heavy assault was launched against the V-1 sites and on 14th January 1944 a total of 552 four engined American bombers escorted by 645 fighters laid waste to a total of 21 such sites. On 21st January 1944, 792 four engined bombers and 628 fighters raided V-1 sites in the Somme, Pas-de-Calais and Lower Seine regions.

Two Doullenaise, Paul Rovillain and Fernand Neuville, had a terrifying experience from which they had a very lucky escape on 23rd January 1944. Little in the way of vehicles could move those days without attracting the attention of marauding Allied fighters looking for any target of opportunity. On that Sunday morning, the two men were returning from the coalmines, their vehicle laden with coal, when their lorry broke down; however the fault was not serious and they quickly made repairs and continued. Further up the road they were joined by a German army truck, also going in the direction of Doullens. As they were travelling through the valley on the right-hand side of Lucheaux, two Spitfires passed overhead, climbing steeply, then banking and coming back. Just as the two vehicles approached a farm, both men noticed spouts of fragmented road surface and dust shooting up. Machine-gun bullets raced everywhere, ricocheting off the coal in the back and passing through the driver's cabin. The German truck in front caught the full force of the attack; as its tyres burst, it literally fell to pieces.

Paul Rovillain and Fernand Neuville immediately stopped their vehicle. Under the impact of the bullets, one of the cabin doors was torn off and the two men jumped out, rolling into a ditch. Absolutely terrified, they looked at the two planes above and then broke into a run, a run of the like they had never experienced before, desperate to reach cover of the farm outbuildings. The two Spitfires flew off, much to the relief of the two men, but Fernand Neuville's arm was soaked in blood. Fortunately, it was just a flesh wound; a bullet had passed close enough to graze the skin and left a small scar, but nothing serious. Back on the road several German soldiers were injured, one severely. The two pilots involved in this incident were Flight Lieutenant G. D. Robertson and Flying Officer P. A. McLachlan, both from 421 Squadron flying Spitfire IXs on an armed reconnaissance mission.

In February 1944, the raids continued. Hundreds of American bombers were seen flying overhead returning from raids on Germany. The railway complex at Amiens / Longueau was attacked in February by B-26 Marauders; however, the raid was unsuccessful due to inclement weather conditions. Another notable raid was conducted against the V-1 site at

Siracourt, which was attacked by 94 B-24 Liberators. After much aerial activity in the first half of February, there was a lull, most likely attributable to the damp misty and cloudy conditions. Snow came towards mid February, causing congestion on roads and an almost total cessation in flying activity over this region of northern France.

By 18th February, the weather had improved and the bombers returned. To the south of Doullens, several waves of Mosquitos were seen, hedgehopping as they skimmed over the flat fields. Their slipstreams caused the frozen twiggy treetops to waver and clatter; no one who saw these aircraft could guess what their target was. In just a few moments, the attack on Amiens Prison would start; an attack planned in the most meticulous detail and executed with great precision. The objective, as history records it, was to release more than one hundred prisoners who had been condemned to death and were due to be executed imminently. So, on that Friday, began one of the most famous and daring of low level attacks; its fame perpetuating until the present day. However, it also posed questions as soon as it had been completed and many more questions in the following years. Just what was the true purpose of this mission? Was it solely the release of important French Resistance prisoners; or was there a deeper, far more significant, purpose behind the attack on the prison at Amiens?

LOCAL RESISTANCE ORGANISATIONS AROUND AMIENS

From 1940, Amiens and its surrounding regions had been regarded by the British Intelligence agencies as an important Resistance strong point and, to some extent, the occupying Germans thought the same. Resistance activities were numerous and consequently, by late 1943, arrests were increasing, a factor noticed by British Intelligence. Although there were established Resistance networks operating in the area, there were probably many locals operating who were not linked to an official organization but who just wanted to harm the occupier. 'Resistance Activities' was an extremely broad term and it must not be forgotten that thousands of minor uncooperative actions by locals could also be classed as resistance: even if it was only wilfully being late delivering eggs to Glisy aerodrome.

There is evidence of some widespread Resistance networks in the Amiens area. One of the most prominent Resistance networks in this area was the 'Sosies' led by the Ponchardier brothers, Pierre and Dominique. Dominique, in particular, became inextricably linked with the Amiens Raid and its after-effects. There is also evidence for SOE agents and their W/T operators (known as 'Pianists') being present in the region.

PART ONE

THE FRENCH STORY

THE PRISON

The prison at Amiens had originally been built as a civilian penal facility. It was of a standard design, a central cruciform shaped building, surrounded by several small outbuildings all encompassed within a 7 metre high security wall. Built of blue-grey brick, it naturally looked very dowdy, bleak and imposing. It usually housed both male and female prisoners who had committed crimes such as petty theft, burglary, arson, and capital offences such as murder. Occasionally, executions had been carried out there, some using a guillotine that had to be brought all the way from Paris. However, from 1940, the fact that France was occupied by the Germans brought along a whole host of new categories of offence under both military and civil law. For example, after 1940, Amiens Prison housed prisoners who had been found guilty of crimes such as 'Resistance Activities' and 'Black-Marketeering'. The crimes of murder and 'serious resistance', though both capital offences, resulted in the offenders being shot rather than hanged or guillotined. The prison was only ever intended for short duration sentences and was not built to adequately house the numbers of inmates that came in later. Problems arising from this included overcrowding, prisoner neglect and poor administration; all aggravated by a very simple sanitary system. Amiens Prison was divided into French civilian and German military / political sections that were further subdivided into male and female quarters. However, these sub divisions were not rigid; space and other factors often meant that a certain prisoner category or type was temporarily housed in a non-relevant section. Further to this, local Gestapo and Milice* arrests were often not recorded or even reported to the administration. So, prisoners could find themselves in detention for weeks before they were processed. These Gestapo and Milice arrests make it difficult to ascertain an accurate figure for the number of prisoners present at any one time, including 18th February 1944. One must not forget that, although under German administration, the prison itself remained a French prison; having both French and German administrative and guard staff.

The Milice (French Militia) had been created in January 1943 by the Vichy Regime to aid the Gestapo combat the French Resistance. Members of the Milice participated in torture, executions and in rounding up Jews for 'transportation' and were considered more dangerous than their German counterparts as, being French themselves, they knew the country and its people.

INSIDER INFORMATION

It does appear that some information about the interior layout of the prison and experiences of interned prisoners had filtered to the outside as early as September 1943, but unfortunately it had not been sent to England. Under the organization and planning of Maurice Genest (known as 'Henri'), a railway worker and Resistance member imprisoned in Amiens, several ideas had been considered, the chief one being to cause a large explosion that would assist the release of prisoners. Unfortunately at least part of this plan to escape fell into the hands of the Gestapo: Roger Collerais, a Resistance member using the codename 'Serge', had part of the plan with him when he was arrested whilst in a café with other Resistance members near Amiens station. The arrest destroyed the possibility of any escape plan associated with 'Serge'. However these early vestigial escape plans had no connection with the Mosquito raid. Information on timings, the number of guards and their day-to-day routines was slowly leaking out of the prison and being carefully compiled.

Maurice Genest had started to work out a plan by evaluating the German presence within the prison. A document exists that appears to have been written on 17th September 1943 and contains hand written details on sheets of school paper. One section of this document indicates that the German team on duty during the day of 17th September 1943 only consisted of six people; a French-speaking woman of Prussian extraction, who was the guard for the women interned by the German authorities, an Adjutant, an interpreter, a warrant officer, and two Austrians.

It is possible that this document is incomplete, but it does seem likely that the German detachment at Amiens was minimal. Other documents mention two warrant officers by name (Hubert and Otto). However, four German soldiers were seen cycling to the prison at 22.00 hours each evening. They were armed with sub machine-guns and one machine-gun. They left the prison at 06.00 hours every morning. Estimates of the number of weapons held on site during the night indicated four to six revolvers, four to six rifles, four sub machine-guns and one machine-gun. It was reported that the German guards slept in a room in the administrative buildings and that, on average, four soldiers slept in the German dormitory at any one time, with one or two doing the rounds along the corridors in shifts. They were recorded as being less on the defensive during daytime, generally staying within the administrative complex. The German presence at Amiens was therefore far lower than the British authorities believed.

From the evidence of Francis Moitie it also seems that a partial draft of a prison plan was produced at this time, albeit a very simple and somewhat distorted draft. However one must consider that if, as most likely, this plan was drafted by an internee who was locked up for long periods with limited access to the whole complex, the inaccuracies can be easily forgiven. The information that had come out of the prison was very detailed.

The following is a literal translation of a section from it:-

According to the information which I have been able to get so far, all the guards including their chief would be sympathetic towards the FN.* The night watchman at the door is appointed each day by the Germans. (None of the guards therefore know which one will be selected for this shift). At 9 each evening the Gendarme or police officer opens the door and one needs to be very wary at this time as there are always five Germans in their office (See plan) there are men and women held in the German section, whilst the condemned and the suicidal are retained in the section under French guards.

Later in the evening at 22.00 hrs four Germans on bicycles arrive armed with sub machine-guns or rifles; they stay until 06.00 hrs. For a period of 9 hours or so it is necessary to ask permission from the 'Feldgendarmerie' or 'German police force' for any access to the prison. The distance from the entry door to the German offices is about 30 metres. The guard opens the main door and a second security grill with a set of two keys. The one used for the security grill is the same key that opens all the cells. The French guards present are not armed. Any teams of prisoners working locally are guarded by civil police who have three rifles, upon return these rifles are given to the Germans for storage in their offices.

The probable compliment of guards totals eight men. When the bell is rung for access there are possibly two procedures:

1) A German armed with a machine-gun goes to the door with the guard and 2 others remain observing, both are armed.

2) As soon as the bell is heard the German guards go to the door and then head over to the German offices. At 6pm a policeman with a revolver is present.

Total weapons available are probably 4-6 revolvers and 4-6 rifles, in the evening added to this are machine-guns and sub machine-guns.

---

* *Front national de l'indépendance de la France, often shortened to Front national, was formed in 1941 by members of the French Communist Party.*

PRISON OCCUPANTS

According to the British report compiled on 8th September 1944 the number of prisoners held at Amiens rose to around 700 men and women in February 1944: 520 of these were political prisoners and those guilty of petty crimes as decreed by the French authorities, 180 were political prisoners as decreed under German law.

According to a prison plan also submitted to the investigation team, the four wings were generally occupied as follows:

North Wing: political prisoners.

West Wing: female prisoners.

East Wing: male prisoners.

South Wing: German administrative offices.

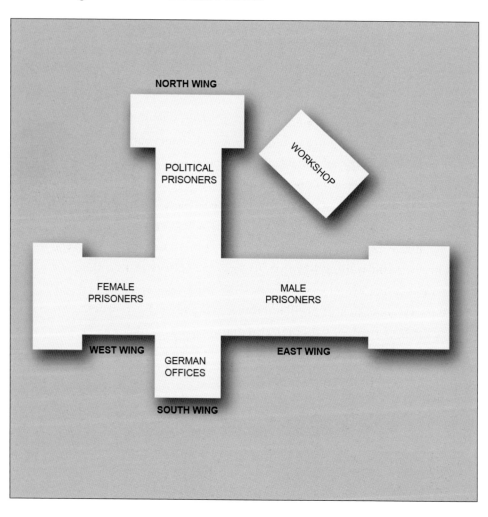

An isolated building located between the north wing and the east wing was a workshop.

The prisoner distribution as detailed here was only a generalization as an individual prisoner may have committed a variety of offences and crimes under differing laws.

The German administrative offices were actually in the south wing of the main building complex and not in the buildings annexed to the east and west wings, as the Mosquito crews would be told at the briefing. Furthermore, despite the original estimate that the number of German soldiers in the prison would be high, the numbers were relatively low from the beginning of 1944 onwards. Although political prisoners were being incarcerated at Amiens by the Germans, Amiens was still essentially a 'French Prison' functioning with French personnel and guards; the Germans simply provided a small staff of supervisory personnel. Interestingly, neither the French guards nor the prison governor were armed, only a police officer taking the guard change at 18.00 hours carried a revolver.

AMIENS - THE SCENE AT NOON ON 18TH FEBRUARY 1944

Shortly before midday a siren located on the Town Hall began to sound its dull drone. Several people hastened to their shelters, but such warnings were commonplace and many inhabitants did not bother to stop what they were doing.

Pierre Maille was standing on the doorstep of No.36 Route de Paris in Amiens when he was surprised to see a British aeroplane. He could clearly see its roundel markings as it flew past at low altitude. Just a few seconds later Michel Olen, standing in Rue de Beauvais, saw the same aircraft accompanied by several others. The siren was still wailing when pupils from the college in Rue Duprez also saw the aircraft passing by.

At the same time, Henri Ducellier (brother of the author) left school on his bicycle heading for No.4 rue Louis Braille, where he was living with his uncle and aunt. At 12.03 hours he heard the first explosions; the attack on Amiens Prison had begun. Arriving home, he would normally have gone straight down to the shelter, but his aunt, Germaine Daussin, was rushing around trying to collect her valuables, such as her handbag, before descending the cellar stairs. At this moment three Mosquitos were pelting in from the east and flashed over the prison at low level. Only two people were on the route d'Albert, there were no parked vehicles or anything else.

INSIDE THE PRISON

"I heard a plane fly very low and it came right over the prison. I thought that it was a German one being chased by Allied fighters, and coming this way to get some protection from the light anti-aircraft guns in the area. Running over to the window, I saw the plane had roundels, and immediately a massive explosion threw us to the ground. The second explosion blasted the door from our cell, it was almost impossible to see anything due to the thick dust.

I then saw Maurice Holleville who grabbed my arm and clutched me hard saying, 'Come on, we must get out."

Jean Beaurain – prisoner

Perhaps just a second or two after 12.03 hours on Friday 18th February 1944 the first 500lb bombs fell on Amiens Prison. One bomb fell against the south wall, just to the west of the large door, creating a large breach. The second bomb fell against the east frontage of the south wing of the main building complex where the German administrative offices were situated.

The explosions followed one after the other with a lull of about two minutes between the first and second waves.

The first testimony comes from Achille Langlet, a gendarme who was imprisoned at Amiens by the Germans: *

On the 18th February 1944 it was very cold in the prison. As soon as dawn broke I saw snow falling that eventually covered all the roof tops. To keep warm, my colleagues and I in the cell covered ourselves with blankets. Once the morning arrived there was again that oppressive feeling as only one who has experienced waiting for death will know. The crashing noise of cell doors opening, voices, a general hubbub of noises, as one door opens another slams shut. At 11.45 I was listening intently, my wife was due to bring a parcel of fresh laundry and some food for me. A German warrant officer appeared in the doorway, his name was Hubert and whilst offering a parcel said simply 'For Langlet'. I tipped the contents onto the straw mattress and filled the bag with dirty laundry that would be given to my wife who remained in the visiting room. Midday was when we were given some soup; the officer in charge of its distribution was called Otto and he shouted and howled along the corridors. He was one of the most unpleasant of the guards. The soup container reached

* These eyewitness accounts were published in the Courrier Picard and are reproduced thanks to Michel Collet, Director of Publications.

the second floor; this was unusual, normally for the three months I had been there the soup distribution started from the odd numbered cells to the left of the building.

Suddenly I heard the sirens start to wail. So, I clambered up to the head of the bed and looked out of the window, just in time to see the belly of a plane complete with British roundels. The plane then headed off to the Boulevard Roubaix . I remember the sounds of engines, but can only recall one explosion that blew in the windowpanes of my cell. Immediately, black dust and a thick cloud of smoke filled our cell and I received a violent impact against my knee. Noticing a tear in my trousers and that it felt wet I realised that I had been wounded. Twice the planes passed over the prison releasing more bombs and I sustained another two wounds, both to my face, one being just below my left eye. The cell I was in was number 15 - which I shared with Louis Sellier, a city councilman from Amiens, Maurice Merienne and another man named Roland Bossi.

I decided then not to make an escape, but to see if I could assist those who had been badly injured.

In the corridor, beneath the rotunda, I met my good friend Noll Guillemant. He was somewhat dazed and did not recognize me, later he was hospitalised and then sent to Germany. From the other side of my cell, I could hear shouts from the area of cells 1-24. Checking, I found the entire staircase had been smashed by the blast. It was necessary to climb down a dangling iron girder. In cell 24, I found Leon Duchatelle who had sheltered under a table that had collapsed onto him. Unable to do anything for him, I went off to see if I could find any tools to help release other prisoners who were trapped. Whilst searching for tools, I was met by two German guards who said I should tend my own knee wound. After I had bandaged it and washed my face I walked past one of the large holes in the wall through which many of my comrades had made it into the surrounding fields. I met up with another friend, Henri Dieu, and together we went back to help the prisoners trapped in cell 24.

After the bombing, there hardly remained any Germans in the prison compound, almost all had been killed. I remember two German survivors named Horst and Hubert. Many dead Germans were situated around the tables in the administration section. At 14.30, the Germans of the 'Sicherheitspolizei' arrived at the damaged prison and placed a cordon around the entire complex. These security services were surrounded by interpreters and many French collaborators in the pay of the Gestapo. They walked around all the cells and ordered the Firemen and Civil Defence persons to remove the bodies of the dead and take them to the nearby cafe.

By 5 p.m. I was exhausted. My wounds had begun to hurt as well. I was invited as one of the rescue party over to the Saint-Victor old peoples' home.

I travelled there in the back of a van with Dr Mans' secretary, a Mme Vignolle. Here, about fifty survivors were placed in an old section of the building without heating or blankets, several of us lay on the cold floor. Our experience was, however, made considerably easier by the actions of the French Red Cross directed by Mme Duc, who supplied large amounts of food ...we were spoilt. On Saturday the 19th, I asked for permission to visit my cousin Adrien Langlet, which was granted, and there I managed to have a bath and a shave. He also supplied writing paper and envelopes so that I could inform other members of our family that I was safe. On Sunday 20th February, I worked with several other volunteers to search amongst the debris. Upon arrival, however, I found that the parcel from my wife had been stolen.

At the time of the raid the prison held approximately 180 political prisoners and 640 ordinary prisoners. 92 wounded persons were transported to hospital or various clinics in the town. A document distributed by the local Police chief for general information on 19 February, announced the exemplary attitude of certain prisoners who had not attempted to escape, but had stayed behind to assist and rescue people from the prison. Following this, I was granted my release, which was actioned on February 29th 1944, along with my friends Bompas, Pache and Oudin. A few days, later my friend Henri Dieu was also released.

The following is a list of people that I know were in the prison at the time of the raid, who I did not see again afterwards. Some were killed, others died whilst deported and others are still alive: Gontier, Fore, Guerin, Piguiloli, Guelton, Leboeuf, Choquet, Mlle Verdy, Lefur, Dazevedo, Massoule, Dobel, Vandenbergh, Chretien, Suard, Hardouin, Dejean, Dr.Beaumont, Malterre, Gruel, Bellemère and lastly Lucien. Finally, I would ask all to have a thought for all those who have been killed or have suffered so that France may live again.

Another account is provided by Henri Moisan, also imprisoned at Amiens at the time of the raid:

At mid-day the distribution of the soup began, a laborious chore that took ages. Whilst I waited for them I decided to read. Suddenly there was the noise of powerful engines approaching. A khaki plane approached just over the roof tops, its roundels clearly visible. An explosion occurred in the courtyard. Frightened, we all moved back to the cell door. More explosions followed and then I was surrounded by falling debris and building material, bricks and concrete beams; soon I was buried a few metres below it all. Despite this, I was still conscious. Totally pinned down from all sides I was unable to move, I choked due to the pressure on my chest and was unaware that I was wounded. As the bombing continued I hoped for all those who I would leave behind should I be killed, that the bombs would not reach them. I managed to loosen the surrounding debris, affording a little space in which to breathe just a little.

I started to call to one of my cell mates to show I was still alive. Later, I discovered that of all the occupants in my cell I was the only one to be buried. My colleague had run away in sheer fright, and the bombs still kept falling. Why was this happening? Why kill us who are members of the Resistance? Finally, the bombing stopped, in fact it only lasted a few minutes. All about me, there were cries of the wounded or trapped, all desperate to attract the attention of the rescuers.

Time passed; I cannot recollect how long, and I tried to control my breathing and only called out occasionally. Gradually I heard voices, indistinct at first, but getting clearer… it was my rescuers! My shouts attracted them and they spotted one of my fingers beneath some bricks. There was some confusion as to where actually my body was lying as my hand was sticking up vertically. Cautiously, not to cause any further collapses, they removed rubble and my head was free, then my body. My legs were trapped beneath a huge concrete block which, had it fallen a few more centimetres, would have crushed my legs completely. Finally, I was free. Instantly I recognized one of my rescuers as Louis Sellier, another prisoner.

He could easily have run away himself, as it took at least fifteen minutes for the Germans to seal the prison complex, but bravely he stayed put to assist in my rescue. Later, Louis was deported to Germany but, thanks to God, returned safely at the end of the war. I was laid down gently onto a stretcher, a little dazed, I was then offered a drink. I refused the offer, gesticulating wildly, however at least this confirmed nothing appeared to be broken anywhere. I had several surface wounds to the face and head, which gave me a mask of blood; combined with the dust it looked like I had not shaved for eight days. With my torn clothing, I had the appearance of a dying man, which in fact was quite useful; carried past on the stretcher, the Germans paid me no attention at all - they thought I was dead. Civil Defence personnel and ambulances arrived at the scene, some actually assisted people to escape before the Germans came along. However, I could not walk so missed the opportunity for freedom. Instead of being taken to the hospital I was taken to Dr Filachet, my brother-in-law.

The third account is provided by René Vanwinck. René had been imprisoned a month earlier for patriotic opinions and actions which had upset the occupying administration. He occupied Cell 9.

It was snowing and I was awaiting the soup distribution. In the corridors, the sound was of doors opening and closing continuously. My cell, number 9, was on the ground floor, just opposite the staircase and, including myself, had four occupants. I had awoken very early this day. At about five in the morning there had been a noisy departure from the prison. Afterwards, the morning proceeded normally, through the bars one was able to make out the German guards in the courtyard. At mid-day, we gathered behind the door to await the meal.

Suddenly a terrible roar of engines was heard, a plane had just missed our building. Immediately afterwards there was a huge explosion and we were forced to the floor. I truly believed this was my last hour and remained on the ground and said a small prayer. The cell grew dark with choking dust, the explosions seemed to last forever. The walls were crumbling and I could hear the screams and cries. Someone shouted 'They will kill us all'. After that and the explosions all was chillingly quiet, except for the cries of the wounded... it was terrifying. In cell 9 everyone was okay, the cell door was blasted, but remained in place. The four prisoners managed to smash it down. Outside was a scene of desolation and destruction. The staircase leading to the gangways was smashed apart, the building itself was largely destroyed, there were huge piles of shattered brickwork.

All I could see was open sky, all was chaos and disorder; guards, prisoners, Germans, everyone was all over the show. There were bodies strewn all over the ground, one of whom was a friend of mine. People I recognized were running and, in a split second, I made the decision to leave as quickly as possible.

Giving himself a few seconds to put his shoes and overcoat on, René ran towards freedom, his sole obsession to leave this cursed place.

I ran past the German administration office, noticing it was shattered. It was really difficult to clamber up and over all the debris. I actually clambered over a huge table, some said later that numerous dead Germans were underneath it, but I did not see any.

There was confusion and chaos everywhere in route d'Albert. The Civil defence arrived and transported the wounded to the nearest houses, whilst the Germans tried to establish a basic level of security. After finding refuge in a friend's house at Rue Lemerchier, René later walked to Lamotte-Brebière railway station, where he travelled to Albert. He hid on a family-owned farm there until the Liberation.

An internal view of the central area of the prison taken shortly after the raid showing the devastation caused by the 500lb bombs.

The only known image of Jean Beaurain*, charged with theft, but an active Resistance member.

Another account came from Jean Beaurain,(see page 24), originally from Mers-les-Bains. Jean's mother owned a café in Mers-les-Bains called 'Le Populaire' which was visited by many Resistance members and even some Allied airmen. He was imprisoned for 'stealing official parts and items'. In Amiens Prison Jean joined his half-brother, Roger Lheureux, who had already been in the prison a few weeks for the theft of a bicycle from Amiens. Marthe Lheureux, their mother, was also in Amiens Prison. Jean occupied a cell with three other prisoners.

On 18th February as the bombs started exploding in the prison, a fellow prisoner Maurice Holleville grabbed Jean's arm and urged him to get out. Seeing their chance to escape in the chaos, the two runaways did not encounter any real difficulties leaving the prison compound. Jean Beaurain was accompanied by two of the other occupants of his cell. One was a Resistance member from Abbeville and the other a local Amiens resident. The 'Amienoise' colleague took them to the district of Saint-Roch, where he gave them money and told them to catch the train to Beaucamps-Le-Vieux. There they were provided with a hiding place as well as some simple temporary work.

Mme Lheureux, Jean's mother, had been injured during the attack on the prison, but managed to escape from the hospital where she had been admitted. Several days later, Maurice Holleville also took her to Beaucamps-Le-Vieux.

A fifth account was provided by Raymond Bompas. Raymond was arrested on 4th January 1944 for possessing forged identity papers; he was placed in Cell 24 shortly afterwards.

The weather was poor and everywhere looked grey. The humming of a plane was suddenly heard. Afterwards, it all happened very quickly. There was an explosion and I believed that the plane had actually crashed on the prison. The walls trembled. There were more explosions, cries of pain, and calls for help. I was wounded by glass splinters from the windowpanes as they were blasted in. Nobody, myself included, had any idea of what

Jean Beaurain is often linked to train derailments - see page 159.

was going on, and it took some time to gather our wits. We tried to smash our door down, but this was not possible. Eventually we heard the sound of keys; our door was open. A fellow prisoner had found the keys on a dead German. Whilst leaving, I saw opposite my childhood friend Pache, he was trying to free some colleagues from a pile of fallen debris. It was soon clear we could not get down the stairs, as the staircase lay mangled and twisted.

Raymond Bompas got to the ground floor by sliding down the damaged staircase. The whole prison was a spectacle from 'the apocalypse'.

When I arrived in the courtyard, I saw a large woman. She had badly cut legs.

Roger Lheureux, half-brother of Jean Beaurain, member of the Resistance, but imprisoned for stealing a Bicycle.
He is believed to have been found dead in his cell after the attack.

Some of the prisoners fled through the adjacent fields, whilst some were picked up and taken into safe hiding by the inhabitants of Rivery. Others remained at the prison, offering their services to the Civil Defence personnel to help look for survivors. Raymond and several of his comrades were quickly led into the basement of the town hall, before being taken to Saint-Victor where they spent the night. The following day Raymond Bompas and his comrades were transferred to the Citadelle.

The sixth account is from Emile Watel, a fireman, who was one of the first people to go into the shattered prison buildings from where the cries of the injured could clearly be heard.

Suddenly, between two broken sections of wall, I could see a man standing upright on a section of flooring of what remained of the second floor of the building. The man, who was not wounded, said to me, 'I'm Leon Gontier.*' This man said very little and I asked him whether he wanted to run away. 'I've only got three more weeks of my sentence, I'd prefer to stay,' he said. Just a few days later Leon Gontier was deported to Germany and never returned.

---

* *Born in 1886, Leon Gontier had been a head clerk in the Prefecture until he was stopped and arrested for Resistance activities.*

VICTIMS AND INJURED PRISONERS

Louis Vandenbergh had been stopped and arrested on 1st February 1944 for the distribution of 'terrorist' leaflets. He was sent to Amiens Prison and was placed in cell 36. Roger Lheureux from Mers-les-Bains, Emile Tavernier from Vismes-Au-Val and one other man from Pierrepont were also in this cell. The explosions threw Louis Vandenbergh to the ground and he was half buried in rubble. He later escaped from the prison compound through one of the breaches in the walls. He was soon captured and placed in a van that took him to the Citadel. From there he was deported to Germany. It is reported that the body of Roger Lheureux was found in the cell.

Maurice Genest, alias 'Henri', had been sentenced in his absence to penal servitude for life in May 1942 by the Special Section of the Court of Justice of Amiens. He was finally stopped and questioned by French gendarmes on 8th October 1942. Initially, he was imprisoned at Clermont and classed as a 'terrorist' but was transferred to Amiens in December 1942. As the explosions occurred, he took shelter under the washbasin in his cell; he was buried under tons of masonry, but was later rescued by firemen. He was then placed on a stretcher and taken to hospital. He managed to escape and took refuge at the home of Therese and Renaud Debuigny. Mme. Duserre, Maurice Genest's sister, was actually taking a parcel to the prison at the time of the raid and was slightly injured, a small cut to one of her legs.

Another similar case is that of Mme. Colette Platel, a resident of Albert, who was also in the prison at the time of the raid. Her husband, George Platel, had requested a pass from the Gestapo that morning to make a repeat visit to his wife who had been imprisoned there for a month. Mme Platel and another young lady, Mireille Duparc, had been accused of typing 'terrorist' leaflets for circulation, following the distribution of the leaflets. It appears that Mme Platel was mistaken for someone else but, nevertheless, she was imprisoned at Amiens with Mireille Duparc.

Just before mid-day, George Platel passed through the main door in the enclosure wall. He then crossed the courtyard and the heavy iron grill was opened, allowing him access to the interior of the prison building. Walking inside he arrived in a large area used as a visiting facility. This was in the southern wing, adjacent to the ground floor near the rotunda where there was an office used by the Germans. According to George, a French guard was involved in a heated argument outside the office with two Germans dressed in civilian clothes. They all moved into the office, including George, where there were three more German soldiers, and George started to explain his business. George remembered it perfectly; at 12.03 hours there was a huge roar overhead from an aeroplane, followed by a colossal explosion. The blast was intense and literally demolished the office in which George was standing. The walls fell down and the ceiling collapsed, burying everyone.

The bomb that had just struck the east-facing frontage of the southern wing, most likely in its lower regions, had just destroyed half of the building. This was the section located more towards the route d'Albert. The remainder of the wing, where the German administrative offices were located, was also wrecked.

A broken-down door inside the prison.

Four long minutes passed whilst the explosions followed one another. More walls collapsed. Finally, it all calmed down. Then the screams, cries and howls for help began to start.

A huge block of cement fell next to George, his feet and legs were covered with rubble, but he was alive. He was surrounded by carnage; the bodies of people he was with just a few minutes ago lay crushed under blocks of stone, bricks, and cement. Hundreds of loaves of bread were scattered all over the place. George was concussed, but managed to extract himself, just leaving a crushed shoe behind, stuck under a large concrete block. Near him, nobody moved, no one cried out. Was it possible that he was the only survivor?

George managed to stumble to the area beneath the rotunda. Everything was devastated, the central walls had come down and the roof had collapsed. Looking at a huge pile of debris, George was horrified to see the body of his wife amongst the jumbled masonry. The bomb had crashed through the roof of the central section at the corner of the northern and western wing and had exploded inside. Colette had been released from her cell and was coming down the staircase to see him. Desperately grappling with the debris, George tried to reach his young wife. When he finally reached her, the gravity of her wounds was only

28 year-old Victor Roullé from Mers-les-Bains, local head of the Front National. Participated in blowing up 525,000 litres of alcohol to be used for synthetic fuel on 11th November 1943. He was betrayed, arrested, tortured and sentenced to death. He died in his cell during the attack.

too clear to him; both her legs had been smashed by a huge concrete block. George remembered a man wearing a hat running over to help his wife, this may possibly have been Dr Anton Mans. Meanwhile, Mireille Duparc, who had been arrested with Colette, had luckily escaped any injury. Other people finally arrived to help and gradually Colette was released from the rubble. She was then placed in a car. The scene was almost surreal, George was following this group in the courtyard when one of the German guards mistook him for an escaping prisoner due to his appearance. The guard raised his rifle but then, seeing that George was associated with the badly injured woman, let everyone leave without further ado. Colette was taken to the New Hospital in Amiens where later she underwent surgery to remove her legs. She died at midnight on 18th February 1944, just twenty-five years old.

Constance Detaille had been arrested and imprisoned for pro-Resistance activities in July 1943 and was subsequently imprisoned in Amiens. After the raid, she was never seen again. Other people whose deaths were confirmed were Jean Dufrénoy, M. Derobertmazure, M. Bellemère and M. Longuet.

Many uninjured prisoners played an active part in the release of their comrades, until the arrival of Gestapo and Feldgendarmerie, who made them take the injured to the Saint-Victor old people's home before imprisoning them in the Citadel.

André Tempez, born on 22nd January 1897, was responsible for Civil Defence. He also worked for the Resistance, which led to his arrest on 12th November 1943. He escaped being killed in the raid and bravely led rescue parties all over the ruins to help the wounded. Despite these dedicated acts, he was subsequently shot in May 1944. His body was later identified amongst those in a mass grave just outside Arras.

Dr. Anton Mans also made no attempt to escape. He was later deported to Germany. Many other people chose to forego the opportunity to escape and remained to help their wounded comrades and friends.

The Bishop of Amiens, accompanied by Canon Duhamel, arrived at the scene to bring comfort to the victims; these two gentlemen were later joined by the Abbott of St-Pierre and two vicars from the same district. Abbot Wyplier, the prison chaplain, helped to move the wounded to the New Hospital. Amidst such scenes of chaos, some organisation seemed to be re-forming.

A view from the courtyard showing the devastated north wing.

CONTEMPORARY NEWSPAPER REPORTS

This was how the Amiens regional press reported the casualties during the three weeks that followed the raid. The press was under German control, but was well informed about the situation at the prison and about the search and recovery operations.

On 19th February 1944, the day after the raid, there were no articles mentioning the attack on the prison. As usual, the Germans took time to censor the journalists' text. The first articles about the attack on Amiens Prison appeared in the 'La progrés de la Somme' and in 'Le journal d'Amiens' on Sunday 20th and Monday 21st February 1944.

'La progrés de la Somme'

THE ENGLISH COME AS 'LIBERATORS'

BOMBING THE AMIENS PRISON
40 DEAD AND 90 WOUNDED

The death toll lengthens as the difficult work of clearing up continues.

One loses oneself in conjecture about the significance of the bloody attack that English flyers carried out, in broad daylight, taking the route d'Albert Prison as their objective.

It is no secret to anyone that, apart from the common criminals incarcerated at the Prison, there were also people whose actions had caused difficulties to the occupying authorities.

Consequently one can ask oneself, since it is clearly and irrefutably established that the prison was the target assigned to the aviators, what hidden motive led to the order?

If it were about a 'massive release' the many corpses that lie bloodied, torn and crushed under the debris, attest to the complete 'success' of the cynical enterprise.

***

The English attackers - the aircraft flew so low that their roundels were clearly visible - attacked Amiens on Friday a few minutes after 12 noon. It seems certain that their objective was carefully chosen - the route d'Albert prison.

Clouds made it possible for the enemy flyers to arrive at low altitude near the prison and they targeted the buildings, launching their bombs. It is not difficult to imagine the consequence of this kind of concentrated attack, which caused very significant damage.

Undoubtedly, the numbers of dead and wounded are extremely high. The Prison of Amiens sheltered some hundreds of prisoners. The precise number of prisoners and casualties must be estimated for some prisoners working outside the prison had not returned for the midday meal. It is also necessary to add those who escaped during the attack and who fled either to the fields, or towards the city. Others were recaptured in the enclosure itself.

***

At 4 p.m., about fifty casualties had been evacuated and 15 dead recovered from the debris. There were unfortunately others ... many others. Here, two atrociously mutilated corpses lay in a cell, crushed under the weight of the blocks of cement and bricks; there, one endeavoured to release other victims who could be heard. Everywhere people probed the tangled rubble and desperate digging started immediately.

In a relatively short time, the French and German authorities, all the rescue organizations, the medical departments and the ambulances, the firemen and police were mobilised. Among this crowd, were the anguished relatives of the prisoners.

Let us not omit to mention that a bomb fell on one of the houses of the St Victor Hospice old people's home, where two were wounded. Other bombs fell on nearby houses. Two houses were completely destroyed. A rain of shrapnel fell on the area, but there were no casualties. The work of clearing rubble continued through the night with lights powered by a generating unit of the civil defence. It is necessary to emphasise the devotion and the courage of the teams of rescuers who endeavoured to pull out the dead.

This Saturday morning, the provisional assessment of the victims is established as follows at 10 a.m. - about forty dead - and approximately a hundred wounded. As these very difficult rescue operations advance, new corpses will be discovered. The absence of any identity papers makes it very difficult to identify the victims. Four wounded died at the New Hospital where they had been taken.

During the air raid on Amiens, Mme. Jeannot, wife of the Divisional Police Commissioner, was seriously wounded in the right arm by a machine-gun bullet. Mme. Jeannot was in the kitchen when the projectile that went through the living room and the dining room struck her. Dr. Pauchet, who tended her, thinks he will be able to save the limb.

<u>Two of the planes were shot down</u>

Towards 12h20, immediately after the bombing and the following aerial combats, two of the attacking planes were shot down, one in Poulainville, the other in Saint-Gratien. Each plane contained a crew of 2 men. Three of the occupants were killed, the fourth, a wounded pilot, was hospitalized under the care of the occupying army.

The journalist made a couple of errors, excusable under the conditions they were working under. The planes were not shot down at 12.20 hours. One Mosquito was shot down over Saint-Gratien at 12.05 hours, whilst the other aircraft was an escorting Typhoon which was shot down over Poulainville. There was also confusion over a second Mosquito, which was shot down over Villeroy. This is where the reference to three of the four crew members being killed came from, as the pilot of this aircraft was taken prisoner.

On Monday 21st February 1944 '*Le journal d'Amiens*', another daily Amiens newspaper, featured a violent diatribe by its leader-writer J. Picavet against the Allies. It also gave some additional details about the raid:

BRITISH AVIATORS BOMB AMIENS PRISON AND AN OLD PEOPLE'S HOME

Initial rescue attempts made it possible to release 37 bodies and nearly a hundred casualties.
<u>The Liberators passed</u>
The gangsters of the air, for the second time in less than a month, attacked Amiens on Friday.

The prison destroyed, several individual houses destroyed, so many victims that it is not yet possible to quantify after 24 hours of clearing the debris, but it is not far from 200; such is the scale of this aggression.

It is war, said some stubborn Anglophiles. War? With whom? Germany? Well, then! In what way can this destruction and these murders hasten the end of the war? We ask this of the men of right spirit and balanced judgment.

It is war, certainly, but war on the civilian population, war on our doorsteps, war on France, a cowardly war because France is disarmed, a wild and barbaric war.

Why was the prison so clearly targeted? Was it to deliver the elements of disorder that are the best aids to England? It is possible.

But then the goal was exceeded. They freed more than they wished, they were freed 'permanently'.

Is this is not a warning? The liberators have passed. They have brought the only liberation that they can give, that which they have reserved for France itself.

J. Picavet
Le journal d'Amiens, 20th and 21st February 1944

THE WORK OF THE LIBERATORS

Friday, a little after midday, several light British bombers flew over the city at very low altitude in the middle of the anti-aircraft guns and dropped a number of bombs on the Saint-Pierre district.

The military prison objective.

The departmental prison that seems to have been main objective of the attackers was entirely destroyed and the victims are numerous there. The vast building which sheltered several hundred prisoners offers a tragic sight now. Through the breaks of the enclosing wall one can see the extent of the damage. The house of the chief warden, the entrance buildings, the Western, Northern wings and the central rotunda are literally shattered. The high walls collapsed burying a great number of prisoners. There were no victims among the staff. Only a few were very slightly wounded: Mme Magiras, wife of the chief warden, M René Clerc, registrar; M Gaston Brasseur, guard, Mme. Vve Renee Thuillier, guardian, M Albert Foré and M Marius Delcourt, policemen, were all hospitalized as was M. Jules Cuvillier, member of the Civil Defence, wounded by the collapse of a section of wall.

In a neighbouring street, 19 buildings were damaged. Numbers 15-17-19 were destroyed. One resident, Mme. Etienne Letien, aged 40 years, was killed in her house. There are some wounded: Jacqueline Lecocq, 23 years, the young Jean Claude Louette, 2 years, and Mme Pauline Lefebvre.

On the road, a bomb exploded on the pavement at the corner of a garage and another in the garden of number 411 without causing casualties. In this main road, 23 houses were affected.

Saint-Victor old people's home.

Projectiles reached the old people's home Saint-Victor, Boulevard Beauvillé , of which one of the houses was seriously damaged. There are only two wounded.

Rescuers

Throughout the night, under extremely difficult conditions and in intense cold, the teams of Civil Defence, the firemen and the rescue teams worked like navvies, clearing the debris of the prison. It is unfortunately impossible to even roughly evaluate the number of victims, but the funeral list lengthens hour by hour as work continues.

The majority of the bodies are stripped of identity papers, which makes identification difficult. The back room of the Defruit cafe, 375 route d'Albert, was turned into a temporary mortuary, where the remains of the victims were laid out. 37 corpses have already been identified.

Saturday morning, 37 corpses of prisoners were identified, of whom 7 were identified at the mortuary of the New Hospital. Among the latter, one was recognized as a station master recently convicted of the theft of parcels intended for prisoners.

A number of people are still alive in the basement of the prison. In addition, 170 uninjured prisoners were transferred to a safe place.

Many local dignitaries went to the disaster scene, in particular M P. Baube, Prefect of the Somme and his principal private secretary M. Berson, M Dewas and Dr Perdu, deputies to the Mayor, Civil Defence Director Collignon and Director Thérasse Urban.

Le journal d'Amiens, 20th and 21st February 1944

On Tuesday 22nd February, under the by-line of its leader-writer G-S Savigny, 'Le progrès de la Somme' continued to speculate about the motive for the raid. In another article published on the same day, the newspaper continued its account of those tragic days:

A prison is not a military objective and, at first sight, one does not understand the attack by planes on such a building. One understands it even less when one recalls that many of the inmates of such establishments are partisans of the perpetrators of the raid.

Precisely, object the Anglophiles: the confusion created by the bombing allowed several prisoners, such as Gaullists or Communists, to make a clean getaway.

If that were the objective, it is far from being achieved because the majority of those intended to be released found only death during the bombing of the prison. It was the political section that suffered the most, so much so that the majority of dead or wounded were those who were expected to be released. They were obviously released in the most tragic way.

It is undeniable that some prisoners did nevertheless escape, but they will not enjoy a long freedom. It is not thought that the English or American planes took them on board to take them back to England.

For lack of means, they will not be able to reach distant provinces and the majority of them, obliged to remain in the area, will be tracked down rigorously. It will be necessary for them to live carefully and, as there are not only partisans but also suspect elements among them, they will give themselves away by thefts, plunderings, or perhaps more serious acts.

Some killed, some condemned to wander in the countryside under the threat of being recaptured, that is the clearest result of this release by bombing.

G-S Savigny
Le Progrès de la Somme, Tuesday February 22nd, 1944

BOMBING OF AMIENS PRISON
The rescuers released new corpses
LATEST ASSESSMENT - 71 DEAD

All day Sunday the crowd never stopped arriving at the prison where work of clearing continued, day and night, without respite.

New corpses were pulled from the debris, but it appears now that means, other than shovel and pickaxe, will have to be used to remove the tangle of rubble, concrete blocks and

A view from the main road to Albert showing the breach in the front wall.

girders. The last victims – in double figures undoubtedly - whose terribly crushed bodies, are still being found, only limbs and heads are visible. Atrocious sights have driven the determined workers on for three days, to complete this difficult work.

While the undertakers carry out their work the personnel of the prison endeavour to reconstruct the files of the records office.

During Friday and Saturday nights, the search continued for any survivors still buried under the rubble. No shouts or cries were heard and those who were rescued during these tragic hours were the last.

As bodies were found they were transported to a nearby room where, on Saturday afternoon, the identification proceeded, as far as possible. It was an extremely difficult task due to the almost complete absence of papers.

The assistance of the prison warders and that of the specialized personnel of the Criminal Investigation Department made it possible to identify some of the bodies.

At the end of Sunday afternoon, 62 bodies, of whom 37 were identified, had been transported to the mortuary. To this figure it is necessary to add 9 dead at the New Hospital, including six identified bodies, which brings the number of dead to 71.

But when we left the ruin of the prison, which is completely destroyed, the firemen were working to free several more bodies buried under enormous blocks of masonry. Other workers with a tractor from the General Stores, continued clearing the collapsed buildings, an enormous pile of rubble under which there are certainly more corpses that will not be reached for several days.

Let us add that from the earliest hours a field kitchen has been working, where hot drinks and snacks are provided for the workers.

Gradually the bodies were put into coffins and transported to Jean-Macé school, for the funerals which will take place on Tuesday at the expense of the city.

Le Progrès de la Somme, Tuesday February 22nd, 1944

FUNERALS WILL TAKE PLACE ON TUESDAY

Municipal funerals of the victims of the last air raid will take place on Tuesday February 22nd at 10 a.m., in the courtyard of the girls' school in Rue Jean-Macé.

Le Progrès de la Somme, Tuesday February 22nd, 1944

On Wednesday, February 23rd, 1944, a new article appeared in 'Le Progrès de la Somme'.

THE BOMBING OF AMIENS PRISON

The municipal administration communicates:

The bombing of the prison suddenly presented the Civil Defence with a heavy task.

Its many services, which worked unceasingly, as well as its additional organizations, were able to intervene immediately with remarkable effectiveness. Thanks to the admirable devotion of their members, of whom some did not hesitate to risk their lives, very many casualties buried under heaps of debris were saved from death under often hazardous conditions and were looked after without delay.

Unexploded bombs increased the general risk further.

Clearing continued without interruption - apart from a few fifteen minute breaks - until Sunday evening, when it appeared with certainty that no more survivors were under the debris.

Several team members were injured, fortunately not seriously, during rescue operations.

The municipal administration addresses to all its thanks and its congratulations. It warmly thanks the tradesmen who agreed to bring food and assistance to help the rescuers in their task.

81 dead

Work of clearing of the prison continued without halt all day Monday.

In spite of the difficulty of their task and the risks that they ran, the rescuers discovered and freed new corpses.

This Tuesday morning, the official figure of deaths had reached 81. It is unfortunately feared that this figure will grow. Indeed, several cells are still under the debris and it is known that they were occupied. At the hospital, the health of the wounded improves and no new deaths have been reported.

Municipal funerals, for the newly-found victims of the bombing of last Friday, will take place tomorrow Thursday, February 24, at 10 a.m., at the girls' school in Rue Jean-Macé.

This ceremony, as it was for the first, will be followed, at 11.00 by a religious service in the cathedral.

On Tuesday, the operations of clearing continued at the prison. Searchers discovered six new corpses, which currently brings to 87 the total number of victims.

Le Progrès de la Somme, Wednesday February 23rd, 1944

On Thursday 24th February 1944 'Le Progrès de la Somme,' reported the funerals of the first victims, which had taken place on Tuesday 22nd February.

AMIENS GAVE THE PRISON BOMBING VICTIMS AN EMOTIONAL FUNERAL

In the large courtyard of the girls' school in Rue Jean-Macé, transformed into a funeral chapel, 67 coffins containing the remains, sometimes incomplete, of the pitiful victims of the English raid of last Friday had been gathered, attended by the young people of the emergency teams of the Red Cross.

On Tuesday, long before 7 p.m., a downcast and silent crowd began its procession, which had to be stopped to allow the lifting of the bodies by the clergy of the church Saint-Anne.

There was a tragic silence in the immense hall, a silence that was sometimes split by sobs that were impossible to suppress, while the groups of the Civil Defence, teams of the Red Cross and Firemen transported coffins of oak.

M le. Baube, Prefect of the Somme, assisted M Tournié, Secretary-General and M Berzon, Chief of the Cabinet; M. Rollin, Mayor of Amiens, his colleagues of the Town Council and chiefs of the services of the Prefecture and the Town Hall, as well as many senior departmental officials were first to bow in front of the victims and members of their families.

All along the route to the cathedral, the painful procession stretched between double ranks of Amiénois massed in several rows to pay their last respects to the victims of an unjust act.

Religious service

At the cathedral, 49 coffins were brought in and arranged in the nave. Mgr Martin, Bishop of Amiens, assisted by Mgr Fourcy and Canon Quentin, presided over the ceremony, while the organ played and the choir sang.

Before giving absolution, Mgr Martin, addressed a short speech to the dignitaries and the crowd said their prayers, moved by those in sorrow he assured them of the profound compassion of the church.

Never had the cathedral seen gathered together so many victims of a cruel and mysterious bombing, said Mgr Martin, who finished by expressing the wish that all these deaths and all the suffering would be for France, the Peace and the Union of all its sons.

The bodies of most of the victims were then buried in the various cemeteries around the city.

Eighteen other bodies remained in the courtyard in Rue Jean-Macé awaiting completion of documentation.

Le Progrès de la Somme, Thursday February 24th, 1944

According to 'Le Progrès de la Somme' of Friday, February 25th, 1944, the number of victims reached 88.

AFTER THE BOMBING OF THE PRISON OF AMIENS

During clearance work, the workmen discovered on Wednesday, the body of one of the victims of the bombing last Friday. This discovery brings the number of dead to 88.

Funerals

On Thursday morning, in a repeat of the funerals of Tuesday, 24 new victims were taken to their last resting-place, in the presence of the representatives of the authorities and of an emotional crowd.

Le Progrès de la Somme, Friday February 25th, 1944

On Saturday February 26, 1944, the number of the victims was changed to 89.

AMIENS - FUNERALS OF THE VICTIMS

For the second time, as we briefly indicated yesterday, a moving ceremony took place in the courtyard of the Rue Jean-Macé school, for new victims of the bombing of Amiens Prison. This time the twenty-four coffins, which were placed on four trucks draped with black hangings, and the funeral procession, like Tuesday, proceeded to the cathedral, preceded by the dignitaries of the Town of Amiens and the clergy of Saint-Anne.

At the head of the procession came M Le Baube, Prefect of the Somme and Dr Christian Perdu, representing the Mayor of Amiens, a delegation of the Municipality and the representatives of the principal public services. The Fire Brigade (except for those on call) the teams of the Civil Defence and of the Red Cross formed a double rank on both sides of the cortege. As on Tuesday, Mgr Martin, Bishop of Amiens, conducted the ceremony and gave absolution, then the coffins were transported to various cemeteries.

Following the discovery of a new corpse in the debris of the prison, the number of deaths is now 89.

The search thus continued without interruption under the direction of the Municipality represented by M le Maire and M Dewas, assistant, M Therasse, urban director, Blin, chief of sector and Herbet, chief of the clearing of the Civil Defence, assisted by several technical advisers of which M Duday, Simon and Antoine, Doctor Fafet, medical chief, Jardillier, chief of the flying teams and M Timbert, Afsi, Privileggio and Debuigny, chiefs of sector.

The firemen were led by their captain M Monnier, assisted by Lt Raquet and their adjudant Mahiou and the rescuers of the Red Cross by M Perschair, chief of the emergency teams and M Martigny, chief of the first-aid workers.

Let us announce finally the magnificent effort provided by the Secours National and M Boulanger, rue de Noyon who undertook to ensure the supply of the team-members on the clearing site.

Le Progrès de la Somme, Saturday February 26ᵗʰ, 1944

On Monday February 28ᵗʰ, 1944, '*Le Journal d'Amiens*' told of the appearance of two new victims. The newspaper reported the total number at 90, but it may have been 91- as 89 had been recorded two days earlier.

BOMBING OF THE PRISON OF AMIENS

Two wounded died in the hospital, which brings to 90 the number of victims.

For two days, the work of clearing the ruins of the prison in route d'Albert has not made it possible to discover any other bodies. It is not, however, certain that there will not be more during days to come; work is currently reaching places not yet explored.

It has been announced that two seriously injured died at the New Hospital on Friday. The total number of deaths thus now reaches 90, about the same number as hospitalized casualties.

'Le Journal d'Amiens' Monday February 28ᵗʰ, 1944

LATEST ASSESSMENT OF THE BOMBING: 94 DEAD

The latest count of the victims of the bombing of the prison on February 18ᵗʰ, 1944 brings to 94 the number of dead (85 bodies recovered), 8 casualties died at the hospital and one person was killed outside the prison. There are currently 86 wounded in hospital and 20 who are being cared for at home or in private clinics.

25 probation prisoners are working on the clearing. 30 are on bail.

'Le Journal d'Amiens' Tuesday February 29ᵗʰ, 1944

AFTER THE BOMBING: 95 DEAD

Work of clearing the debris of the prison is temporarily suspended because of the danger that sections of wall and the roof might collapse on the workmen.

The characteristic smell from the rubble reveals that corpses are still hidden there.

On Tuesday body parts were transported to the mortuary. It was impossible to identify them.

The death of a casualty in a private clinic of the city brings to 95 the provisional number of the victims of the bombing of February 18th, 1944.

'Le Journal d'Amiens' Thursday March 2nd, 1944

The provisional number of dead from the bombing of the prison on February 18th 1944 has reached 96 after the death of M. Jules Bajus, who was being treated at the hospital.

'Le Journal d'Amiens' Thursday March 9th, 1944

A view of the northern side of the prison taken by a low flying reconnaissance Mustang just two days after the raid. The extensive damage is clearly visible.

REPORTS BY THE POLICE CHIEF OF THE SERVICES

The reports compiled during the days after the raid by the Police Chief of the Services (General Information), in particular Police Chief Divisionnaire Jeannot,[*] give the official view of the casualties.

MINISTRY FOR THE INTERIOR
Regional direction of National safety
Police station of the general Information Amiens No.398

Amiens, February 19, 1944.
to the Director of the General Information,
Ministry for the interior, Vichy
the Prefect of the department of the Somme, Amiens,
the Police chief,
Chief of the service régional of the General Information, Saint-Quentin.

INFORMATION PAPER

With reference to my telephone call on February 18th, 1944, relating to the bombing of the prison of Amiens, I have the honour to make known to you the following:

On February 18th, 1944, about midday, the 'Allied' planes released bombs on the northern part of the town of Amiens, completely destroying the prison, located on route d'Albert, numbers 15 and 17 of rue Voltaire, as well as part of the Saint-Victor hospital, transformed into 'Lazaret' by the German authorities.

The aircraft bombed the prison on several runs and thirty bombs fell as much on the buildings as on the immediate neighbourhood.

The prison contained roughly 640 ordinary prisoners and 180 prisoners imprisoned by the German authorities. It has not been possible, until now, to give an exact number of the prisoners, the files being destroyed.

[*]This police officer lived at 92 rue Louis Thuillier (a street located in the southern districts of the city). By an extraordinary coincidence, his wife was at home at the time of the raid and was the victim of a cannon shell that undoubtedly came from an FW190 attacking a Mosquito.

- 37 dead recovered from the debris by this morning. Amongst them, is Dr Guyot, of Bray-sur-Somme and Dr Beaumont, of Warloy Baillon. Only six or seven have been identified up to now.

- 92 wounded have been transported to the hospital and to various clinics.

M. Bellemere, a solicitor from Amiens, was seriously wounded and was pulled out today at 1 o'clock.

A great number of prisoners benefited from the bombing to escape. Amongst them, 231 have been recaptured by the French and German police force, of which:

- 163 ordinary prisoners are imprisoned temporarily in the Lebel factory, in the suburb of Hem;

- 50 prisoners detained by the German authorities, are locked up in the Citadel;

- 18 women are at Drury and the new hospital.

The work of clearing up is being carried out day and night by the firemen, the teams of the civil defence, and workmen. It is believed that, under the enormous mass of rubble, still lie a significant number of prisoners, about thirty certainly.

In addition, a woman was killed in her residence, rue Voltaire; as for the victims of the Saint-Victor hospital, the number is unknown.

The number of escaped prisoners not yet recaptured cannot be given exactly, but will certainly climb to several hundred. M. Vivant, sous-prefect of Abbeville, has disappeared. He was held by the German authorities for a few days. The police services are continuing, on one hand, with the identification of the victims; on the other hand, they are conducting searches, both day and night, with a view to finding the escaped prisoners.

One should note the exemplary attitude of certain prisoners who, after their release, cooperated in a very active manner with the rescue of other prisoners; among those of particular note are Dr. Mans, M. Tempez and Gendarme Langlet, of the Nesle brigade.

The Police chief
Head of department.
(Signature illegible)

PREFECTURE OF THE SOMME
Cabinet of the prefect

Amiens, February 21, 1944

Le préfet de la Somme

A Monsieur le chef du gouvernement, ministre de l'Intérieur (secrétaire général au maintien de l'ordre, directement de la défense passive), à Paris ;

A Monsieur le préfet, délégué du ministère de l'Intérieur, à Paris ;

A Monsieur le préfet, chef du S.I.P.E.G., à Paris

A Monsieur le préfet de la région de Laon (cabinet), à Saint-Quentin

I have the honour to confirm to you my telephone call of Friday 18th February, informing you that on 18th February, a little after midday, some Anglo-American planes, flying at low altitude, launched on the district of Amiens, in the northern part of the city, a number of explosive bombs.

The objective seems to have been the prison, which was entirely destroyed.

About thirty houses located in the immediate surroundings of this establishment were also damaged; two buildings were partially destroyed and, in one, a person was killed. In addition, part of Saint-Victor hospital, which was used as a hospital by the troops of the occupation, was partially damaged.

Two of the attacking planes were shot down following an aerial combat.

The prison contained approximately 640 ordinary or political prisoners and 180 people imprisoned by order of the occupying authorities. Of this total, a hundred worked outside on various building sites.

So far, 77 corpses have been recovered from the debris and 78 people have been hospitalized, of whom many are seriously wounded; but these victims are prisoners, the personnel of the prison not having been reached. However, these figures are only provisional; the clearing of the debris, which continues actively, not being completed yet.

Among the civil servants who had been held by the German authorities, and who died during this bombing, was M. Gruel, head clerk to the Prefecture, who had been held since November 1943.

In addition, I make a point of mentioning to you the disappearance of M. Raymond Vivant, sub-prefect of Abbevîlle, held by the services of Sicherheitspolizei since February 14th, 1944, and who had been sent, that very same day, to the prison at Amiens.

According to information emanating from the German authorities, M. Vivant was seen unharmed a few moments after the bombing.

Since the news of this air attack, help was organized at once, and the various services of the civil defence began to release the victims and clear away enormous amounts of rubble.

Lastly, the police force and gendarmerie carried out searches, both day and night, in order to find the many people who had used this bombing to escape.

At the present time 192 prisoners, who were imprisoned by order of the French authorities had been recaptured, as had 54 prisoners of the German authorities and a score of women also held by the occupying authorities.

The number of escaped prisoners cannot yet be exactly determined, because of the impossibility of identifying many corpses and the number of victims that are still under the debris.

I believe it my duty to underline the considerable difficulties now facing us regarding the imprisonment of ordinary and political prisoners, following the destruction of the only penal establishment in the town of Amiens. Prisoners, at the moment, are imprisoned temporarily in an old factory which does not present any guarantee against the risk of escape.

The German authorities were approached with the view to reassigning to this use several buildings currently occupied by them, such as the Citadel or the barracks, but they did not succeed, and I fear that they will be refused. Undoubtedly, the condemned will be forwarded to other establishments by the order of the Director of the Penitentiary District of Poissy. However, the prisoners cannot leave Amiens, where they are at the moment. The absence of a prison would present a serious inconvenience.

Under these conditions, and in agreement with the Director of the Penitentiary District of Poissy, I envisage the installation, not far from the destroyed prison, of barracks surrounded by barbed wire, intended to be used as a provisional prison. Monitoring of this camp, whose construction will take time, will not be difficult to carry out and will require, undoubtedly, recourse to the police force of the city, whose manpower is already insufficient in the current districts.

The Prefect
Signed
Le Baube

PS. At the time I address this communication to you, I have just been advised that the German police force continues its search to discover a building suitable to contain the French and German prisoners.

Information provided by M. Jeannot

Police Chief

Situation of the prisoners at the prison on 23rd February 1944.

Before the bombing:

French section (men)		448
French section (women)		72
German section (male and female)		180
	Total	700

Population after the bombing

recaptured		182
52, rue de la republic (women)		26
German district at Dury (women)		8
citadel (men)		48
at the hospital (casualties)		74
at the disposal of chief warden		20
killed.		87
	Total	445

Which gives from a population of 700 people, 255 absent.

Amiens, February 24, 1944.

to M. le Délegué in northern zone of the Secretariat

General for the Maintenance of law and order (Cabinet), Paris

With reference to my report of February 21st on the bombing of the prison of Amiens, February 18th, 1944, I have the honour to make known to you that, since the news of this air attack, the police force and gendarmerie of my department have carried out searches in order to capture the prisoners who had escaped as a result of the bombing.

In the hours that followed, they apprehended 165 prisoners, of which 22 were apprehended by the gendarmerie in Amiens, Péronne, Villers-Bretonneux and in other localities.

For its part, the police force apprehended 18 prisoners, 9 during the day and 9 in the evening. Moreover, the French police force collected 56 people who had been imprisoned by the German authorities, of whom a number were women.

The total figure of recaptured prisoners, which currently amounts to 284, increases unceasingly, with many prisoners making known the place of their residence to the town halls or the gendarmerie squads.

I make a point of adding that, with regard to the effects of this bombing, M. Melin, who is in charge of the mission to the regional prefecture, was alerted at 2 p.m. by the departmental director of the civil defence of the Somme.

In addition, the police force immediately alerted the regional services Paris, while the gendarmerie warned all the neighbouring departments.

The prefect
signed
Le Baube

PART TWO

THE RAF STORY

Ramrod 564

18th February 1944

Previous page; Group Captain Pickard (centre) who led the raid on the Amiens prison on 18th February 1944. Behind him are Mosquitos of 464 Squadron which also took part in the raid.

PLANNING AND CREW BRIEFINGS

THE ORIGIN OF THE ORDERS

Air Vice-Marshal Basil Embry (Air Officer Commanding 2 Group) and his staff led the initial planning stages for the attack. However, neither he nor his staff actually made the decision to confirm these plans and go ahead with the operation. The decision to bomb the prison at Amiens was made official and effective on Thursday 10th February 1944. The staff of the Allied Expeditionary Air Force received a letter, dated the 10th, addressed to Air Marshal Trafford Leigh-Mallory - the Commander-in-Chief of the AEAF - from the Air Ministry.

Air Vice-Marshal Basil Embry, A.O.C. 2 Group

On Friday 11th February 1944, Brigadier General A.C. Strickland, writing under the authority of Trafford Leigh-Mallory, wrote to Air Marshal Arthur Coningham, Commander-in-Chief of 2 TAF (Second Tactical Air Force). Strickland forwarded Coningham a copy of the letter from the Air Ministry asking him to prepare an attack against 'a certain important objective in France'.

**HEADQUARTERS, ALLIED EXPEDITIONARY AIR FORCE
KESTREL GROVE, HIVE ROAD
STANMORE, MIDDX**

11 FEBRUARY 1944,

REF: AEAFI/MS.13110

SUBJECT: Special Operation

TO: Air Marshal Commanding, Second Tactical Air Force.

    1.   Attached is a copy of Air Ministry letter 55/44/D of I (R) dated 10 February, 1944, which requests that a certain important target in France be attacked before the 16th of February.

    2. The Air Commander in Chief has accepted this commitment and desires that the mission be given to your Air Force for accomplishment. He believes the operation deserves our best efforts and intends that you employ any combination of your forces required to ensure its success.

    3. Arrangements have been made for a representative from Air Ministry Director of Intelligence (Research) to visit your headquarters at Uxbridge at 1100 hours on Saturday, the 12th of February, to give you all information necessary to brief the crews of the unit or units that you may assign to the task.

For the Air Commander in Chief
Allied Expeditionary Air Force

A. C. Strickland
Brigadier General
D/S.A.S.O.

N.A. Doc Ref. AIR 37/806

This 'most secret' letter from the Headquarters of AEAF does not reveal the reason for the raid on the prison at Amiens, but it does give some interesting clues.

The orders came directly from the Air Ministry. This should not be taken to suggest or imply that the officers of this ministry actually planned the attack. The Director of Intelligence simply took on the responsibility for transmission of the details to those who needed them. The decision to attack military or other objectives always passed through the Air Ministry, therefore it is not at all surprising that the order to attack should emanate from them. What is surprising, however, is the level of secrecy attached to the transmission of these orders from one staff member to another. The name of the objective is not quoted in the letter from Brigadier General Strickland and the representative from the Air Ministry would only verbally confirm the details of the operation during the meeting at the Headquarters of 2 TAF. This procedure was unusual. For example, when a V-1 site was selected for an attack, the name of the site, or at least its number and its code, were registered on the list of the top priority targets and this list was then transmitted without the astonishing mystery that surrounds this letter.

The letter from the Air Ministry confirming and making official the decision to attack was dated 10th February 1944, exactly eight days before the raid, indicating considerable urgency.

A final point of interest, is by far the most important. The National Archive files AIR37/806 and AIR37/15 may be considered by some to be complete, but this is not actually the case. Several documents relating to the Amiens raid were carefully and methodically removed from the files. For example, the accompanying note from the Commander-in-Chief of AEAF is present in the file but the Air Ministry letter itself is not on file and is no longer available. From 23rd February 1944, a 'cleaning out' policy seems to have been applied to all files containing documents that related to, or mentioning, the name of Amiens Prison. This 'weeding', however, only relates to the documents that were used for the planning and development of this project. Not all the documents concerning the execution of the operation and other associated details at the time of the raid were destroyed. Evidence exists that confirms that there were at least four copies of this 'missing letter' from the Air Ministry in circulation.

The representative of the Air Ministry Director of Intelligence (Research) went personally to the Headquarters of the 2nd Tactical Air Force in Uxbridge on Saturday 12th February 1944, to convey the details for this operation.

The following day, Wing Commander Pleasance made a hand-written note:

```
Note of action

Ref enc 8A - a meeting was held at T.A.F. at which S.A.S.O. 2 Gp, G/C
Jameson 11 Gp, G/C Palmer DD of I (R), W/C Pleasance and others were
present. The general plan agreed was that R/P Typhoons should breach
the walls and Mosquitos following up should shake up the prison.
Details of the plan were to be worked out by 2 & 11 Gps. The attack
could not take place before Feb 16th as the prisoners could not be
informed before that date. The Air C in C wants to know details of
the prison and results of the attack.

13 Feb 44                                   H Pleasance W/C Ops 1(b)
```

NA Ref. AIR37/806

At this stage it was considered that a first wave consisting of R/P (rocket) equipped Typhoons would be used, each one carrying eight 60lb rockets under its wings to breach the enclosing walls. A second wave of Mosquitos would then bomb the prison building complex. This plan was only a suggestion and the staff of 2 and 11 Groups needed time to consider it.

The initial letter, dated 11th February* states that the attack must be made *before* 16th February 1944. However, in his note Pleasance, who was present at the meeting, clearly states that the attack must be made *not before* 16th February i.e. *after* the 16th.

RECONNAISSANCE

On 20th December 1943, nine Spitfire Mk.IXs from No. 542 Squadron had taken off for various reconnaissance operations over occupied Europe. Of these nine operations, eight were completed successfully and one was considered only a partial success. Two of the missions were related to the 'Bodyline' programme', i.e. the search of the area of the Pas-de-Calais for new V-1 sites. These two missions were also of interest in relation to Amiens:

```
Spitfire IX  EN395. Flt Sgt L.B. Baker. 542 Squadron.
Mission 'Bodyline'. Photograph reco. 11.30/13.25 (1h.55).
Objective Pas-de-Calais. Result photo obtained of targets. Climbed
to 16,000 feet over coast then commenced at 27,000 feet and continued
to 40,000 feet. Had troubles with canopy but managed to take 235
exps. Saw u.i. a/c some miles away but they kept going so I guess
they were ours. Landed OK.
```

* See page 290.

Spitfire IX EN667. Flt Lt J.E. Storey. 542 Squadron.
Mission 'Bodyline'. Photograph reco. 13.20/14.50h (1h30).
Objective: Pas-de-Calais. Results: Photographs obtained of the
objectives. Tried for a dozen 'Bodyline' objectives but other than having
seen Cap Gris Nez and knowing I was in the right area the remainder was
covered by 7-8/10 cloud so could not pin-point any targets. Took 130
exposures by chance through holes in the cloud layer.

Remarkably, whilst neither of the two 'Bodyline' pilots had been ordered to photograph Amiens Prison, the prison is quite clearly evident on exposures 3141 and 3142 taken of northern Amiens, where it appears on the route d'Albert. This was incredible good fortune. However, this was an area and feature of no particular interest at the time so the exposures were classified, indexed and filed. When planning began for the raid on Amiens Prison in 1944, Group Captain Palmer hurried to find a photograph of the building itself.

The PRU Spitfire pilots flew alone and unarmed, often having to search for gaps in the cloud to reveal a glimpse of their objectives.

Surprisingly, it appeared that Amiens Prison had never been photographed before. It was not considered a military objective as it was accepted that the Germans placed prisoners there, as with many other penal institutions in the occupied territories. However, the staff at the RAF's photographic interpretation centre at Medmenham retrieved the two photographs of the prison taken by the 'Bodyline' pilots from their files.

A section of exposure 3141 showing the Citadelle mid-left) and the prison (bottom right).

On Monday 14th February 1944, Group Captain Palmer from the Air Ministry arrived at 2 TAF headquarters in Uxbridge with the two aerial photographs of the northern area of Amiens and an assessment report compiled from an analysis of both pictures.

Photo 3141 had been taken at a very high altitude; it covered a considerable area totalling some 2,500 square metres. Needless to say, the prison itself was very small on that exposure. The second exposure (photo 3142) below, from the same Spitfire covered much the same area, but slightly further to the east.

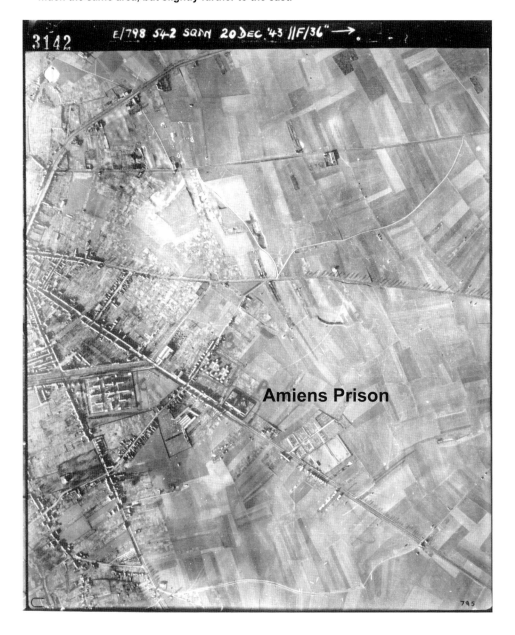

11 Group,
2 Group
2 T.A.F. Main.

From: Air Ministry, D.D.I.2.
Ref: DDIS/70/44.
Date: 14th February, 1944.

PRISON BUILDINGS - AMIENS AREA.

       With reference to the meeting which took place in No.2 T.A.F. Main Headquarters on Saturday, 12th February between representatives of the addressees and D.D.I.2., herewith an interpretation report by Medmenham on the building concerned.

       Some additional information has been included referring to nearby groups of buildings.

       A/V/M. Embry. D.S.O., A.F.C. has taken a personal copy of the interpretation report.

                     Palmer
                     Group Captain

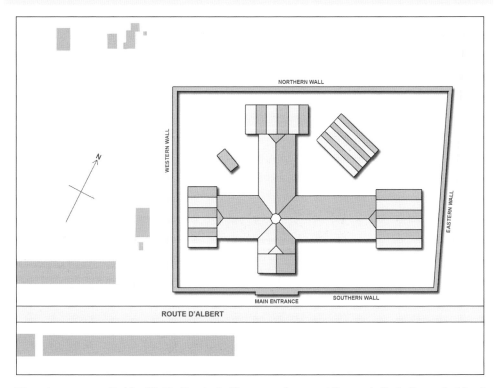

The prison was easily identifiable thanks to it's cross shape and its proximity to the main Albert road out of Amiens.

Although the image of the prison was small, the specialists at Medmenham were able to enlarge it considerably. In addition, they had sophisticated methods of interpreting the exact scale of buildings according to the shadows they cast. A whole series of calculations were carried out, based on the position of the aircraft, its altitude, the hour the image was taken and the known position of the sun. These extraordinary methods had their limits, but form the basis for the report reproduced below.

MOST SECRET
14.2.44.

INTERPRETATION REPORT Z 59 (R)

This report gives certain specified details of the buildings marked A, B and C on the attached photographs (Nos 3141–3142 of Sortie E/798).

Building A

Cross-shaped building (prison).

i) The height of the surrounding wall is 22 feet.

ii) It is difficult to make any accurate measurement of the thickness of this wall. The wall does not appear to be unusually thick for its height and as may be expected is thicker at the base than at the top. It can be stated, however, that the wall does not exceed 4 feet in thickness and is probably considerably less than this.

iii) Dimensions of area enclosed by the wall are as follows:

North side	425 feet.
South side	410 feet.
(adjoining main road)	
East side	325 feet.
West side	315 feet.

iv) The height of the main building to the eaves is approximately 48 feet and to the ridge 62 feet. There are therefore four or five storeys but the exact number cannot be ascertained from the photographs.

v) No machine-gun posts are visible in the immediate neighbourhood of the building but these could of course be concealed.

Buildings B

This appears to be a small housing estate consisting of a number of semi-detached two storey dwellings with gabled roofs. The layout is regular, each house having a small garden. There is no photographic evidence to suggest that the buildings are used otherwise than as private houses.

Building C

      The buildings are marked on the town plan as 'HOSPICE ST VICTOR' and their layout and design would correspond to that of an institute for the poor and aged. The grounds are surrounded by an 11 feet wall but there is no photographic evidence of military occupation. Outside the grounds about 80 yards to the north there is a trench near the road junction.

MOST SECRET   DISTRIBUTION

R.A.F. STATION,   A.D.I. (Ph)   4
MEDMENHAM   File   1
                                         5

NA Ref. AIR37/806

The officers of 2 TAF had at their disposal two vital tools for assessing the target:

1) The aerial photography of the northern district of Amiens and its associated reports.

2) A general plan of the town of Amiens.

The town plan had been extracted from an old Post Office publication from 1939, which also served as a tourist guide. This 'tourist guide' included the plan and population details which stated that the population of Amiens in 1939 was 93,207 inhabitants. The position of the prison had also been marked in red pencil on this plan. The plan was particularly useful in identifying the St Victor Hospice and houses in rue Voltaire.

Upon receipt of the report from Medmenham, Embry authorized the building of a model of the prison. This was a crude model, but was invaluable for showing the scale and proportions of the prison complex. This model would later prove to be essential in showing the aircrews a three-dimensional representation of the target, hopefully making their attack that much easier. Combined with the photographs, this model was studied over and over again. For some time, Embry had been very pro-active in requesting model mock-ups to be made, especially for low-level attacks on V-1 sites, as models for these had proved to be very useful to the aircrews and made them feel that the target was already familiar.

However, despite the factors mentioned above, the information available regarding the target was still sparse. Only approximate information was known about the following:

A crude model of the prison was made to help the aircrews familiarise themselves with its layout as seen from the air.

1) The external shape of the prison buildings.

2) Their external dimensions.

3) The nature of the buildings located in the vicinity.

Although the map indicated that some of the buildings close to the prison off the Boulevard Beauvillé belonged to the St Victor Hospice, the planners did not know that this had been transformed into a Luftwaffe hospital.

Thus, the basic details available for the briefing were that,

a) The principal prison building was in the shape of a cross.

b) Additional buildings were supported on the east, west and northern ends.

c) An isolated building was in the courtyard.

d) All the above was surrounded by a wall.

There was no information that related to the specific use or purpose of the buildings.

There was some debate about the number of storeys in the main building and no information was available at all about the internal structure and materials used for construction of the main prison building. When looking at the photographs taken after the raid, it is clear that the model contained many minor errors. However, given the information that was available when the model was built, it must be regarded as a very good effort.

Overleaf. The original town map as used by the planners with the prison highlighted.

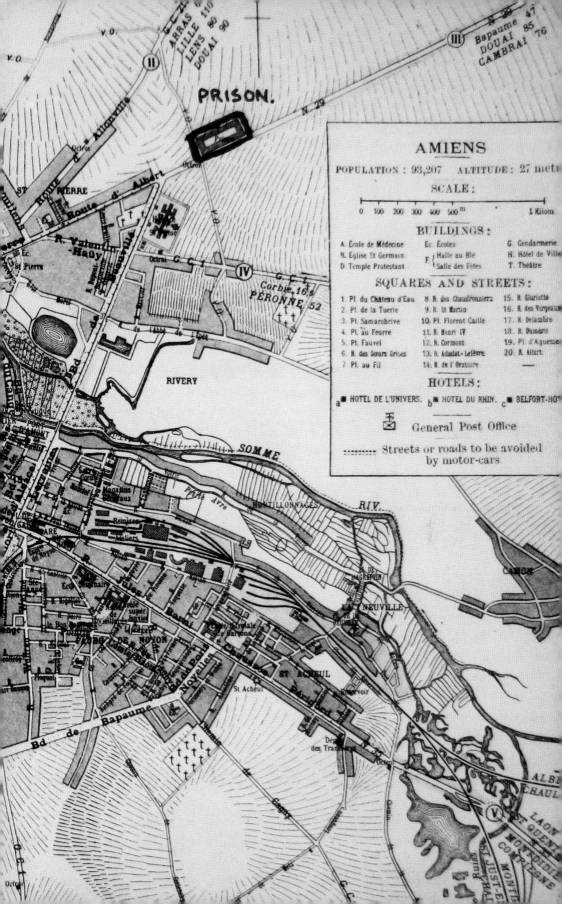

PRISON.

AMIENS
POPULATION : 93,207   ALTITUDE : 27 metr[es]
SCALE :

0   100   200   300   400   500 m   1 Kilom.

BUILDINGS :

A. École de Médecine   Ec. Écoles   G. Gendarmerie
B. Église St Germain   F. Halle au Blé   H. Hôtel de Ville
D. Temple Protestant   Salle des Fêtes   T. Théâtre

SQUARES AND STREETS :

1. Pl. du Château d'Eau   8. R. des Chaudronniers   15. R. Gloriette
2. Pl. de la Tuerie   9. R. St Martin   16. R. des Vergeaux
3. Pl. Samarobrive   10. Pl. Florent Caille   17. R. Delambre
4. Pl. au Feurre   11. R. Henri IV   18. R. Dumaril
5. Pl. Fauvel   12. R. Cormont   19. Pl. d'Aguesseau
6. R. des Sœurs Grises   13. R. Adadat-Lefèvre   20. R. Allart
7. Pl. au Fil   14. R. de l'Oratoire

HOTELS :

a. HOTEL DE L'UNIVERS   b. HOTEL DU RHIN   c. BELFORT-HO[TEL]

⌖ General Post Office

------- Streets or roads to be avoided
        by motor-cars

During the briefing, it was explained to the Mosquito pilots that the additional buildings at the east and west ends of the main building were the areas where German soldiers and staff were located. Pilot Officer Lee Howard recalled Group Captain Pickard saying:

We have a model of the prison, which you are all going to study in detail shortly. You will notice that the prison itself is in the form of a cross, and that at its east and west ends are small triple buildings which, according to our information, are the quarters of the Nazi prison guards.

It is now known that these buildings had nothing to do with the German guards or staff and that most of the Germans were actually located in the south wing. Therefore, whatever source this 'information' came from, it was incorrect. This particular information was not included in the original AO 241 message about the attack upon the prison either. It is possible that it was simply a case of Pickard motivating his crews and perhaps trying to deflect their thoughts from the large numbers of prisoners who could be killed as a result of the attack, many of whom were believed to have willingly assisted Allied airmen who had been shot down over France.

The senior officers of 2 TAF responsible for planning the raid:
l-r. Air Commodore D F W Atcherley, Group Captain Wykeham-Barnes,
Wing Commander H P Shallard and Air Vice-Marshal Basil Embry.

THE GROUNDING OF AIR VICE-MARSHAL BASIL EMBRY.

Air Vice-Marshal Basil Embry was a man who had an extremely high level of responsibility and involvement in the many tasks that he supervised. These were always planned meticulously and completed to very high standards. Previously he had even flown on missions to observe the performance of his aircrews so that he could select men for particular posts and promotions.

On 22nd December 1943, 41 Mosquitos attacked the V-1 site at Saint-Agathe-D`Aliermont in the Lower Seine area for the first time. The commander of the operation was Group Captain Percy Charles Pickard DSO** DFC, flying in lead position in the first wave. His immmediate superior, Air Vice-Marshal Basil Embry flew just behind him, leading the second wave. Embry and his navigator, Flight Lieutenant 'Ted' Sismore, then used their experiences of this raid to plan the Amiens mission along the same lines.

It was Air Marshal Trafford Leigh-Mallory, Commander-in-Chief of the AEAF who, stopped Embry taking part in the Amiens raid. The official reason for this was because he was too senior to risk being shot down and captured. Furthermore, Embry had escaped from captivity in France in 1940 and his re-capture could possibly endanger escape routes. When questioned about this in 2011, 'Ted' Sismore believed that Embry's seniority was *not* the reason for his removal from the raid, rather he knew something that could not fall into enemy hands. Exactly what this was he was never told, but he assumed it was something to do with the raid, or details of the coming invasion plans.

It is of course a fact that on 22nd December 1943, Trafford Leigh-Mallory had not prevented Embry from taking part in the V-1 raid, when surely the risks were just as high and of the same nature. It must be considered that Embry`s removal from participating in this raid is of some significance.

THE SCENE AT RAF HUNSDON ON 18TH FEBRUARY

At 09.00 hours on the morning of 18th February 1944, nineteen highly trained crews, each consisting of a pilot and navigator, were anxiously awaiting orders specifying the nature and the objective of their operation that day.

The crew list had been compiled by Group Captain Pickard who was the Officer Commanding 140 Wing which had been entrusted with the operation. On this particular February morning, a carpet of snow covered the airfield and more was still falling. The snow seemed to absorb all the sounds from the surrounding countryside and all lay quiet. However, this was not the case inside the confines of the airfield. Normal pre-raid

Group Captain P C Pickard DSO** DFC was a highly decorated pilot who was well known to the British public, having appeared in the very popular propaganda film 'Target for Tonight'.

procedures for the ground crew had been under way since the early morning: re-fuelling, bombing up, checking the engines and the radios. The nineteen aircrews totalled 38 men, each one in a state of tense anticipation; the snowfall in England had already led to the cancellation of several other missions and the situation did not look promising.

The last operational flight of these crews had been on 15th February. They had participated in *Ramrod 558*, a low-level bombing run on some V-1 sites at Bonnetot and Ardouval in the Lower Seine region of France. This attack had been entrusted to six Mosquitos from 464 Squadron RAAF of 140 Wing (Hunsdon) and six Mosquitos from 613 Squadron of 138 Wing. Other squadrons had flown on 16th February when *Ramrod 561* took place against a V-1 launching site at Hambures and *Ramrod 562* against V-1 sites at Bonnetot, Écalles-sur-Buchy and Belleville-en-caux. *Ramrod 563* involved attacks by B-26 Marauders on another series of V-1 sites. Poor weather conditions on 17th February had curtailed any further operations.

By Friday 18th February the weather had not improved at all, more snow had fallen and Hunsdon was still covered; conditions were further worsened by winds that were increasing, carrying snow flurries that reduced visibility further.

A roster of crews had been posted for a mission that morning; however, most crews were bewildered at this when looking out at the weather. Lee Howard, the navigator of the Film Production Unit Mosquito that would film the raid, later recollected: *"In addition, it was snowing heavily outside - certainly very poor flying weather - and we were all fairly convinced that any normal trip would have been cancelled from the weather point of view alone. This one must have been different, with a vengeance"*.

The snow continued to fall, swept along by an icy wind. The aircrews looked out of the windows at the fractured grey clouds scudding low over the snowbound airfield, surely confirming that no mission could possibly take place that day. The majority of men shared this view, thinking that surely anything planned must be cancelled, unless it was an especially important mission. However, whatever the final decision, the mechanics, armourers and engineers still had to conduct all the rigorous pre-flight checks and adjustments to ensure that every aeroplane was at the height of readiness if required. These checks were rigidly applied, each member of the ground crew knew how vital they were and thought of themselves as custodians of their machines; responsible for the reliability of their aeroplanes and the lives of the crews who flew in them. Nothing was left to chance, as chance had cost lives all too often.

At this stage the senior officers in 2 TAF who took overall command of such missions were fully aware of the target and most likely whether the mission would be carried out. Pickard had already been informed by Embry of the full details relating to this difficult mission and just how the desired results could be achieved.

The secrecy surrounding such operations was vital; however, two others, apart from Pickard, had a fair idea of what was happening on this day. Contrary to strict orders several people had received some information prior to the normal pre-flight briefing. This information only became known after the cessation of hostilities. The two crewmen who claimed they had been told were Squadron Leader Philippe Livry-Level (a navigator in No. 21 Squadron) and Pilot Officer Lee Howard. According to Livry-Level, Pickard had spoken of the issue earlier, on or about 10th February, saying, '*Philippe, I am annoyed, we have friends in prison in Amiens, it is necessary that they escape.*' Pickard must have had extreme confidence in Livry-Level to even raise the topic in view of the strict secrecy surrounding the raid and knowing that Livry-Level, as a Frenchman, would be passionate about such an action.

Squadron Leader Livry-Level was himself quite a character, very tall and with a large black moustache. He was highly decorated (Croix de Guerre in the 1914-1918 war and he would receive the DSO, DFC and Bar and American DFC during the 1939-45 war). Originally from Normandy, this father of five decided to escape after the German invasion

74

and travelled via Portugal to England. By April 1941, Philippe Livry-Level was 45 years old, too old to be considered for aircrew. So, when he met the Recruitment Officer, Livry-Level informed him that he was only 35 years old. The deception was successful and resulted in him being selected for the RAF. Following a navigator's training course Livry-Level became a navigator in Coastal Command with No. 53 Squadron. He was then posted to No. 161 Special Duties Squadron, as a navigator. He took part in many clandestine operations with this squadron, often involving the dropping of equipment to the French Resistance, and became acquainted with Pickard who was also flying with 161 Squadron at the time. They met again when

The '35 year old' Phillippe Livry-Level was accepted by the RAF for aircrew training despite actually being 10 years older!

A 487 Squadron Mosquito photographed shortly after the Amiens raid.

Livry-Level joined 21 Squadron which was part of 140 Wing commanded by the newly promoted Group Captain Pickard.

Pilot Officer Lee Howard too had been given information prior to the briefing:

Unlike most of those present, I had been given preliminary details of the raid the evening before, because there are certain additional preparations the film cameraman had to make which take time.

Most of the other members of air crew were quite used to my knowing what was happening long before they did, and several of them asked me what the raid was all about.

Normally I would have answered their questions; but this time, when I had seen Group Captain Pickard the evening before, he had done nothing other than indicate the nature of the attack in the most general terms.

He had told me where it was; he had told me the route by which we were getting there; and he had told me that I would like the raid. "It's going to make a grand story for you", he said. "You should get some damned good pictures; I think you'll find it's very photogenic".

"A big factory of some kind?" I hazarded.

"Well - something like that, in general," he replied. "You'll understand the need for absolute secrecy when you hear all about it at the briefing."

Of the 19 crews, 18 were scheduled to fly Mosquito VIs as attack aircraft. These were armed with two 500lb bombs in their bomb-bay and another two, externally mounted under the wings. This combination of internal and external stowage was made necessary by the 20mm cannon breech mechanisms intruding into the bomb-bay.

The nineteenth crew was to fly a Mosquito IV for the FPU (Film Production Unit). This specialist aircraft was parked away from the rest of the Mosquitos as its ground crew made their final adjustments.

In addition to the FPU Mosquito, cameras were installed in at least two other aircraft. One was fitted in Pilot Officer Sparks' Mosquito and another was installed in Pickard's Mosquito. The camera installed in Sparks' aircraft was to be used for filming the bomb impacts from the lead bomber.

THE CREWS SELECTED FOR THE OPERATION

No. 487 Squadron Royal New Zealand Air Force

Pilot W/C I. S. Smith DFC	Navigator Flt Lt Barnes DFM
Pilot Flt Sgt S. Jennings	Navigator W/O Nichols
Pilot P/O M. N. Sparks	Navigator P/O Dunlop
Pilot P/O M. L. S. Darrall	Navigator P/O Stevenson
Pilot P/O D. R. Fowler	Navigator W/O Wilkins
Pilot Flt Lt B. D. Hanafin	Navigator P/O Redgrave

No. 464 Squadron, Royal Australian Air Force

Pilot W/C R. W. Iredale DFC	Navigator Flt Lt J. L. McCaul DFC
Pilot Sqn Ldr W. R. C. Sugden	Navigator Flg Off A. H. Bridger
Pilot Flg Off K. L. Monaghan DFM	Navigator Flg Off A. W. Dean DFM
Pilot Sqn Ldr A. I. McRitchie (NZ)	Navigator Flt Lt R. W. Sampson
Pilot Flt Lt T. McPhee	Navigator Flt Lt G. W. Atkins
Pilot Gp Capt P. C. Pickard DSO** DFC	Navigator Flt Lt J. A. Broadley DSO DFC DFM

No. 21 Squadron Royal Air Force.

Pilot W/C I. G. Dale	Navigator Flg Off E. Gabites
Pilot Flt Lt A. E. C. Wheeler DFC	Navigator Flg Off N. M. Redington
Pilot Flt Lt E. E. Hogan	Navigator Flt Sgt D. A. S. Crowfoot
Pilot Flt Sgt A. Steedman	Navigator Flg Off E. J. Reynolds
Pilot Flt Lt D. A. Taylor DFC	Navigator Sqn Ldr P. Livry-Level DFC (France)
Pilot Flt Lt M. J. Benn DFC	Navigator Flg Off N. A. Roe

Film Production Unit (FPU)

Pilot Flt Lt A. (Tony) Wickham DFC Navigator P/O L. Howard

Wing Commander I. S. 'Black' Smith DFC was to lead the attack.

THE BRIEFING FOR THE BOMBER CREWS

At 09.40 hours on Friday 18th February, the Tannoy system in the Mess crackled into life. It announced that there was to be an immediate meeting in the briefing room for all the crews who had been selected. The weather was still a major concern and most still thought that any mission scheduled for that day would be cancelled. As always, entry into the briefing room was kept strictly to those giving the briefing and those selected to attend. Once inside, they all took a seat looking at the large blackboard; next to this, and of far more interest, was a large map of Northern France. The following description provided by Pilot Officer Lee Howard allows us an insight into the pre-mission environment:

The mystification of the air crews was increased somewhat by the very elaborate precautions to maintain the secrecy of which Group Captain Pickard had spoken. There were Service police guarding the briefing room; the one by the door had a list of the names of those entitled to enter, and even when one was inside the target model was still hidden from view.

Finally Group Captain Pickard came in, followed shortly afterwards by the Air Vice-Marshal commanding our Group*, who stood at the back of the room and listened.

    * AVM Embry

Wing Commander R. W. 'Bob' Iredale DFC (right) and his regular navigator Flight Lieutenant J. L. McCaul DFC (left) were to lead the second wave over the prison. *AWM UK0848*

The aircrews sat down in the briefing room with its curtained windows. They did not have long to wait; soon voices were heard and, in the general hubbub, the staff officers came into the room, some of whom represented the intelligence and meteorological departments. All now paid attention to what was said. Pickard was first to speak; carefully placed on the desk in front of him were some papers, one of which was the Broadcast Emergency Form B - AO241. This form had only just come off the teleprinter and gave final details and authorization for the mission to proceed.

'Form B' was the standard form used for the orders coming in from Group. However, this one differed from the usual form in that the word 'Emergency' could clearly be seen in bold print. The original document still exists in the files at the National Archive, Kew, (AIR37/806) where it can be examined today and, for the modern researcher, it provides both irrefutable and tangible details of the raid.

Once again, it is the personal account of Pilot Officer Lee Howard that allows a glimpse of the briefing proceedings:

"Your target today", said the G.C. "is a very special one from every point of view. There has been no little debate as to whether this attack should be carried out, and your A.O.C. more or less had to ask for a vote of confidence in his men and his aircraft before we were

given the chance of having a crack at it. It could only be successfully carried out by low-level Mosquitos; and we've got to make a big success of it to justify his faith in us, and prove further, if proof is necessary, just how accurately we can put our bombs down".

The experiences and accounts of Pilot Officer Howard were used, at least partially, to compile an official history of the raid (albeit heavily censored) that was made public on 28th October 1944. Pilot Officer Howard's is only one account of the briefing and, in itself does not record all the facts and details that were placed before the aircrews at the briefing.

This is part of the original text of Pilot Officer Howard's account. Research shows that this version agrees perfectly with the accounts of other aircrew and attendees of this briefing.

"The story is this: in the prison at Amiens are one hundred and twenty* French patriots who have been condemned to be shot by the Nazis for assisting the Allies. Some have been condemned for assisting Allied airmen to escape after being brought down in France. Their end is a matter of a day or two. Only a successful operation by the R.A.F. to break down their prison walls can save them, and we're going to have a crack at it to-day. We're going to bust that prison open."

"If we make a good job of it and give the lads inside a chance to get out, the French underground people will be standing by to take over from there.

"There are eighteen of you detailed for this trip. In addition, the Film Unit's special aircraft is coming along to see what sort of job you make of it.

"The first six of you are going to breach the walls. Now, these walls have got to be broken down if the men inside are to get out successfully. This will mean some real low-level flying; you've got to be right down on the deck. The walls are only about twenty-five feet high, and if we're not damned careful our bombs are going to bounce right over them and land inside the prison and blow everybody to smithereens.

"We have told the men inside of the risk, through the underground movement, and they're fully aware of the possibility.

"We've got to cut that risk down to the minimum. You've got to be below the height of the wall when you let them go; down to ten feet, if possible. There are no obstructions in the way on your run up, so you should be able to make it.

"We have a model of the prison, which you are all going to study in detail shortly. You will notice that the prison itself is in the form of a cross, and that at its east and west ends are small triple buildings which, according to our information, are the quarters of the Nazi prison guards.

"The second six aircraft are going to prang those quarters. I don't suppose all the Nazis will be inside at once, but we're sure to get some of them and it'll add to the general confusion and give the prisoners a better chance.

*Changed in pencil on the draft to 'many'.

"The film aircraft will follow this second formation and will orbit the target, filming the results of the raid."

The Group Captain looked at my pilot. "We're dropping 11 second delay bombs, Tony", he said. "You will have to lose a minute or so near the target to give them a chance to go off before you run over the prison. Then you can make your runs as the cameraman wants and as you consider expedient".

Tony nodded.

The Group Captain continued: "The first six aircraft are on target at exactly midday. The second six will attack three minutes later.

"Now, the last six will arrive 10 minutes after this second attack. Their job will depend entirely on the success or failure of the first two sections. If the job has been well done, they will pass north of Amiens and set course for home, bringing their bombs back with them."

The Wing Commander who was leading the last six aircraft stood up. "Who is to decide whether the attack is a success or not, sir"? he asked.

Group Captain Pickard considered. "I shall be flying towards the end of the first twelve", he said. "When I've dropped my bombs I shall pull off to one side and circle, probably just to the north of the prison. I can watch the attack from there; and I'll tell you by radio. We'll use the signals 'red' and 'green', repeated three times; so that if you hear me say 'red, red, red' you'll know you're being warned off and will go home without bombing. If I say 'green, green, green' it's clear for you to go in and bomb.

"As an additional precaution, the film aircraft will have just as good a view as myself of the whole show - perhaps even a little better - so it can act as cover. If you don't hear me give the signal and hear the answering acknowledgment, Tony, you can give the 'red' or 'green' yourself before the third six come in to bomb."

Eventually the briefing was nearly over. We had studied the route again and again; we had studied the model of the prison until we knew it better than our own homes; the navigators, of which I was one, had checked and counter-checked their work. Hot tea was brought around; and, as we rested a moment from the high-speed work and concentration of the last three hours, the G.C. had a final word to say.

"It's still snowing, and the visibility is not so good; but we can get off the deck all right. I've just had a final word with Group on the phone and they've given us the O.K. to go. This is one raid where a cancellation is unthinkable; if the slightest hint of what we are going to try to do were to leak out, every one of those men would be shot instantly. So - let's get going and make a good job of it".

Teleprinter Message 'Form B' - AO 241. (NA Ref AIR37/806)

```
B/CAST + EMERGENCY + FORM 'B'            B  71 11 M/B2/3A   FEB 44
HNO   T   140 A/F
UGI         T        11 GROUP
V GPB GPB 5:18        ''O''         FORM 'B'
```

FROM 2 GROUP 180940 A
TO 140 WING/AIRFIELD
INFO 11 GROUP, HQ TAF MAIN, HQ ADGB, HQ AEAF.
SECRET QQX BT
AO 241 18TH FEB

INFORMATION. MOSQUITOS OF 140 AIRFIELD ARE TO ATTACK THE PRISON
AT AMIENS IN AN ATTEMPT TO ASSIST 120 PRISONERS TO ESCAPE. THESE
PRISONERS ARE FRENCH PATRIOTS CONDEMNED TO DEATH FOR ASSISTING THE
ALLIES. THIS AIR ATTACK IS ONLY PART OF THE PLAN AS OTHER ASSISTANCE
WILL BE AT HAND AT THE TIME.

DATE AND TIME.   18TH FEBRUARY 1944.
                   ZERO: 12.00 HOURS.

ROUTE. BASE - LITTLEHAMPTON - VIA APPROPRIATE LATTICE TO TOCQUEVILLE
- SENARPONT - BOURDON - ONE MILE SOUTH DOULLENS - BOUZINCOURT - 2
MILES WEST SOUTH WEST ALBERT - TARGET - TURN RIGHT - ST. SAVEUR
-SENARPONT - TOCQUEVILLE - HASTINGS - BASE.

BOMB LOAD: 2 X 500 LB. M.C. MKIV FUSED T.D.
                  11 SECS.
                  2 X 500LB S.A.P. FUSED T.D.
                  11 SECS.

METHOD OF ATTACK. ALL AIRCRAFT TO ATTACK AT LOW LEVEL.

1ST. ATTACK. SIX MOSQUITOS AS DETAILED BY O.C. 140 AIRFIELD.
INTENTION. TO BREAK THE OUTER WALL IN AT LEAST TWO PLACES.
METHOD. LEADING THREE AIRCRAFT TO ATTACK EASTERN WALL USING MAIN ROAD
AS LEAD IN. SECOND SECTION OF THREE AIRCRAFT WHEN TEN MILES FROM
TARGET WILL BREAK AWAY TO RIGHT AT SUFFICIENT HEIGHT TO ALLOW THEM
TO WATCH LEADING THREE AIRCRAFT AND THEN ATTACK NORTHERN WALL ON A
NORTH-SOUTH RUN, IMMEDIATELY FOLLOWING THE EXPLOSION OF THE BOMBS OF
LEADING SECTION.
TIMING. ATTACK TO BE AT ZERO HOURS.

2ND. ATTACK. SIX MOSQUITOS AS DETAILED BY O.C. 140 AIRFIELD.
INTENTION. TO BOMB THE MAIN PRISON BUILDING.

METHOD. LEADING THREE AIRCRAFT TO ATTACK SOUTH EASTERN END OF MAIN
BUILDING AND SECOND SECTION OF THREE AIRCRAFT TO ATTACK THE NORTH

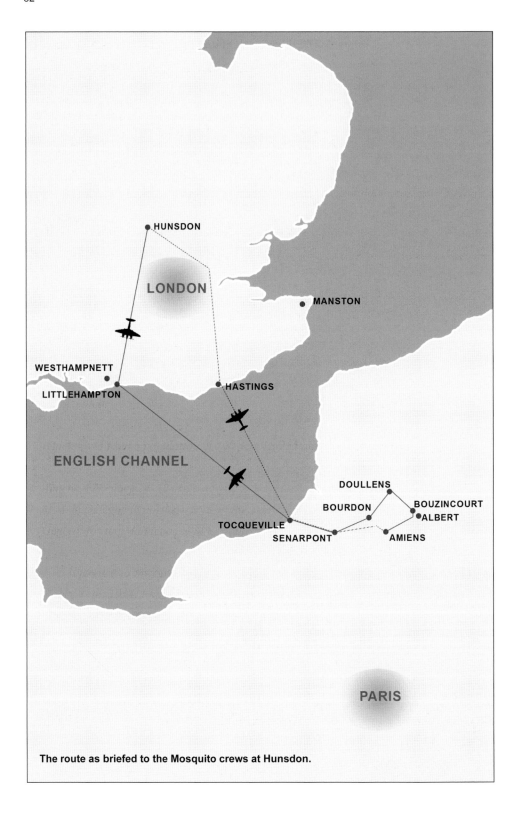

The route as briefed to the Mosquito crews at Hunsdon.

WESTERN END OF BUILDING. ATTACKS TO BE CARRIED OUT IN SIMILAR MANNER
TO 1ST. ATTACK ABOVE.
TIMING: ATTACK TO BE MADE AT ZERO HOURS PLUS 3 MINS.

3RD. ATTACK. SIX MOSQUITOS AS DETAILED BY O.C. 140 AIRFIELD.

INTENTION. THIS FORCE IS A RESERVE, AND WILL APPROACH THE TARGET AS
IN THE TWO PREVIOUS ATTACKS, ONE SECTION FROM THE EAST AND ONE FROM
THE NORTH, BUT WILL BOMB ONLY IF IT IS SEEN THAT ONE OF THE PREVIOUS
ATTACKS HAS FAILED.
TIMING. ATTACK TO BE MADE AT ZERO PLUS 13 MINS.

FIGHTER SUPPORT. EACH FORMATION OF SIX MOSQUITOS WILL HAVE ONE
SQUADRON OF TYPHOONS AS CLOSE ESCORT. FIGHTERS WILL RENDEZVOUS WITH
MOSQUITOS AS FOLLOWS.
      1ST. ATTACK. 1 MILE EAST LITTLEHAMPTON AT
             ZERO MINUS 45 MINS.
    2ND. ATTACK. 1 MILE WEST P X LITTLEHAMPTON
             AT ZERO MINUS 42 MINS.
      3RD. ATTACK. LITTLEHAMPTON ZERO MINUS 32 MINS

SIGNALS.   1ST ATTACK. BOMBER CALLSIGN: DYPEG.
                    GROUND CONTROL CALLSIGN: AILSOME
                    ON 2 GROUP GUARD 1.
                    BOMBER LEADER MAY CALL ESCORT
                    DIRECT IN EMERGENCY ON 11 GROUP
                    GUARD 1.
                    FIGHTER CALLSIGN: GARLIC.
          2ND ATTACK. BOMBER CALLSIGN: CANON.
                    GROUND CONTROL CALLSIGN:BELLFIELD
                    ON 2 GROUP GUARD 1.
                    BOMBER LEADER MAY CALL ESCORT
                    DIRECT IN EMERGENCY ON 11 GROUP GUARD 1.
                    FIGHTER CALL SIGN: CAJOLE.

          3RD ATTACK. BOMBER CALLSIGN: BUCKSHOT.
                    GROUND CONTROL CALLSIGN: GREENSHIP
                    ON 2 GROUP GUARD 1.
                    BOMBER LEADER MAY CALL ESCORT DIRECT
                    IN EMERGENCY ON 11 GROUP GUARD 1.
                    FIGHTER CALLSIGN: DUNLOP.

GENERAL.   EMERGENCY HOMING TO FRISTON ON 2 GROUP GUARD.
            A.V.XXXX A.S.R. ON 2 GROUP GUARD.
            SPECIAL V.H.F. CODEWORD: RENOVATE.

NOTES (1) FOLLOWING EACH ATTACK SECTIONS OF THREE AIRCRAFT OF
EACH FORMATION ARE TO ENDEAVOUR TO REGAIN CLOSE COMPANY AS SOON AS
POSSIBLE.

B.T 180940 A

DIFFERENCES BETWEEN VERBAL AND WRITTEN ORDERS

The teleprinter message AO 241 received at Hunsdon on 18th February 1944 at 09.40 hours is quite clear concerning its objectives.

What can be clearly ascertained is that the official reason for the raid given to the crews by Group Captain Pickard and the details contained in the message AO 241 were the same:

(a) That the 140 Wing Mosquitos were to make an attempt to free 120 prisoners condemned to death for having assisted the Allies.

(b) The air operation was only part of the planned release mechanism for these prisoners, as those who escape would receive help and assistance from local resistance parties, who had already been informed of the attack.

The secrecy that had surrounded the planning of this attack is understandable. Even the flight plans show a frequent change of direction on approach to Amiens to continually deceive German radar plotters of the true target. The flight paths had been carefully chosen in an attempt to minimize Luftwaffe fighter opposition.

The first indication of a difference in objective from Pickard's verbal briefing and the AO 241 message was suggested by Pilot Officer Lee Howard:

You will notice that the prison itself is in the form of a cross, and that at its east and west ends are small triple buildings which, according to our information, are the quarters of the Nazi prison guards.

The second six aircraft are going to prang those quarters. I don't suppose all the Nazis will be inside at once, but we're sure to get some of them and it'll add to the general confusion and give the prisoners a better chance.

The content of the message AO 241 was:

```
2ND. ATTACK. SIX MOSQUITOS AS DETAILED BY O.C. 140 AIRFIELD.
INTENTION. TO BOMB THE MAIN PRISON BUILDING.

METHOD. LEADING THREE AIRCRAFT TO ATTACK SOUTH EASTERN END OF MAIN
BUILDING AND SECOND SECTION OF THREE AIRCRAFT TO ATTACK THE NORTH
WESTERN END OF BUILDING. ATTACKS TO BE CARRIED OUT IN SIMILAR MANNER
TO 1ST. ATTACK ABOVE.
```

Group Captain Pickard (centre) and Wing Commander I G E 'Daddy' Dale O/C 21 Squadron (left) walk past Mosquitos of 464 Squadron at Hunsdon early February 1944. To the right is Wing Commander A G Wilson who handed over command of 487 Squadron to 'Black' Smith shortly before the Amiens Raid.

Here is an important change. The account of Pilot Officer Howard mentioned that Group Captain Pickard explained the significance of the two buildings situated at the east and west end of the main prison building as being where the German prison guards were billeted.

The written orders contained in AO 241 do not mention these two buildings as being included in the objectives or that they were where the prison guards would be located. AO 241 only stipulates the raid is to address the south-eastern and north-western ends of the principal prison building. On a purely military level, this difference is inconsequential; however, it must have had a significant psychological effect on the listening crews.

Other far more important details are:

(a) The place in the formation that Group Captain Pickard would take; at the rear of the second wave.

(b) The method of attack planned for the Third Wave.

Pickard's position would allow him to assess the situation and make two decisions:

(1) Whether the third wave attacked or not.

(2) How it would attack and what its objectives would be.

Message AO 241:

3 RD. ATTACK. SIX MOSQUITOS AS DETAILED BY O.C. 140 AIRFIELD.

INTENTION. THIS FORCE IS A RESERVE, AND WILL APPROACH THE TARGET AS IN THE TWO PREVIOUS ATTACKS, ONE SECTION FROM THE EAST AND ONE FROM THE NORTH, BUT WILL BOMB ONLY IF IT IS SEEN THAT ONE OF THE PREVIOUS ATTACKS HAS FAILED.

Group Captain Pickard was the overall leader of this operation. Theoretically, the place of such a commander was at the head of the formation, the exception being for the 'Pathfinder' operations where the leader followed the 'Scout'. However, the Amiens raid had three quite distinct formations, each having its allocated leader. In the written orders from 2 Group, a higher authority than either Pickard or 140 Wing, the leader of the operation did not receive any orders to orbit the target making assessments as to whether the Third Wave should attack.

'Ted' Sismore, who planned the attack with Embry, recalled that the original plan relied on the crew of the Film Production Unit Mosquito to make the decision as to whether the Third Wave should attack, or not. This was decided upon to minimise the risk to the aircrews who were to leave the target immediately. In a 2 Group briefing film (shown in a 1982 BBC Panorama documentary) a written message states,

21 SQDN. FOLLOWING 10 MINS LATER, UNLESS INSTRUCTED BY F.P.U. RECCO A'C THAT ATTACK WAS SUCCESSFUL TO DESTROY THE PRISON ENTIRELY.

'Tony' Wickham and Lee Howard were to take their FPU Mosquito over the target after the second wave's attack and record the results of the bombing; they were ideally placed to assess the effect of the attack without exposing themselves to any danger over and above that inherent in their own task. Pickard decided that he would make the assessment himself, after being given command.

AO 241 clearly states that the leader of the third wave had the responsibility for choosing the target on his approach. If the first attack on the external walls had failed then these would become a priority for the third attack. Or, if the principal building had not been touched, then this would take priority.

The officers at 2 Group and the Air Vice-Marshal had left nothing to chance when it came to the finer details of their plan. Everything had been thoroughly assessed and worked out; even to the leaving of a ten-minute interval between the second attack and arrival of the third wave to allow the smoke to disperse from the target.

WHY PICKARD DID NOT FOLLOW THE ORDERS FROM GROUP TO THE LETTER?

The choice of pilots to act as leaders in certain roles during wartime was, more often than not, down to personalities. Basil Embry was the most conscientious and meticulous of leaders. There is no doubt that Embry regarded Pickard's past accomplishments highly, particularly his night operations to the French Resistance. However, he may have had reservations about Pickard's capabilities in daytime operations, especially low-level flights, in which Pickard was less experienced. Pickard may even have felt some antagonism at Embry for assuming both overall command of this operation and intending to participate in it. This leadership choice and placement was shown in the original plans, but for a variety of reasons these plans were to be challenged, opposed and would never proceed as originally envisaged. 'Ted' Sismore believes that Embry's position of choice would have been behind the lead bomber, Wing Commander Smith*, had he participated in the raid.

The Amiens Raid was only Pickard's sixth low-level operation. Perhaps due to this inexperience, Embry left nothing to chance and wanted to oversee and control all issues relating to this raid. With something this important, perhaps he considered it too risky to deputise overall responsibility to a junior officer. How this command situation was originally managed and presented, and whether or not Embry himself or Pickard mismanaged the situation, is open to discussion.

Everything was now ready, positions had been assigned, and it was only at the last moment that Air Marshal Trafford Leigh–Mallory, Commander-in-Chief of the AEAF would make an important change and ground Embry.

Embry, having received orders that he was not to participate in the raid, had little option but to give overall command to Pickard. The absence of Embry at this late stage explains the variation between the orders given by Pickard at the briefing and the original orders provided by Embry.

* *Irving Stanley 'Black' Smith; born in New Zealand in 1917 flew with 151 Squadron in the Battle of Britain then converted to night fighters. He was an 'Ace' with 8 victories. He arrived at 487 Squadron earlier in February and the Amiens raid was one of his first low-level daylight operations.*

Pickard was presented with a dilemma when Embry was taken out of the equation. If one accepts Embry's reasoning and planning, it would make sense for Pickard to take his position in the formation. However, if this were so, he would not be in a position to take the decision on the third wave attack, which he now wanted to do instead of entrusting the decision to 'Tony' Wickham in the FPU Mosquito. Pickard seemed to find a satisfactory solution but this placed him, his navigator and their aircraft at a greater level of risk.

Pickard's somewhat riskier 'solution' was to place himself in the number twelve position; in the sixth and last position in the second wave. This position would enable him to take part in the bombing of the prison and then break away from the others and orbit the target area so that he could assess the damage and make the judgement as to whether the third wave, scheduled to arrive ten minutes later, would be required. In theory a commander has every right to position crews where he sees fit at any time during the operation, as well as making combat-influenced judgements. However, he was not usually expected to openly modify the orders from Group to the extent that his crew and others were potentially placed at greater risk throughout the operation.

One major consideration was that the last position in a flight was always the most vulnerable to prowling Luftwaffe fighters. To have this position occupied by a leader did not fit with standard RAF policy of the time. The leader would normally have been covered by a wingman at all times but this role could not be fulfilled with Pickard adopting the position he had chosen – at the rear.*

Pickard stated that he intended to break away from the formation to fly a few circuits over the target; this would also leave him in a dangerous and isolated position, spending far too long over the target. This would increase the possibility of being hit by anti aircraft fire or caught by prowling Luftwaffe fighters. Message AO 241 underlines this:

```
FOLLOWING EACH ATTACK SECTIONS OF THREE AIRCRAFT OF EACH FORMATION
ARE TO ENDEAVOUR TO REGAIN CLOSE COMPANY AS SOON AS POSSIBLE.
```

The RAF, much like the USAAF, considered formation details and in-flight procedure to be rigid, with each leader having strict orders to regain close formation as soon as the attack had been completed. This avoided having aircraft widely dispersed over the combat area and the regaining of formation allowed the aircraft to provide mutual protection to each other if required.

* Embry later 'led' a similar attack on the Shell House in Copenhagen - and elected to fly at the end of the first wave.

Therefore, by taking the decision to orbit the prison, Group Captain Pickard would seem to be in conflict with all recognized and established operational procedures.

Why did Embry not challenge the changes during the briefing? One reason could be that he considered that this might undermine the authority of Pickard in what was already a very dangerous mission and would do little to increase morale amongst the participating crews.

Another reason could simply be that he considered Pickard's decision to be the right and noble one; particularly in view of a last minute change to the orders for the Third Wave.

If called in, the objective for the Third Wave had been altered to 'the destruction of the entire prison', rather than 'backing up' the previous two waves. This change of target is confirmed by documentary evidence and by the reports of participating pilots. Fifty years later, whilst in Amiens, Squadron Leader Ian McRitchie confirmed that the entire building was to be the target for the Third Wave. This decision consolidated the target zone for the crews; no longer would a detailed assessment of structural damage have to be made. If Pickard judged that waves one and two had not completed the task, then all the prison would be targeted. The only decision to be made was whether the target should be attacked or not.

The changes made to the Third Wave's target since the original AO 241 document may again have influenced Pickard to assume total responsibility for the operation, as calling in the Third Wave would undoubtedly result in the death of many French patriots. This life-or-death decision was really for the leader to make and not the pilot of the photographic aircraft.

The sequence of changes was:

AO 241 - Target to be decided by the (Third Wave) leader on approach.

Briefing (as illustrated in the official post-raid film) - Unless instructed by F.P.U. Recco a/c that attack was successful, to destroy the prison entirely.

140 Wing ORB - In the event of failure (by previous waves) it was requested of the crews that the whole of the building be bombed.

Pickard's briefing to crews - "When I've dropped my bombs I shall pull off to one side and circle, probably just to the north of the prison. I can watch the attack from there; and I'll tell you by radio."

So Pickard deviated from official orders because, firstly, he considered such a last minute alteration to be justified and, secondly, he felt the success of the mission was far more important than his own personal safety. Pickard had just been made sole commander of the operation and was quite simply displaying the leadership qualities that had made him the legend he already was. Maybe he also sensed that this subtle but significant change in orders implied that the operation was not just an effort to free prisoners.

Pickard also changed the message to be used to instruct the Third Wave to bomb the target or abort the mission.

The general recall codeword for the entire mission was 'Renovate'. The use of this word would cancel all actions right up until the last minute before the attack, and would result in all aircraft, including the Third Wave, returning to base with their bomb loads. In the text of AO 241, the word 'Renovate' features only as a 'special V.H.F. codeword', however, in another message sent to Fighter Command, it was clearly specified as the bomber recall codeword, to be used to cancel that section of the raid and to recall the participants back to base.

The use of 'Renovate' as a codeword for specifically calling off the Third Wave was therefore not satisfactory for Pickard as there was no positive instruction, only a negative one. This meant that if he was shot down or had radio failure before assessing the damage, the Third Wave would bomb simply on the basis that they hadn't been told not to. Pickard therefore came up with codewords specifically aimed at calling in the Third Wave or not. 'Red' repeated three times was to be used if the Third Wave was not required, 'Green' repeated three times would be the signal to go ahead and bomb.

In his memoirs, Squadron Leader Livry-Level recorded that the amended code words to be used were 'red, red, red, the oranges are ripe'. However, other documentary sources, including testimonies from participants, all agree that the words 'Red' and 'Green' were the correct ones. This is not the only point on which Livry-Level's post-war memoirs differ from other accounts and puts into question his reliability as a source.

It could be argued that Pickard took too many liberties with the orders that had been issued but, to most researchers, Pickard's changes consolidated and clarified an operation already fraught with risk and may have been viewed with relief by the Third Wave crews. Coming in last to finish the job was one issue, but ten minutes was enough to alert any local Luftwaffe airfields that something was happening and the defences would be alerted by the time that the Third Wave arrived. So, with all that to contend with, just to bomb the target would seem a tough enough task.

BRIEFING OF THE FIGHTER ESCORT PILOTS

The message AO 241 B/CAST+EMERGENCY+ FORM B from 2 Group had been received by Hunsdon's teleprinter at 09.40 hours that morning. At the same time it had been sent to the participating fighter bases and also the Headquarters of 2 TAF, ADGB (Air Defence Great Britain - Fighter Command) and AEAF. This message laid down the fighter escort instructions for protecting each of the Mosquito flights. The escorting Typhoon 1bs would rendezvous with the Mosquitos as soon as they had passed over the coast in the vicinity of Littlehampton.

At 10.44 hours the teleprinters of 83 and 84 Group (2 TAF) at Manston and Westhampnett respectively clattered into life with another message.

Manston was notified that 3 and 198 Squadrons must be at a state of readiness and high alert. Westhampnett (16 Wing) was to ready No's 174 and 245 Squadrons.

The Headquarters of the various British and American air forces were also informed of the imminent undertaking (named 'Ramrod 564'). Apart from this, the circulation of these details was restricted.

Fighter escort was to be provided by four squadrons of Typhoons. Three of the pilots seen here in a 198 Squadron photo took part in the raid.

'V   UGI   NP   OPS/1   O   ALL SECTORS NORTHOLT 483 GCC

FOR 16 WING   484 GCC   BEACHY HEAD   WESTHAMPNETT   MERSTON
MANSTON   O-P
XQF   T   16 WING
TAN   T   MERSTON AND WESTHAMPNETT
             1K KX PETT
IAH   T   HQ AEAF AND HQ ADGB
XRQ   T   SAWBRIDGEWORTH FOR 35 WING
XSR   T   34 WING

FROM UGI

TO ALL SECTORS NORTHOLT 483 GCC FOR 16 WING 484 GCC BEACHY HEAD
WESTHAMPNETT MERSTON MANSTON
HQ's Nos 2, 10, 12, 83 AND 84 GROUPS   HQ VIII USAF (Copy FOR COPC)
HQ IX USAAF   HQ IX USAAF BC   HQ VIII USFC   HQ AEAF   HQ ADGB
SWINGATE   HYTHE   GREYFRIARS   SAWBRIDGEWORTH FOR 35 WING
HARTFORD BRIDGE

FOR 34 WING REDHILL   FOR 39 WING   HQ TACTICAL AIR FORCE
BY HAND   SECRET BT
18 FEBRUARY 1944   11C/S500/63/1/OPS
RAMROD No. 564

1.   INFORMATION.
MOSQUITOS OF 2 GROUP ARE ATTACKING
AMIENS PRISON.

2.   EXECUTIVE.
ZERO 1200 HOURS, 18 FEBRUARY 1944.

3.   1ST ATTACK.
6 MOSQUITOS ARE ATTACKING TARGET.

4.   CLOSE ESCORT.
3 SQUADRON   1 TYPHOON SQUADRON FITTED WITH LONG RANGE TANKS.

5.   RENDEZVOUS.
1 MILE EAST OF LITTLEHAMPTON BELOW 500 FEET AT ZERO MINUS 45.

6.   ROUTE AND TIMING.
LITTLEHAMPTON
TOCQUEVILLE
SENARPONT
DOULLENS
SOUTH WEST ALBERT
TARGET...................ZERO
SENARPONT
TOCQUEVILLE
HASTINGS

7.   2ND ATTACK.
6 MOSQUITOS ARE ATTACKING TARGET.

8.   CLOSE ESCORT.
1   TYPHOON SQUADRON   16 WING.

9.   RENDEZVOUS.
1 MILE WEST OF LITTLEHAMPTON BELOW 500 FEET AT ZERO MINUS 42.

10.   ROUTE AND TIMING.
ROUTE AS FOR 1ST ATTACK   TIME ON TARGET ZERO PLUS 3.

11.   3RD ATTACK.
6 MOSQUITOS ARE ATTACKING TARGET.

12.   CLOSE ESCORT.
1 TYPHOON SQUADRON 16 WING.

13.   RENDEZVOUS.
LITTLEHAMPTON BELOW 500 FEET AT ZERO MINUS 32.

14.   ROUTE AND TIMING.
ROUTE AS FOR FIRST ATTACK.   TIME OVER TARGET ZERO PLUS 13.

15.   TARGET COVER.
198 SQUADRON. 1 TYPHOON SQUADRON FITTED WITH LONG RANGE
TANKS TO PATROL NORTH OF TARGET AREA FROM ZERO UNTIL BOMBERS OF
3RD ATTACK ARE WELL CLEAR OF TARGET.

H. BEACHY HEAD TO PASS INFORMATION
WING TO REMAIN AT SEA LEVEL AS LONG AS POSSIBLE.
— NOTE: MOSQUITOS WILL CROSS-CHANNEL AND ENEMY COAST AT 0 FEET. WHEN APPROACHING
TARGET THEY WILL PULL UP AND ATTACK FROM 1500 FEET TO GROUND LEVEL.
WEATHER CONDITIONS PREDICTED ARE 10/10 CLOUD AT 3,000 FEET.

16 SIGNALS ORGANISATION.
1ST ATTACK.

V.H.F. IN BOMBERS.
2 GROUP GUARD.
BIGGIN HILL TO MAINTAIN WATCH ON THIS FREQUENCY FOR COMMUNICATION ON
RECALL TO BOMBERS.

CALL SIGNS.
BOMBERS: DYPEG
FIGHTERS: GARLIC
GROUND STATION: AILSOME

CLOSE ESCORT.
TO OPERATE ON 11 GROUP GUARD 1 UNDER BIGGIN HILL CONTROL
BOMBER LEADER OF EACH FORMATION WILL BE FITTED WITH 11 GROUP
GUARD 1 AND CAN COMMUNICATE WITH ESCORT.

BOMBER RECALL CODE WORD: RENOVATE.

2ND ATTACK.

V.H.F. IN BOMBERS.
2 GROUP GUARD.
483 G.C.C. TO MAINTAIN WATCH TO PASS INFORMATION OR RECALL TO
BOMBERS.

CALL SIGNS.
BOMBERS: CANON
FIGHTERS: CAJOLE
GROUND STATION: BELLFIELD

CLOSE ESCORT.
TO OPERATE ONE 11 GROUP GUARD 1 UNDER 483 G.C.C CONTROL.
BOMBER LEADER WILL REVERT TO 11 GROUP GUARD 1 IF THEY WISH TO
COMMUNICATE WITH CLOSE ESCORT.

BOMBER RECALL CODE WORD: RENOVATE.

3RD ATTACK.

V.H.F. IN BOMBERS.
2 GROUP GUARD
483 G.C.C. TO MAINTAIN WATCH TO PASS INFORMATION OR RECALL TO
BOMBERS.

CALL SIGNS.
BOMBERS: BUCKSHOT
FIGHTERS: DUNLOP
GROUND STATION: GREENSHIP

BOMBERS MAY REVERT TO 11 GROUP GUARD 1 TO COMMUNICATE WITH CLOSE
ESCORT.

BOMBER RECALL CODE WORD: RENOVATE.

TARGET COVER TO OPERATE UNDER SECTOR CONTROL.
EMERGENCY HOMING TO FRISTON ONE 2 GROUP GUARD.

A.S.R. LAYOUTS ALLOCATED AS FOLLOWS:
BIGGIN HILL 11 LAYOUT ON 2 GROUP GUARD
KENLEY NO 1 ON TANGMERE SF.5

ALL STATIONS STAND BY FOR FURTHER B/ST

UBA R 181044 A SL   AR

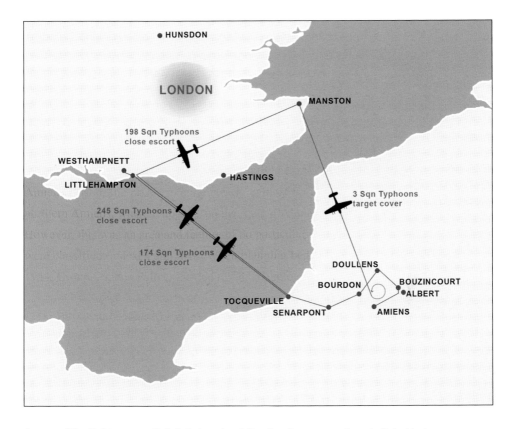

A map of the fighter escort's briefed routes following the ammendments listed below.

In this first message target cover was allocated to 198 Squadron. No. 3 Squadron received orders to provide escort to the first wave of Mosquitos. Both squadrons were to be fitted with drop tanks. The message was received on the morning of 18th February 1944 at 10.44 hours. In this message the code word 'Renovate' is the 'bomber recall codeword' and is the same for *all* three waves of Mosquitos, not just the third wave.

CHANGE TO THE INSTRUCTIONS AT 11.00 HOURS

```
AMENDMENT NO 1 TO RAMROD 564

PARA 4 AMEND TO READ:
CLOSE ESCORT
NO 198 SQUADRON

PARA 15 AMEND TO READ
TARGET COVER
NO 3 SQUADRON
```

Time to prepare for the operation was very short. In addition there had been the last-minute telephone call ordering a 'swap' between 198 and 3 Squadrons just five minutes before takeoff. None of the pilots had been briefed. The teleprinter message confirming the change did not arrive until 11.31 hours, by which time all the pilots should have taken off. This would have grave consequences.

The final escort assignments were:

No.198 Squadron based at Manston, equipped with long-range tanks to escort the six Mosquitos of the first wave.

No.3 Squadron based at Manston to provide cover and patrol to the north of Amiens whilst the attack was in progress. To provide adequate cover time, these Typhoons would also be equipped with drop tanks.

No.174 Squadron based at Westhampnett (16 Wing) to escort the six Mosquitos of the second wave.

No.245 Squadron based at Westhampnett (16 Wing) to escort the third and final wave.

Under normal circumstances, a squadron of fighters comprised twelve aircraft; however this might be reduced in some circumstances due to ongoing repairs or attrition. Unfortunately, 18th February was one of these periods when only eight aircraft were available from both No's. 174 and 245 Squadrons. No.198 Squadron fared even worse, being only able to provide six serviceable aircraft. The number of available aircraft at 3 Squadron is not known.

TAKE-OFF FROM HUNSDON

At Hunsdon all those involved in the briefing left the room and walked across the fine white carpet of powdery snow. The large group of men quickly dispersed into smaller groups and then pairs as they headed off towards each parked plane. At 10.50 hours Hunsdon's runways, perimeters and the surrounding fields were filled with the gathering roar of freshly fired-up Merlin engines. The sound carried for many miles, but few civilians paid any attention to the noise as all those who lived close by were familiar with this vibrant roar that was almost a daily intrusion in their lives.

Right; Ground crew load two 500lb bombs into the bomb-bay of MM403 SB-V which was flown on the Amiens Raid by Flight Lieutenant T McPhee. The Mosquito FBVI was formidably armed, with four .303 machine guns in the nose and four 20mm cannon in the belly. It could also carry four 500lb bombs, one under each wing and two in the fuselage bomb bay.

At 10.50 hours the first two Mosquitos from 487 Squadron taxied onto the perimeter track leading to the runway. Each aircraft was separated by some fifty feet, two more followed and then two more. Soon the streamlined bombers were roaring down the runway, clouds of powdery snow swirling behind each one, engines at full throttle, then they were up. The noise was deafening; flocks of startled woodpigeons rose from neighbouring fields and the hedgerows seemed to empty themselves of finches and chattering sparrows.

Groundcrew about to load 500lb bombs aboard a 464 Squadron Mosquito.
In the background is SB-F MM412 not to be confused with the SB-F LR334 which Bob Iredale flew on the raid. Note the exhaust shrouds have been removed, reflecting the return to daylight operations.

At the head of the six 487 Squadron aircraft forming the first attack wave was:

Mosquito VI   LR333   EG-R   Wg Cdr I.S.Smith, DFC,   Flt Lt Barnes DFM.

Followed in order of take-off by:

Mosquito VI	HX982	EG-T	P/O M. N. Sparks,	P/O A. C. Dunlop.
Mosquito VI	HX856	EG-H	Flt Sgt S. Jennings,	W/O J. M. Nichols.
Mosquito VI	HX855	EG-Q	Flt Lt B. D.Hanafin,	P/O G. F. Redgrave.
Mosquito VI	HX909	EG-C	P/O M. L. S. Darrall,	P/O F. Stevenson.
Mosquito VI	HX974	EG-J	P/O D. R. Fowler,	W/O F. Wilkins.

At 10.53 hours the whole process was repeated; the second wave was off; five aircraft from No.464 Squadron RAAF, Pickard's Mosquito and the Film Production Unit aircraft.

Mosquito VI   LR334   SB-F   Wg Cdr R. W. Iredale, DFC,   Flt Lt J. L. McCaul.

Followed in take-off order by:

Mosquito VI	MM402	SB-A	Sqn Ldr W. R. C. Sugden,	Flg Off A. H. Bridger.
Mosquito VI	MM410	SB-O	F/O K. L. Monaghan, DFM,	Flg Off A. W. Dean DFM.
Mosquito VI	MM404	SB-T	Sqn Ldr A. I. McRitchie,	Flt Lt R. W. Sampson.
Mosquito VI	MM403	SB-V	Flt Lt T. McPhee,	Flt Lt G. W. Atkins.
Mosquito VI	HX922	EG-F	Gp Capt P. C. Pickard, DSO** DFC,	
			Flt Lt J. A. Broadley DSO DFC DFM.	

A seventh Mosquito was tucked in neatly behind Pickard's aircraft; this belonged to the Film Production Unit.

Mosquito IV   DZ414   -O   Flt Lt A. Wickham, P/O L. Howard.

They followed in the disturbed snow tracks of the first wave and once airborne were quickly enveloped in the grey overcast, soon just a dimming distant sound fading in the wind. A few minutes later, just as peace had settled around the snow covered airfield, more Merlin engines opened up in the dispersal areas. This time it was the 'reserve' third wave aircraft from 21 Squadron. The first five Mosquitos took off without incident, but Flight Sergeant Steedman's Mosquito was briefly delayed with a magneto problem which caused him to take off a few minutes after the main group.

Mosquito VI   LR403   YH-U   Wg Cdr I. G. Dale, Flg Off E. Gabites.

Followed in take-off order by:

Mosquito VI MM398   YH-J   Flt Lt M. J. Benn DFC, Flg Off N. A. Roe

Mosquito VI HX930   YH-O   Flt Lt A. E. C.Wheeler DFC, Flg Off N. M. Redington.

MosquitoVI   LR385   YH-D   Flt Lt D. A. Taylor, Sqn Ldr P. H. Livry-Level.

MosquitoVI   LR348   YH-P   Flt Lt E. E. Hogan, Flt Sgt D. A. S. Crowfoot.

MosquitoVI   LR388   YH-F   Flt Sgt A. Steedman, Flg Off E. J. Reynolds.

The three groups assembled in the vicinity and then flew off at low level towards Littlehampton.

MANSTON - WEATHER AND FUEL TANK PROBLEMS

At Manston, despite flurries and heavier snowfall, a group of pilots from 3 Squadron were put on high alert at 10.50 hours. Six minutes before, the teleprinter had printed off message H G/SS-O/63/1/OPS RAMROD 564, ordering the Typhoons to escort the first wave attack on Amiens Prison and the requirement for drop tanks needed to extend their range.

```
4.      CLOSE ESCORT.
3 SQUADRON    1 TYPHOON SQUADRON FITTED WITH LONG RANGE TANKS.

5.      RENDEZVOUS.
1 MILE EAST OF LITTLEHAMPTON BELOW 500 FEET AT ZERO MINUS 45.
```

The late arrival of this message caused problems for the ground crews, as the fitting of fuel tanks to the aircraft took time if they had not been prepared in advance. In addition, the snowfall had become severe and visibility was very poor. Bearing in mind these two issues, Squadron Leader A.S. Dredge (commanding 3 Squadron) categorically refused to allow his aircraft to take off. He was unaware of the critical nature of the mission. The weather and last minute changes were beginning to cause a shambles. Dredge's steadfast refusal caused new problems and the planning officers had to make a tactical decision to change responsibilities for the escort squadrons. Their decision was to issue the order to 'swap' the roles of No's 3 and 198 Squadrons.

This amendment was received by 3 Squadron at Manston by telephone at 11.00 hours before being sent in the form of a Telex at 11.31 hours. However, it did nothing to change Dredge's opinion and he persisted with his refusal to allow his Typhoons to take-off. No.3 Squadron's Operational Record Book records:

After standing by all the morning for an operation which was eventually
cancelled, no flying was possible during the afternoon owing to bad
weather.

NA Ref. AIR 27/34

On the other hand, the ORB of 198 Squadron (also based at Manston) reads:

Original role (target cover) altered to close escort of the 1st
attack, 5 mins before take-off. As it was found that 3 Sqdn could not
be fitted with tanks in time.

NA Ref. AIR 27/1171

The comment about the impracticality of fitting additional fuel tanks in time is correct. However, several officers (Flight Lieutenant Roper and Flight Lieutenant R. Lallemant, a Belgian) confirmed that the real reason for the alteration was that Squadron Leader Dredge steadfastly refused to take off in such poor weather. The Typhoons of No.198 Squadron did eventually take off without tanks fitted, but it was the weather conditions that concerned everyone at Manston.

Additional tanks had been ordered for Manston's Typhoon 1bs because of the distance to the initial rendezvous at Littlehampton. Nos.174 and 245 Squadrons at Westhampnett were considerably closer to Littlehampton and therefore did not require additional fuel. The pilots of 174 and 245 Squadrons were also concerned about their fuel consumption for the mission. From the distances involved, it can certainly be argued that the planes from Westhampnett would have also required additional tanks.

Squadron Leader Dredge had every right to be concerned for his aircraft and could justify his refusal to take off due to the worsening weather. He considered it almost impossible to fly in formation in

Squadron Leader Dredge the Commanding Officer of 3 Squadron.

such weather, let alone be able to locate the Mosquitos he was supposed to rendezvous with at Littlehampton. Visibility was almost zero at Manston. Refusals to obey orders of this nature were unusual, however, Dredge believed that the flight posed an unnecessary risk to his men, especially when he had no knowledge of the mission. The Typhoons of 3 Squadron remained parked, motionless.

TAKE-OFF FROM MANSTON

There was now a state of utmost urgency; things needed to happen quickly in order to have any hope of keeping to the planned rendezvous time to meet the first wave at Littlehampton. 198 Squadron's commander, Squadron Leader Baldwin DSO, DFC (and Bar), was not at Manston so Flight Lieutenant R. Dall took over the role of placing the base at readiness and overseeing its administration before he himself took off. He collated as much information as possible and immediately took it to the waiting pilots; there was little else he could do. Information was so scant that Dall could only tell them that they were escorting a squadron of Mosquitos. Without a proper briefing, the pilots of 198 Squadron started walking out towards their aircraft, six men who would be airborne in a matter of minutes in almost zero visibility and having had no briefing all. The six pilots who took off were:

The Typhoons of 3 Squadron remained parked, motionless as the visibility dropped to almost zero at Manston.

Flt Lt R. Dall (NZ)	Flt Lt J. Scambler (Can)
Flt Lt R. Roper	Flt Lt R. Armstrong
Flt Lt R. Lallemant DFC (Belgian)	Flt Lt J. Niblett

The surface of Manston's runway was in a critical state and it was with no small effort that these men got off the ground without incident. They managed to get into tight formation, despite being further hampered by severe gusts of wind, and at 11.06 hours almost immediately disappeared from view in the snow-flecked grey skies. Flight Lieutenant R. Roper later reported:

We in B Flight were having a quiet morning. No shows had come down from No. 11 Group and the weather was too bad for any flight-testing. Low cloud, poor visibility and thick snow squalls were driving in from the southwest. The well-fed iron stove in our dispersal hut was almost red hot as we clustered around it. Bluey Dall, our Flight Commander, was over at the stores. We didn't know then that something was brewing up and had been for some time. Something that was about as red hot as our old stove...

Anyway, there we were in dispersal and we didn't know that the CO of 3 Squadron had refused to fly at the last moment because of the weather. The operations room was in an uproar and Bluey Dall popped in to see what was going on. He readily said his flight would do the show and had a very quick briefing. When he rushed into our hut all he had time to say was.... There's a show on chaps, escort Mossies, follow me! The snow was now continuous and heavy. On the grass airfield, we could do a close formation take-off. That was the only way to keep in sight of Dall and he was the only one who knew where we were going! *

TAKE-OFF FROM WESTHAMPNETT

By 11.10 hours, there had been a short briefing at Westhampnett and the pilots of 174 'Mauritius' Squadron began to clamber into the cockpits of their Typhoons. The weather was little short of appalling and heavy, intermittent, showers of snow were coming down. Despite this, the conditions were better than Manston was experiencing. The orders from Group stated that two squadrons from Westhampnett would escort the second and third waves of Mosquitos.

The escort to the Mosquitos of the second wave was entrusted to eight pilots of 174 Squadron from Westhampnett.

*Supplied by Seymour B Feldman, an American volunteer in the RAF based in the communications section at Manston who was present on the morning of 18th February.

Blue section:	Typhoon 1b	JR310	Flt Lt F. A. Grantham.
	Typhoon 1b	JP541	Flt Sgt F .E. Wheeler.
	Typhoon 1b	JP671	Flt Lt G. I. Mallett.
	Typhoon 1b	JR133	Flg Off J. E. Renaud.
Red section:	Typhoon 1b	JP308	Flg Off W. C. Vatcher.
	Typhoon 1b	JP793	Flt Sgt H. S. Brown.
	Typhoon 1b	JP303	P/O W. D. Burton (Canadian)
	Typhoon 1b	JP535	Flg Off H. V. Markby (Australian)

The first of the Typhoons slowly rolled down the runway, their huge engines making their characteristic 'chugging' sound and their massive propellers sending up clouds of fine spray. All took off without incident. Eight minutes later, they were due to make their rendezvous with the Mosquitos. By 11.20 hours, all of the Typhoons were fast disappearing into the snowstorm.

The task of escorting the six Mosquitos of the third wave was entrusted to 245 Squadron, also stationed at Westhampnett, under the command of Squadron Leader J. R. Collins DFC. Their take-off and rendezvous with the Mosquitos above Littlehampton was due to take place ten minutes after that of 174 Squadron. The pilots who flew on this day from 245 Squadron were:

Sqn Ldr J. R. Collins DFC	P/O T. L. Jeffreys
Flt Sgt D. J. Lush	Flg Off R. G. F. Lee
P/O K. J. Dickie	Flt Sgt D. C. Nott
Flg Off A. E. Miron	Flt Sgt.E. E. G. Noakes

A quick briefing at 10.55 hours and at 11.20 hours eight aircraft were airborne to escort six Mosquitos on a low level attack on a prison camp at Amiens.

(No.245 Squadron ORB NA Ref. AIR 27/1482)

At 11.20 hours, the first Typhoon took off, shortly followed by the other seven aircraft; they were in the area of Littlehampton in about six minutes, where they met the third wave of Mosquitos.

FROM LITTLEHAMPTON TO THE FRENCH COASTAL TOWN OF TOCQUEVILLE

At 11.18 hours the six 487 Squadron Mosquitos of the first wave split into two sections, each consisting of three aircraft, and were fast approaching the English coast. They were flying at an altitude lower than 450 feet, incredibly risky in these weather conditions. In fact the weather caused them to be between two and three minutes late, as they should have passed over this area at 11.15 hours.

The two sections comprised:

Section 1

Mosquito	LR333	Wg Cdr Smith / Flt Lt Barnes.
Mosquito	HX982	P/O Sparks / P/O Dunlop.
Mosquito	HX856	Flt Sgt Jennings / W/O Nichols.

Section 2

Mosquito	HX855	Flt Lt Hanafin / P/O Redgrave.
Mosquito	HX909	P/O Darrall / P/O Stevenson.
Mosquito	HX974	P/O Fowler / W/O Wilkins.

The escort of 198 Squadron Typhoons from Manston should have appeared to the left of the Mosquitos at this time, but the weather meant that nothing could be seen at all. With the escort not visible, Wing Commander Smith decided to carry on with the planned route. The sky began to clear as they flew towards Northern France and, just occasionally, the Mosquito crews glimpsed a pale sun.

Back over Littlehampton the 464 Squadron Mosquitos of the second wave began to appear, followed by the FPU aircraft. They too were later than scheduled and, at that stage, the bad weather meant that only four planes were in the formation over Littlehampton.

These were:

Mosquito	LR334	Wg Cdr Iredale / Flt Lt McCaul.
Mosquito	MM402	Sqn Ldr Sugden / Flg Off Bridger.
Mosquito	MM404	Sqn Ldr McRitchie / Flt Lt Sampson.
Mosquito	HX922	Gp Capt Pickard / Flt Lt Broadley.

At the same time, the eight Typhoons from 174 Squadron appeared just to the west of Littlehampton, but were unable to see the Mosquitos they were supposed to escort.

After several minutes the 464 Squadron Mosquitos were finally spotted and the escorts assumed their positions just to the rear. Great care was needed, the Typhoons were so close that they could feel the turbulence from the Mosquitos ahead of them.

A few minutes later the two straggler Mosquitos of the second wave also appeared directly over Littlehampton. The latecomers were:

| Mosquito | MM410 | Flg Off Monaghan / Flg Off Dean. |
| Mosquito | MM403 | Flt Lt McPhee / Flt Lt Atkins. |

Flt Lt McPhee (right) and Flt Lt Atkins struggled to catch up with the rest of the formation after being separated in the bad weather.

Aware that they were late, these two increased speed and flew out over the sea hoping to spot their colleagues ahead. Some sixty seconds later the FPU Mosquito of Tony Wickham could be heard flying in the grey skies over Littlehampton before it also streaked away at low level over the sea.

Shortly afterwards the three late arrivals joined their colleagues and the fighter escort some miles out over the Channel. So far, given the weather conditions, so good. Ramrod 564 was well under way.

Pilot Officer Howard, the navigator on board the FPU Mosquito, recalled the early stages of the operation:

I just had time to check over my cameras, and then we were taxying for the take-off. A moment or two after the second six had gone we, too, belted down the runway in a shower of fine snow. Airborne, we climbed to 300 feet and set course. The aircraft ahead were invisible; the ground below us could be seen only vaguely through the swirling snow.

We were about three minutes late at the coast, where we were to pick up our escort of Typhoons. This was the first time I had experienced the joys of a fighter escort; normally Mosquitos operate alone, being well able to take care of themselves, but this target was very near to an enemy-occupied fighter airfield and the boys needed a free hand to ensure their doing a good job of work, so the powers above had provided us with two Typhoons each to chase away inquisitive Huns.

In addition, we were to be given further fighter cover of two squadrons of Typhoons which would be around and about the target when we got there. Being a few minutes late with our rendezvous with the Tiffies I thought perhaps we might miss them. As we tore over the coast - we were going pretty fast, in an endeavour to catch up with the second six - both Tony and I saw aircraft ahead, and as we gained on them we were able to identify them as Mosquitos and Typhoons.

We were still belting along when, as if from nowhere - I made a mental note of it, to remind me how easy it is to be "jumped" by fighters if one doesn't keep a good look out - a couple of the Typhoon boys were sitting, one each on our wing tips.

This is as good a place as any to record our immense admiration of those boys; fighter escort was a novelty to me and I couldn't quite see why we, in Mosquitos, had one; but long before the trip was over I had become an enthusiastic advocate for fighters in general and our two Tiffies in particular. They stuck to us like glue; I'm sure if we'd gone down a railway tunnel they would have come right with us.

It must be remembered that our aircraft behaved differently from all the others. The others attacked and went home; ours stayed at the target and made three runs without dropping any bombs at all. Our two Tiffies couldn't have had the faintest idea what we were supposed to be doing, since no-one had told them we were a film aircraft; but they watched faithfully whatever we did, and when we moved from the scene, along they came again.

At 11.28 hours the Typhoons of 245 Squadron arrived over Littlehampton. Two minutes later they spotted three Mosquitos from 21 Squadron. The two groups made contact and drew up into formation heading out over the Channel. A few moments later a fourth Mosquito appeared and joined the formation. The formation consisted of four Mosquitos and only six Typhoons, because Flight Sergeant Nott and Flight Sergeant Noakes had already got lost in the bad weather; thirty-five minutes after they took off they both decided to abort and return to Westhampnett.

The four Mosquitos were:

Mosquito	LR403	Wg Cdr Dale / Flg Off Gabites
Mosquito	HX930	Flt Lt Wheeler / Flg Off Redington
Mosquito	MM398	Flt Lt Benn / Flg Off Roe
Mosquito	LR385	Flt Lt Taylor / Sqn Ldr Livry-Level

Flight Sergeant Steedman in LR388 had magneto problems and had taken off late; arriving over Littlehampton he was unable to locate his colleagues and made the decision to return to Hunsdon.

Flight Lieutenant Hogan had managed to take off successfully, but LR348 began to experience a whole range of technical problems; the radio and intercom had become unusable and Hogan therefore decided to abort and to return to Hunsdon.

THE FLIGHT OVER THE CHANNEL

The first wave of Mosquitos was now flying out over the Channel without Dall's 198 Squadron Typhoon escort from Manston.

Flight Lieutenant Dall had no time to brief his men before take off and his pilots had insufficient route details. Only Dall had any idea where they were going! Visibility was minimal after take-off and a new turbulent snowstorm was evident within the first 30 miles. The three pilots at the rear of the formation lost sight of Dall, and then with the remainder of the formation, just 15 minutes after take-off.

Series of snow showers. Med. Vis. F/Lt Dall led 6 Typhoons of 198 to escort Mosquitos on a special mission to the Pas-de-Calais. The formation divided in a snow storm S.W. of Manston and 3 a/c returned to base. The remaining 3 a/c carried out the operation uneventfully and returned to Tangmere because of the bad weather conditions at Manston.

(198 Sqn ORB, NA Ref. AIR 27/1170)

30 miles S.W. base, a/c encountered 10/10 clouds at zero feet with heavy snow and visibility less than 400 yards causing 3 a/c to lose contact and return home independently. Remaining 3 continued and landed back at Tangmere.

(198 Sqn Appx, NA Ref. AIR 27/1171)

The pilots who returned to base at this time were:

Flg Off R. Armstrong - took off at 11.00 hrs and returned 11.30 hrs.

Flt Lt R Lallemant DFC (Belgian) - took off at 11.00 hrs and returned 11.15 hrs.

Flt Lt J. Niblett - took off at 11.00 hrs and returned at 11.15 hrs.

There is no question that these three pilots could have done anything else but return to base once they lost contact, as they were not aware of their destination. Several previous publications have drawn conclusions about why these pilots returned, which are neither correct nor historically accurate. Flight Lieutenant Roper's report clarifies the situation and conditions:

The snow was now continuous and heavy. On the grass airfield, we could do a close formation take-off. That was the only way to keep Dall in sight, and he was the only one who knew where we were going. Scambler was on one side of Dall and I was on the other. We all got off alright, although I couldn't see the others. All my attention had to be riveted on Dall's plane with our wingtips just a foot or so apart. I couldn't glance at my instruments nor at the others and all my controls, mixture, pitch, rad flap, trim etc had to be done automatically. It was a good job we had had plenty of experience with formation flying and flying in cloud. As it turned out the other three planes lost touch and managed to land back at Manston almost right away.

Dall was forging on at high speed at what appeared to be very low level. When he changed course, or the air got bumpy, there was a lot of work to do with both throttle and stick in order to keep position. We seemed to be flying through a white void to an unknown destination. Dall was never a man who inspired a great deal of confidence either in his flying or his judgement. He was always coming back with evidence of his 'goofs'.

One day he ran into our barrage balloons off the Thames Estuary and came back with a big dent in his spinner and marks of the wire hawser along one wing. He had thought he was somewhere else. He swore blind he was leading us over Calais on a previous show and we were actually over Dunkirk! Here was I and Jack Scambler trusting every move of his wing tips and every fluctuation in his speed, but we had little alternative. This blind formation flying seemed to go on for a very long time and then, suddenly, we were out in the clear. Blue skies surrounded us and the Channel was blue. We were very close to the waves and there was no indication of where we were. Presumably, we must have been near the rendezvous point, as Dall started circling around, but still no other planes were in sight. We were quite close to the French coast and we had to keep radio silence and keep low to avoid the radar. We must have been circling around for 5 or 10 minutes.

Unfortunately, the Mosquitos they were scheduled to escort were nowhere to be seen. They therefore began a series of wide circles just off the French coast, but did not penetrate inland.

SUMMARY OF THE FIRST STAGE OF THE OPERATION

First wave

Six Mosquitos of 487 Squadron.

Flight mainly to plan, but delayed by some 2-3 minutes.

These Mosquitos missed the rendezvous and proceeded to Northern France unescorted. Of the six Typhoons of 198 Squadron scheduled to escort these bombers, three lost contact and returned to base, and three failed to locate the Mosquitos.

Second wave

Five Mosquitos of 464 Squadron and one from 487 Squadron flown by Group Captain Pickard, the leader of the operation.

They managed to follow the first wave according to plan and without incident. There was a delay of some two minutes in getting to Littlehampton. Eight Typhoons from 174 Squadron were met as planned. The FPU Mosquito followed the second wave.

Third wave

Four Mosquitos of 21 Squadron.

Took off 10 minutes behind according to orders. From the original six aircraft that had taken off, two returned to Hunsdon due to technical problems. Six Typhoons from 245 Squadron provided escort.

Target Cover

Air protection above Amiens as specified in the original plan was not provided because the commanding officer of No. 3 Squadron (Squadron Leader Dredge) refused to take off due to the severe weather conditions.

THE ARRIVAL OVER TOCQUEVILLE AND ONWARDS TO AMIENS

487 Squadron - The First wave

In order to avoid detection by German Radar the Mosquitos and escorting Typhoons were to fly at very low level, in fact just a few feet above the wave tops, and cross the coast at 'zero' feet.

The crews finally spotted a long hazy line that gained increasing clarity as it broke from the colour of the Channel. The sky was a deep blue and the sun could clearly be seen when they approached the coastal district of the Seine. The Mosquitos began to climb slightly. As they flew over the cliffs, they noticed a small group of trees beside a rural farm. This small farm had become a landmark for the experienced crews penetrating into this area of Northern France. It was the farm of Neuvillette, located some two kilometres west-south-west of Tocqueville-sur-Eau. Surging inland, cloud cover appeared again turning the skies pale grey and blending the horizon smoothly with the snow covered landscape below. The road from Le Tréport to Dieppe flashed by, its dark surface contrasting clearly against the white fields and hedgerows. The Mosquitos skimmed over the fields, passing over the Forêt d'Eu and over the valley of Bresle, heading south-east to their first turning point at Sénarpont. Reaching Sénarpont at 11.47 hours, the crews then altered course north-east towards Bourdon. Having dropped to the lowest possible level they flew so low that flurries of snow were sent swirling from wavering treetops, their leafless branches clattering in the slipstreams. Visibility then improved to some four to six miles with a cloud base between 1,500 and 2,000 feet.

By 11.52 hours they were in the valley of the Somme. In front of the planes lay Hangest-sur-Somme, on the far side was Bourdon (the third turning point); swinging to the left, they headed towards Doullens. At 11.53 hours, they saw a main road. On this road between Flixecourt and Belloy-sur-Somme, they spotted a large German convoy of military vehicles, heavy artillery and tanks. The vehicles were heading towards Amiens.

> … Between Flixecourt (M 9573) and Belloy-sur-Somme at 11.53. 50 feet. Large convoy of heavy guns, MT and Tanks travelling towards AMIENS.

Having spotted this convoy, the six 487 Squadron Mosquito pilots kept to just 50 feet. They once more split into their two sections: First section: Smith, Sparks and Jennings. Second section: Hanafin, Darrall, Fowler. With their objective being of prime importance, the pilots of the first section did not consider turning their attention to this convoy and flew onwards. Any action against the convoy would have increased German awareness of their position and would, in all probability, have caused unnecessary complications.

When the second section approached the vehicle convoy Flight Lieutenant Hanafin and Pilot Officer Darrall passed straight over, but the temptation proved too great for Pilot Officer Fowler. Flying 'J-Johnny' in sixth position, he lowered the nose of the Mosquito slightly so that the German vehicles filled the whole of his vision and opened fire. Just in front of the convoy small but violent powdery bursts of snow and dark soil started to erupt. These smaller burst were accompanied by the bright flashes of the larger 20mm shells smashing into the frozen soil. As the shells reached the asphalt road surface, small greyish dusty puffs from strikes could be seen along with vividly contrasting bright flashes from the explosive 20mm shells. As all this was happening, the shells found a vehicle. In a split second its fuel tank was punctured, resulting in a white flash, then an almighty orange fireball burst skywards topped with black billowing smoke and debris.

> J/487 also attacked a lorry which was part of a very large convoy composed of heavy guns, M.T. vehicles and tanks travelling towards Amiens. One lorry was hit by cannon fire and burst into flames.

(140 Wing / Airfield HQ. NA Ref. AIR 26/204)

Within a second or two, Fowler climbed and rejoined the formation heading towards Doullens, Canaples and then Bonneville. The Mosquitos then passed between Candas and Beauval.

At 11.56 hours the pilots of the first wave saw a small valley. At the far end of the valley, situated at the top of its north-eastern slopes, was a large vertical radio mast that was much higher than the Mosquitos' current altitude. They were just south of Doullens and passed close by the radio mast. The mast was positioned outside a large building at the intersection of the Route 16 road (Doullens - Beauval) with the road heading towards Terramesnil[*]. The mast had been erected by the Germans earlier in the war and had been observed and monitored by reconnaissance aircraft for some time. It was even indexed in British information files as code 5002 E/K/13.

In the summer of 1941 the German army installed an immense metal radio transmitter pylon in the locality of Doullens and Beauval. This gigantic antenna was visible from 20 kilometres away and was believed by the local population to be a station intended to scramble the radio broadcasts from London. Built on a slight slope, it seemed to rest on a fragile base formed from four girders, each of which was approximately two metres long. The actual pylon itself was perhaps only 50 centimetres wide, leaving just enough space for a man to climb up on the inside. A metal panel gave access to the top section. Twelve large cables provided support on four sides, so that it did not seem to sway at all in high winds. Several local 'Doullenaise', including Robert Lagache, were conscripted to assist with its construction. The antenna was finally dismantled in August 1951.

Although it was a tempting target, they ignored it. The Mosquitos then flew northwards, arriving at their fourth turning point approximately one mile south of Doullens. The first wave (487 Squadron) Mosquitos emerged from the valley in very neat formation and executed a slight change in course. To their left were the Valley L'Authie and the small town of Doullens. They executed a sharp turn in a south-easterly direction and headed in the direction of Bouzincourt.

BOUZINCOURT TO AMIENS

It was in this area that Flight Lieutenant 'Titch' Hanafin informed Wing Commander Smith, the first wave leader, that his aircraft was experiencing difficulties. Hanafin's port engine had failed. He made an attempt to re-start the problematic engine, but it overheated and he decided to feather the airscrew. Hanafin therefore made the decision to abort. Despite being so near to the target an attack would place a severe strain on the remaining engine, especially at so low an altitude. There would be no room for even the slightest error and he considered it would severely hamper his ability to perform successfully over the target.

At 11.58 hours Hanafin left the formation, departing for the homeward journey back to Hunsdon. The remainder of the formation continued onwards, passing nearby the villages of Terramesnil and Beauquesne. Wing Commander Smith gave the order to the remaining two pilots of Hanafin's section to carry on despite the reduction in their number.

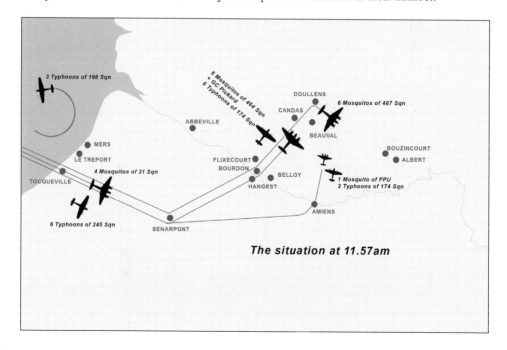

The situation at 11.57am

The remaining five aircraft of the first wave passed over Arquèves, Léalvillers, Varennes and Hédauville, arriving over Bouzincourt at 11.59 hours and 30 seconds. Heading south they made for the final turning point near Albert. However, they all slightly overshot the turning point and were heading straight for a light anti-aircraft *Flak* battery.

On the western side of the town of Albert there were two German controlled factories, a BMW plant manufacturing aero engines and GSP - a factory producing machine tools. Naturally, there were a number of light anti-aircraft defences around the periphery of these two plants equipped with 20mm and 37mm guns, which were particularly adept at combating low-flying aircraft.

Apart from the factory defences, there were other Flak batteries, some manned all the time, some only infrequently. On Friday 18th February, the Flak battery the Mosquitos were heading towards was manned. Normally, aircraft arriving in close formation at low level would surprise such batteries and the planes would pass overhead quickly, too fast for the gun crews to react. On this occasion though, the battery crews reacted with speed and skill. As the Mosquitos approached, the sky was filled with wavering lines of multi-coloured tracer shells and medium sized white-oily-coloured bursts. Deceptively slow at first, then streaking past, the tracer was mesmerizing, but the pilots held formation and emerged unscathed. Moments later the five swung west - towards Amiens. They were lined up for their final run in to the target, the straight line that is the route d'Albert into Amiens.

Walking on the route d'Albert at 12.00 hours, Henri Heraud watched the Mosquitos for about 30 seconds, just before their attack on the prison. They were also seen by Raymond Letoquart, another local man, who watched as they swung round and changed course until they went out of sight over the fields towards Amiens. The Mosquitos flew down the long, straight, tree-lined route d'Albert at 50 feet. They were some three minutes behind schedule.

464 Squadron - The Second Wave

The fifteen aircraft crossed the French coast at 11.44 hours and headed towards Sénarpont. They flew over the French coast without incident and followed a route identical to that flown by the first wave a few minutes earlier.

Whereas the Mosquitos of the first and second waves flew at very low altitude in accordance with their orders, the FPU Mosquito pilot, Pilot Officer Wickham, was authorized to fly at whatever level was determined to be appropriate. The same applied to the Typhoon pilots of 174 Squadron who flew at 5,000 feet and then descended rapidly when over the French coast in the area of Tocqueville.

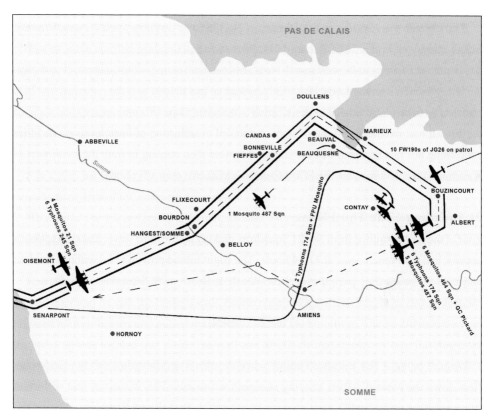

The situation at 12.01hrs as the first formation of Mosquitos located the Albert Road and turned onto its course which would lead them directly to Amiens and the prison.

As the formation flew on the FPU Mosquito, escorted by two Typhoons from 174 Squadron, remained detached from the main group. At 11.49, the second wave flew over Sénarpont. By 11.54 hours, they had arrived at the third turning point at Bourdon. By 11.58 hours, they were nearing Doullens, the fourth turning point, and took note of the large antennae mast visible to the south of Doullens. At exactly 12.00 hours, they passed over Bouzincourt and approached the fifth turning point. At 12.03 hours, they were above the route d'Albert.

The FPU Mosquito and its Typhoon escort had flown directly from Sénarpont to Amiens and arrived early. The Mosquito and its escorts swung north and flew over Amiens heading north-north-east - away from Amiens towards Doullens where navigator Pilot Officer Howard hoped to find the other aircraft. Howard does not make any reference to this deviation from the course in his notes. However, several independent witnesses have been traced who confidently recall the arrival of planes above route de Paris and heading towards the rue Beauvais *before* the attack on the prison.

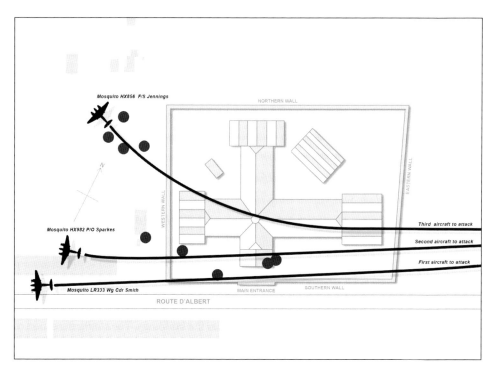

The first wave - first section attack - Smith, Sparks and Jennings.

The third Mosquito, flown by Jennings, attacked the wall from slightly higher - 20 feet. It appears that the bombs overshot the prison and the west wall to fall in the adjacent fields.

Sparks' Famous Photograph

As Sparks released his bombs a camera automatically took a series of exposures. The photograph was taken just as the first two bombs landed - one at the base of the south wall just to the west of the main entrance; and the other against the east frontage of the south wing of the main building, where the German administrative offices were located.

The dust has just started to rise and two people are still standing upright and have not been thrown to the ground or taken cover. One is in the road, where the snow had started to thaw, practically opposite the main entrance. The second is on the pavement opposite. There are no parked vehicles or anything else, which contradicts the post-war accounts of help being on-hand to release the prisoners.

The camera itself was not mounted below and facing to the rear, rather a mirror was fitted at 45 degrees to enable a standard vertical camera to be used.

The original Air Ministry caption for this photograph states, 'A Mosquito which took part in the operation made three runs over the target and secured this picture'. This has lead many to believe that it was taken from Tony Wickham's FPU Mosquito and some even to believe that the second Mosquito is Pickard's.

However, it is clear from the lack of damage and smoke that this was taken in the first seconds of the attack. Wing Commander Smith's bombs have just landed near the main gate, this photo has been taken from Sparks' aircraft, which means the other Mosquito is that of Jennings - the third aircraft over the prison. The bombs have yet to explode. After 11 seconds (the delay set on the fuses) these Mosquitos would be much further away from the prison than they are in this photograph..

First Wave - Second Section Attack

Following the first section, the two Mosquitos of Darrall and Fowler forming the second section had passed over the small hamlet of Petit-Camon and swung right to prepare for their north-south bomb run. From their higher vantage point they could see the first signs of the attack to their left; large grey-brown bursts of smoke and debris were billowing upwards. Banking steeply into a tight turn, the two crews then saw a large dark building that contrasted with the surrounding snow covered fields. For the first time they noted the large enclosure wall, a dark and sinister barrier that they had come to destroy. Coming closer, the individual courses of the brickwork were visible and the wall appeared to fill the whole scene in front. They dropped their bombs from 70 feet on a heading of 150 degrees and skimmed over the roof of the main prison building. The smoke from the previous bomb-bursts was picked up and forced into vortices, like thick whirling serpents. Pulling round into a tight right-hand turn Darrall and Fowler swept over the St Victor hospice and snow dusted roofs of Amiens in pursuit of the leading section. 11 seconds later, their delayed action bombs exploded.

Of the eight bombs released by these two Mosquitos, six landed right on their briefed targets. The attack on the eastern section of the northern enclosure wall was a success and it had been breached.

One of Darrall's bombs had penetrated the northern wall and exploded behind it; a huge plume of smoke and bricks erupted into the air and a broad breach could easily be seen when the dust had settled. Another bomb, dropped a little too late, smashed into the northern face of the building. This exploded, removing a huge section of the roof and smashing the interior. Another bomb may have fallen in the courtyard adjacent to a small workshop. The position of Darrall's fourth bomb is unknown; there is a possibility that it was the bomb that destroyed part of the St. Victor Hospice, which was a Luftwaffe Hospital at this stage of the war.

Fowler later claimed to have placed his bombs on the western part of the eastern wall, however, this breach was actually caused by a bomb from the second wave. Photographs taken on 20th February by a reconnaissance aircraft show four craters made by Fowler's bombs a few metres short of the wall without making any breach.

The Second Wave Attack

The six Mosquitos of the second wave had been running slightly late, but as they approached Albert they had made up time and were on schedule. At precisely 12.02 hours, the six Mosquitos lined up over the route d'Albert for their final approach. accompanied on each side by their escort of Typhoons from 174 Squadron. Unfortunately the first wave

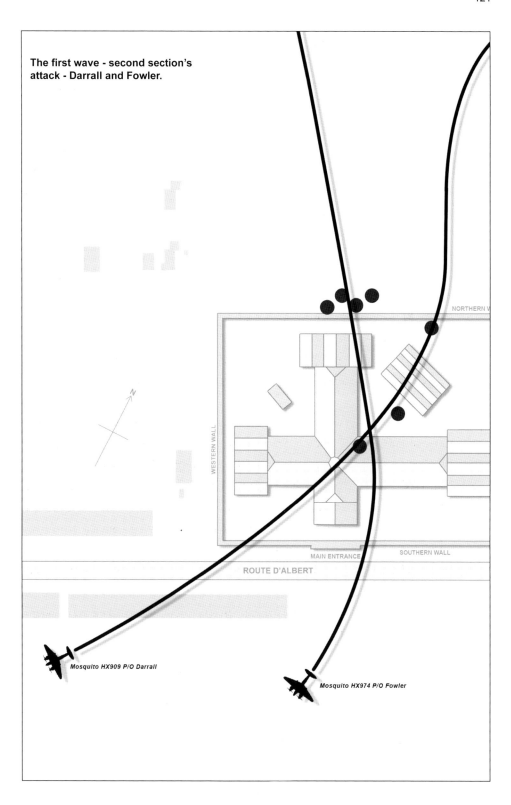

The first wave - second section's attack - Darrall and Fowler.

NORTHERN W

WESTERN WALL

N

MAIN ENTRANCE   SOUTHERN WALL

ROUTE D'ALBERT

Mosquito HX909 P/O Darrall

Mosquito HX974 P/O Fowler

was running three minutes late and Wing Commander 'Bob' Iredale* and his second wave crews were taken aback to see the aircraft of the first wave only slightly ahead of them - far too close!

According to orders, the Mosquitos of the second wave should have adhered to the same flight plan as the first wave. However, Iredale observed that, if this plan were followed rigidly, then the three Mosquitos of his first section were very likely to be over the target area as the first wave's bombs were exploding and would also be at risk of a collision with aircraft from the first wave's second section bombing the target from the north.

In a split second decision Bob Iredale led his formation into a left-hand circuit to lose time. Squadron Leader Sugden wrote:

As we commenced our run up to the gaol, down the road leading southwest from Albert, either the leading squadron was a few seconds late, or ours a few seconds ahead of time, which would have meant probably being over the previous squadron's bomb bursts. So Bob Iredale very wisely took us left around a 360 degree turn, which also brought us over the airfield at Glisy, where we collected a fair amount of light flak, fortunately no casualties, and we were able to do a good bombing run.

The aircraft of the second wave flew over the hamlet of Petit-Camon and headed towards Lamotte-Brebière; from here, they could clearly see the twin runways of the airfield at Glisy. As the six Mosquitos flew over the countryside to the north of Glisy, a light anti-aircraft battery opened fire. The fire was accurate but the Mosquitos were flying at speed, were turning and were soon gone, heading towards Bussy-lès-Daours. Swinging further round they completed the 360-degree turn and rejoined the route d'Albert a little to the west of Querrieu.

At 12.04 hours, the second wave split into its two sections. Wing Commander Iredale lead Sugden and Monaghan down to 50 feet above the route d'Albert and headed towards the target. Squadron Leader McRitchie and Flight Lieutenant McPhee followed hard on their heels, but Pickard's Mosquito was not there. During the 360-degree orbit, a Focke-Wulf 190 had slipped out of the cloud cover and latched onto the tail of the rearmost Mosquito flown by Pickard and fired a burst of cannon fire. Pickard immediately broke formation and took evasive action but a second burst of fire severed the tail section and the Mosquito plummeted to the ground near Saint-Gratien, killing both Pickard and Broadley instantly.

The combat was so brief that none of the other aircraft of the second wave were aware of the fighter or of Pickard's loss until much later on.

Australian Robert Wilson Iredale, born 1913, a former salesman in Victoria.

Second Wave - First Section Attack

The orders given to the second wave for the attack on the prison were similar to those given to the crews of the first wave, the only difference being which aircraft should bomb the wings of the principal building:

INTENTION. TO BOMB THE MAIN PRISON BUILDING.

METHOD. LEADING THREE AIRCRAFT TO ATTACK SOUTH EASTERN END OF MAIN BUILDING AND SECOND SECTION OF THREE AIRCRAFT TO ATTACK THE NORTH WESTERN END OF BUILDING. ATTACKS TO BE CARRIED OUT IN SIMILAR MANNER TO 1ST. ATTACK ABOVE.
TIMING: ATTACK TO BE MADE AT ZERO HOURS PLUS 3 MINS.

Pickard had told the crews at the briefing:

You will notice that the prison itself is in the form of a cross, and that at its east and west ends are small triple buildings which, according to our information, are the quarters of the Nazi prison guards.

The second six aircraft are going to prang those quarters.

Iredale, Sugden and Monaghan were rapidly approaching the target. They could see the prison out in front and the palls of smoke drifting sideways from it. The aircraft roared down the tree-lined road, the prison was right in front of them and they could see the east wall; it was still intact. They could see smoke billowing from the main buildings, but the wall was not even damaged. Swinging slightly south, Iredale decided to tackle the building at the end of the east wing himself (as briefed), whilst giving the order to Sugden and Monaghan to bomb the wall in front of them. Iredale opened the Mosquito's bomb bay doors and released the two bombs as well as the two wing mounted bombs from 50 feet.

The Mosquito pulled up steeply, hurtled over the compound, and was gone. Just a few seconds behind, the other two Mosquitos approached the prison a little to the north. They too released all eight of their bombs and 'jumped' the wall. Eleven seconds later the prison was shrouded in dust, debris, smoke and flying bricks from the explosions.

The angle of attack calculated to hit the south-eastern end of the building had been perfect. The trajectory and impact of two of Iredale's four bombs could be observed. The first bomb flew over the enclosure wall and exploded in the courtyard between the southern enclosure wall and the south frontage of the extension to the east wing of the prison. The second bomb also passed over the wall and totally demolished the extension. The effects

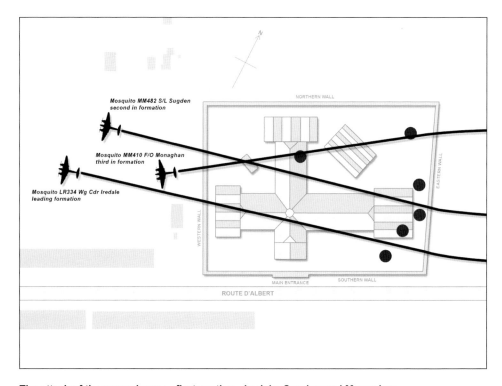

The attack of the second wave - first section - Iredale, Sugden and Monaghan.

of the third and fourth bombs cannot be ascertained as they fell into areas already damaged extensively. It is entirely possible that they did not explode at all.

This building was one of those Pickard selected for attack initially and therefore its demolition was a particular triumph. However, the east wall had still not been breached.

Squadron Leader Sugden, bombing from 100 feet, missed the east wall with all four bombs:

The first exploded near the building at the end of east wing, dispersing its debris even further. The second exploded a little more to the north, near the north-east corner of this same building.

The third passed straight over the enclosure wall and probably landed just in front of a workshop building. (There is a possibility that this crater may have been caused by the earlier attack of Pilot Officer Darrall of the second section of the first wave.)

The fourth bomb was probably responsible for the massive structural damage to the east wall of the north wing of the main prison building.

The third Mosquito, flown by Flying Officer Monaghan, approached the northern end of the east wall. One of his bombs shaved the top courses of brickwork off the east wall and exploded in the north-eastern part of the courtyard. Another bomb smashed through the enclosure wall, leaving a four-foot wide ragged hole, and landed in the courtyard without exploding. A photograph taken on a reconnaissance flight on 23rd March 1944 shows work undertaken in this area allegedly associated with the extraction of an unexploded bomb. The location of Monaghan's third and fourth bombs is uncertain, but it seems likely that one exploded against the eastern frontage of the north wing and totally destroyed it. There is a possibility that the fourth bomb exploded in No.17 rue Voltaire, as it is almost certain that this explosion was caused by a bomb dropped by the first section of the second wave.

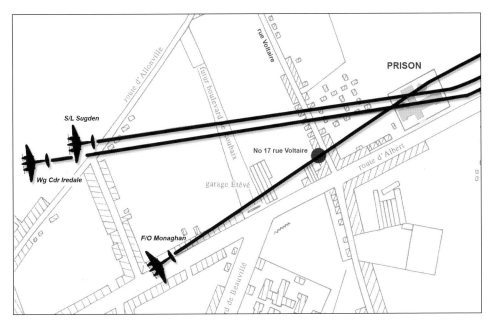

It is likely that Monaghan's fourth bomb was the one that fell on No. 17 rue Voltaire.

Second Section - Second Wave Attack

The second section was tasked to attack the north-western end of the prison building.

McRitchie and McPhee swung to the north over the south-west area of Cardonnette in order to be able to make a north-to-south approach and headed for the prison.

McRitchie aimed at the west end of the northern prison wall and released the bombs just before passing over it. His Mosquito rose up and over the buildings in the north-western area of the prison. Seconds later McPhee approached from the north-west at 100 feet, dropped his bombs and leapt up and over the rooftops in a now familiar style. The attack lasted only a few seconds, but was responsible for some huge explosions as the bombs detonated and the sound and blast waves reached outwards, travelling to the outskirts of the town.

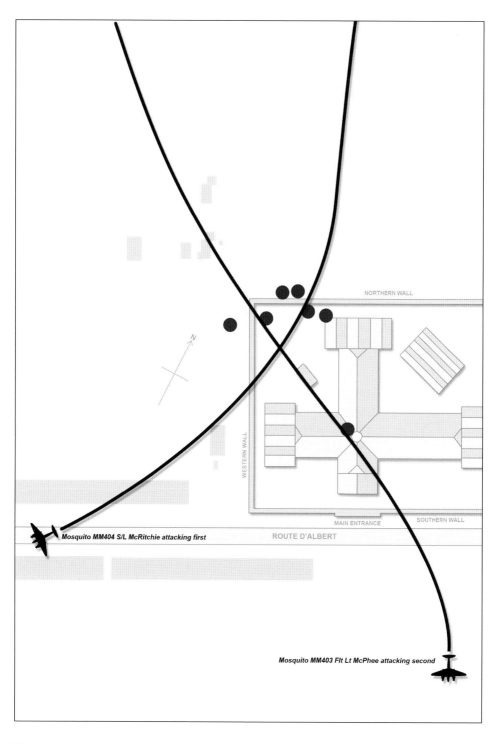

The second wave - second section - McRitchie and McPhee.

Squadron Leader McRitchie had approached from the north and released his bombs at 50 feet whilst banking slightly to starboard, with the right wing down. All four bombs exploded near the west end of the northern enclosure wall. Photographs taken of the target two days later allow an extremely accurate analysis of this aspect of this attack.

The bomb underneath the left wing was the furthest from the ground on release. It was this bomb that smashed through the wall and exploded in the courtyard. The wall did not collapse at the point of impact but remained in situ with a large hole punched straight through it. The bomb that was on the left of the bomb bay punched through the wall slightly more to the west, at a lower

Flight Lieutenant Tom McPhee

level, exploded in the courtyard and made a massive breach in the wall. The bomb in the bay on the right hand side fell and exploded outside the enclosure wall, causing little damage. The fourth bomb, located under the right wing of the Mosquito, also exploded outside the enclosure wall to the north-west, causing no structural damage.

McRitchie's objective, set by Group Captain Pickard, should have been the annex at the west end of the prison. The bombs did not achieve this goal, but did create a broad breach in the north wall.

Flight Lieutenant McPhee came in from a more westerly position. The first bombs exploded on the north-western corner of the enclosure wall forming a breach in the west wall at its corner with the northern wall. Another one of the bombs hit the main prison building at the junction of its north and west wings. This created an enormous hole and totally destroyed the building beneath it.

A Brief Summary of the Second Wave

The second wave attack was due to commence at 12.03 hours, but was delayed and took place between 12.04 and 12.06 hours. The first section was briefed to bomb the east wing of the prison, the second section to bomb the west wing of the prison.

The three Mosquitos of the first section bombed and destroyed the annex to the east wing of the main building. Iredale diverted Sugden and Monaghan to the still intact east enclosure wall which was hit, but not breached. It is likely that this section was responsible for devastating the north wing of the prison.

The two remaining Mosquitos of the second section attacked the west end of the main prison building. One of the bombs created a large breach in the north wall while another left just a hole in the north wall where it penetrated without exploding. The other Mosquito created a breach in the north end of the west wall. It is probable that a bomb from this aircraft exploded on the roof of the west and north wings, causing considerable damage.

This analysis of the attack is based on assessment of the reconnaissance photographs taken during and after the attack, as well as eyewitness testimonies and military documents. The diagrams plotting the impacts of each bomb are the most precise ever attempted and are believed to be the most accurate reflection of what actually occurred. There are several explosions that can be attributed to more than one aircraft and this has been indicated where appropriate.

The Arrival of the Film Production Unit Mosquito over Amiens

The FPU did not have specific aircraft allocated to it, but used aircraft chosen from operational squadrons. The aircraft on this raid, DZ414, belonged to 21 Squadron and became operational as an FPU plane after various modifications and camera installations had been made. The purpose of the unit was to make a visual record of effects of bombing upon targets, for both propaganda and future training purposes.

In the case of the Amiens raid, the FPU footage would provide a future reference for the capabilities of the Mosquito in this role, as well as showing exactly what had been achieved. However, Flight Lieutenant Wickham was not tasked to film the raid in its entirety. His original task was simply to fly over the prison in as short a time as possible, avoiding anti-aircraft fire and enemy fighters. Staying over a target whilst it is being bombed would be hazardous for any crew. Furthermore, the presence of the FPU aircraft in such a position might have impeded the progress of the bombing and would have created an additional risk of collision over the target.

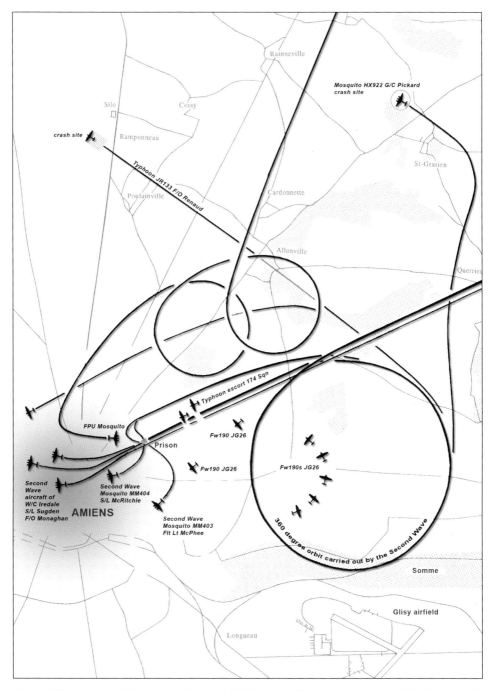

The position of aircraft between 12.04 and 12.06 hours. The second wave is attacking and the FW190s of JG26 have entered the stage, shooting down Group Captain Pickard and one of the Typhoon escorts. The FPU Mosquito is about to commence his first photographic run over the devastated prison.

At 11.59 hours, classes had just finished at Amiens College on Rue Desprez in the south-western district of Amiens when the air raid warning sirens began to sound. Almost as soon as they started, a Mosquito and two Typhoons passed over at low level, disappearing in the direction of the town hall. People stared upwards and glimpsed the blur of British roundels on the fuselage sides.

This was Flight Lieutenant Wickham's FPU Mosquito and his Typhoon escort.

According to the original plan, neither the Mosquito nor its Typhoon escort should have been over this part of Amiens, at least not at this time and not heading in this direction. However, since the arrival of these three aircraft behind the second wave over the French coast, their navigation had been hampered by the featureless, snow-covered landscape which resulted in them flying too far to the south-east. When the course was changed to the north-east as planned, it brought them over the south-western district of Amiens.

The three aircraft carried on north-east towards Doullens, separated from the second wave and further to

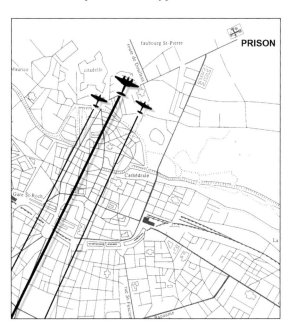

The path of the FPU Mosquito and its Typhoon escort over Amiens prior to the attack.

the east than originally planned. They flew parallel to the main road south of Puchevillers, then turned south-east, and consequently were far further south than was originally planned. However, at 12.01 hours, following the advice of his navigator, Wickham began a very wide right-hand turn. In the distance they both noticed small mushroom shapes of smoke; the attack had started. At this stage Wickham decided to head back to the Puchevillers road in order to give the second wave time to release its bombs.

The two Typhoons followed, as always, sticking closely to their Mosquito.

In the Chateau de Contay, situated near Herissart, Madeleine Liscourt spotted a group of aircraft. She remembers that they were very low and heading north. At the time she was unaware of the attack on Amiens Prison and only later associated the planes with the raid. What Madeleine Liscourt saw was actually the FPU Mosquito and its Typhoon escort.

At 12.03 hours, just to the south of Herissart, Serge Chatelain was outside, looking towards the south when he also saw the FPU Mosquito. A few seconds later he heard distant explosions coming from the area of Amiens. At the time, he estimated that the explosions had come from the direction of Falise Wood, but they were actually a lot further away. Wickham now turned left south of Rubempre and headed for Amiens. At 12.04 hours Wickham realised that he needed to lose yet more time and began two left-hand circuits north-west of the prison that he completed as the second wave bombed.

... and when we came up to the target we did a couple of fairly tight circuits to the north of it to allow the remainder of the bombs to explode. I went down into the nose to do the filming and as I peered out of the side, I saw the Group Captain's a/c orbiting near us. I believe this is the last time he was positively seen by anyone on the trip. He did not return from the operation.

I had just time to note the Gp Capt's a/c and to think I'd never seen so many Typhoons apparently looking as if they were figure skating over the target, when Tony's voice warned me, 'Here we go'.

At this time there were eight Typhoons of 174 Squadron flying in the area north of Amiens, including the two escorting the FPU Mosquito

The Actions of the FPU Mosquito over the prison

By 12.07 hours, the last Mosquitos (McRitchie and McPhee) had released their bombs and had disappeared over Amiens. An enormous cloud of smoke billowed from the western section of the prison, rapidly streaming over the surrounding area.

A few seconds later the FPU Mosquito approached the prison from the west at an altitude of 400 to 500 feet in a shallow dive. The 174 Squadron Typhoon escorts were also passing over the route d'Doullens, though at a slightly lower altitude than the FPU Mosquito. In the nose of the Mosquito, Pilot Officer Lee Howard positioned himself as comfortably as possible and, looking through the Perspex nose, he began to film.

I switched on the fixed cameras and started operating the one in my hand, too.

The target was a remarkable sight. There was a strong east wind blowing and smoke was streaming in thick clouds across the western end of the prison; but the hole in the wall, a beautiful round hole - ideal for getting out of prisons - stared us straight in the face. We could both see tiny figures running like mad in all directions; then we were over and racing round in a tight turn.

"Going round again", said Tony; and round again we went.

route d'Albert

eastern wall

COLLAPSED
EAST BUILDING

eastern wing

COLLAPSED
STRUCTURE

SMOKE

BREACH

DEBRIS

Mosquito 1st Wave
2nd Section lead position
P/O Darrall

COLLAPSED
NORTH BUILDING

northern wing

northern wall

allotments

BOMB HOLE

bomb craters

BREACH

DEBRIS

western wall

bomb craters

BREACH

Mosquito 1st Wave
2nd Section 2nd position
P/O Fowler

Mosquito 2nd Wave
2nd Section lead position
S/L McRitchie

Mosquito 2nd Wave
2nd Section 2nd position
Flt Lt McPhee

A still from Pilot Officer Lee Howard's film of the prison just minutes after the attack.

Again I stared, more at the hole in the wall than anything; it fascinated me. We were so tightly banked in this turn that I could scarcely move; but it was obvious that things were happening very quickly down below, and that the band of patriots who had to escape were standing not upon the order of their going.

Breaches had been blasted through the northern wall, but it was the breach in the western wall that had attracted Howard's attention. Another large, almost round hole, close to the northern wall breach had been punched through by a falling bomb, but was not nearly so large and was several metres from the ground.

"Like another"? asked Tony; so we made our third and final run. It was as we did this that I realised how one could tell Nazis from prisoners; on our every run the Germans threw themselves flat on their faces, but the prisoners went on running like hell. They knew whose side we were on.

```
Ramrod 564. One Mosquito / FPU 1151h / 1300h.

Mosquito circled target three times between 1203 and 1210h from
400/500 feet using cine camera but carrying no bombs. He reported a
breach in the western centre of the north wall and a hole through the
wall to the east of the breach. A hole in the northern side of the
eastern wing of the main building, a breach in the northern end of the
western wall and considerable damage to extension building at west of
main building as well as damage to western end of main building. A
number of men were seen in the courtyard near the separate building
which appeared to be a workshop and three men running into fields from
large breach in northern wall.
```

Although this report states that the three runs took place between 12.03 and 12.10 hours, this is incorrect. Flight Lieutenant Tony Wickham was north of the route d'Albert at 12.02 hours. At 12.03 hours, he was watching at a distance as the bombs of the first wave exploded in the prison area. He then turned south of Herissart and completed two orbits over the north of Amiens. It is absolutely certain that the FPU Mosquito did not pass directly over the prison until at least 12.07 hours.

In addition, Pilot Officer Howard's official report, compiled during his debriefing, states that he had problems with the hand held cine camera because of the high 'G' forces in the tight turns. This report also gives us the altitude of each pass:

```
12.07 hours, altitude 3,000 feet, the first pass over the prison
commences.
(Author's note: the cloud ceiling was in general estimated at 2,000
feet. Perhaps a slight over estimate here)
12.09 hours, 400 feet, the second pass is completed.
12.11 hours, third pass is completed at 200 feet.
```

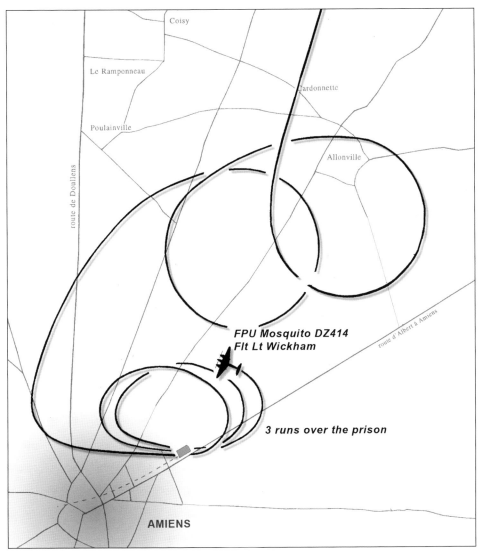

The flightpath taken by Tony Wickham in the FPU Mosquito.

The Third Wave Cancelled

For more than sixty years, it was universally accepted that Group Captain Pickard orbited above the prison after the bombing, indeed, this was the account provided by the British authorities when they gave an 'Official Press Release' on 28th October 1944. However, Pickard's Mosquito crashed before he bombed the prison.

When Pilot Officer Howard stated that he saw Pickard's aircraft for the last time, this could only have been when the FPU aircraft began its turn near Puchevillers. Unfortunately,

The FPU Mosquito was a MkIV version which had a glazed nose, ideal for filming operations such as this.

Howard does not give the precise time that he spotted the aircraft. It is also possible that Howard spotted Pickard's aircraft after Wickham had completed the two circular sweeps over the north-eastern districts of Amiens, but at this time the attack of the second wave would have already begun. Had Howard seen a Mosquito at this stage then he would have assumed it was Pickard's aircraft, but in fact it was McPhee's aircraft which attacked in the last position, the position Pickard would have been in. Howard may have confused the two aircraft for, according to what Howard had heard at the briefing, the aircraft in that position should have been Pickard's. Finally, Howard himself said it was just a glimpse before greater issues took his attention:

Pilot Officer Howard in his own account states;

As we flew away from the prison Tony switched on the radio and gave the 'red, red, red' signal that sent the last formation home with their bombs.

Flight Lieutenant Wickham had cancelled the third wave attack. This was exactly what Group Captain Pickard had requested at the end of the briefing, if the circumstances merited it. Howard did not specify the exact time that this message was sent. We can be sure that it was not before 12.11 hours, but more likely one or two minutes afterwards. The message was received by the pilots of the third wave when they were only between two and four miles from the prison.

The reports from the various pilots are not detailed in the squadron's Operational Record Book (ORB) as usual, because this operation was scheduled as a special mission and classified as Secret. Only the generalized version of their reports are available from 2 Group:

```
Four aircraft of 21 Squadron received V.H.F. messages from "F", 464
Squadron, and F.P.U. aircraft when between two and four miles from
the target, instructing them not to bomb. Target was seen covered
with smoke: they brought bombs back.
```

The aircraft referred to as 'F', 464 Squadron is Mosquito 'F for Freddie' flown by Group Captain Pickard. However, the instruction not to bomb was issued at between 12.11 and 12.13 hours, some eight or so minutes after Pickard's death. The author has had access to the original report, compiled after Flight Lieutenant Wickham's debriefing,[*] which contains evidence proving that it was actually Wickham who gave the cancellation order. The confusion about who issued the order almost certainly arose because the formation did not know that Pickard had been shot down. Even at the de-briefing stage, the crews were still under the impression that the order originated from Pickard.

Why has the myth been allowed to carry on for so long? Obviously, at the time of the incident, the British authorities would not have been aware of the time of Pickard's death. It seems that, if a doubt as to who gave the order existed later on, then under the circumstances, it was deemed more appropriate to say it was Pickard who issued it.

It seems also that no one was prepared to amend the records, as they all gave credence to the myth, even sometime later on when the facts began to percolate through. After all, if Pickard had bombed the prison, as the myth perpetuates, then he would have cancelled the third wave himself.

At 12.13 hours the aircraft of the third wave were halfway between Albert and Amiens, the estimate of between two and four miles specified in the report is a slight under-estimate. What is certain is that the third wave was on its final approach when the crews received the 'red, red, red' message cancelling their attack.

---

[*]Contrary to the other reports, this document is still preserved at the Imperial War Museum.

A still from Lee Howard's camera in the FPU Mosquito showing the damage to the north-west corner of the prison.

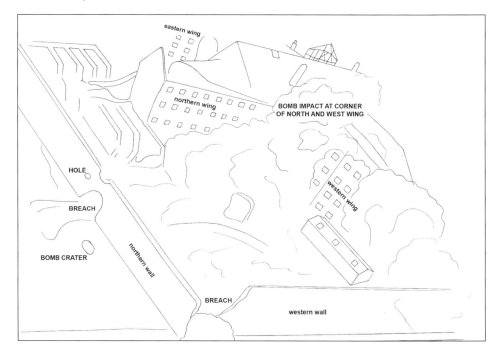

Under great stress, Flight Lieutenant Wickham had waited until the very last minute, hoping finally to hear Pickard's voice. Wickham waited and waited for the order that could never come. Wickham's responsibility therefore was paramount; had he given the order and then Pickard counter commanded it, there would have been total confusion. On the other hand, the cancellation could not be given too late; it had to be heard by the pilots of the third wave before they began their attack.

The Third Wave

After crossing the French coast, the aircraft of the third wave had headed inland towards Sénarpont just as the two waves out in front had done. The original schedule for them, according to the message AO 241, was:

```
INTENTION. THIS FORCE IS A RESERVE, AND WILL APPROACH THE TARGET AS
IN THE TWO PREVIOUS ATTACKS, ONE SECTION FROM THE EAST AND ONE FROM
THE NORTH, BUT WILL BOMB ONLY IF IT IS SEEN THAT ONE OF THE PREVIOUS
ATTACKS HAS FAILED.
TIMING. ATTACK TO BE MADE AT ZERO PLUS 13 MINS.
```

As the first wave was making its attack, the third wave was approaching Airanes. By 12.04 hours they passed over Bourdon and as the second wave began its attack they passed between Flixecourt and Vignacourt, heading for Doullens. At 12.08 hours the third wave passed over Bonneville, where the crews could see tracks from German army vehicles down below:

```
1208. Bonneville. (M 08 78). Military training ground with many tank
tracks visible in snow on high ground.
```

By 12.09 hours they had passed the radio mast at Doullens, heading for Bouzincourt. At 12.12 hours they passed over the Albert to Amiens road and headed straight for the prison.

Wing Commander 'Daddy' Dale,* leading the formation, had still not heard the signal 'red' or 'green' as the small formation raced along the road, skimming over the treetops. Then came the signal; 'red, red, red'.

Dale swung his formation to the north. The attack had been cancelled and they had to re- focus on the journey back to base. The Typhoons headed west.

*Englishman Ivor Gordon Easton Dale was given the name 'Daddy' on account of his 'great' age
- he was 38. He was killed on a night ground attack over Holland on 2-3rd February 1945.

THE RETURN HOME

By 12.16 hours the attack was over and the last aircraft involved were heading for home.

The Return of Flight Lieutenant B.D. Hanafin, No. 487 Squadron RNZAF

Flight Lieutenant Hanafin had been leading the second section of the first wave in Mosquito HX855 EG-Q for 'Queenie'. Its port engine had overheated and Hanafin therefore decided reluctantly to abort the mission. He radioed Wing Commander Smith, the leader of the first wave, to advise that he was obliged to give up the mission.

At 11.58 hours Hanafin moved away from the formation at an altitude of 50 feet and flew westwards. He passed over Beauguesne and crossed the Amiens-Doullens road to the south of Beauval.

At 12.01 hours Hanafin's Mosquito arrived in the area of Canaples / Naours and he released his bombs to save weight. Two of the bombs were 500lb MC TD fitted with 11-second fuses and the other two were 500lb SAP, also with 11-second fuses. The bombs were not armed and fell safely into the fields. According to Hanafin they fell over position NR 0476. Many bombs had already fallen in this area due to the increased attacks on V-1 sites: most exploded, but a few had not. On Tuesday 22nd February, four 500lb unexploded bombs were found in the area of Naours. It is almost certain that these were the bombs released by Hanafin.

The Mosquito had been flying very low, but had not made good time because it was only flying on one engine. The crew followed the route they had used for the inward journey, having passed the area only some ten minutes beforehand. Having jettisoned the bombs, the Mosquito was lighter and gained some height, flying fractionally to the north-west of its incoming route.

The solitary Mosquito was flying close to the village of Allery at 12.05 hours when it came under fire from machine-guns and light anti-aircraft guns hidden in a small patch of woodland. Hanafin was taken completely by surprise and had no time to react to avoid the fire directed at him from so close a range.

One of the machine-gun bullets smashed a section of Perspex, crossed the cockpit and embedded itself in Hanafin's shoulder and neck. With half his body paralysed with pain and losing blood, Hanafin still managed to maintain level flight with the help of his navigator. He managed to make it back to England and made a good landing at Ford airfield, whereupon Hanafin was immediately transferred to hospital. Their Mosquito was later assessed and was found to be damaged category 'AC' requiring more than 36 hours of repair.

During the subsequent preparation of the official history, the officer in charge of collating the crew testimonies wrote:

On his way home on one engine, Flt Lt Hanafin flew through intense flak and received a bullet or piece of shrapnel in the shoulder which for some time paralysed one side of his body so he came home 'on one engine, one leg and one arm' and made a landing at a south of England base.

The return of Smith, Sparks and Jennings (No. 487 Squadron)

Having attacked the prison at 12.03 hours Smith, Sparks and Jennings flew over the site of the future Boulevard Roubaix and up the route d' Albert to the north of the St-Pierre district, flying over the St-Maurice district to the area of Saint-Sauveur for the 'Return Point'. By 12.04 hours they were some 8 kilometres away from Amiens Prison. From the 'Return Point', the aircraft took a west-south-west course over Breilly-Riencourt and Avesnes-Chaussoy. By 12.09 hours they had reached Sénarpont, the last turning point before leaving France. At the north-western end of a large wood near Sénarpont, there were many small sandy hills and slopes. Before the crews could speculate about the nature of this strange site, numerous German soldiers opened fire at them with rifles.

```
Haute Foret d'Eu (M 52  67) At NW end of wood, many small sand banks
sited in woods resembling dumps. Soldiers opened fire with their rifles
at the planes.
```

The Mosquitos quickly departed from the area and at 12.14 hours, still flying at an altitude of only 50 feet, the Mosquitos passed into the coastal area. They noticed a green painted pill box on an escarpment and saw the tell-tale flickering of guns firing from the slot. As the Mosquitos passed over, Sparks' Mosquito (HX922 EG-T) took a direct hit on the cowling of the starboard engine. The same shells also stripped away some of the wing surface, creating an exit hole over two feet across. The Mosquito absorbed the shock of the explosion and flew on with full rudder trim; fortunately the engine itself had escaped damage. Sparks was well aware that the damage was affecting the Mosquito's behaviour and his flying skills could be tested to the full at any second.

At 12.15 hours the planes crossed the coast of France, heading towards Littlehampton. The weather deteriorated as the three aircraft approached Ford, but Wing Commander Smith and Flight Sergeant Jennings managed to make good landings amidst flurries of snow and sleet. The next to land was Mosquito HX982 flown by Pilot Officer Sparks.

Sparks approached Ford very fast, braked heavily, but still had to swerve off the runway to miss another aircraft. The Mosquito came safely to a halt, but was declared damage category 'AC', yet another candidate for more than 36 hours of repairs.

The return of Darrall and Fowler (No. 487 Squadron)

After Hanafin's departure, Darrall and Fowler attacked the prison and flew over the boulevard de Beauvillé before taking a westerly flight path towards the route d'Abbeville 'Return Point' above Saint-Sauveur.

The planes kept low from Saint-Sauveur onwards to Sénarpont and Tocqueville. They were joined by the two Typhoons of 174 Squadron 'Red 1' (Flying Officer W.C. Vatcher) and 'Red 2' (Flight Sergeant H.S. Brown). All of the planes returned to England without further incident and landed at Ford.

The return of Iredale, Sugden and Monaghan (No. 464 Squadron)

After releasing their bombs, Iredale, Sugden and Monaghan flew north-west towards Saint-Sauveur. The return route was exactly the same as the first wave's and they departed from the French coast at 12.18 hours, flying over the British coast at 12.45. Monaghan decided to land at Ford, whilst Wing Commander Iredale and Squadron Leader Sugden carried on to their home base of Hunsdon. They made safe landings at Hunsdon at 12.54 and 12.55 hours.

The return of McRitchie and McPhee (No. 464 Squadron)

After McRitchie and McPhee attacked the prison it seems likely that they were pursued and fired upon by an FW190 after releasing their bombs. The shells from an FW190 hit the kitchen of No.92 rue Louis Thuilier, seriously wounding a woman in the kitchen. The two Mosquitos managed to lose the FW190 and headed homewards via Sénarpont.

Near the town of Fresneville, the pair suddenly ran into a hail of light flak. Miraculously Flight Lieutenant McPhee and his navigator Flight Lieutenant Atkins got through unscathed and, accompanied by his Typhoon escort, McPhee left France in the vicinity of Tocqueville and headed towards Littlehampton, finally landing at Ford at 12.45 hours.

McRitchie and Sampson however had not been so fortunate. A direct hit on the right side of the cockpit killed Sampson instantly and badly wounded McRitchie. With his last available strength, McRitchie managed to crash land his crippled Mosquito in a field and was soon taken to hospital by German troops.*

See page 244.

The return of the No.21 Squadron Mosquitos from the third wave

The four Mosquitos flown by Wing Commander Dale, Flight Lieutenant Benn, Flight Lieutenant Wheeler and Flight Lieutenant Taylor aborted the raid as instructed. Three landed at Ford due to the poor weather conditions and Wheeler returned to Hunsdon.

The return of the FPU Mosquito DZ414

Despite spending more time than any other aircraft over the target Wickham and Howard's Mosquito escaped any ground-fire and they did not report seeing any German fighters. Their return flight was uneventful and they left the coast of France at approximately 12.20 hours.

They soon spotted three Typhoons orbiting over the sea, almost as if they had been waiting for the Mosquito. However, when Wickham headed for Littlehampton the Typhoons did not follow him. The Typhoons were from 198 Squadron and

Squadron Leader McRitchie and Flight Lieutenant Sampson were shot down on the way home near Fresneville. McRitchie survived the high-speed crash landing but Sampson was already dead, killed by a direct hit to the right side of the cockpit.

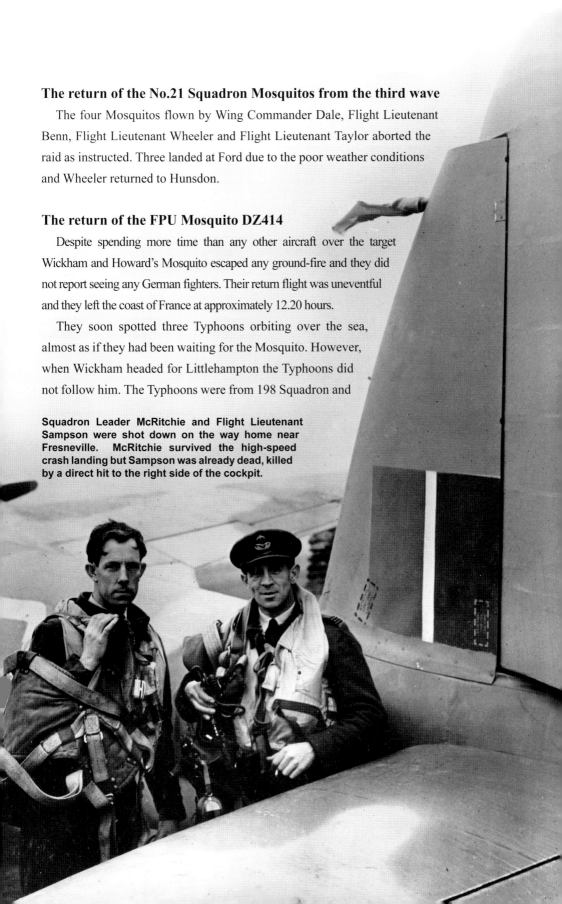

The offical 2 Group log of operations for Ramrod 564

Take-off	Sqn	Time up	Target	Landed	A/C Letter	Pilot	Successful
		1051		Ford	R	W/C Smith	√
				Ford	H	F/S Jennings	√
Hunsdon	487		Amiens Prison	Ford	T	P/O Sparks	√
				Ford	Q	F/L Hanafin	
				Ford	O	P/O Darrall	√
		110½		Ford	J	P/O Fowler	√
		1057		Ford	U	W/C Dale	
				Ford	J	F/L Benn	
				Base	O	F/L Wheeler	
Hunsdon	21			Ford	D	F/L Taylor	
				Ford	F	F/S Steedman	
				1132	P	F/L Hogan	
		1106		Base	O	F/L Wickham	√
		1057		Base 1254	F	W/C Iredale	√
				Base 1255	A	S/L Sugden	√
Hunsdon	464		Amiens Prison	Ford	U	F/O Monoghan	√
					T	S/L McRitchie	√
				Ford	V	F/L McPhee	√
		1106			F	G/C Pickard	

Following reported by FPU "O" F/L Wickham:- Large breach in eastern centre of North wall & hole through wall to east of breach. Hole in northern side of eastern wing of bldg. A breach in northern end of western wall and considerable damage to extension bldg. Individual targets were:
1) Eastern Wall. 487 "R", "T", "H". 464 "U", "V". 2) Northern Wall. 487 "O", "J". 3) Main Building. 464 "T", "U", "V".
FPU a/c circled target three times at times and heights stated. Photographs were taken by cine-camera.

Notes	Attack Time	Attack Height	Bearing	No. Bombs	Size	Type
	1203	10'	250°	4	500	
Belly Landed. Cat AC	1203½	20'	260°			
	1203	10'	250°	4	500	SAP
Abandoned 1158.50' Port engine seized. Hit by Flak. Pilot wounded. Cat. AC Bombs jettisoned 'safe' N.0476						
Hit by Flak. Pilot wounded. Cat. AC	1203½	70'	150°	2 2	500 500	SAP MC
Bombs jettisoned 'safe' N.0476	1203½	70'	150°	4	500	GP
Instructed not to bomb by "F" Returned with bombs.						
As for "U"						
As for "U"						
Abandoned Littlehampton - late, states, failed to contact section.						
	1203 1210	400' 500'	No bombs carried.			
	1204	50'	250°	4	500	MC
	1204	100'	250°	4	500	SAP
	1206	50'	150°	2 2	500 500	SAP GP
S/L McRitchie P.O.W. Nav F/L Sampson killed						
	1206	100'	150°	2 2	500 500	SAP GP
Missing, Nav F/L Broadley Both definitely killed						

Weather. Fine. Whisps of cloud 2000'. Visibility 4 - 6 miles.

From 2 Group - NA Ref. AIR37/23

remained over the Channel to see if they could find the other planes from their squadron as they headed back. 'O for Orange' carried on alone until it was over Littlehampton and then headed inland, eventually arriving at Hunsdon with its vital photographic material.

The return of the No. 174 Squadron Typhoons

Flt Lt F.A. Grantham	Typhoon lb JR310	Blue 1	landed at Hawkinge.
Flt Sgt F.E. Wheeler	Typhoon lb JR541	Blue 2	landed at Lydd.
Flt Lt G.I. Mallet	Typhoon lb JP671	Blue 3	landed at either Hawkinge or Lydd but there is no record of his landing.
Flg Off J.E. Renaud	Typhoon lb JR133	Blue 4	shot down near Amiens
Flg Off W.C. Vatcher	Typhoon lb JP308	Red 1	landed at Westhampnett
Flt Sgt H.S. Brown	Typhoon lb JP793	Red 2	lost in the Channel
P/O W.D. Burton	Typhoon lb JR303	Red 3	(Canadian) landed at Westhampnett
Flg Off H.V. Markby	Typhoon lb JP535	Red 4	(Australian) landed at Westhampnett

Blue Section

Blue 4, piloted by Renaud, was shot down by a Focke Wulf 190 flown by Oberleutnant Radener and made a forced landing near Ramponneau.* The other three pilots were not aware of any combat and, when they heard Renaud's message about a forced landing, they all believed that he was the victim of anti-aircraft fire.

Flight Sergeant Frank E. Wheeler reported that they attacked some boats during the return journey, probably in the Somme valley. The flight over the Channel passed without incident, apart from the rapidly deteriorating weather that became so bad that the pilots lost visual contact with each other.

Red Section

Flying Officer Vatcher and Flight Sergeant Brown joined up with the Mosquitos of Darrall and Fowler. They crossed the French coast without incident, but then ran into bad weather. The Typhoons then left the Mosquitos that carried on towards Littlehampton. Both Typhoon pilots then entered a patch of very violent turbulence and Vatcher saw Flight Sergeant Brown climb into cloud - it was the last time he was ever seen.

Pilot Officer Burton, and Flying Officer Markby passed to the north of the prison, having orbited to the east of the city. Markby then headed westwards and was surprised to see two FW190s climbing quickly towards the clouds. The two German aircraft flew towards the north-east, but Markby was too far away to engage them. Burton and Markby continued

* See page 250 for full details.

their planned route to join up with the Mosquitos flown by McRitchie and McPhee and saw McRitchie's Mosquito hit by machine-gun fire right in front of them. Almost immediately, one of its engines burst into flames and a long smoke stream was seen. The Typhoon pilots then escorted McPhee to Ford, whilst they landed at Westhampnett.

The return of the Typhoons from No.198 Squadron

The three 198 Squadron pilots led by Flight Lieutenant Dall that were circling in vain looking for their Mosquitos finally gave up after 20 - 25 minutes. It is likely that none of these pilots knew precisely where they were, but they were probably north of Tocqueville. The arrival time is hard to estimate, but was probably around 12.00 hours. On its return flight the FPU Mosquito crew spotted the Typhoons at 12.19 hours. Flight Lieutenant Roper reported:

We must have been circling around for 5 or 10 minutes when a lone Mosquito turned up. Flying very low and fast we formated close enough to it to make out it was a photographic plane. Dall pulled away and we kept circling for a while. I was getting low on fuel, formation flying always used up more than usual, then we finally turned for home.

We landed back at Tangmere, as Manston was in the middle of the snow storm. It was only after we landed that Bluey Dall told us what had been going on. We later learned that the raid had been a success, the walls of the jail had been breached by the bombs and many of the prisoners got out to freedom.

Flight Lieutenant Dall also explained the whole course of the mission during the debriefing and the latter was recorded officially:

```
6 Typhoons took off and when 30 miles sw of base they encountered 10/10
cloud at zero feet with heavy snow causing three a/c to lose contact
and to return to base independently. The remaining 3 a/c eventually
met the bombers when they were crossing over French coast.
```

NA Ref AIR25/208)

The return of the No.245 Squadron Typhoons

Two of the original eight Typhoons from 245 Squadron became lost in the snow-laden skies before the attack and quickly returned to Westhampnett. The remaining six Typhoons led by Squadron Leader Collins followed the four 21 Squadron Mosquitos of the third wave throughout the operation. All six pilots returned to base without incident. The squadron Operational Record Book noted;

A quick briefing at 1055 hours and at 1120 hours eight aircraft were
airborne to escort six Mosquitos on a low level attack on a prison
camp at Amiens. Only 3 Mosquitos arrived at rendezvous two minutes
late and after cruising round France for 45 minutes the Mosquitos
returned without locating target or dropping bombs.

(NA Ref. AIR 27/1482)

This ORB entry once again illustrates the lack of information that was available to the fighter pilots involved in the mission. Since the pilots had not witnessed the Mosquitos dropping their bombs, they concluded that they were unable to find the target.

SUMMARY OF THE FIGHTER ESCORT

'Ramrod 564' was completed successfully, but one of the biggest failures of the operation was in the provision of fighter cover over the target. This was considered essential for this type of operation as the higher flying escort fighters could keep any enemy fighters busy enough to allow the bombers clear passage over the target. Had this escort been available, it is probable that they would have engaged the prowling FW190s, so diverting attention from the Mosquitos. Given this lack of fighter cover it is fortunate that the Mosquitos did not suffer greater losses.

So who was responsible for the lack of target cover? Initially, it would appear that Squadron Leader Dredge of No.3 Squadron should take responsibility, for it was he who refused to take off. However, the answer is not quite so simple. An officer has responsibilities both to his men and to his aircraft; he must make decisions accordingly, even if this may sometimes countermand orders from his superiors. This would be appropriate where the officer had more up-to-date information or direct experience of conditions and felt that the mission could not be accomplished. Dredge considered that the snow storm at Manston was too risky for what he believed was the limited likelihood of being able to rendezvous with the Mosquitos, let alone being able to provide adequate cover for them. Unknown to Dredge the snowstorm was far worse in the area of Manston than it was at Littlehampton.

A report from 160 wing (245 and 174 Squadrons) commented:

Warning was received of a fighter sweep of 280 miles so no tanks were
fitted. Forty minutes before T/O the target was given as Amiens and
the task as close escort to Mosquito bombers. This gave an air mileage
of somewhere about 380 miles. The result was that all aircraft of
Nos.174 and 245 Squadrons that took part were short of fuel and two
were lost, Flg Off Renaud and Flt Sgt Brown of 174.

Lack of fuel was not responsible for the loss of the Typhoon flown by Flying Officer Renaud, but it might have been the reason for the loss of Flight Sergeant Brown, who disappeared in the English Channel.

According to some reports, Squadron Leader Dredge also pointed out that the distance from Manston to Amiens was greater than the distance from Westhampnett to Amiens. Planes from Manston would therefore be at greater risk of running out of fuel if additional tanks were not fitted. It is clear that it was too late to fit the Typhoons with drop tanks by the time that the details of the operation and the route were given.

So who, then, should take the responsibility for the problems caused by last minute alterations?

It should certainly not be Squadron Leader Dredge or Flight Lieutenant Dall of 198 Squadron. Rather, the blame must lie with the organizers and planners of 'Ramrod 564'. The mission plans and contents had been kept secret and only seen by a few who simply did not appreciate the operational problems. The mechanics and ground crew at Manston had not been given warning that the additional fuel tanks would be required.

A further operation, 'Ramrod 565' involving 613 Squadron's Mosquitos, was cancelled because it was considered that the fighter escort would not be able to take off due to the poor weather. The cancellation of 'Ramrod 565' was received at Lasham airfield shortly after Dredge had refused to take off; perhaps his decision had already had an impact upon those responsible for authorizing missions.

It seems, therefore, that bad weather and the failure to supply target cover had dire consequences.

However, once the orders had been issued a plan had been set in motion and could not be stopped. It had been made clear that 120 prisoners were due to be executed the following day - the operation had to go ahead; no matter what the weather, misgivings or doubts.

It had to go ahead for a greater plan to succeed.

PART 3

THE REAL STORY

Previous page: A view from the main road near the entrance to the prison, showing the first breach in the wall created by a bomb dropped by Wing Commander Smith.

WHY ATTACK AMIENS PRISON?

There can be no doubt that the men who attacked the prison did so in the firm belief that they were attempting to free members of the Resistance facing imminent execution. The written orders and verbal briefing had made this abundantly clear to the Mosquito crews. If any airmen were to be captured during the raid (as McRitchie was) or on subsequent operations they may have revealed the purpose of the raid to their interrogators. Should this have happened then German intelligence would have been bemused; for they had no knowledge of any plans for such a 'mass execution'.

Amiens was liberated on 31st August. Just a week later, on 8th September, an RAF investigator arrived to discover why the attack was requested and who requested it. He did not succeed in either task, but he did establish that no 'mass execution' was planned.

When details of the raid were made public eight months after the raid, the execution story was revived. Historians and authors have quoted from and repeated the story as published in October 1944 ever since. However, it can now be shown that there was to be no mass execution and there was no 'call for help', a revelation that challenges the long held beliefs of many.

THE 'OFFICIAL' ANSWER:

The first occasion that a 'reason' or justification for the attack appears is in the order AO 241 from 2 Group, briefing 140 Wing for the attack. Here it is clearly stated, MOSQUITOS OF 140 AIRFIELD ARE TO ATTACK THE PRISON AT AMIENS IN AN ATTEMPT TO ASSIST 120 PRISONERS TO ESCAPE. THESE PRISONERS ARE FRENCH PATRIOTS CONDEMNED TO DEATH FOR ASSISTING THE ALLIES. Prior to this message there is no mention of the reasoning behind the attack, only details of the target. This justification is stoically maintained in the press release eight months later and must therefore be regarded as the 'official' reasoning for the attack.

Assessing the 'Official' Reason for the Raid

The author's first line of enquiry was to establish the identity of the '120' prisoners about to be executed. In short, this appears to be a total fabrication.

As with many similar penal institutions, executions did take place from time to time, but *not* at Amiens prison itself at this time. On 17th January, 1944 Jean Roy of Nesle was executed in the Citadelle in Amiens; André Dumont of Mers-les-Bains was shot on 5th February, 1944. Earlier on 2nd August, 1943, eleven members of the Resistance had been shot at the Citadelle.

If one excludes the summary executions that took place towards the end of summer 1944 in what was known as 'The Massacre of Gentelles', when 27 people were killed, the execution of the eleven Resistance operatives shot on 2ⁿᵈ August 1943 was the largest mass execution in this area.

On Thursday 17ᵗʰ February 1944, a request from the French Attorney General arrived at the offices of the National Gendarmerie of Amiens. Eight people (seven men and a woman) imprisoned in the prison at Amiens were to be brought to the Special Section of the Court of Appeal for judgement. The Special Section of the Court of Appeal at Amiens was responsible for passing judgement on the fate of the so-called 'political' prisoners held in Amiens Prison.

22 year-old André Dumont. Member of the FTP executed on 5th February at the Citadelle.

```
GENDARMERIE NATIONALE
LEGION DE PICARDY
COMPAGNIE DE LA SOMME
SECTION  D`AMIENS
OBJECT extraction speciale
Amiens February 17, 1944

The Captain F…in charge of the section and the Major in charge of the
company of gendarmerie of the Somme. Amiens.

Reference Article 78 of the decree of May 20, 1903.

I received from the Attorney General a request to remove from the
prison at Amiens, eight individuals accused of terrorist activity
and arson who must appear on the 26th February at 14.30 hrs before
the Special Section of the Court of Appeal.
Because of the nature of the crimes committed, I estimate that
special measures of security must be taken. I have the honour to
propose that this removal is carried out by twenty (20) gendarmes and
will require that a van be placed at the disposal of the brigade on
February 26 as from 1.30p.m.
```

The raid took place on 18th February and a period of general confusion naturally followed. On 26th February 1944, the same captain of the gendarmerie advised the Attorney General that:

```
The eight people who were to appear before the Special Section have
not been able to be located among the prisoners currently held in
Amiens Prison, nor among the identified corpses recovered from the
debris of the destroyed prison that was destroyed on 18 February. It
is to be assumed that these individuals have escaped.
```

The names of these eight people are registered in this report, but none were known Resistance leaders. Records of the affairs of the prison do exist, as illustrated by the above correspondence, but there is no reference to any large scale execution being planned.

WAS THERE A CALL FOR HELP?

It is claimed that the raid had its origins in a request from 'the Resistance', pleading for help to release members who would be executed in the near future. But is there any evidence to support this?

At the beginning of January 1944 General Emmanuel d'Astier de la Vigerie, Commissionaire of the Comité National des Forces Francaises de L'Interieur, began a whole series of requests to the Allies, claiming with determination that help was required for the Resistance which was under-equipped and under-manned. During the entire month of January 1944, General d'Astier de la Vigerie called upon London, and Washington, ending up by personally obtaining a meeting with Winston Churchill on 27th January 1944.

```
War Cabinet
Minutes of meeting held at No.10 Downing Street,
SW1, at 3pm on Thursday 27th January 1944

Present:
The Rt. Hon. Winston S. Churchill M.P. Prime Minister and Minister of
Defence (In the Chair)
The Rt.Hon. Sir Archibald Sinclair, The Secretary of State for Air.
The Rt Hon. The Earl of Selborn, Minister of Economic Warfare
Marshal of the Royal Air Force, Sir Charles Portal, Chief of the
Air Staff
Lt. General Sir Hastings Ismay, office of the Minister of Defence
Mr. W.H.B. Mack, Foreign Office
Mr. R.L. Speaight, Foreign Office
Mr. H. Sporborg, S.O.E.
Brigadier E.E. Mockler-Ferryman, S.O.E.
Mr. Emmanuel d' Astier de la Vigerie, Commisioner for the Interior,
```

French National Committee
M. Boris, French National Committee
Major D. Morton, Personal Assistant to the Prime Minister
Secretary:
Lieut Colonel D. Capel-Dunn

ASSISTANCE TO THE RESISTANCE MOVEMENT IN FRANCE

The Prime Minister stated that he had called the meeting to consider what could be done to assist the resistance movement in France during the coming critical months.

He understood from M. d' Astier that considerably more help than had recently been provided was required if the resistance movement was to produce the results of which it was capable.
The Prime Minister attached high importance to this matter.
The Minister of Economic Warfare said that S.O.E. were giving every assistance in their power but their help was limited by the number of aircraft that the Air Staff could make available for these purposes
The Secretary of State for Air asked if the Prime Minister would give the Air Ministry authorization so that the efforts of Bomber Command during the month of February should be directed primarily to the bomber offensive but that the priority for other activities of Bomber Command should be as follows:
a) assisting the Maquis
b) other operations for S.O.E.
c) crossbow operations
d) mining

The German defences were becoming stronger and it would in his opinion be deplorable (The Chief of the Air Staff) if anything were done at this stage to upset our bombing effort and thus affect the spirit of those taking part in it.

THE MEETING AGREED:
1) That during the month of February 1944 the primary effort of Bomber Command should be directed to the bomber offensive against Germany and that, subject to the needs of S.I.S., the priorities of other operations of Bomber Command during that month should be as follows:
a) assisting the Maquis
b) other operations for S.O.E.
c) crossbow operations
d) mining

2) Invited the Minister of Economic Warfare in consultation with M. d' Astier and the Air Staff to enquire into the air facilities that could be made available for S.O.E. operations in support of the Maquis resistance movement during February and to prepare an outline plan of assistance and to submit a report to the Prime Minister by Monday the 31st January.

At this meeting a long discussion was held during which General Emmanuel d'Astier de la Vigerie explained that the assistance given to the Resistance would not increase friction between the various political groups. Such problems would most likely only be a cause for concern after the Germans had departed. The answer he received was positive: despite the lack of available aircraft an effort was to be made to assist the Resistance. In fact two American units (the 36th and 406th Bomb Squadrons) would be taken away from USAAF combat units operating against enemy submarines and would be used to reinforce the parachute supply drops instead.*

The Secretary of State for the Air Ministry then asked if the Prime Minister would give his agreement that Bomber Command should concentrate first on the bombing offensive against Germany, but that subsequent priorities could be directed to the four objectives outlined above.

The meeting of 27th January 1944 has been outlined here in order to illustrate the repeated requests of General d'Astier de la Vigerie. The requests related only to one topic; additional assistance to the Resistance, and nothing else.

Dominique Ponchardier, head of the 'Sosies' Resistance network, did make a claim after the end of the war that he had been involved in requesting the raid, but no evidence can be found to substantiate his claim. Eventually Dominique Ponchardier refused to make any further comment.**

None of the Resistance organisations claimed responsibility for requesting the raid; each suggests that another was responsible. From a French perspective this is hardly suprising. Whilst it is now possible to look at the raid in the knowledge that 102 people were killed and 258 escaped, that outcome could not have been predicted. The death toll may well have been much higher had a greater number of bombs struck the prison building; and certainly far higher had the third wave carried out its task to destroy the prison entirely. Had the walls not been breached, and all six of the third wave Mosquitos attacked, 700 prisoners would have been confined in the building when 12,000lbs of bombs were dropped. Would anyone from the Resistance movements near Amiens have requested such an attack on a prison containing 700 of his own countrymen?

Whilst the lack of evidence of the much reported 'call for help' is unusual in itself, it should be considered that the RAF was not in the business of carrying out attacks on demand; particularly on an insignificant civilian prison.

*In fact, the first 'Carpetbagger' operation had already been flown from Tempsford on the night of 4-5th January 1944, the first of its kind to be flown by B-24s, but General d'Astier de la Vigerie was totally unaware of this.

** See page 157.

To persist in the belief of these reasons for the raid today, one must be convinced of the following series of events:

1/ That a person or persons 'understood' or was erroneously led to believe that a large number of prisoners were facing imminent execution in Amiens - when no one else, French or German did.
2/ That no one, during the war or since, knew who this person was.
3/ That this unknown person had the ability to communicate this to senior British Intelligence officers from within occupied France.
4/ That British Intelligence decided to take action immediately, without further corroboration of the information.
5/ That all of this left no credible evidence, verbal or written, in either Britain or France.

THE 'UNOFFICIAL' ANSWERS:

No sooner had Amiens been liberated, on 31st August 1944, than the story of a 'mass execution' began to unravel. Two other stories then began to be heard; that the raid had been requested by the Resistance to free a senior officer, or ordered from London to eliminate a British agent.

THE RESISTANCE STORY:

It is true that some important Resistance leaders were imprisoned at Amiens, such as Leon Bourdon from the Picardy Resistance group, Andre Tempez, Dr. Antonin Mans, Henri Moisan and Raymond Vivant among others. But this does not make Amiens Prison unique in Occupied Europe as members of the various Resistance organisations were imprisoned, and executed, in other prisons. This, then, is not a reason in itself to justify the raid. However, two names appear repeatedly in connection with this story; Raymond Vivant and Jean Beaurain.

Raymond Vivant

Squadron Leader Houghton who carried out the enquiry on behalf of 2 Group on 8th September was led to believe that the raid had been requested to free Monsieur Vivant, the Sous-Préfet of Abbeville. Vivant was certainly a key member of the Resistance and well connected. He was one of the successful escapees and by September 1944 was already in

Paris working under General de Gaulle. This idea has been repeated in several publications, however, it has now been established that plans for the raid pre-date Vivant's arrest by four days. Raymond Vivant could not have been the focus of the raid.*

Jean Beaurain - saboteur extraordinaire?

Another name often associated with 'high level' prisoners is Jean Beaurain. Indeed Pierre Ponchardier suggested in a French document dated September 1944 that his brother Dominique, head of the 'Sosies' Resistance network, organised the raid solely to free Beaurain.

Jean Beaurain's story:

My father was away in Compiègne during the first hours of the occupation, as he was attending a Communist function. My half-brother Roger Lheureux was arrested for stealing a bicycle. I was being sought by the Gestapo and all the local gendarmerie for a false accusation relating to the murder of a German soldier. I was eligible for deportation to Germany for work.

Thus, one day in 1943, Jean Beaurain gathered a pair of shoes, a small amount of money and arrived at the station to catch a train to Berlin.

I took the shoes and the money, but I did not leave from the station. A member of the FTP called Lemaire (who was later shot) managed to conceal me and hide me away in Amiens. I eventually joined the Maquis near Tergnier and was soon involved in train derailments and other actions to harass the Germans.

Colonel Rémy first described Beaurain's exploits in his book *L'operation Jéricho*. According to Rémy, Jean Beaurain took part in two derailments on the Amiens-Tergnier line, two more on the Amiens-Montdidier line, two on the Amiens-Compiègne line and a further nine derailments on the Amiens-Arras line. One of the derailments took place at Grandcourt, near Miramont, on the night of 29th July 1943. On this night, they unbolted many rails and a large train carrying German troops was overturned. This derailment would probably not have had such enormous consequences had it not been for a goods train travelling in the opposite direction that collided with the derailed train.

Dr. Dhotel, then doctor at Achiet-Le-Grand, was called to the incident to look after the casualties. According to him, the derailed train comprised forty coaches with approximately 600 soldiers on board. 180 soldiers were killed and another 100 were injured as a result of the derailment.

* See page 188.

'We never used explosives. The rails were dislodged by removing the coach screws and operations only took place at night, when only the troop trains used the lines. We never killed one French civilian', Jean Beaurain declared proudly.

However, can this story be as straight forward as it seems?

Although a well known story, the author became suspicious of the grandiose scale of Beaurain's exploits and now believes that they were, at the very least, embroidered by Rémy. The local French resistance organisations worked in small groups, now better known as 'cells', for security. Should any one group become known to the Gestapo, the amount of information regarding other groups that could be extracted from its members was limited. Beaurain claims to have quickly joined a group near Tergnier, far from his home town, then to have derailed trains in no less than three French Departments; Somme, Pas-de-Calais and Aisne. Derailments and other acts of sabotage were almost always performed by small groups that restricted their operations to their own areas where they had the advantage of local knowledge. They knew the best place for an ambush, or stretch of railway line to dismantle, and where they could hide and melt back into the community without arousing suspicion by being outsiders. Yet according to Rémy, Jean Beaurain, now based in the small village of Grandcourt north of Amiens, derailed trains near Montdidier (48km south) Tergnier (60km south-east) and Combles (15km south-east).

At the end of 1943, it is claimed that Jean and his colleagues were betrayed to the Germans and went on the run, taking refuge at Albert. One day shortly before Christmas 1943, Jean set off for his home town of Mers-les-Bains but was stopped, questioned and later imprisoned at Amiens, but on charges of petty theft! Rémy claims that the Germans never discovered that he had been involved in sabotage or train derailmnets.

Who was 'Colonel Rémy'? Is his account to be believed, and why should he need to embroider Jean Beaurain's exploits?

'Colonel Rémy' was in fact Gilbert Renault, who died in 1984 at the age of 79. He was also known as Raymond, Jean-Luc, Morin, Watteau, Roulier and Beauce, and was one of France's top 'secret agents' in WW2. He escaped from France upon the German occupation in June 1940 and joined General de Gaulle in London. He claimed that he had met Pickard in England, which he may well have done. He was flown back to France in a Lysander from 161 Squadron - which Pickard was attached to - on 26th March 1942 for an SOE mission code named 'Operation Baccarat II'. He returned to England by boat with details of the German channel defences, but the Gestapo arrested his mother, brother and five sisters. By 1944 he was the London head of the BCRA* (Bureau Central

* *The organistaion later became the BRAL - See pages 165 and 333.*

de Renseignements et d'Action) or Central Bureau of Intelligence and Operations. The BCRA worked with Stewart Menzies' MI6, and Maurice Buckmaster's SOE. Renault specifically created an information gathering and dissemination network in France using the likes of Dominique Ponchardier's 'Sosies'.

If any Frenchman knew the real purpose of the raid on Amiens Prison it would have been Renault (Rémy), but not surprisingly he maintained the cover story of freeing important members of the Resistance in his book *L'operation Jéricho* - and Jean Beaurain's 'exploits' suited this cause very well.

'Colonel Rémy' was in fact Gilbert Renault - a top French secret agent.

THE SECRET AGENT STORY

Working in London with Renault in the BCRA / BRAL was Commandant André Manuel - de Gaulle's Head of Intelligence. In an interview for a BBC Panorama programme in 1982 André Manuel was asked what he believed the purpose of the Amiens Prison raid was. He replied:

I was told that this unusual action, because I think it was the only action during the war against a prison, was decided by Winston Churchill himself. The reason to my mind is that amongst the prisoners in that jail was one man who was very important who had been told on account of his importance the exact date of the [Normandy] landing. And the British knew quite well that even a first class man cannot resist the torture the Germans were inflicting on their prisoners and therefore Winston Churchill decided on the 'Jericho' operation in order either to help him escape or to kill him.

Asked, who was the man? Manuel replied:

I do not know. Because he was not part of the French Secret Service. He was part of a British branch of Secret Service working in France.

When asked, which branch? Manuel said simply:

Headed by Mr Buckmaster.

By which he meant Maurice Buckmaster's SOE.

It is often suggested that there were agents from British services in the prison whom it was vital to release or 'silence' at all costs. An SOE (Special Operations Executive) agent was arrested at the end of 1943 and other associated arrests took place in the St Quentin sector, which at that time was included in the administrative region of Amiens.

Colonel Rémy wrote in his book *L'operation Jéricho* that two agents of the British Intelligence Service were imprisoned in Amiens on 12th February 1944.

It is highly improbable, given the level of security surrounding the planning for D-Day, that anyone with highly classified knowledge would have been placed in a position where he might risk capture, as was the case when Embry was prevented from flying on the Amiens raid. Furthermore, the 'exact date' of D-Day had not been decided at the time of the Amiens raid. However, if German intelligence officers could be convinced that someone in the prison *did* have that knowledge, it would suit the aims of British Intelligence very well.

It would appear that there are as many stories behind the origin of the raid as there are people to tell them yet, with nearly 70 years of hindsight and the availability of more information than has previously been available, all can be dismissed. It is probable that at least one of the men quoted here knew what really happened, but maintained the cover story and took the answer to his grave - that was and is the nature of Military Intelligence.

The following section sets out to establish the real motives behind the attack and peers into the dark, murky, heart of Allied intelligence and the planning for the invasion of Europe itself. The conclusions reached are wildly at variance to the accepted history of this attack; but when the stories of 'releasing Resistance workers facing execution' and others have been dismissed, one is left asking the question – what was the purpose of the attack?

It is the author's belief that the real reason for the raid on Amiens Prison was to support the attempt to deceive the intelligence services of the Reich in Occupied France. It was a key part of the plan to persuade German intelligence that the Pas-de-Calais area was to be the location of the Allied invasion.

THE PLAYERS

THE BRITISH INTELLIGENCE ORGANISATION

LONDON CONTROLLING SECTION (LCS)

The organization was established in June 1942 within the Joint Planning Staff at the offices of the War Cabinet. Its purpose was to devise and co-ordinate deceptions for military strategy and cover plans. The first Controlling Officer of the LCS was Lieutenant Colonel (later Colonel) John Bevan. Bevan moved in the same circles as General Lord Ismay, (Military Deputy Secretary of the War Cabinet and Chief of the Chiefs of Staff Committee within the War Cabinet) and Sir Stewart Menzies, (head of MI6). He also had a direct channel to Churchill and indirectly via Churchill's Chief of Staff; Ismay. The only permanent RAF member was Dennis Wheatley, author of many thrillers and books on the occult.

The LCS acted as a clearing house to coordinate Allied efforts to deceive the *Abwehr* and therefore the OKW as to when and where the landings would take place - 'Plan (or Operation) Bodyguard'. The LCS was also heavily associated with the code-breakers of Bletchley Park, with their intelligence (code-named Ultra) and the Twenty Committee Double Cross Agents. It also co-ordinated plans to use local French Resistance groups in support of the deception plan.

TWENTY COMMITTEE

The task of deceiving German intelligence was given to the unusually named 'Twenty Committee'. This 'committee' of leading lights in British Intelligence from MI5, MI6, RAF, Army and Navy met weekly in MI5's London offices to discuss how to pass misleading information to the Germans, and plan deception operations. It also discussed how best to employ the many double agents run by section B1(A) of MI5, the so called 'Double Cross' network - or XX - twenty in Roman numerals - hence the 'Twenty Committee'. The very naming of the department in charge of deception illustrates the tortuous minds of its larger-than-life members. Chairman was Oxford don, John Masterman.

SPECIAL OPERATIONS EXECUTIVE (SOE)

The SOE was created at the request of Winston Churchill in July 1940, in order to specialise in warfare conducted by means other than direct military engagement. SOE was an amalgamation of three secret departments that already existed: Section D, a sub-section of MI6 (also known as SIS - Secret Intelligence Service), a War Office department named MI R and a propaganda section named Department EH. Its headquarters was situated in Baker Street, which led to it acquiring the nickname 'The Baker Street Irregulars' after Sherlock Holmes' fictional spies. There was much rivalry between SOE and MI6 (SIS), which hindered effectiveness and co-operation. The first chief of SOE was Sir Frank Nelson, who was replaced in 1942 by Sir Charles Hambro. Sir Charles was often quoted as saying of the SOE, 'It was not good for democracies to know what their governments did in times of war.' He resigned in 1943 to be replaced by Major General Colin Gubbins.

Two London-based sections controlled operations in France: F section was under British control (Colonel Maurice Buckmaster), whilst RF section was linked to the exiled Free French Government of General de Gaulle. The section under French control was BCRA (Bureau Central de Renseignements et d'Action)

MI5 (MILITARY INTELLIGENCE - SECTION 5)

MI5 was responsible for security operations in Britain and dates back to before WW1. It was not prepared for its tasks at the outbreak of war and in early 1940 Winston Churchill replaced MI5's long-standing head, Vernon Kell with Brigadier Harker. He was quickly replaced by David Petrie (from MI6) but Harker stayed on as his deputy. As the threat of German invasion receeded, MI5 concentrated on the 'Double-Cross' network of 'turned' German agents.

MI5 sent bogus 'intelligence' to the *Abwehr* via the Twenty Committee.

SECRET INTELLIGENCE SERVICE (SIS)
MI6 (MILITARY INTELLIGENCE - SECTION 6)

Dating back to 1909 MI6 was responsible for secret operations overseas, and in particular Germany. During WW2 the highly secret operations of MI6 in occupied Europe were compromised by the dramatic accomplishments of the SOE. Increased German security hampered and endanged the work of MI6's agents. This led to an almost total breakdown of relations between the two organisations.

The head of MI6 was known as 'C' - at the time of the Amiens raid this was General Sir Stewart Menzies.

BUREAU CENTRAL DE RENSEIGNEMENTS ET D'ACTION (BCRA)
BUREAU RENSEIGNEMENTS ET D'ACTION LONDRES (BRAL)

The French equivalant of the British secret services, the BCRA (Central Bureau of Intelligence and Operations) was established in London after the fall of France in 1940 under General de Gaulle. It was commanded by Major André Dewavrin, known as 'Colonel Passy'. Head of the intelligence section was Captain André Manuel (known as 'Pallas') who worked with MI6. Other sections worked with the SOE and MI5.

The BRAL was created from the BCRA when it was divided between Algiers (North Africa) and London. 'Colonel Passy' headed the Algiers operation and Gilbert Renault - 'Colonel Rémy' - author of *L'operation Jéricho* - was a senior figure in 1944.

THE GERMAN INTELLIGENCE ORGANISATION

The *Abwehr* was the intelligence-gathering arm of German Intelligence and dealt exclusively with human intelligence, especially raw intelligence reports from field agents and other sources. The Chief of the *Abwehr* reported directly to the German High Command. *Oberkommando der Wehrmacht* (OKW) that produced intelligence summaries and distributed the summaries via its Operations Branch to the *Oberkommando Des Heeres (OKH)* Army, *Kriegsmarine (OKM)* - Navy, or *Luftwaffe (OKL)* - Airforce. The *Abwehr's* Headquarters was located at 76/78 Tirpitzufer, Berlin, adjacent to the offices of the OKW.

THE GAME

COVER and DECEPTION PLANS

"All warfare is based on deception. Hence, when able to attack, we must seem unable; when using force, we must seem inactive; when we are near, we must make the adversary believe we are far away; when far away, we must make him believe we are near. Hold our baits to entice the adversary, feign disorder, and crush him."

Sun Tzu 'The Art of War' (around 722–481 BC)

There is an important difference between a 'cover plan' and a 'deception'.

A 'cover plan' is designed to persuade the enemy that something true (such as the landings in Normandy) is false.

A deception sets out to convince the enemy that something false (such as landings in the Pas-de-Calais) is true.

Cover conceals truth; deception conveys falsehood. Cover induces non-action; deception induces action.

Since behaviour is that which is to be influenced, the enemy does not have to actually believe what is being projected. It is only necessary that the enemy is so concerned that he must provide for it.

To influence behaviour, the target of deception is the enemy commander, and the consumer of the deception is the commander's intelligence organization. For example, for strategic deception in Europe, the target of deception was Adolf Hitler himself through the Supreme Command of the Defence Forces, Oberkommando der Wehrmacht (OKW). The consumer was a branch of the intelligence staff of the High Command of the Army, Oberkommando Des Heeres (OKH), the Foreign Armies West, Fremde Heere West (FHW).

(Thaddeus Holt: The Deceivers: Allied Military Deception in the Second World War)

PLAN BODYGUARD

Churchill used the phrase; "In wartime, truth is so precious that she should always be attended by a bodyguard of lies" at a meeting with Stalin at the Tehran Conference in November 1943.

'Bodyguard' was prepared by the LCS and was the 'overall' deception plan for operations against Germany in 1944. The objective was 'to induce the enemy to make faulty strategic dispositions in relation to operations by the United Nations against Germany.' The aim was to keep German forces away from the invasion in Normandy. If German intelligence could be confused as to where and when the invasion would take place then their forces would be spread thinly all the way from Norway to the Mediterranean. After the Normandy landings did take place the aim was to stop troops being moved to Normandy by persuading the commanders that Normandy was an elaborate diversion to draw their troops away from the 'real' landing area. It was hoped that German commanders would be reluctant to move their forces for fear of 'leaving the back door open' by rushing to Normandy, exactly what the deception plans for the landings in Sicily had achieved in July 1943.

'Bodyguard' itself had several sub-operations to persuade the Germans that invasions would come in various locations including:

'Fortitude North'; landings in Norway launched from Scotland.

'Fortitude South'; landings in the Pas-de-Calais.

'Zeppelin'; landings in the Mediterranean.

'Vendetta'; landings on the French coast between Sete and Narbonne.

'Ironside'; the capture of the port facilities at Bordeaux.

In the context of the raid on Amiens Prison, it is the plan aimed at keeping German forces held back in the Pas-de-Calais after the Normandy landings that is of interest. This plan began life as 'Plan 'Mespot' and went through three drafts before the code name was changed to 'Fortitude' in February 1944 - at the time of the Amiens raid.

PLANS MESPOT and FORTITUDE SOUTH

The purpose of 'Mespot' which evolved into 'Fortitude South' was to ensure that the German XV Army stayed in the Pas-de-Calais, even after the landings in Normandy. This was made easier by the preconceptions of the German High Command (OKW) who considered it unlikely that the Allies would attempt to cross the English Channel anywhere other than at its narrowest point - the 22 miles of the Straits of Dover. A crossing in force anywhere else would, they considered, be too hazardous when distance and sea conditions were taken into account.

The German coastal defences were strongest in the Pas-de-Calais region and troops were stationed ready to repel the expected attack that they had come to believe was very likely to take place in February 1944.

There were many intricate cover plans and deception schemes employed to reinforce the beliefs held by German intelligence. Most famously an entire phantom army called the First US Army Group was conjured out of little more than dummy planes, vehicles and landing craft. Supporting this 'physical' evidence was an entirely realistic stream of radio messages to, from and between the imaginary units making up FUSAG that the German listening service could pick up and pass to the *Abwehr*.

XX Agents were given messages by B1(A) section of MI5, to send to their German masters. B1(A) also used a less controllable avenue to get their messages to German intelligence; spreading rumours via civilians and the French Resistance!

HOW IT WORKED

To understand how the Amiens Prison Raid played a key role in the deception plans behind the Normandy landings, one must go back to 1943 and the Allied invasion of Sicily.

To allow Allied troops time to establish an invasion beachhead it was proposed to deceive the defending German forces into believing that the landings were to take place in Sardinia and Corsica. By doing this the defending forces would be concentrated away from the real landing area, Sicily, thus ensuring the initial attack met less resistance than there might otherwise have been. Taking the idea still further, if the Germans could be persuaded that the landings in Sicily were merely a diversion in advance of a much larger invasion of Sardinia and Corsica, then reinforcements would be held back and not sent to counter the actual landings. The German forces may only be deceived by a few days, but the time gained was critical in establishing a defendable beachhead.

Secretary to the Twenty Committee, the section under MI5 charged with fooling the *Abwehr*, was 25 year-old Flight Lieutenant Charles Christopher Cholmondeley (pronounced Chumly - as he was keen point out) who had read Geography at Oxford and joined the RAF, but his very poor eyesight precluded him from flying. Six feet three inches tall with a large pointed moustache, this eccentric observer of mating insects possessed a mind capable of dreaming up highly original ideas. This talent led to him being recruited into MI5 as 'ideas man'. His opposite number in Naval Intelligence was Ian Fleming; Personal Assistant to the Director of Naval Intelligence and post-war creator of James Bond. Working with Ian Fleming was Ewen Montagu. Lieutenant Commander Montagu was a 42 year-old Cambridge graduate and son of an aristocratic Jewish banking family. All worked in the upper echelon of British Military Intelligence and had access to the most secret information, such as the 'Ultra' decrypts of German coded signals provided by Bletchley Park.

In 1943 Flight Lieutenant Charles Cholmondeley had been developing plans to mislead the German Military Intelligence service - the *Abwehr.* The *Abwehr's* role was to gather intelligence from what would now be called 'human sources' be that agents, informants or by interrogation. Intelligence gathered was presented to the OKW *Oberkommando der Wehrmacht*, which in 1944 was responsible for the overall command of all forces in the west. Cholmondeley proposed that a radio set would be planted within German intelligence by dropping the dead body of an 'agent' with a failed parachute into France. It was hoped that the *Abwehr* would pretend to be the 'agent' and attempt to use the radio; through which British Intelligence would then feed its misinformation. That plan was not used, but Cholmondeley began to work with Lieutenant Commander Montagu on the Twenty Committee and a similar idea was formulated.

'Operation Mincemeat' was carried out in April 1943 and 'planted' the body of a fictitious Major into the hands of German intelligence as part of the deception plan 'Operation Barclay'. 'Barclay' was the to plan to deceive the Germans as to where the invasion of southern Europe was to take place nearly three months later - in July 1943. In this case a body carrying the identity of Major William Martin R.M. was set adrift from a submarine to be washed ashore in Spain. He had on him papers that led the *Abwehr* to believe that the coming invasion would be made in Sardinia and Corsica. Cholmondeley and Montagu went to great lengths to ensure that 'Major Martin' had an identity and 'life' of his own so that, even though fictional, any attempt by the *Abwehr* to verify his identity would prove him genuine in every way. Even after 'Operation Husky', the biggest amphibious landing to date, went ashore in Sicily, German forces were held back, waiting for the 'real' landings as detailed in the papers that had been found in Major Martin's briefcase. The deception had worked beautifully.

'Operation Mincemeat' remained a closely guarded secret, but the general idea behind this deception plan began to leak out with a fictional account, based on fact, published in 1950. Ewen Montagu - co-creator of 'Mincemeat' - wanted to publish his own account, but was prevented from doing so by British Intelligence. Eventually it was decreed that Montagu should write an edited account - as a spoiler to a story being prepared by a journalist. It was claimed that Montagu would provide an 'accurate account' of the operation and stifle the journalist's story that was likely to be 'inaccurate'. In fact Montagu's story, when it finally appeared, carefully steered around any sensitive issues, such as the deception of the Spanish Government and the Catholic Church, Ultra, and how the body that became Major Martin was obtained. There was concern in British Government and Intelligence circles that the journalist's account might reveal too many secrets and be too close to the truth.

The precise details and the identities of the personalities involved only became public knowledge in 2010 with the publication of Ben Macintyre's book, 'Operation Mincemeat'. Macintyre traced Montagu's son who allowed him access to his father's war-time papers. Remarkably, the papers included the MI5 file on 'Mincemeat'.

Montagu had been allowed to keep one of the three copies of the secret report on 'Mincemeat' by the head of MI5, in case he should at some time in the future be permitted to publish the story. It is thanks to this remarkable breach in security that Cholmondeley, Montagu and the details of the deception were finally revealed - 67 years after the event.

This unusual breach in MI5's security provides a rare glimpse into the world of deception, but relates only to 'Operation Mincemeat'. Cholmondeley, Montagu and the Twenty Committee then slip back into the shadows, their subsequent war-time work is still a closely guarded secret. However, after the success of 'Mincemeat' there can be little doubt that Cholmondeley and the Twenty Committee were next given the task of preparing a similar deception plan for the coming invasion of Europe - 'Operation Overlord' - D-Day.

For a window on the deception work behind D-Day one has to rely on the literary work of another retired officer from the top echelon of British deception, Roger Hesketh. Hesketh, an Eton - Oxford educated barrister, was recruited onto the Ops(B) section of the COSSAC - Chief of Staff to Supreme Allied Command - and became the brain behind Operation Fortitude, the deception plan supporting D-Day. Hesketh, Ops(B), worked with Cholmondeley's B1(A) section of MI5 and XX organisation - the Twenty Committee, to feed misinformation to the Germans by whatever means possible. Like Ewen Montagu, Hesketh had been allowed to retain a copy of his post-war analysis of his work. At first he did not attempt to publish his work, but he changed his mind in 1973 after a journalist wrote 'The Counterfeit Spy' - based on Hesketh's own report! There was little interest in Hesketh's own account when he approached publishers and it remained unpublished at his death in 1987. It was another twelve years before Hesketh's wish was realised and his account, 'Fortitude' was published. Written in the immediate post-war years 'Fortitude' does not identify the men involved, nor does it detail the small scale operations under the umbrella of 'Fortitude' - as 'Mincemeat' was under 'Barclay', for 'Husky'.

Hesketh's role in Ops(B) was to handle 'controlled leakage' of misleading intelligence to the Germans, by what was known as 'Special Means'. The information was passed largely via the 'London Controlling Section'.

WHY CHOOSE AMIENS PRISON?

Before exploring the detail of the plan behind the bombing of Amiens Prison, consider what would have happened if the tables had been turned:

In the summer of 1940 - at the height of the German threat to invade Britain -18 German bombers attack a British prison, let's say Wormwood Scrubs. 100 prisoners are killed, many others escape. British Intelligence officers are at a loss to explain why such a deliberate precision attack took place and are seeking answers. One of their informants provides the answer, straight from Berlin; a German agent was in the prison – he had to be silenced at all costs. Do they believe their informant - and what he subsequently tells them?

It is the author's belief that the bombing of Amiens Prison was linked to efforts to pass 'misinformation' to German intelligence via their own informants.

Whilst it was a relatively easy matter to use the XX agents and other 'Special Means' to pass on their carefully scripted misinformation to German intelligence this, in itself, would not be sufficient to guarantee the credibility of the information. If an independent route into German intelligence could be exploited, then this would add to the veracity of the intelligence information the *Abwehr* was receiving.

There are three identifiable phases to this plan.

1/ To 'Turn' French collaborators in the Somme region to circulate rumours to German intelligence. Once these rumours were in place, the quality of the information was reinforced by making one become reality – by bombing the prison.

It is an unpalatable fact that there were collaborators in France and by early 1944 the Gestapo had penetrated the Resistance networks. Information was now being passed to the Germans. The French collaborators may have had many reasons to work with the occupying forces, be it ideological, threats to families, or personal gain. This unusual, if unreliable, source could be exploited by LCS - and turned to their advantage. In this 'twist' the collaborators were actually more useful to the British deception planners than the loyal Resistance!

By using the SOE to distribute rumours among Resistance members in the Amiens area at that time there was a very good chance that the rumours would end up in German hands. Exactly how this was done is not known, but the idea of an attempt to free Resistance members from Amiens Prison by some way in the near future would not have seemed unreasonable to the Germans. At that stage the rumour would have aroused German curiosity and, from LCS's point of view, hopefully ingratiated the informants to their local German intelligence officers. The vagueness, in terms of means and time would not endanger the coming air attack which would not, of course, have been made known.

British Military Intelligence sent information via the SOE 'Pianists', the clandestine radio operators, who were in regular contact with London.

2/ Persuading the Germans to believe further information from their sources.

The bombing itself facilitated the second part of the plan. After the raid the *Abwehr* intelligence officers would be searching for a reason behind the devastating attack. It can be imagined that a very specific attack on this scale would demand a very good reason, as the Germans had no knowledge of the 'mass execution' story briefed to the Mosquito crews. The informant, or informants, who provided them with advanced warning of the attack would appear to be a solid source of information being well connected, as they must have appeared, to British Intelligence. The quality of the information now seemingly verified, LCS was able to feed entirely believable misinformation via the collaborators to the *Abwehr,* which would reinforce that from other sources. The main aim, as always with Mespot / Fortitude, was to keep the XV Army away from Normandy.

That little evidence of the first parts of plan have come to light is hardly surprising. German collaborators would hardly broadcast their actions, particularly in the light of post-war recriminations. Little detail of the work of the LCS and the sections working under its umbrella has been released, save for the glimpses afforded by Ewen Montagu and to a lesser extent by Roger Hesketh.

3/ After the liberation of Amiens an entirely different story was sent to loyal members of the Resistance to cover-up the real reason behind the attack.

More detail behind the third, less controversial, part of the plan can be seen. To cover the possibility of the reason behind the bombing becoming public knowledge, known members of the French resistance were primed to make it known that they were involved with the planning and execution of the attack. One only has to recall the extent to which British Intelligence went to cover-up 'Mincemeat' to see the lengths to which they would go to save embarrassment. In the case of 'Mincemeat' little real harm had been done other than the potential embarrassment of the Spanish Government and the Catholic Church. In the case of Amiens, 100 French civilians had died. Any suggestion that the bombing was carried out for a reason other than the cover story of freeing Resistance workers on the request of their own organisations could not be allowed to become known.

Each of the three aspects outlined above can be analysed and explored in detail.

Maurice Genest (known as 'Henri' in the Resistance) had been imprisoned in Amiens and proposed several schemes for a prison break. The most plausible scheme, to set off a large explosion outside the prison, was proposed in September 1943. Some details of this plan for an escape fell into the hands of the Gestapo when Resistance member Roger Collerais, codename 'Serge', had part of the plan with him when he was arrested whilst in a café with other Resistance members near Amiens station. This escape plan had no connection with the raid, but it did demonstrate that attention was being focussed on the Prison. Whilst Genest and Collerais were not collaborating with the Germans, further news from others of a planned attack would not have come as a surprise.

It would be interesting to uncover detail showing how the transmission of misinformation via the British Intelligence Services to their German counterparts was conducted. Perhaps messages were deliberately left lying around at the time of searches, or coded messages intended for the Resistance were voluntarily surrendered to the Germans. Whatever it was, they must have been discovered in a manner that made the German intelligence agencies believe that they had only been located due to their steadfast and competent efficiency!

Just a few days before the attack, information about the forthcoming invasion was received by Jacques Piette, the man in charge of the Resistance Group 'Liberation Nord'. On 21st February 1982 Piette was interviewed by Pierre Yves Morvan of the French television channel FR3. Morvan wanted to have a conversation with a resistance man who he believed to be absolutely honest and who did not embellish on the subject. Piette recounted an episode during his days in the Resistance that related to the bombing of Amiens Prison. However, only Morvan paid attention to Piette's testimony. No-one else appeared to be interested in what Piette had to say. So how can it be that the narrative of Piette was of no interest to anyone at that time? Perhaps it was because the reminiscences of Piette were wholly contrary to, what had become, accepted facts? For Jacques Piette, there was no doubt at all; after all he had been there and was recounting what he had both seen and known.

So what information had Jacques Piette received at the beginning of February 1944?

According to Piette himself, it was information that certain prisoners held in Amiens Prison were privy to the details of the invasion plans; such as where it was going to take place. Piette went so far to say that the invasion was definitely going to be in Normandy. He also suggested that it was imperative that these persons be eliminated, although it was not specified as to how this would be done.

In relation to the area of Amiens at that time this was surprising, as the vast majority of people believed the invasion would occur in the Pas-de-Calais region. This belief remained steadfast after the raid, and many people believed that there were some very important prisoners being held in Amiens, who had information on the Pas-de-Calais invasion. Although Piette's account was neglected by historians and researchers, not everyone was quite so quick to dismiss the account. Morvan later entrusted this recording to the French Audio-Visual National Institute. Although Morvan recounted to the author just what had been said by Piette, who had since passed away, there was a desire to actually hear the tape. So the author applied to the Audio-Visual National Institute. After some research the listings of all recordings for the year 1982 were examined, and all tapes listed corresponded to those present; except one. The tape of Morvan's interview with Piette had disappeared. A link between the Amiens raid and the plausible circumstances Piette had described had been lost.

It is difficult to ignore the coincidence between the disappearance of the Piette tape and the mystery surrounding the raid. It is obvious that the information provided to Jacques Piette and his staff could only have originated from British Intelligence, perhaps one of LCS's rumours.

It may seem strange that German intelligence had been deliberately made aware that Normandy was the proposed invasion area. It had to be given equal standing to the other deception areas to avoid German attention being drawn to it by the *lack* of information from their sources!

Adding to the potential for confusion, British information and intelligence services such as MI5 and MI6 under the LCS successfully 'created' agents, making the enemy believe that fictitious agents were operating. Sometimes this was done with the assistance of double agents. Here it is interesting to consider the roles that Montagu and Cholmondeley may have been playing in the deception plans. Was a fictitious 'agent' created in Amiens to play a role similar to 'Major Martin' in 'Mincemeat'? It would have been a remarkable feat of what is now termed 'lateral thinking' to go one better than planting a body; by having no body at all! It was the sort of thinking that they would doubtless have been capable of, given that something would have to be found to 'trump' their previous efforts. German intelligence could not be expected to fall for the same trick twice, but there is no account, even in the most general terms, of anything that would achieve the same ends – an odd omission. The roles played by Montagu and Cholmondeley in the deception plans surrounding D-Day have never been made known and, unless the equivalent of Montagu's stash of MI5 files is found again, might never be. It took 67 years for 'Mincemeat' to surface, and only then due to a rare lapse in security.

The author believes that no British Intelligence or Resistance agent who had important knowledge worthy of the efforts of the raid was actually in the prison. It would have been foolhardy to allow anyone with high-level knowledge of the real invasion plan (or the deception) to be at any risk of capture. It is now known that roughly half of the prisoners were either killed or freed, which suited the aims of British Intelligence. This outcome was considered to have been a great success, however, *if* the raid were to have been arranged to eliminate an agent, it means that there would have been only a 50/50 chance of that agent being freed or killed.

The raid, having originated within the framework of 'Mespot / Fortitude', was only to convince the Germans that there was such an agent. To the Germans, the urgency to validate and find reasons for the raid was imperative, they would also become far more receptive to a whole variety of information that could be, and was, passed deliberately to them.

The logic of bombing a civilian prison crammed with 700 inmates lent much credence to the suspicion that someone of very great importance had been captured and, insultingly for the Germans, that they had been unaware of their prize.

The architects of the attack must have been both delighted and hugely relieved at its outcome. Had things not gone so well; the walls not been breached and the third wave had destroyed the prison with even greater loss of life, what cover story might have been created? The outcome for the British Intelligence services in support of Mespot / Fortitude would have been the same - the *Abwehr* would be wondering who was so important, and what knowledge did he posess, that it was worth this sacrifice.

French 'Secret Agent' 'Colonel Rémy', in his book *L'operation Jéricho*, made it clear that Dominique Ponchardier believed that two British Intelligence agents had been imprisoned in Amiens Prison on 12th February 1944. Whilst it is often best to be sceptical of these kinds of declarations, Ponchardier may well have received (or been fed) this information by the SOE to support the Mespot/Fortitude plan. Or it may be another example of 'facts' being deliberately sown to hopefully fall, by whatever means, into the hands of the *Abwehr*. Since this action would have fallen under the general umbrella of 'Special Means', it can in no way be accepted as proof of such agents existing within the prison.

There does remain one significant question; if the Germans had been coerced into believing in the presence of prisoners holding critical invasion information, would they not have attempted to pinpoint who they were? The execution of Andre Tempez in May 1944 has been linked to this. He was shot in the ditches surrounding the citadel at Arras, could there have been a connection? Did the Germans suspect that he may have been a key holder of information? All considerations deem this unlikely as, if they did, it is improbable that he would have been shot outright, surely all manner of methods would have been tried to extract the information from their suspect.

To create the cover story the author believes that SOE 'set up' someone as the person responsible for the attack. There is a strong belief that both René Chapelle (an electrician with the French railways and member of the FTP) and Dominique Ponchardier were implicated in this way with the aim of implying that the French Resistance requested this operation.

Dominique Ponchardier, head of the 'Sosies',* presented himself in his book *Les Pavés de l'enfer* **'The Paving Stones of Hell' (albeit in somewhat vague terms) as being the man who instigated the bombing of the prison at Amiens and who followed the whole business from its beginning to the end, in total co-operation with the British.

* *The 'Sosies' Resistance network was initially organized by Commander Nomy at the request of Lt André Devigny to undertake the coastal resistance. Lt Devigny was arrested in April 1943 so Pierre and Dominique Ponchardier took over organizational control. Dominique Ponchardier took the command of the Northern zone along with Lieutenant Rivière. Dominique Ponchardier was in contact with both Colonel Groussard in Geneva as well as SOE with whom he communicated via their agents. He stated that he was also in contact with the 'Alibi' resistance network. This is interesting as the 'Alibi' network was set up by the British intelligence.*

** *Les pavés de l'enfer: from the French proverb "l'enfer est pavé de bonnes intentions" or " la route du paradis est pavée d'enfer". Applied to WW2, it would mean 'the path to victory goes through hell'.*

Dominique Ponchardier came to prominence in early 1941 when he began to organise propaganda and intelligence networks. He was arrested in Paris in December 1942, but escaped. In 1943 he and his brother Pierre began to organise the 'Sosies' network that spread across France. Hunted by the Gestapo and Milice, he was injured by machine--gun fire in Dieppe in April 1944. Both he and his brother were arrested again in September 1944, but overpowered their guards and escaped. After the war he wrote spy-fiction books under the pseudonym of Antoine Dominique; was a special advisor in the war in Algeria, Ambassador to Bolivia and High Commissioner of Djibouti. He died in 1986.

Ponchardier also declared that he sent information about the prison to Britain to help in the planning of the attack.* The fact that the plan for the air attack was based solely on the examination of aerial photographs and many details such as the location of the German staff were incorrect, is evidence that no input from the French was passed to Britain to help in planning the raid.

Dominique Ponchardier has become closely associated with this tragic incident. Indeed, it seems that the British authorities knew him very well. He was photographed at the preview of the film 'Jericho' in Paris in 1946, clinking glasses with the RAF officers who had taken part in the attack on the prison.

It was only very late in the production of 'Jericho' that Ponchardier was consulted about the realism and the plot. The British officially invited him to the preview of the film, but asking his counsel on the scenes to be filmed was another matter entirely. It seems plausible that, even in the post-war years, British Secret Services were working in the background, even if at the time Ponchardier did not realize it.

The overly dramatic release of hostages as portrayed in the film 'Jericho' certainly lent further credibility to the British claim about the main reason for the bombing of a civilian prison. However, the film producers claimed at the time that the film had no real connections with the Amiens raid.

According to Rémy, both Dominique Ponchardier and René Chapelle were involved in the attack. Ponchardier and Chapelle both went to Amiens with Phillipe Livry-Level in 1954 to mark the tenth anniversary of the raid on the prison. During the visit journalists

*Repeated in 'And the Walls Came Tumbling Down' Jack Fishman - Souvenir Press, 1982.

questioned Livry-Level about the raid and asked if the Resistance had been involved from the outset. They were answered with a 'yes' from Ponchardier. Unfortunately 1954 was the last time that Dominique Ponchardier appeared in public in connection with any aspect of this raid. Indeed Ponchardier, whenever questioned about the issue subsequently, always replied 'There is no point, the page has turned, Rémy has already covered the subject very well in his book.' Of course Ponchardier has the unquestionable right not to answer any question he chooses. However, to refer to Rémy, whose account is no longer believed to be accurate or factually based, seems somewhat unusual.

Did Dominique Ponchardier realize that in all probability he had been used and manipulated by British Intelligence? Could this explain his sudden and prolonged silence?

WHY WAS AMIENS PRISON CHOSEN AS THE TARGET?

The choice of Amiens is relatively simple. The Pas-de-Calais and the Somme, in the broad sense, were areas naturally threatened by an Allied invasion due to their geographical position. Amiens was, and is, an important administrative centre for the region.

The selection of any other type of target, perhaps more obviously military in nature such as a factory, port or airfield, would not arouse German curiosity. Selecting a target of no obvious military value would cause the Germans to search for an answer to this very question, 'why attack Amiens Prison?' And that was the aim - to arouse German curiosity, then provide answers that British Intelligence chose to feed them.

From a tactical point of view Amiens Prison was also ideal. Once the Mosquitos had reached the route d'Albert it would lead them straight to the target - the first building on the right - unmistakable.

WHY 18TH FEBRUARY 1944?

It was imperative that the date chosen to carry out the bombing of the prison was to be around the middle of February 1944 for two reasons.

The Germans were expecting an invasion in the area during February. A German intelligence report 'Lagebericht West No. 1173'* dated 12th February 1944 stated, '*To sum up, the continuation of invasion preparations of every kind is to be seen, which, according to present opinion, points for the first time to the second half of February as a critical period.*'

* *Fortitude – Roger Hesketh.*

Plan Mespot/Fortitude placed as much emphasis on the timing as location. Bombing Amiens on 18th February 1944 fitted the aims well and helped convince German intelligence that the invasion would come when and where they themselves expected. When it did not appear, information was provided by 'Special Means' that the invasion had run into unexpected difficulties and had been postponed. All along, the Germans remained convinced that the landing would take place in the Pas-de-Calais - and they remembered the significance of Amiens.

There were several occasions during January and February 1944 when various Allied officials, especially Churchill, made successive statements that were seemingly unconnected. However, when one assesses them as a whole, it can be established that these statements were made in two distinct phases.

Between 17 January and 18 February 1944
The first phase focused on making the Germans believe that the invasion was imminent.

Between 18 February and the end of February 1944
During the second phase, the Allies apparently admitted to troubles and unforeseen circumstances, therefore implying that the invasion would not be possible for several months.

These two phases were only one part of the colossal Mespot / Fortitude deception. The pivotal date between the two phases was 18th February 1944, the date of the bombing of Amiens Prison.

Information collated by German intelligence seemed to indicate that the threat to Norway, by Fortitude North, might be real. The Germans were well aware that the Allies could not undertake two invasions at once so, when combined with the elements of misinformation, it seemed as though the invasion planned for somewhere on the French coast had been postponed.

By the end of February 1944 the Germans no longer regarded the threat of invasion in the Pas-de-Calais as imminent. Instead, the German intelligence network was concerned with identifying any snippet of information directly or indirectly related to the Amiens raid that might shed light on why an invasion had been postponed. Psychologically they were 'prepared' to be very receptive towards any information, true or false, that might pass their way. The postponement of the invasion plan, and swift about-turn, indicated to the *Abwehr* that a European offensive would not be possible until the Russian Summer Offensive in mid-July 1944.

Perhaps one of the greatest successes of this policy of deception and misinformation was that the OKW, German High Command, always stuck firmly by its belief that the invasion would take place in the Pas-de-Calais area, even though Rommel always believed that the Allies would land at Normandy. Once again the bombing of the prison served as a tool to add credibility to the information that the Germans obtained by their own diligence and intelligence networks.

ROMMEL'S VISIT

The second reason for the date of 18th February was closely linked to the first, but came through pure chance. Hitler had requested a conference at his Headquarters with the senior commander defending this famous 'Atlantic Wall' Field Marshal Erwin Rommel. Rommel had been named by the Führer as the person responsible for developing and maintaining the Atlantic Wall defences back in December 1943.

Although Field Marshal von Rundstedt was Commander-in-Chief of the Western Front, Hitler charged Rommel with carrying out this mission. One of Rommel's first acts was to issue orders for the building of shore based obstacles and laying of numerous minefields. Rommel believed that the enemy must be forced back from the beaches before gaining any foothold whatsoever, whereas the majority of the OKW General Staff believed that the inland defences should be strengthened to repel the attack.

Once Rommel had issued these orders, they were followed up by a series of in-depth visits and on-the-spot inspections. These visits were usually carried out with Rommel seated in his hugely powerful Horch motorcar, followed a short distance behind by Admiral Friedrich Ruge in his Merkury. These distinguished officers were accompanied by a group of other civilian and military officials; the cars themselves being escorted by considerable numbers of soldiers. The coastal roads were cleared of civilian vehicles so that the visits to each location could be made at high speed.

Hitler's conference was planned for 21st February 1944. This is confirmed by Admiral Friedrich Ruge who, in his memoirs, wrote 'The commanders of the West were to meet on February 21st at the HQ of the Führer'. It is likely that the LCS, via Ultra decrypts, were aware of this conference and of Rommel's tour of inspection.

ROMMEL'S ITINERARY

January 16th, 1944, Rommel visits the defences of the Normandy beaches in the area of Pont-Leveque - Deauville - Trouville and Cabourg.

January 17th 1944; Rommel goes up towards the North along the coasts of the Lower-Seine region. Bolbec, Fécamp, Saint Valéry-en-Caux, Dieppe arriving at Abbeville in the evening and spending the night there.

January 18th 1944; inspection of Tréport then of Cayeux up to Montreuil-sur-mer, Hardelot-Plage finally spending the night at Le Touquet.

January 19th 1944; Berck-sur-mer and a return to his headquarters which were then situated in Fontainebleau.

From the 23rd to 25th of January 1944; inspection of the coastal section of Brittany and its fortifications.

January 30th to 31st 1944; an inspection in Normandy along the beaches of Caen to Cotentin.

From the 3rd to the 4th of February 1944; inspection at Hardelot-Plage while passing by Beauvais to Boulogne and Calais then a visit to General von Salmuth at Tourcoing.

February 7th; This time Rommel made an outward journey and inspected the south-eastern zone of France. Lyon - route nationale 7 - Avignon - Marseilles then the west coast of the Mediterranean - Narbonne before skirting the Pyrenees to arrive at Rayonne on February 9th at midday.

Bordeaux on February 10th 1944.

La Rochelle on the 11th February and a return to Fontainebleau.

On the **14th and 15th of February** Rommel once again inspected Normandy, where he visited the 9th SS Armoured Division, a unit recently withdrawn from the Russian front to be brought into Normandy.

On the evening of 15th February Rommel returned to Fontainebleau with his staff, after having visited the Chateau de la Roche Guyon, the location for his new headquarters. The Allies listened to all the German communications, including those which were in code, so they must have been aware of Rommel's approximate

Rommel during his inspection of the coastal defences.

location even if they did not know the exact details as changes could be made minutes before departure. In addition the local press announced these inspections after they had occurred and once Rommel was back safely at Fontainebleau.

16th February 1944 Rommel, seemingly untired, set out again for a new inspection, this time to the beaches of the Channel coast to the west of Dieppe and to the beaches of Pas-de-Calais held by the XV Army. Rommel remained in this area for two days, February the 16th and 17th. Regrettably Admiral Ruge stayed at Fontainebleau during those two days and did not record the visit, so the usually precise details of Rommel's visits and inspections are lost to the historian on this occasion.

'**Rommel in Amiens**', note the fresh tracks in the snow, this must have been taken around 17th February 1944.

Whilst Rommel was inspecting the Pas-de-Calais area for the first time that year, a heavy snowfall occurred during the night. A series of photographs published under the name of the 'Rousseau Collection' in Jacques Béal's book 'The Somme in the war 39/45' show Rommel walking in the snow beside a large heavy artillery coastal battery in the Pas-de-Calais, whilst a second photograph captioned 'February 1944 - Rommel in Amiens' shows the Field Marshal crossing a snow-covered street where the imprints of wheels in the fresh snow are visible. Unfortunately it is impossible for us to identify the buildings visible behind Rommel's car.

It is thus wholly possible that he passed through Amiens on **17th February 1944.**

Rommel returned to Fontainebleau once more before leaving the headquarters on the morning of **Friday 18th February 1944** to visit General Blumentritt, Chief of Staff to von Rundstedt, in Paris and to go on from there to make a last inspection, this time in the area of St-Nazaire, Lorient, and Brest.

As the prison was being attacked, Rommel would have been approaching Saint-Nazaire.

There is no doubt at all that the Allies were very interested in the visits and inspections being made by this very senior member of Hitler's military staff. It is quite logical to assume that the British Intelligence services knew about Rommel's visit to the Somme coastal sector and that they assessed from this the likelihood that Rommel may well pass through Amiens itself. After this visit Rommel departed for Germany for his meeting with Hitler on 21st February. However, this was suddenly cancelled by the Führer and deferred to a later date.

Could the urgency with which the raid was planned and undertaken - eight days 10th to 18th February, have been dictated by Rommel's tour? The timely opportunity to impress and make a bold statement to Rommel, the *Abwehr* and the OKW immediately prior to the meeting with Hitler was most fortuitous. Rommel, Blumentritt and von Rundstedt were taken by surprise at the location of the landings on the Cherbourg peninsula. Later Blumentritt said, "The disposition would more truly be described as 'coast protection' rather than 'defence'! As we did not anticipate that any landing would be made on the west side of the Cherbourg peninsula, that sector was held very lightly - we even put Russian units there." - Clearly the Mespot/Fortitude plan had been a total success.

Once the cover plan behind the Amiens Prison raid had been set in motion it could not be stopped, even after the end of World War Two. Anglo-French relations in the immediate post war years were already strained. A major diplomatic incident would have arisen from a British admission that a prison had been targeted, and 100 people killed, simply to support a deception plan.

With the continuing confusion as to objectives of the Amiens raid, it is fascinating to consider that a plan, hatched in 1944, is still working very well today.

PART 4
POST RAID MYTHS AND COVER UPS

Previous page: A 1944 view of Whitehall where many of the decisions behind the Amiens Raid were taken.

THE BRITISH INQUIRY AT AMIENS, 8 SEPTEMBER 1944

On 6th June 1944 the long awaited D-Day invasion began on the coasts of Normandy. By 31st August 1944 Amiens had been liberated. On Friday 8th September the 2 Group investigator, Squadron Leader Edwin Houghton, arrived at Amiens. Curiously, the Amiens Prison raid investigation began within eight days of the town's liberation, whilst the investigation of the effects of new 12,000 lb bombs at Albert did not take place until five months after the liberation of the district.* Needless to say, this does emphasise the importance given to the raid by the 2 Group.

The fact that the raid on Amiens Prison was investigated is, in itself, most curious. The question must be raised as to why it was thought imperative to establish the details of the raid – surely the RAF knew? It is tempting to think that the curiosity of some senior officers had already been raised as to the true purpose of attack.

Air Commodore Atcherley, Senior Air Staff Officer at 2 Group, sent Squadron Leader Edwin Houghton to Amiens. He began his investigation there on 8th September 1944 to observe and record the reaction of the 'Amiénois' after the bombing of the prison. Houghton was also tasked to determine which Resistance member or party was at the origin of the request to bomb the prison, the actual numbers of prisoners condemned to death, the reason(s) for their sentence and when these executions were due to be carried out.**

Despite an investigation that looked at documents from the Prefecture of Amiens and interviewed local members of the Resistance, no satisfactory answers to these questions were obtained.

Squadron Leader Houghton remained in the area until 10th September. He submitted a report detailing his conclusions about the bombing and the deaths of Pickard and Broadley. He also believed that he had discovered the origin of the raid:

---

* *617 Squadron had bombed the BMW and GSP factories at Albert on 2nd March 1944 using special 12,000 lb bombs. The RAF needed to assess the results to decide whether the continued use of these bombs would be beneficial.*

** *Houghton's report appears on page 297.*

On Friday, 8th September, 1944, I visited the Prefecture de la Somme
in AMIENS and examined the files relating to the attack on the prison
and extracted copies of correspondence attached at Appendix B.

I interviewed the following Frenchmen:-
1. Henry Delaunay
2. Monsieur Magiras Louis, Head Warden, Amiens Prison.
3. Monsieur Henri de Bailliencort, Haulage Contractor - who lived
close to the prison.
It was not possible to discover from this source the reason for
the detention of the Political prisoners arrested by the Germans
because in all the records the reason was stated to be unknown
nor were the French ever told when the Germans intended to
execute the Political prisoners. One point was clear - that the
most important prisoner to escape was a Monsieur VIVANT, the Sous-
Prefect of ABBEVILLE, who was arrested by the Gestapo on the
14 February, 1944. 4 days before the attack or at about the same time
that we were asked to carry out the attack. Monsieur VIVANT is now
in the Ministry of the Interior, Place Beauvau, Paris, in General de
Gaulle's government. (Without having seen Monsieur VIVANT, I think it
probable that we were asked to carry out the attack by the French in
London, mainly to effect his escape. Monsieur VIVANT was a key member
of the Resistance at ABBEVILLE and probably had in his possession
important secrets of the Resistance organization).

Houghton also took back to England a list of prisoners under the headings 'Communists, Terrorists or belonging to some type of secret society'. Despite all his efforts, Houghton appears to have found nothing to persuade him that there was anybody else in the prison who would have merited such an effort. The fact that Vivant became a member of de Gaulle's government after the Liberation reinforced Houghton's belief that the release of Vivant was the primary reason for the raid.

If we look at the facts surrounding Vivant's arrest, a number of anomalies arise that seriously flaw Houghton's theory. Most importantly, Vivant was arrested on Monday 14th February 1944, four days after the official decision had been made to go ahead with the raid on Amiens Prison. Raymond Vivant had not even been arrested when the decision to bomb the prison was finalised.

Houghton's report continued:

From all sources it was clear that the population of AMIENS had
wondered why the attack had been carried out, more particularly since
the section of the prison occupied by Political prisoners was the
most seriously damaged, but that within a few days, when it became
known that Monsieur VIVANT had escaped, together with so many other
Political prisoners, the attack was generally applauded.

In spite of Houghton's assumptions about Vivant, he still continued to conduct interviews and probed the situation further. One of those interviewed was Doctor Machoire:

> On Sunday morning, 10th September, 1944, I visited Doctor MACHOIRE, No. 6, Place St.Michel, AMIENS, Chief of the F.F.I. in AMIENS, who had until then been visiting Paris to see General LE CLERC. I wanted to establish with him who the request for the attack had come from and how many people were due to be executed and the successes of the attack. He said that the request had not come from him but that the F.F.I. worked in water-tight compartments for security reasons and it was probable that the request had come from within the prison through our agents, but that he would get in touch with Monsieur VIVANT and other members of the Resistance Movement who had escaped from the prison and establish the facts for us. I said that someone would call on him in a fortnight's time when he would have the facts ready.

Few of these questions have been answered over 65 years later.

HOW MUCH DID THE RESISTANCE KNOW OF THE RAID BEFOREHAND?

> 'This air attack is only part of the plan as other assistance will be at hand at the time.'

AO 241 - the orders for the raid 18th February 1944.

In pre-raid briefings the impression was given that the Resistance in Amiens had been told of the forthcoming raid, but was that so?

Can any evidence of this advanced knowledge be found in the Resistance having a presence outside the prison at the time of the raid as was claimed?

No additional information about this co-ordination can be found in any of the numerous files and documents examined. We have seen the photograph taken at 12.03 hrs above the prison and there are only two people in evidence on the route d'Albert. All accounts and testimonies agree to the fact that those who managed to escape had to make their own way amongst the general confusion. It is known that Civil Defence and first aid organizations did offer limited vehicular assistance in some cases. But this was offered later as they arrived and took note of the situation;

it had not been prearranged. However, this does not rule out the possibility that several Resistance workers might have been walking, or even been secreted, nearby waiting to assist.

In 1980 a report published in 'Le Courier Picardy' under the signature of R.J. Glaudel gave two testimonies claiming that organised assistance was provided.

On the 18th February 1944, I received a visit from an unknown person at my office of the Civil Defence, at the town hall of Amiens where I was then employed. The unknown person said to me 'In one hour, the prison will be bombarded. I have come to warn you so that with your friends of the Organization, you can go to recover friends as much as possible.

Another source, Jacques Rennesson - a local Amiens Resistance member, stated just before his death that:

He had just left the boulevard Beauvillé on his bicycle, only minutes after the prison had been bombed. As he looked along the route d'Albert he clearly saw a Citroen car, two men ran across the fields towards it, clambered into it and it then drove away at some speed. Jacques then spotted two more escapees and letting one onto his bicycle with another running behind he sped away to a secure address where these two men stayed for some fifteen days after the raid.

The eyewitness account of the Citroen car could be, and most likely was, an example of a passing motorist offering help having encountered a most extraordinary situation. However the encounter of the 'unknown' person one hour before the raid by R.J. Glaudel is something of a different nature - if this is a true and accurate memory.

Surely this 'unknown' person could not have been the only person to have received information of this nature from Britain? How could someone know that the prison would be attacked at so a precise a time without the raid being placed in jeopardy? This account remains a mystery. It is possible that one of the SOE radio operators in the Amiens district could have been informed at the last minute. Even if the Germans had intercepted the transmission, the raid would have been over before they had decoded it.

MESSAGE OF THANKS FROM THE RESISTANCE - A FAKE

The following message of thanks was allegedly forwarded to the British authorities on 23rd February 1944 by the Amiens Resistance:

```
Message, dated 23 February, 1944.

"I thank you in the name of comrades for bombardment of prison. The
delay fixed for the attack was too short; we were not able to save all.
Thanks to admirable precision of attack the first bombs blew in nearly
all the doors, and 150 prisoners escaped with the help of civilian
population. 12 of these prisoners were to be shot on the 19th. Bombing
was too violent; 37 prisoners were killed, some of them by German
machine-guns. 50 Germans also killed. To sum up it was a success. No
plane down over Amiens, but we are having pilots looked for."
```

Of all the files and information studied, this is the only example of a message allegedly sent by the Resistance. The more one studies this message the more interesting it becomes. On the face of it, it does seem to prove that the Resistance was informed of the raid and that they even had some input in the planning of the raid. It also suggests that the Resistance may actually have requested the raid as it thanks the aircrew for their precision. So do we finally have proof of Resistance involvement in the raid? Not at all; this document is a 'fake'.

How is it that this one document survived after all the 'spring cleaning' of the files? It survived because it was designed to be seen to bear witness and support 'facts'. To all outward appearances the information contained would have had to originate from a source close to the prison attack. Further analysis of this document is particularly interesting.

First, the message states that 50 Germans were killed. This is a figure that was often quoted at the time and has been quoted regularly since. It is a comfortable figure that seems to capture the ultimate success of the mission. However, we know that the number of Germans who actually died inside Amiens Prison was probably fewer than ten and, even if one includes the victims in the St-Victor Hospice, the overall total was probably fewer than 14. The message also announces that 12 prisoners escaped who were due to be executed the next day. We have already seen the court records and other accounts that show this figure was purely fictitious. (By curious coincidence 12 people were arrested after the revolt at the power station at Eysses on 19 February 1944). The message states that prisoners were also killed by German machine-gun fire, but we know categorically that no machine-guns were used against the prisoners and that no shots were fired even after the raid.

One statistic in the message is particularly curious. The claim that 37 prisoners were killed matches the figure given in the first report by the Police Chief on 19 February and later given to the Prefecture. Could a British agent on the spot or a member of the Resistance have passed on this figure? It is unlikely. After all, the Resistance was noted for sending precise, and on the whole extremely accurate, information. By the time that the message was allegedly transmitted on 23rd February the death toll had risen twofold from this figure. This was no secret; two local newspapers carried this information for all to read on 22nd February. Surely, if a local agent had sent the message, he/she would send the more accurate figure of 80 plus deaths and not the 37 claimed on 19th February.

Finally, the sentence, '*No plane down over Amiens, but we are having pilots looked for*' would be ridiculous. Pickard's crash only a few kilometres from Amiens was well known to the 'Amienoise' - but not to the British.

It is obvious that the message was not written in Amiens.

A letter discovered during the research for the 1982 Panorama documentary revealed the source of the message.

```
MOST SECRET
                                       2nd March 1944
Dear Air Vice-Marshal,

I have been asked by "C" to express his gratitude and the gratitude
of his officers for the attack carried out on Amiens Prison on 18th
February, and also sympathy for the relatives and comrades of the
air-crews who were unfortunately lost

Before writing I wished to ascertain what the result of the attack
had been. This has taken some time: however, we have now received
certain messages from France to the following effect:

"I thank you in the name of comrades for bombardment of prison. We were
not able to save all. Thanks to admirable precision of attack the first
bombs blew in nearly all the doors, and 150 prisoners escaped with the
help of civilian population. Of these 12 of these prisoners were to
be shot on the 19th February. In addition, 37 prisoners were killed,
some of them by German machine-guns and 50 Germans also killed.
       To sum up, the operation was a success, although the bombing
was too violent. No aircraft were shot down over Amiens, but we are
searching for the missing aircraft."
```

"C" is now known to be the head of MI6 (or SIS - Secret Intelligence Service), at that time General Sir Stewart Menzies. The letter was addressed to Air Vice-Marshal Basil Embry.

In 1982 many of the key personalities were still alive and the BBC researchers got as close as anyone has to the source of the order to attack Amiens Prison.

Maurice Buckmaster - Head of SOE (French Section) who, although not always easily, worked with MI6, LCS, BCRA / BRAL etc. was asked by reporter Michael Cockerell what he thought was the real purpose of 'Operation Jericho':

Buckmaster, *Well, its always been a bit of mystery to me, we were, so to speak, the lucky side beneficiaries of an attack which was organised and thought of by someone else, and I don't know who.*

Cockerell, *There is a letter which actually says, 'I have been asked by C to express his gratitude and the gratitude of his officers for the attack carried out on Amiens Prison.'*

Buckmaster, *Oh - Yes.*

Cockerell, *So C is the Head of MI6.*

Buckmaster, *Is he.*

Cockerell, *You know that!*

Buckmaster, *I believe it's true, yes.*

Cockerell, *So doesn't that letter at least suggest that MI6 was involved?*

Buckmaster - clearly unsettled, *Yes. I have never seen this letter or heard of of it before, until you mentioned it just now, but that could well be. Yes. I just don't know. I mean, it's not my kind of work at all.*

Cockerell, *But the SIS didn't mount this operation at your instigation?*

Buckmaster, *Oh no. Not at my instigation. I don't know who mounted it I'm afraid.*

The renowned SOE and British Intelligence historian M. R. D. Foot was asked to comment on C's fake letter of gratitude, and why it was sent:

Foot, *All part of the cover.*

Cockerell, *All part of the cover?*

Foot, *Most certainly. If you're going to do something like this, you do it properly. To support the myth. Is C any good? Of course he can write a cover letter - and a very good one!*

Foot stated that the raid had nothing to do with releasing prisoners:

I now believe there can hardly have been any single person, or even group of persons, in the prison of such importance to the intelligence service that were worth risking a lot of airmen to get out.

But asked if it was worth the risk as part of deception plan, Foot replied:

In order to secure the safety of the major landing in Normandy, four months later, of course it was! Think of all the lives they saved. Hundreds of thousands of lives were saved by Fortitude. Because the Germans remained so impressed with the whole of the Fortitude idea, it wasn't until after the end of June 44 that they moved a single man west of the Seine.

THE OFFICIAL HISTORY OF THE RAID ON AMIENS PRISON

Given that the raid appeared to be an overall success, it was decided to publish an official history of the raid. The responsibility for organizing and collating the details was given to Air Commodore H.A. Jones, Director of Public Relations for the Air Ministry, who was based in King Charles Street, Whitehall. Jones recorded the accounts of the aircrews who had participated in the raid and examined the files relating to the air attack, including the records brought back from Amiens by Houghton. He then forwarded a proposal for the draft text to Air Vice-Marshal Basil Embry.

Jones's draft did not meet with either Atcherley or Embry's approval. Atcherley expressed particular concern;

"We know the French are a bit out of sympathy with the purpose of the operation, and it is reasonable to assume that if uninformed and misleading criticisms (verbally or Press) from France are to be anticipated, we shall have to make certain of the intelligence 'facts' in the D.P.R.'s official account".

What a curious remark to make.

```
Obviously the D.P.R. intends the story to be splashed across the
British newspapers.
We know that the French are a bit out of sympathy with the purpose
of the operation and it is reasonable to assume that if uninformed
and misleading criticism (verbally or Press) from France is to be
anticipated, we shall have to make certain of the intelligence
'facts' in the D.P.R.'s official account.
I suggest we can make the facts incontestable if Shallard visits
Tubby Grant at once and obtains from him the revised Monk Street
opinion — if it is revised.
We need their estimate of the number of prisoners held prior to the
attack including the number who were due to be executed. We also
need the figures of casualties (killed and wounded) and the number of
successful escapes resulting from the attack.
You will note that these important details figure in the account of the
operation forwarded.
Firstly, therefore, will you permit the suggested visit?
```

(NA Ref. AIR37/15)

It seemed that Jones was portraying the event in a way that emphasized the skill, courage and bravery of the RAF, whereas Embry and Atcherley were more concerned about how the raid would be perceived. They had planned the raid, weighed up its consequences, and difficulties and were both aware that many questions remained unanswered.

Atcherley made several other specific criticisms. One point of particular interest made on 14th October relates to the disappearance of Group Captain Pickard and shows how far the truth would be distorted in order to give Pickard a fine obituary:

```
In any case this operation more than any other merits its own
treatment. Pick deserves a decent obituary with some references to
his superb career and his talent as a leader.
On this last point. Let us suppose that he left the escort and the
principal formation with the intention to make investigations in the
area of the crash landing of McRitchie and Sammy.
He was aware in that by doing so it was giving increased opportunities
to enemy fighters. While he was occupied looking at the ground in
the search of survivors of this first crash landing, he was probably
attacked by the 2 FW 190 that the French eyewitnesses have claimed to
have seen chasing him (in a northerly direction) and who eventually
shoot off his tail.
As you know, we have in our possession the shell cases (German)
collected consequently by the same French family which later will
transport the bodies of Pick and Broadley and later follow the German
funeral arrangement so they are able to mark and to photograph the
graves.
If some additional lines can find a place in the official history, I think
that it would not be irresponsible to include them there. It would have
been typical of Pickard to leave his formation to follow one of his
lame ducks. I feel reasonably sure that this is what happened and how
he met his end. It will do no harm and probably a lot of good to let
it be recorded as so.
```

Admittedly, the FW190 pilot's report was not available at that time and neither Atcherley nor Embry knew the exact time that Pickard was shot down. However, this is quite an astonishing suggestion considering that Atcherley was well aware of most of the facts about the raid by this stage. The fact that Air Commodore Atcherley and Air Vice-Marshal Basil Embry knew both the missing pilots very well is illustrated by the use of nicknames to refer to them ('Pick' for Group Captain Pickard and 'Sammy' for Flight Lieutenant Sampson).

Atcherley sincerely believed that Group Captain Pickard was shot down after attacking the prison and not before. He also believed that Pickard's Mosquito was shot down whilst it was orbiting the prison. He knew that Pickard had decided on his own initiative to fly in the twelfth position and then to orbit above the prison, even though the original orders from

Embry did not envisage anything like this. Pickard and Broadley would obviously have been in prolonged danger by orbiting over the prison after bombing and yet Atcherley made no suggestion that Pickard was shot down during these manoeuvres, preferring to state that Pickard was looking for McRitchie. In all the reports available the place where McRitchie was seen to be in trouble was clearly stated. His aircraft was seen with one engine on fire in the area of Oisemont, and that he crashed near the village of Fresneville.

Embry and Atcherley were aware that McRitchie's aircraft disappeared in the south-western sector of the Somme, not between Amiens and Albert. How, therefore, does one explain Atcherley's account of Pickard orbiting above McRitchie's crash site to the south-west of Oisemont, knowing full well that Pickard had crashed at Saint-Gratien to the north-east of Amiens?

Air Vice Marshal Basil Embry (right), seen here in 1945 with Wing Commander Bob Iredale leader of the second wave.

The reports compiled from the aircrew debriefings were kept secret. Only a general report was published and the circuit carried out to the south of the route d'Albert did not feature in this report. That this circuit was flown, and the direction taken by Pickard's aircraft was known, is undeniable. It must have been decided to withold this information, rather than publicize it.

It is entirely possible that Embry was annoyed that Pickard had chosen to place himself in such a dangerous place within the formation. Atcherley, aware of this, may have made an attempt to calm the situation by drafting a more positive account that absolved Pickard and reflected well upon Embry, who was largely responsible for many aspects of the mission.

The memo drafted by Atcherley ended with the conclusion that it was absolutely necessary to improve and clarify certain points in the first draft:

```
I believe Iredale and Shallard could collaborate to write a much
better account of the operation than the one enclosed and I strongly
recommend you to let them do it.
Perhaps you will write the portion relating to Pick yourself. I feel also
that the account would be incomplete without the following photographs
(all already in existence or possible to obtain).
1) the model of the prison used for briefing.
2) stills from the film taken of the actual attack.
3) close ups of the actual damage and breaches effected on the prison
buildings and its walls, taken from the ground now. The prison is
still unrepaired.
```

Note that Atcherley suggested that Embry write the section about Pickard.

Further letters and correspondence, some quite abrupt in tone, were exchanged between the Director for Public Relations and Embry. The majority of these letters contained only minor suggestions and alterations to the text, but meant that considerable time had to be spent altering the text and the publication date of the official history was delayed by some eight days.

On 28th October 1944, in bulletin No.16106, the Air Ministry officially published the history of the raid for the first time.

NOT FOR PUBLICATION, BROADCAST IN OVERSEAS BULLETINS OR USE ON CLUB TAPES BEFORE 2330 B.S.T. ON OCTOBER 28 (I.E. FOR SUNDAY PAPERS). NOT TO BE BROADCAST IN THE MIDNIGHT NEWS OF OCTOBER 28/29. OVERSEAS MESSAGES SHOULD BE PREFACED WITH THIS EMBARGO.

Air Ministry News Service   Air Ministry Bulletin No. 16106

ATTACK ON THE AMIENS PRISON

AN EPIC R.A.F. OPERATION.

"Mosquitos are to attack the prison at Amiens in an attempt to assist more than 100 prisoners to escape.

"These prisoners are French patriots condemned to death for assisting the Allies."

This was the briefing one day of air crews at an Allied Expeditionary Air Force intelligence room, and it was the prelude to an epic operation by the Royal Air Force. For security reasons it has not been possible until now to give a full account of the exploit.

Frenchmen were lying in the jail awaiting death for their brave efforts in the Allied cause. Some of them had been condemned for assisting Allied airmen to escape after they had been brought down in France. It was clear that nothing less than a successful operation by the R.A.F. to break down the prison walls - even at the risk of killing some of the patriots they wished to rescue – would afford these men any reasonable prospect of escape.

The R.A.F. undertook this exacting task, accepted the risk of killing people who, in any event, were to be put to death by the enemy, and eventually learned that as a result of their attack on the jail, many prisoners escaped and considerable casualties were caused among the German guards.

The prison was a cruciform building in a courtyard, surrounded by a 20 feet high wall, some 3 feet thick. The yard was fenced internally to segregate the prisoners while they were at exercise. Accuracy in attack was regarded as essential, for whereas on the one hand the walls and buildings were required to be breached, on the other, in order to reduce casualties to a minimum, it was important that the least possible force should be used.

The jail was guarded by German troops living in a special wing, the location of which was exactly known. The attack had to be sufficiently discriminating to ensure that decisive force was used against this part of the building. The timing factor, too, was important, for the escaping men were to receive valuable assistance by patriots from outside if these patriots could be warned of the exact time of attack.

The task, therefore, called for secret and detailed planning, and a model of the prison and its surroundings was made from photographs and other information already in the Air Ministry's possession. Thus, in planning and briefing every aspect was studied.

To carry out this exceptional operation, the task was entrusted to a Mosquito wing of the R.A.F. Second Tactical Air Force comprising British, Australian and New Zealand squadrons, and including R.C.A.F. airmen, commanded by Group Captain P.C.Pickard D.S.O. and Two Bars, D.F.C., one of the most outstanding and experienced bomber pilots in the R.A.F.

It was decided to allocate two fighter squadrons for escort duties, from a fighter group that played a memorable part in the Battle of Britain.

The task added to the many difficult and diverse operations which the Mosquitos of the Second Tactical Air Force have performed - operations which have included the destruction of the single-building German Headquarters of Civil Administration in the centre of the Hague, numerous enemy army barracks, or chateaux converted for occupation by German troops in France, German army headquarters in the field, electric power stations and other targets which demanded the most exacting precision attacks.

Of all these operations, however, the Mosquito air crews counted as the most intricate the action against the Amiens prison on 18th February, 1944. On the morning of that day the aircrews rose before dawn for their very careful briefing, to find the airfield covered with snow and low cloud, and with little prospect of clearance.

Once the plan was outlined, the crews, the most experienced from each squadron, were determined to press home their attack in spite of the adverse weather. It was obvious that the prison walls must be broken in at least two places to enable any escape whatsoever to be made. At the same time, both ends of the main building had to be hit to release the prisoners from their confinement. Accordingly, the first wave of six aircraft was detailed to breach the wall, on its north-east and north-west perimeter. The second wave of six aircraft was to divide and open up both ends of the jail, and to destroy the German guards' quarters. A third wave was available should any part of the plan miscarry.

To obtain the accuracy required, it was necessary to bomb from "deck level" and each wave had to be so timed that the results were achieved in their right sequence and to avoid casualties by collision over such a small target.

A Mosquito was allotted to the operation to make film and photograph records of the attack.

It was an hour before midday when the squadrons left their snow covered airfield to rendezvous with their fighter escort on the south coast of England. From there the formation flew at sea level to the French coast, swept round the north of Amiens and approached their objective along the straight Amiens-Albert road on which the prison is located. The second wave, on approaching the target, saw that the first wave had been successful.

Through the dust and smoke of the bombing the corners of the jail were seen, enabling an accurate attack to be made. This, too, was so successful that Group Captain Pickard, circling the target, was able to send the third wave home without any necessity for its attack. The photographic Mosquito, making three runs over the objective, saw the breaches in the wall, the ends of the building broken, prisoners running out through the breaches, Germans lying on the ground, and on the last run, some patriots disappearing across the snow on the field outside the prison.

The operation was not completed without loss, however, for two Mosquitos, one of which carried Group Captain Pickard and his navigator, Flight-Lieutenant J.A.Broadley, D.S.O., D.F.C., D.F.M. of Richmond, Yorkshire, were shot down by enemy fighters, as also were two of the fighter escort. Saddened as they were by this loss of their leader and other colleagues, the aircrews who took part in the operation felt that the sacrifices had not been in vain when it became known that a high percentage of patriots had escaped. Although, as was unavoidable, some of the patriots were killed by German machine-guns as well as by bombs, it is known that the Germans themselves suffered casualties from the attack.

Since the successful liberation of France and subsequent relief of Amiens by the Allies, it has been possible to collect certain details, particularly of our losses, which had hitherto been unobtainable. All that was originally known of Group Captain Pickard's fate was that his aircraft was last seen circling over the prison slightly above the height at which the three waves of Mosquitos were attacking.

His purpose was to decide whether or not sufficient force and accuracy had been achieved by the first two waves and to order the reserve wave to attack or withdraw, accordingly. It was for this reason that he had detached himself from the main formations to a position which, though it was dangerous, he could best see and direct the operations.

It now seems certain that when he had ordered the last wave to withdraw without dropping its bombs, he saw one of his Mosquitos brought down by the fierce light flak put up by the German defences. Determined to investigate the crash, to discover the fate of the crew, he was himself "bounced" by a pair of F.W.190's sent up to intercept our aircraft. Caught thus pre-occupied, and detached from the friendly fighter escort, which by then was covering the withdrawal of the main formations, he fell a victim to the enemy fighters.

He was shot down a few miles from Amiens and his body, with that his navigator, was subsequently recovered by friendly villagers, who had seen the whole action. The Germans forced the villagers to hand over the bodies but were unable to prevent them attending the burial in the cemetery alongside the prison.

As soon as his comrades reached Amiens after the invasion, seeking news of the aircrews' fate, the villagers presented them with photographs of the graves and a few personal belongings which they had secreted from the Germans for the months before the invasion in order that his identity and that of his navigator might be established. Tragic though Group Captain Pickard's loss is, there is consolation in the knowledge that it occurred while he was leading probably the most successful operation of his gallant and brilliant career. The attack on Amiens prison will remain one of the most memorable achievements of the Royal Air Force.

There are seventeen points on which comments can be made:

1) "Mosquitos are to attack the prison at Amiens in an attempt to assist more than 100 prisoners to escape. "These prisoners are French patriots condemned to death for assisting the Allies."
As previously explained there were not 'more than 100' prisoners condemned to death at Amiens Prison in February 1944.

2) The R.A.F. undertook this exacting task, accepted the risk of killing people who, in any event, were to be put to death by the enemy,..
We now know that no death sentences were planned in the prison of Amiens on, before or after 18 February 1944. The main threat at this time was deportation which, depending on the type of work undertaken after a deportation, could (and indeed did) result in death for many.

3) The prison was a cruciform building in a courtyard, surrounded by a 20 feet high wall, some 3 feet thick. The yard was fenced internally to segregate the prisoners while they were at exercise.
The fact that the wall was some three feet thick was only known as a result of Houghton's investigation after the raid. The separation of the courtyard emphasized the need to make two breaches in the enclosure wall. (See Point 8) In theory two or more breaches would have been required anyway as one breach could have been quickly isolated and brought under control by the guards. Several breaches would allow the maximum chance of escape. Multiple breaches would also ensure that the Germans would believe the attack was an effort to assist one or more key prisoners to escape.

4) Accuracy in attack was regarded as essential, for whereas on the one hand the walls and buildings required to be breached, on the other, in order to reduce casualties to a minimum, it was important that the least possible force should be used.

As previously established, 48 or 72 bombs seems excessive for such a small target. Even the official history notes that the target was of a small size. The overly heavy use of bombs was quite simply a guarantee that the raid would not fail and that the goal of release of one or several inmates was made obvious.

5) The jail was guarded by German troops living in a special wing, the location of which was exactly known. The attack had to be sufficiently discriminating to ensure that decisive force was used against this part of the building.

Nobody knew that the Germans were gathered in the southern wing of the prison building. One or two bombs from the first wave missed their objective (the enclosure wall) and smashed into and exploded on the southern wing. The location of the Germans was only ascertained by Houghton's investigation on 8ᵗʰ September 1944. Previously the southern wing had never been considered as part of the target objectives. According to Pilot Officer Lee Howard's account and testimonials from other aircrew, Pickard had said that the Germans had their offices in the additional buildings against the east and west wings of the principal building. According to the orders from Group, the pilots were encouraged to bombard these parts of the prison, not the southern wing.

6) The timing factor, too, was important, for the escaping men were to receive valuable assistance by patriots from outside if these patriots could be warned of the exact time of attack.

This sentence does seem to correspond to the fact that an unknown individual (probably an SOE agent) went into the offices of the Civil Defence in Amiens one hour before the bombing to inform Jacques Rennes that a raid was imminent.

7) It was decided to allocate two fighter squadrons for escort duties, from a fighter group that played a memorable part in the Battle of Britain.

In fact four squadrons were originally designated, but only two of them actually managed to fulfil this role.

8) It was obvious that the prison walls must be broken in at least two places to enable any escape whatsoever to be made. At the same time, both ends of the main building had to be hit to release the prisoners from to their confinement.

It was stated that two breaches in the enclosure wall were required because the courtyard was segregated by a fence. Research has since indicated that there was no separating fence dividing the courtyard. If this was the case perhaps two or more breaches were deemed necessary in order to make escape easier and because there would be a greater degree of visible damage. These would be results that would convince the German authorities that the aim was to facilitate escape rather than any other purpose.

9) The second wave of six aircraft was to divide and open up both ends of the jail, and to destroy the German guards' quarters.
The whereabouts of the German guards' quarters was not known at the time of the raid.

10) To obtain the accuracy required, it was necessary to bomb from "deck level" and each wave had to be so timed that the results were achieved in their right sequence and to avoid casualties by collision over such a small target.
Once again the report refers to a 'small' target. Why, then, were 48 or even 72, 500lb bombs used for an attack on such a small establishment?

11) Through the dust and smoke of the bombing the corners of the jail were seen, enabling an accurate attack to be made.
The south-east and north-west parts of the principal building were not hit by the bombs. On the other hand the additional buildings located against the east and west wings of the principal building were devastated.

12) This, too, was so successful that Group Captain Pickard, circling the target, was able to send the third wave home without any necessity for its attack.
Pickard did not orbit above the prison because he was shot down before arriving at the objective. Pickard could not, therefore, have given the order for the third wave to return home. In truth it was Flight Lieutenant Tony Wickham in the FPU Mosquito who gave the order.

13) The operation was not completed without loss, however, for two Mosquitos, one of which carried Group Captain Pickard and his navigator, Flight-Lieutenant J.A.Broadley, D.S.O., D.F.C., D.F.M. of Richmond, Yorkshire, were shot down by enemy fighters, as also were two of the fighter escort.
Group Captain Pickard's Mosquito and an escort Typhoon were shot down by German Fighters. Squadron Leader McRitchie's Mosquito was shot down by light AA fire. The second escort Typhoon that was lost disappeared in a snowstorm above the English Channel during its return, possibly having run out of fuel.

14) Although, as was unavoidable, some of the patriots were killed by German machine-guns as well as by bombs, it is known that the Germans themselves suffered casualties from the attack.

We know that no French patriots were killed by German machine-guns after the bombing, indeed, no firing of any sort took place during or after the raid. Furthermore, whilst the Germans did have casualties, they were minimal.

15) All that was originally known of Group Captain Pickard's fate was that his aircraft was last seen circling over the prison slightly above the height at which the three waves of Mosquitos were attacking.

It is absolutely certain that the aircraft seen to orbit the prison could only have been the FPU Mosquito. If Pickard's plane was seen then it was off at some distance and could have been nowhere near the prison.

16) His purpose was to decide whether or not sufficient force and accuracy had been achieved by the first two waves and to order the reserve wave to attack or withdraw, accordingly. It was for this reason that he had detached himself from the main formations to a position which, though it was dangerous, he could best see and direct the operations.

Embry's original plans did not envisage a situation whereby Pickard detached himself in this manner. The wording of the official report in the section written by Embry nonetheless explains that Pickard took this decision and put himself in greater danger. Whilst outlining Pickard's bravery it does also discreetly outline the fact that the move was not originally / officially envisaged. Today we know that Pickard was shot down before he reached the target whilst flying in the last position, a tempting target for attacking fighters and an unusual position for a leader.

17) It now seems certain that when he had ordered the last wave to withdraw without dropping its bombs, he saw one of his Mosquitos brought down by the fierce light flak put up by the German defences. Determined to investigate the crash, to discover the fate of the crew, he was himself "bounced" by a pair of F.W.190's sent up to intercept our aircraft. Caught thus pre-occupied, and detached from the friendly fighter escort, which by then was covering the withdrawal of the main formations, he fell a victim to the enemy fighters.

Having pointed out that Pickard took risks while orbiting above the prison, Embry then pretends to believe in Pickard's search for McRitchie. From this statement we can see that Embry took Atcherley's advice to write a decent obituary for Group Captain Pickard. We see no other possible explanation for this statement as Embry knew the circumstances of both Pickard's and McRitchie's losses, and McRitchie was shot down by AA fire some distance from where Pickard's plane was lost.

THE PUBLICATION OF THE ATTACK IN THE BRITISH PRESS ON 29 OCTOBER 1944

On Monday 29 October 1944 the 'Sunday Graphic' featured the raid.

This was 'F for Freddie's' Greatest Exploit

FRENCH WERE TO DIE — RAF SMASHED JAIL

The most amazing pictures of the war reached London last night revealing how the R.A.F. attacked the prison at Amiens, flew in at 'deck level' and blew a hole in the wall to assist the escape of a high percentage of the 100 French patriots who had been condemned to death for assisting the Allies.

Group Capt Pickard (of 'F for Freddie' fame) led the attack — and lost his life doing it. Briefing his men he said. 'It's a death or glory job, boys. You'll have to bust that prison wide open.'

The article that followed reported the history of the attack on the prison of Amiens. Obviously it contained the same errors found in the official version published the day before.

At the end of October 1944 the BBC made a radio broadcast which included interviews with men who participated in the raid, explaining their mission and their opinions of it. With this press interest the attack entered history and Group Captain Percy Charles Pickard - already famous in England for his involvement in the film 'Target for Tonight' - became a legend.

This Was 'F For Freddie's' Greatest Exploit

FRENCH WERE TO DIE—RAF SMASHED JAIL

Pacific Score Mounts

27 Jap Ships Sunk-Official

LATEST figures of Japanese sinkings announced by General MacArthur last night bring the total of enemy losses in last week's 48 ships sunk or damaged.

A U.S. official announcement early to-day said 27 enemy ships had been destroyed off the Philippines. Later unofficial reports placed the total much higher.

Gen. MacArthur's communiqué claimed 16 warships—two battleships, four cruisers and ten destroyers sunk in the battle of Leyte Gulf, one of the three great actions of the Western Pacific.

A B.U.P. correspondent aboard Admiral Mitscher's flagship reported last night that the entire Japanese complement of four aircraft carriers engaged were destroyed in a second action off the Northern Philippines.

Bulgar Armistice

An armistice agreement between Bulgaria and the Allies was signed in Moscow yesterday, says B.U.P.

DENTURE COMFORT with CONFIDENCE Do you suffer pain and embarrassment by wearing a denture which has become loose through gum-shrinkage? Dentists recommend KOLYNOS DENTURE FIXATIVE to make false teeth fit firmly—to restore confidence and to enable you to masticate food properly. A tasteless powder, harmless to denture and user, it will hold your dental plate in correct position, thus obviating painful and embarrassing situations. From all chemists—1/3 & 3/3.

KOLYNOS DENTURE FIXATIVE Also the KOLYNOS DENTURE POWDER for cleaning false teeth, 1/6

"MOSQUITOES are to attack the prison at Amiens in an attempt to assist more than 100 prisoners to escape."

This was the order given in an R.A.F. Intelligence Room one day.

Among the men to receive it was Group Captain P. C. Pickard, D.S.O., D.F.C., of "F for Freddie" film fame. It was to be his last and most daring operation.

Frenchmen were lying in the jail awaiting death for their efforts in the Allied cause.

Nothing less than a successful operation by the R.A.F. to break down the prison walls could afford them any prospect of escape.

Accuracy and timing were vital. The crews were specially picked. Models of the prison were examined by the airmen.

On the morning of February 18 the attack was made.

Walls Were Blasted

It was snowing, but the attack could not be delayed. At any moment the Frenchmen, many of whom were caught while helping R.A.F. men regain freedom, were due to face the firing squads.

The first wave of six aircraft swooped in low and crashed their bombs on the north-east and north-west walls.

The second wave dived. Walls at both ends of the jail were blasted and other carefully-placed bombs landed squarely on the quarters of the German guards.

There was no need for a third and reserve Mosquito squadron to perform. Pickard sent them home with their bombs.

Overhead all the time a single Mosquito watched, its cameras working. Through the gaps in the walls and in the midst of the confusion the prisoners made their break for freedom.

Most Escaped

Most of them, helped by patriots outside escaped. Others were mown down by German machine-guns, and some died as the bombs exploded.

And "F for Freddie" Pickard, shot down over the target as he tried to help another plane in trouble, did not return.

But many Frenchmen who were to be executed were free.

French villagers saw it all. They found the body of Group Captain Pickard. The Germans forced them to hand it over, but could not prevent them from attending the funeral.

In Amiens cemetery Group Captain Pickard was buried, alongside the broken prison walls.

Afterwards the men who snatched

Greek Isle Freed

British troops have occupied Piskopi Island, north-west of Rhodes. The Germans are making extensive preevacuation demolitions in Salonika.

the Frenchmen from their death cells talked it over.

A Navigator said: "It was the sort of job that gave you the feeling that if you did nothing else in this war you had done something.

"It was as though each pilot had determined that whether he lived or not those Frenchmen were not going to be executed. It all went off like a Hendon display."

HEN HOUSE FAMILY MOVE

After a fortnight in a poultry house, the Clark family, of Saffron Walden, Essex, have now a real home.

A solicitor who read about their case got into touch with a house-owner who agreed to let it to the Clarks, and they will move in tomorrow.

Since being ejected from their cottage, Mr. Clark, 59-year-old horseman, his wife and two daughters, one with a baby, have been living in a poultry house in a field.

The Mayor of Saffron Walden said yesterday there were other cases in the district.

Tito Captures Naval Base

Yugoslav troops have captured the important Dalmatian port and naval base of Split after three days of fierce fighting, stated Marshal Tito's communiqué last night, quoted by Reuter.

With its capture 125 miles of the Dalmatian coast is now in Partisan hands. The Germans lost 1,500 dead and 1,300 prisoners in the battle.

Many German officers committed suicide when enemy columns were encircled by Yugoslavs in the Neretva Valley where the Germans lost 4,000 dead and 1,700 prisoners.

German Prisoners Leave Wanstead

Wanstead German prisoners of war camp, against which residents had made protests, was closed yesterday.

Residents complained of the brilliance of the searchlights used to illuminate the camp and of the Germans singing. It had been in use for two months.

POST-WAR CONFUSION

'Jericho' – the film

The most remarkable misunderstanding of the attack on Amiens Prison is the repeated use of 'Operation Jericho' as a code-name for the attack.

Jericho was never used during WW2 in relation to Amiens and, obviously, never appears in any documents. The attack was 'Ramrod 564' – nothing more.

'Operation Jericho' first appears in 1946 as the title of a French film directed by Henri Calef. The reference to Joshua leading the Israelites into Canaan, laying siege to Jericho and bringing the walls down by a combination of trumpets and his people shouting in around 1400 BC, may have had some resonance, but it had nothing to do with air attack on Amiens! The film, was, however, dedicated to Group Captain Pickard and the Royal Air Force.

Jericho is complete 'fiction', to describe it as a 'dramatisation' would be to stretch a point. The plot of the film is set just prior to the Normandy landings when a German train loaded with petrol has stopped at a station. To deter French saboteurs blowing up the train the Germans take 50 hostages who will be executed should the train be attacked. The Resistance do blow up the train and the hostages are duly lined up before a platoon of German soldiers. At the eleventh hour, just as the Germans raise their rifles, Group Captain Pickard's Mosquitos attack the prison and release the prisoners who escape in lorries waiting nearby. The film ends with our hero's Mosquito crashing to the ground.

The main set for the film was constructed near the studios at Epinoy and 'resembled' the prison at Amiens. It reportedly cost 2 million Francs and was, of

Above and opposite page: Two photos taken during the filming of 'Jericho' showing the pyrotechnics rearranging the '2 million Franc' film set!

course, spectacularly blown up when the Mosquitos 'attacked' and huge breaches created in its walls. The RAF gave their full co-operation and Pickard was played by the English actor Bruce Seaton who, apparently, bore a striking resemblance to him. It premiered at Palais de Chaillot in Paris. Among the many high ranking officers and dignitaries in the audience was Dominique Ponchardier (of the Sosies Resistance network). Ponchardier appears in photographs taken at the event clinking glasses with Squadron Leader McRitchie, Wing Commander Smith and other Mosquito crew members who participated in the raid.

On 10th April 1946 the film was shown in Amiens and the *Courrier Picard* reported on the event:

The film commemorates the actions of the R.A.F. 'Jericho' was shown on Wednesday at the O.C.M. M Jacquiot accompanied by M. Moisan, received his guests among whom we recognized M. Cuttoli, prefect of the Somme, M. Vast, mayor of Amiens, General Denant representing the Northern Liberation movement, as well as the representatives of the other Resistance groups.

Whilst it is known that the idea of the Jericho film had as its starting point the bombardment of the prison of Amiens, and this is clearly one of the central points, the film has little to do with the actual event.

Apart from the film set of the prison, which resembles that of Amiens, the film tells the heroic and tragic history of the resistance in an anonymous city.

The passage of time since the bombardment has been essential. It would have been in extremely bad taste had the most tragic attack that we have known served as a pretext for voyeuristic curiosity.

The director, H. Calef, has ignored many things likely to bring back the tragic day of the 18 February 1944 and enabled us to appreciate 'Jericho' more

A damaged Mosquito rear-fuselage used during the filming.

objectively. It is not overstated but dramatic, realistic and technically brilliant. This production contains some real qualities, which classify it among the most significant of Allied war films.

Two days after the film's premiere Basil Embry, accompanied by many local dignitaries, visited the graves of Pickard and Broadley where he laid a wreath and held a minute's silence. He then went on to open an exhibition in Amiens showing the close working relationship of the RAF and French forces during the war. After the Marseillaise and God Save the King had been played, Embry gave a speech in which he made particular mention of the dangerous work carried out by many Amiénoise who sheltered downed airmen and aided their escapes. He recalled he had parachuted from his aircraft in this area himself and was sheltered for three days in a house by the Amiénoise. The RAF, he said owed a debt of gratitude to the French Resistance.

The English Channel, Embry pointed out, had been crossed only twice, once by William the Conqueror, and the second time by Montgomery! He then asked for all to raise their glasses to the future prosperity of France and Amiens.

Opposite: Two film posters for 'Jericho' confirming the emphasis on the men and women of the Resistance rather than the raid itself.

THE ANNUAL COMMEMORATIONS
AND STILL MORE QUESTIONS?

After the publication of the official history in the United Kingdom by the British Press on 28th October 1944, it was published on 18th November 1944 in the local newspaper *'Picardy Libre'*.

The first anniversary of the raid was marked, not at the prison, but at the crash site of Pickard's Mosquito. Many RAF officers and local dignitaries were in attendance.

On Sunday 4th March 1945, a ceremony was held outside the prison itself, when a marble plaque was unveiled. It reads, 'To the French Patriots martyred on 18th February 1944, in this prison where they were held by the Nazis".

M. Moisan, a survivor of the bombing spoke, *'Alas the number of dead and the casualties were appalling and the Resistance paid a heavy price. Our Allies, on their part, were tested by the death of Group Captain Pickard and his companion Flight Lieutenant Broadley."*

LAC Albert Sullivan and Marie Yvonne tending Pickard and Broadley's graves in 1945.

Two photographs of the 1945 ceremony.

Monday 18th February, 1946 saw the second commemoration of the raid on the prison. The *Courrier Picard* reported:

To the memory of the killed patriots on February 18, 1944... Two years have passed since a formation of RAF aircraft, for reasons which have never been officially known, bombed the prison of Amiens.

Alas, although one of the bombs fell on the German guards, many others exploded in other parts of the prison. It was a dark hour - 97 killed and many other casualties...

It was to honour the memory of the victims of this bombardment that the municipal administration of Amiens went at midday yesterday to the prison where a short but moving ceremony was held.

It is not recorded that any RAF representatives came to this event, but earlier that morning another ceremony had been held at the Pickard's crash site, with members of his family in attendance.

George L. Collet wrote for the *Courrier Picard* on Sunday 16th February 1947. His article is particularly interesting as it perfectly illustrates the local view of the raid; and the reasons behind it;

The 1946 commemoration at the cemetery.

On a snowy day three years ago the RAF breached the walls of Amiens prison and gave the inmates a chance of escape. At the same time the RAF lost a remarkable pilot in Group Captain Pickard.

In the context of the war this event is not very significant among the death and destruction seen elsewhere. But for us it marks a moment in the history of the Resistance in Picardy. Partly because it gave some the opportunity to escape, but also because of the destruction and death it brought and the strangeness of its motives. We have not learned of the reason for the bombing; perhaps we were the victims of an experiment of war? We can see our ruined houses and count our dead, but the bombs that fell at midday were a surprise to all and no-one could understand the reason behind it. One could perhaps understand if it were to free those imprisoned, perhaps the rescuers who worked so feverishly to free those trapped under rubble would understand.

Why the bombing? What was the RAF aiming at? And if it really was the prison, why then and not earlier or later? What was the ultimate aim?

Was it to release prisoners? Or was it to make some symbolic gesture to boost morale? If that were the case it was an error.

The press release tells us of the careful planning, the photo reconnaissance, the model of the prison, but after that nothing else is known.

Dorothy Pickard with Robert Cagnard (centre) mayor of Saint-Gratien in 1944 and George Cagnard (right) who helped carry the bodies to the village - at the cemetery in 1974.

Even now explanations provided with the film 'Jericho' cannot disguise the facts of the bombing; the curious smoke screen that surrounds the brutal attack on the population of Picardy and especially the Amiénois.

This day marks a personal moment of remembrance of the war and the Resistance.

Three years away is a good vantage point from which to reflect on the events of February 18, June 6 and August 31, and the long – hard winter of 1944, and to look forward to a new future.

In 1948, on the fourth anniversary, political concerns overshadowed the commemorations as protesters used the occasion to criticize the Government over its broken promises. A second service was held by veterans of the Civil Defence and first aid organizations outside the prison. At eight minutes past twelve a fire engine parked exactly where it had done in 1944.

There were no British representatives at the 1947 or 1948 commemorations, but a Captain Archer of the RAF appeared in 1949. He remarked on the preparations for the raid and said that Britain was proud to have heroes like Group Captain Pickard and Flight Lieutenant Broadley, but France could be proud of its heroes, its martyrs and the Resistance.

Again, two commemorations were held in 1950. M. Louis Sellier chair of 'Northern Libé' one of political prisoners who survived the bombing, spoke from a platform draped with a tricolor. He put the question; *'What exactly were the motives that prompted the commanders to organize and to carry out this operation? We are reduced to making guesses'.*

A brass band led the 1951 procession of many veteran's associations and organizations representing families who had loved ones who died during the war; they processed from the Saint-Pierre church along the route d'Albert to the prison.

The 'line' of associating 'Jericho' – the film – with the actual event was first crossed in 1951 by none other than Philippe Livry-Level – navigator aboard one of the Mosquitos. In his book 'Missions in the RAF' he details several operations that he took part in, one of which he entitled, 'The Jericho Mission'. The line had been crossed and from now on Jericho and Amiens Prison became interchangeable.

Dominique Ponchardier also merged the two in his book, 'The Paving Stones of hell'. He applied the appellation 'Jericho' to the actual raid, then writes; *A false idea was given by the film which bears the official name of the Jericho operation'* thereby implying that the actual raid was 'Jericho' and the film stole it!

As the years rolled by the annual commemorations continued. In 1954 the usual participants were joined by Dominique Ponchardier, Phillipe Livry-Level and René Chapelle a former Resistance member and author of 'The Joined Hands' that also referred to the raid. Colonel Rémy's book, *L'operation Jéricho* had just been published and named Dominique Ponchardier as the instigator of the attack, according to this book it was Ponchardier who asked the RAF to break down the prison walls.

The film 'Jericho' was broadcast on French television on Wednesday 19th February 1969, followed by a discussion with Colonel Rémy, René Chapelle and of three survivors, the Sous-prefect Raymond Vivant, Henri Moisan and René Alavoine. The debate did not shed any new light on the subject. The man who had previously had so much to say, Dominique Ponchardier, declined an invitation to take part.

On the thirtieth anniversary R. J. Glaudel wrote in the *Courrier Picard;*
Thirty years on one does still not know who originated this operation. Jericho, it seems, was assembled by the British High Command. A Resistance worker named Gad, alias Brittany, now deceased was always of the conviction that it originated from the 'Intelligence Services' or a network working directly with them. Gad declared that it was an operation planned by the English; 'In any case people who worked in espionage never talk, even after thirty years'.

Over the years, commemorations on the anniversaries of the raid have taken place, this one in 1994 took place in similar weather conditions to those experienced 50 years before.

One of the principal persons in charge of the Resistance in Picardy declared; 'One can only repeat that what is known as 'Jericho' was not an operation organised by the Resistance as a whole. All who worked with the Resistance will attest to this. No one in the Picardy Resistance was involved in this operation.'

Colonel Rémy wrote that 'The Resistance had mobilized trucks to evacuate the political prisoners during the attack'. It is a joke when one remembers the war. I would love to know who in the Resistance could have had trucks available! It was beyond the Resistance and combat units' wildest imagination.

There was no contact or consultation with the Resistance. Had anyone been aware of the attack then it might have been possible to help the escapees, perhaps even with a truck. After thirty years the veterans of the Resistance wonder if they might have benefitted from the operation; and never knew it.

Jack Fishman's book, 'And the Walls Came Tumbling Down' was published in 1982 and again the story was debated on television, but was particularly disappointing for anyone seeking historical fact. Once again Dominique Ponchardier declined an invitation to take part.

The *Courrier Picard* published another story on Sunday 17th February 1991 – the 47th anniversary;

Was it a question for the British opening a breach in the walls of the prison to make it possible for some prisoners to escape? Would the British secret service, on the contrary, have deliberately sought to eliminate some prisoners by bombing the prison? It will probably never be known. One thing is sure. A member of the British Intelligence service was in the prison of Amiens. A particularly valuable prisoner in the eyes of the Germans who, if one believes a witness who explained, 'Immediately after the bombing one could see the chief of Amiénoise Gestapo opening the coffins and gasped in relief when he saw the body of Mr. X.'

And in 2001;

Though the operation was carefully prepared, one is still unaware of the reasons that led the English to carry out this raid. The files of the Secret Intelligence Service, the instigator of this mission, remain completely inaccessible to this day.

Every year, near the anniversary, The Courrier Picard continues to question the motives behind the bombing of the prison at Amiens on 18th February 1944. Hopefully this book will at last provide some of the answers that have been sought for over 60 years.

Often looking sad and neglected, this small memorial outside the prison is the only permanent reminder of the loss of 102 lives.

APPENDICES

APPENDIX I

CRASH INVESTIGATIONS

THE LOSS OF PICKARD'S MOSQUITO VI HX922 EG-F 'FREDDIE'
487 SQUADRON / 140 WING

At 11.25 hours on 18th February British radar plotted a training flight of six or seven aircraft near Cambrai, to the north of Amiens. Then, at 11.47 hours, the British wireless listening service, the Y Service, picked up radio messages between the fighters and their ground control - ten to twelve aircraft were flying at between 3,000 and 4,000 feet, five miles south-west of Cambrai.

Group Captain P. C. Pickard DSO DFC photographed in front of the Mosquito in which he died. The black shape under the fuselage could be the mirror attachment for the vertical camera to enable it to take rear-facing shots similar to the Sparks photo on page 119.*

The RAF was not the only one observing the enemy's activity, for the Luftwaffe had plotted the Mosquitos as they came over Tocqueville. Orders were issued for the German fighters to assemble over the base and immediately head for Amiens.

British radio monitoring and radar services monitored the situation:

```
1159 hrs. German a/c have sighted Mosquitos.
1200 hrs. Allied a/c 7 miles N.E. Amiens course S.S.E. height 200
feet.
1203 hrs. German a/c reported 4 Typhoons and Mosquitos over Amiens.
```

(11 Group ORB, NA Ref. AIR25/208)

At 12.03 hours the Luftwaffe correctly reported the presence of Ramrod 564 over Amiens. At that time 'Bob' Iredale was leading his six Mosquitos in the wide circuit south of route d'Albert to lose time before making the bombing run. Pickard was flying 'tail-end Charlie' at the rear of the formation.

Some distance behind Pickard's Mosquito, a FW190 dropped below the cloud cover its pilot had been lurking in. When Feldwebel Wilhelm Mayer emerged from the cloud he spotted the six Mosquitos below him. Naturally he selected the last plane in the formation to 'pick-off'. His quarry broke away from the formation towards Querrieu-Fréchencourt - closely followed by Mayer.

The gap closed, but the Mosquito took no evasive action and carried on flying straight and level at hight speed. Pickard was in an impossible position. Having spotted the fighter behind, his only option was to jettison his bombs* and open his throttles in an attempt to outpace his pursuer. To weave would have slowed him down and presented an easier target as he turned across the fighter; to climb would have slowed him even further and would again have made it easy for the fighter to shoot him down.

Around 45 seconds passed from the time the fighter appeared and Pickard broke away from the formation to the first burst of fire - 15 seconds later the second burst of fire shot the tail from the Mosquito.

*Pickard had jettisoned the bombs, unarmed, along the line of Bussy-Les-Daours - Querrieu Fréchencourt - Saint-Gratien. There have been no reports of unexploded bombs found in this area, but the entire area was heavily bombed later in the war when the airfield at Glisy and a neighbouring large ammunition dump were targets for bombing raids. Perhaps one day a local farmer or builder will unearth Pickard's bombs, but 500lb bombs can penetrate to great depths and it is likely they will stay hidden forever.

Mr Descamps in 2007, last witness to the combat, stands where he had been in 1944.

Below the aerial activity, on the road from Querrieu to Saint-Gratien, four horses led by Gilbert Descamps were quietly pulling an old farm cart. Gilbert was 22 years old and had managed to avoid the S.T.O.* deportations to Germany the previous year, continuing instead to work on the family farm on rue Cavee in the village of Querrieu. Progress was slow due to the icy road and Gilbert did not want to rush the horses.

The sound of aircraft engines began to fill the surrounding sky. Gilbert stopped, looked up and saw a group of aircraft flying low just beyond the trees towards Amiens. The aircraft flew on, the sounds from their engines gradually diminishing. Gilbert resumed his journey and took a left-hand turning a little way along the road, heading along the old route to Rainneville. Just at that moment the sound of machine-gun fire could be heard clearly. Gilbert immediately stopped the horses. Looking to the south he saw an aircraft approaching at low level followed by another smaller aircraft. The smaller aircraft was firing and tracer bullets and shells were creating a striated smoke pattern through the sky. Several of these bullets and shells struck the area where the horses were and exploded. In a split second Gilbert clambered underneath the cart for protection. The two aircraft passed over the crossroads of Rainneville and Saint-Gratien.

The two planes reached L'Equigna wood, just east of the wood at Querrieu, and were flying between the wood and the village. On this particular morning Jacques Bruaux, a farm labourer who had also avoided the S.T.O. deportations, was cutting wood in a small thicket north of the bois du Chateau. Jacques looked up at the sound of aircraft engines. He saw an aircraft coming from the south pursued by another and heard the sound of gunfire. Jacques looked on in amazement as the aircraft in front lost its tail and disintegrated. Looking over to Donchel Wood, Jacques could see a large plume of black smoke quickly billowing up.

* *Forced Labour (Service du Travail Obligatoire) introduced early in 1943.*

Edgar Durand was 20 years old at the time and working on a farm in the village of Saint-Gratien. He had stopped work when he heard the sound of gunfire and had run into the road to get a better look at what was happening. He saw two aircraft flying from an east-south-east direction. Both planes appeared to be flying at an altitude of about 200-300 metres. There was hardly any distance between the two planes. The German aircraft began to fire at the Mosquito and it broke in two. The tail plane whirled around as the front section flipped up and then dived straight into the ground at the northern end of Donchel wood. There was a large explosion and smoke rose quickly from the impact point.

Pierre Cagé provided a similar account. Pierre lived in Saint-Gratien and worked for Léonce-Cagnard. He was east of the village, near the Frechencourt road. The sound of aero-engines and gunfire caused him to stop work and look up. At first, he saw nothing, then two aircraft appeared from the southeast. They were flying very close to each other and Pierre estimated that they were flying at about 100 metres altitude. The plane to the rear then opened fire; the tail of the aircraft in front broke away and fell straight down, whilst the engines, wings and cockpit fell a little further on.

These accounts show that Pickard was not shot down by the first burst of gunfire from Mayer, but that it took at least two bursts to destroy the Mosquito.

The men ran to the scene of the crash. Passing the crossroads and then over the fields, they saw fragments from the Mosquito lying strewn about the area. The tail section was located on a slight slope and further on they came upon the main impact point of the front section.

The Focke-Wulf 190 was a fast and highly agile fighter which could easily out-manoeuvre a Mosquito at low level. Just one hit from its explosive 20mm cannon shells could be enough to bring an aircraft down, especially the wooden built Mosquito.

Amongst the first to arrive at the scene were Saint-Gratien inhabitants Laurent Cagnart, Bernard Cagnart, Serge Cagé, Christian Labateux, and Pierre Cagé. Others who arrived soon after included Nicolas Hennebert, Gisele Cagé and her father, all from Molliens-au-Bois. A little later still Gabriel Souhait from Bavelincourt, Marceau Souhait from Cardonnette, Jacques Bruaux, Emile Rîoux and others arrived at the site. The wreckage was on fire and the heat was intense. No one could get close to the plane and they withdrew some distance when ammunition started to explode.

After several minutes, the sounds of detonating ammunition ceased and the villagers moved towards the inferno. Watching as it abated, two dark forms could be seen in the flames, but it was hard to make out what they were. Gradually, the shapes of two bodies could be made out.

Several men headed into the woodland to cut down some long sticks to push the bodies away from the flames before they were totally consumed by the fire. Recovery was difficult, but eventually the men managed to push the bodies clear. The two badly burned bodies lay in the snow, one of them in the sitting position, with his arms in the air as though they were still holding the control column .*

Bodies that have been subjected to intense heat often take on this appearance, which is known as the 'Jockey Position'. This is most likely the case in this instance rather than the body retaining an in-flight posture.

The locals continued to search through the wreckage using the poles to pull out anything that looked curious. A cigarette case was found, some French money, and a wristwatch. Finally, a scorched driving licence bearing the name Alan Broadley was recovered.

Did Pickard orbit the prison before the crash?

It has been assumed that Pickard carried out his attack on the prison, made another run over the target to assess the situation, then called off the third wave. However at 12.05 hours, before the second wave bombed, Pickard's Mosquito was shot down. Evidence of this timing comes from several sources:

A battered and burned wristwatch was found in the wreckage with its hands stopped at precisely 12.05.

Mayer reported that his victory occurred at 12.05 hours.

The British 'Y Service' picked up a message at 12.07 hours reporting two victories; given that pilots would not instantly get on the radio, as they were still in the combat area.

The second wave attack did not start before 12.06 hours and probably took place 20 or 30 seconds after this time. The cancellation message given to the third wave by Tony Wickham after his three passes over the prison came around 12.13 hours, around eight minutes after Pickard's death.

French civilians with the wreckage of Pickard's Mosquito

Several pilots later reported that they had seen Pickard's aircraft orbiting to the north, close to the prison. However, these sightings must relate to the FPU Mosquito that was circling in that area waiting for the second wave to finish their attack. Only Pilot Officer Lee Howard stated that he saw Pickard's plane 'orbiting' but he did not specify where this was. The timing of the sighting indicates that Howard may have seen Pickard's aircraft, but there are no other reports that Pickard's aircraft was definitely seen.

German view of the attack

The FW190s that arrived over Amiens came from the German fighter unit 7./JG26.* Leading the formation was Oberleutnant Radener who ordered his men to drop below the cloud layer to look for the raiders. This was a good tactic, as it enabled them to make swift observations and would give them the element of surprise if they encountered any enemy planes. At 12.04 hours Mayer and Radener came out from the cloud layer and spotted several Mosquitos and Typhoons.

This denotes the 7th Staffel of the fighter unit Jagdgeschwader 26. At the beginning of 1944, Jagdgeschwader 26 was divided into four groups providing air defence for northern France. The Geschwader Stab was based at Lille-Nord from the beginning of September 1943. It was a small unit consisting of four aircraft, two of which were kept in a state of readiness. Its commander was the celebrated Oberleutnant Josef Priller.

I Gruppe had been based in Florennes since December 1943. Its commander was Hauptmann Hermann Staiger and it had a compliment of some 20-30 FW190s in readiness for operations. II Gruppe had been based at Cambrai-Épinoy since the beginning of October 1943. Its commander was Major Wilhelm Gath. Like I Gruppe it had some 20-30 operational FW190s, including some A5s, A4s and a few of the newer A6 types. III Gruppe was based at Lille-Vendeville and Denain and was commanded by Major Klaus Mietusch.

II Gruppe was originally formed from the 4th, 5th, 6th, and 10th Staffeln. From October 1943 onwards, the 6th Staffel was redesignated as the 7th Staffel. The 7th Staffel was officially based at Cambrai-Épinoy, but appears to have been based temporarily at Grevillers, some 27 kilometers from Cambrai, due to the number of air raids on Épinoy. In February 1944, Oberleutnant Waldemar Radener was the commander of the 7th Staffel and he was very familiar with the Amiens area. On 5th January 1944, his Staffel shot down a B-17 Flying Fortress from the 95th Bomb Group over Mesnil-Martinsart and, on 4th February, he shot down a B-24 Liberator from the 446th BG over Bray-sur-Somme.

Waldemar Radener came out of the cloud behind a group of Typhoons, while Mayer found a group of Mosquitos in a turn ahead of him. The leading Mosquito crews did not appear to notice Meyer as they were concentrating on the raid unfolding in front of them. The last Mosquito crew spotted the attacking fighter and broke away from the rest. This did not put Mayer off his attack. The Mosquito was clearly visible to Mayer; its fast dark form contrasting against the snow-covered fields below. Mayer opened fire but missed with his first burst.

Mayer closed in to about 150 metres and fired again. The FW190 shuddered with the recoil of the cannon fire, but his sight was firmly fixed. Bright flashes appeared on the Mosquito's tail section and small pieces of fabric and wood flew back past Meyer as some of the larger 20mm cannon shells punched and blasted their way through the rear structure of fabric, glue, plywood, control cables and handmade brass screws. The armour piercing shells passed straight through the weakened tail to land in the frozen soil below. At 12.05 hours precisely, 7./JG26 had obtained its 130th aerial victory and this was triumphantly recorded on the Staffel's scoreboard.

Squadron Leader Houghton's report does differ from this version of events:

```
After the bombing of the prison was completed, 1 Mosquito flew
E.N.E. towards QUERRIEU (2062) and BEHENCOURT (2266). It is possible
that the machine was already slightly damaged, although still under
control, from small arms fire emanating from the German hospital near
the prison.
```

However, Houghton does not not appear to have been made aware of the time of the crash from the watch, and would not have known the time of Mayer's combat.

The Eyewitnesses

The testimonies of Laurent Cagnart, George Cagnard and Gisele Cagé, are particularly interesting and evocative of those times.

Laurent Cagnart's account:

About midday an aerial combat took place above our village. A plane fell in flames at the end of Donchel wood between Saint-Gratien and Molliens-au-Bois. There was snow everywhere that day. I left with others at once towards where the plane had crashed. The tail

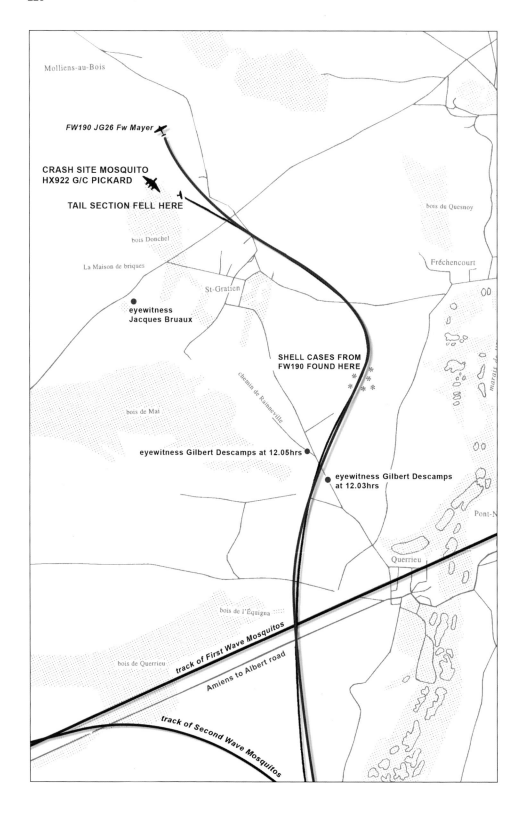

Molliens-au-Bois

FW190 JG26 Fw Mayer

CRASH SITE MOSQUITO HX922 G/C PICKARD

TAIL SECTION FELL HERE

bois du Quesnoy

bois Donchel

Fréchencourt

La Maison de briques

St-Gratien

● eyewitness
Jacques Bruaux

SHELL CASES FROM FW190 FOUND HERE

chemin de Rainneville

bois de Mai

eyewitness Gilbert Descamps at 12.05hrs ●

eyewitness Gilbert Descamps at 12.03hrs ●

Pont-N

Querrieu

bois de l'Équigna

track of First Wave Mosquitos

bois de Querrieu

Amiens to Albert road

track of Second Wave Mosquitos

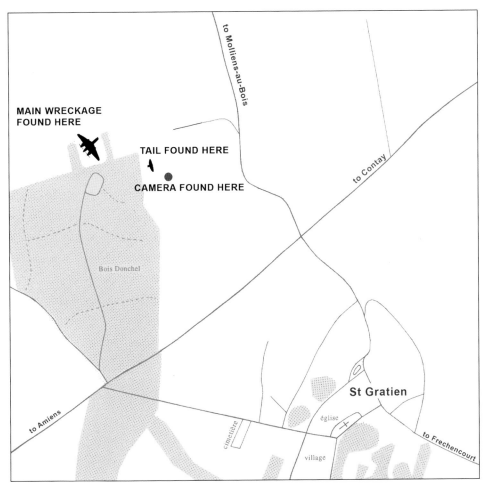

of the plane fell a hundred meters away from the main wreckage. Whilst looking at the tail
I saw a black camera and film roll container on the ground. At once I took them and placed
them in a rabbit burrow in woodland close by.

Returning to the subject of the plane, we could not get near because of the
bursting of the shells from the guns. When we judged that there was no more danger,
we looked in the remains and we saw a dark mass. We saw one, then two airmen.
We removed them, placed them on the grass, and then covered them with a piece of parachute,
which we found on the spot. The men who withdrew the bodies from the fire were: Laurent
Cagnart, Bernard Cagnart, Serge Cagé, Christian Labateux and Nicolas Hennebert. Then
the Germans arrived and told us to leave. We went back to the village. The next morning
we returned to the scene to see the two bodies were still where we had left them the day
before. We returned to the village to get two stretchers and brought back the bodies to the
Town Hall. While returning to the village, we made a brief stop and we photographed the

team and the bodies. At around three o'clock in the afternoon, a German van arrived at the village; The Germans demanded the bodies of the airmen whom they then put in coffins for burial at the Saint-Pierre cemetery in Amiens.

On 28th November 1944, Laurent Cagnart gave the camera to the British authorities in the company of Henri Fournier, a local policeman. Lieutenant A. Gray received the camera and made out a receipt for Laurent.

It might be assumed that this was simply a gun camera. The Mosquito VI was not equipped as standard with a camera that could have been used to film the raid but it was fitted with a gun camera mounted in the nose. Its primary use was to record the effects of shooting at ground targets or during aerial combat. The detailed accounts of Laurent Cagnart, Bernard Cagnart and Pierre Cagé show that the camera they found was not a gun camera, but an additional camera similar to that fitted to Sparks' aircraft. Laurent Cagnart's account therefore reveals that Group Captain Pickard's Mosquito had a ventral camera. The decision to have a camera mounted in Sparks' plane was Pickard's and it had been installed so that the results of the bombs from the lead aircraft of the first section could be recorded. When Pickard stated that he would fly in the twelfth position and orbit over the prison, it seems likely that he was intending to record the final result of the bombing himself, perhaps using these photographs as evidence to support any decisions he made relating to the cancellation, or use, of the third attack wave.

Gisele Cagé did not actually see the aerial combat, but she arrived at the scene of the crash very soon afterwards:

On February 18, we heard the bombs close to Amiens, the noise of the planes and saw a large black cloud of smoke between Molliens and Saint-Gratien, about one kilometre from our house. We ran at great speed in the hope of being able to be of some assistance. Alas nothing could be done.

My husband Gabriel, who was in the fields elsewhere, did see the aerial combat.

Gisele Cagé's husband was near the village of Bavelincourt to the east of Montigny-sur-L'Hallue (which is about 4-5 kilometres from Saint-Gratien). Coming from a south-south west direction, he spotted a twin engined aircraft flying at low altitude. Behind this was a German single engined fighter. Turning left, the two aircraft flew off in a westerly direction. The noise of the gunfire from the German aircraft echoed all around the surrounding woodlands.

Gisele's account continues:

A hundred metres further into the wood and perhaps the plane would not have caught fire if it had fallen into the trees. My husband Gabriel rode up on his bicycle and arrived at the scene.

My father and I were amongst the first ten people to arrive on the spot. The plane was burning or more exactly the engines burned, because the Mosquito was made of wood and this had been all smashed to pieces at the time of the impact and all the pieces had dispersed far and wide. A variety of other objects such as a camera, charts and parachutes were also scattered.

My father grabbed the charts and after having a brief examination of them, he threw them into the flames because we constantly expected to see the Germans arriving and he did not want them to gain information from the charts. My husband saw another person who found some French currency, which was later given to the Mayor. Through the smoke, we could now make out two forms between the engines. We thought they were the airmen. With long poles freshly cut from the surrounding woodland, the men began to push and pull, this was very dangerous because the heat was exploding the bullets in all directions. Later, however, they finally managed to get the bodies from out of the fire and placed them on several pieces of broken wooden structure from the plane. I covered them with their parachutes.

French villagers prepare to take the bodies of Pickard and Broadley to Saint-Gratien.

This page and opposite:
The bodies of Pickard and Broadley were brought in from the fields by this group of French villagers, Julien Pinket took his camera to record the events.

First stretcher
At the front: Léonce Cagnard and Jacques Mortel.
At the back: George Cagnard and Pierre Cagé .

Second stretcher
At the front: Laurent Cagnart and Bernard Cagnart.
At the back: Arthur Joly and Christian Labateux.

The body of Captain Pickard still had a few pieces of uniform attached and I cut the RAF wings and decorations from his jacket to make the identification of the bodies by the Germans even more difficult.

The uniform of Lt Broadley was completely ablaze and was nothing more than ashes when he was withdrawn from fire.

The bodies themselves had not burned, they were just slightly swollen from the heat and the wounds evident had no sign of blood.

I never saw photographs of Captain Pickard or of Lt Broadley but I am certain of being able to recognize them.

We are certain that the two men were killed by the impact. They had remained in sitting position and one of them had two raised arms and contracted hands. It was to hold the two handles in the cockpit. Undoubtedly the plane was above the wood when it broke apart and they fell to the ground immediately.

The bodies were transported to the town hall of Saint-Gratien and were kept by the French for as long a time as possible.

Later Gisele Cagé managed to obtain the address of Dorothy Pickard, Group Captain Pickard's widow, and wrote her a very moving letter. She enclosed the RAF wings and decorations in the envelope and posted the letter at Molliens-au-Bois. Alexander Hamilton, who wrote Group Captain Pickard's biography, informs us that Dorothy Pickard wrote a letter of thanks for the gesture. However, this was a time of great disruption and chaos and Mrs Pickard's letter never arrived. Gisele Cagé waited 30 years before she found out that the valuable little package had been received by Dorothy Pickard, when they met in Amiens for a commemoration of the raid and confirmed that she had received the package.

The account of George Cagnard, a farmer living at Saint-Gratien at that time.

On the 18th February 1944, I was in Amiens and shortly before midday the town shook as huge explosions took place. It was the bombing of the prison on the route d'Albert by English planes. They were bombing it to assist in the release of resistance prisoners who were going to be tortured.

Whilst returning later that evening to the farm, I learned that an English plane, an RAF Mosquito, had crashed after being shot down by a German fighter. The English plane had come down near Donchel Wood. It had broken in two: the front with its two occupants and the tail, the sections being approximately 250 metres apart. Many locals went to the spot before the occupation soldiers arrived. This made it possible to remove the bodies from the blazing wreckage and also find and remove several items. One of these was a wristwatch that had stopped at 12.05 hours; a cigarette case was also found, as well as French money and some papers belonging to Alan Broadley. The other body was more seriously burned and its papers had been consumed by the fire and therefore we had no idea of his identity.

The following morning I decided to return to the crash site accompanied by my brother-in-law, Julien Pinket. Arriving there we saw nobody was guarding the site. The German soldiers' campfire had long gone out. The two bodies lay, abandoned, wrapped in their parachutes with a light covering of snow over them. We had brought along coffee heavily fortified with alcohol to offer the Germans, in the hope they might let us remove the two bodies. Since nobody was there, we returned to the village to get a car to transport the bodies back to the village. On the way back we met several local persons and it was discussed and decided that we would take two stretchers up to the site instead and carry the bodies back. The two airmen deserved to be treated with some honour. A slow and laborious procession now passed through the snowdrifts to collect the bodies and take them to the town hall. The photographs taken by Julien Pinket record this event.

Then it was time to decide what to do with the bodies, assembling a group of locals as a 'Guard of honour', obtaining some coffins and making funeral preparations. However, this did not take into account the Germans. They arrived at about one o'clock in the afternoon. They were not pleased at all that the bodies had been removed and to save my father any stress I explained and justified our actions, further outlining that soldiers who have fallen in combat should be accorded appropriate respect.

They accepted this and asked that I accompany them to the town hall to see and collect the two bodies. Two oak coffins arrived and, so that they could be distinguished later, I marked a coffin with my knife. I knew it contained the remains of Alan Broadley. After all, in the future if anybody opened the coffins, who would be able to recognize who they were?

As to being permitted to bury them in the village cemetery, this was flatly refused. There were already six French soldiers killed in 1940 buried there and the Germans said they were not allowing French and English personnel to be mixed in the same cemetery. At the time the Germans were absolute masters, so there was little we could do. We decided we must know where they were going to bury them. By pure chance, one of my friends later spotted a truck whose driver had stopped for a coffee break between Saint-Gratien and Querrieu and he reported that he believed the two bodies were inside it. Without a moment to spare I saddled up a mare and rode out to the area. Finding the truck I watched patiently, but was unable to wait much longer as I had to return to the farm. We still had to know where the Germans intended burying the bodies. The next morning I contacted a good friend of mine, M. Pierre Deflandre, who lived opposite the Saint-Pierre cemetery in Amiens. I asked him if he could see the cemetery supervisor and ask if any British airmen had arrived for burial recently. Reluctant at first to confirm this, eventually he did. Later, during the British investigation, a jeep arrived at our farm to ask where the two bodies had been buried and I informed them.

It was at this stage I learned that one of the dead airmen had been the famous Group Captain Pickard. Later I went with the investigation team to the Saint-Pierre cemetery at Amiens to show them where the two graves were. At the time one of the team must have photographed me without my being aware because, years later, I saw a picture of myself in the book written by Livry-Level

Shortly afterwards a simple cross was erected in the space between the two apple groves at the point where the Mosquito had hit the ground. This remained for several years, but eventually fell down.

Location of the Crash Site

The eyewitnesses interviewed by Squadron Leader Houghton confirmed that the Mosquito that crashed was seen flying from the direction of Querrieu (i.e. coming in from the southeast). He was subsequently able to find the precise co-ordinates where various parts of Pickard's Mosquito fell and recorded it in his report. The figures quoted in this report are grid references. This area was mapped in zones 10 squares by 10 squares each identified by letters of the alphabet, for example the southern zone of Abbeville was in square 'M', the east of Amiens/ Doullens fell in square 'NR'. The tail of Pickard's Mosquito fell at NR 178 662, exactly 125 meters to the east of the corner of Donchel wood. The engines and cockpit fell at NR 175 663, exactly 75 meters to the north of the northern edge of Donchel wood and approximately 125 meters to the north-west of the northeastern corner of this wood. In 1944 two thickly planted lines of apple trees existed at the northern edge of Donchel wood. The front of the Mosquito crashed between these two lines of fruit trees, which have since been cut down and grubbed out. The tail section fell 100-250 metres away from the engines.

Accounts supplied to the British investigator

When Houghton arrived in Saint-Gratien to continue his investigation many people were interviewed about the crash:

```
The son of the Mayor at ST. GRATIEN, Monsieur GAGNARD-PINKET went
out to see the crash and found both occupants burnt up. On one
body he found a motor licence with the name JOHN ALLEN BROADLEY
(Group Captain PICKARD'S Navigator) and the body had the back
of the head broken open. The other body was too burnt up to be
recognisable, but there was a shoulder strap with 4 stripes.
He took away the effects which he has since handed over to a
Major of the R.A.M.C., acting on behalf of Wing-Commander Wilson.
Two hours later a party of Germans arrived who sent them away. They
went out next morning and found the bodies still there with no guard
and so brought them back into the village and had coffins made. Later
that day the Germans returned with Oak coffins and admonished the
French for interfering. The Mayor's son marked the German coffin
containing the remains of BROADLEY with 4 scratches. The Germans took
the coffins and buried them in the cemetery at ST. PIERRE, just East of
Amiens Prison (120595). A Friend of the Mayor watched the internment
and the graves are in the British part of the Cemetery, marked with
crosses on the sketch at Appendix D. It would be necessary to examine
the scratches on the coffins to establish which grave is which. The
graves are well cared for.
```

Another eyewitness account was included in his report:

```
A farmer, Monsieur DOURFAUT, at MONTIGNY (2166) saw a single-engined
enemy aircraft on the tail of the Mosquito and saw the Mosquito's
tail shot away, whereupon the Mosquito spun in, the tail falling
at 178662 and the engines and forepart at 175663. Empty cartridges
which had fallen from the enemy fighter were recovered by a farmer
at 198645.
```

The author has tried in vain to trace M. Dourfaut or anyone with a similar surname from Montigny. Houghton may have written down the name phonetically and it is the author's belief that the witness may have been named Dufour. Interestingly, M. Dufour, Edgar Durand's father-in-law, lived in Pont-Noyelles in the district of Montigny at the time that Houghton was compiling his report.

F-Freddie's crash site lies in the field just off the wing tip (Pierre Ben).

Epilogue - The Commemoration of the first anniversary of the deaths of Group Captain Pickard and Flight Lieutenant Broadley

At the end of January 1945, 140 Wing of the RAF (comprising 487 Squadron of the RNZAF, 464 Squadron of the RAAF and 21 Squadron of the RAF) was based at Rosieres-en-Santerre, where it remained until April 1945. The close proximity of these squadrons meant that they were able to participate in the memorial service for Pickard and Broadley held at Saint-Gratien on 18th February 1945. This ceremony was a very large affair attended by locals, civic dignitaries and RAF colleagues alike. An article from the *Courrier Picard* published on 19th February 1945 gives an idea of the scale of this ceremony.

The journalist of the *Courrier Picard* noted '*The Mayor, M. Lagache stated the whole aim was to honour the two dead Allied airmen, all those who have died in combat and those who are still dying each day.*'

Saint-Gratien paid homage to the two RAF aviators that fell in the district.

Yesterday it has been one year since the prison of Amiens was bombed by the RAF. One remembers how this raid was responsible for releasing a certain amount of Resistance operators who had been sentenced to death; alas the raid itself also caused casualties. One day a ceremony will take place to honour them. Yesterday at Saint-Gratien a ceremony for

The commemoration held near the crash site in 1945 involved locals as well as serving Mosquito pilots who had taken part in the raid and who were now based nearby. See also the top photo on page 213.

two others who died on this day, RAF Group Captain Pickard, leading the raid and his navigator Flight Lieutenant Broadley. The English newspapers devoted many articles to them both as they are well known in England. We will not undertake to describe this raid, which passes for one of most remarkable of those that the R.A.F has achieved, and our fellow paper the 'Picardie Libre' has given a full account.

Pickard was attacked by a German fighter after he had just made a third circuit at very low altitude over the objective to note the results of the bombing and had just told Livry-Level, who commanded the third wave, to return home without dropping their bombs.

For the population of Saint-Gratien, Mayor M. Lagache said we honor the two dead Allied airmen and with them all their brothers in arms who died and who die each day so that finally there can be peace in the World. The sister of Pickard had asked that a mass be said in his memory.

The population of Saint-Gratien wanted to pay homage to these men, who were amongst a group of airmen who had attempted to restore freedom to France.

Both French and British forces were well represented; so who organized such an impressive ceremony - and why? Ceremonies on this scale were not the norm, even for highly regarded officers.

The Mayor of Saint-Gratien was responsible for any type of civic or commemorative ceremony that took place in his area. Much credit is certainly due to the Mayor and villagers for initially recovering the bodies and for showing due respect after the crash. There was a huge wave of emotion at this service, and George Cagnard later wrote:

... The rustic cross that the villagers erected at the crash site has long since fallen down. At the impact point a pilgrimage was made a year later with friends of the airmen such as Livry-Level and of course the Pickard family. The area now is cultivated and only old men such as myself can remember this sad memory. When we meet at a festival or other gathering we often like to recount amongst ourselves that fateful day.... I myself will never forget it.

However the presence of many senior officers at the event implies that it was more than just a local affair planned by the Mayor. Many British and American airmen and crew were killed in the district, and yet none has received such publicity or marked concern.

Courrier Picard

Close to where the plane fell a simple oak cross was erected, and yesterday all the population came to dedicate the cross and attend mass held by Abbot Cossin, Vicar of Saint-Remi in Amiens.

Captain Ollivier, the liaison officer, represented the prefecture of the Somme. General Brading, in command of the area, had come from Dieppe to represent the British Army. He was accompanied by Major Combes and Captain Williams representing Colonel Ashley. Finally there were many RAF personnel present: Commandant Livry-Level. W/C Iredale, W/C Vincent, W/C Oats, S/Ldr Sismore and Anderson along with many other officers and even ground crew and mechanics.

After short speeches by M. Lagache and Livry-Level, a bugle and a drum sounded 'Au Drapeau' while all around resounded the cries 'Long live England - Long live France. M. Masson, who identified the graves, Miss Hunt, Mrs Bayne and Miss West also attended the service. Flowers were laid at the base of the cross and a wreath made up in the French colours placed there to honour the two airmen killed by German bullets and who are, for us, brothers in arms.

Percy Charles Pickard, 1915-1944

Pickard was born on 16th May 1915 at Handsworth, Sheffield, to Percy and Jenny Pickard and was educated at Framlingham College in Suffolk. His RAF commission began in 1937 with the Service Number 39392 and his long operational career spanned many of the RAF's most daring and difficult episodes. On 19th June 1940, he was at the controls of a No. 99 Squadron Wellington returning from a raid on Germany. He ran into a particularly strong pocket of Flak. The aircraft was severely damaged and eventually it crashed into the North Sea. Pickard and his crew were fortunate to vacate the stricken aircraft immediately after it had landed on the water, and were later picked up by a lifeboat. Strong leadership and determination were the hallmarks of 'Pick's' character, for which he was very much admired. These characteristics made him an obvious choice to play Squadron Leader Dickson in the 1941 film made at Mildenhall and High Wycombe called 'Target for Tonight'. The legend of Pickard was created by the success of this film.

Pickard was a tall, fair-haired man, mild mannered with an ever-present pipe in his mouth. He played a key role leading twelve Whitley bombers acting as paratroop carriers in 'Operation Biting', the airborne commando raid on the German Radar installation at Bruneval. Later he began flying sorties for SOE, dropping agents into occupied Europe. By December 1943 he had been promoted to the rank of Group Captain and took over 140 Wing of the 2nd Tactical Air Force under the direct control of AOC 2 Group, AVM Basil Embry.

Today he lies buried in Plot 3 Row B Grave 13 in the Saint-Pierre Cemetery at Amiens, barely 300 metres from the prison. Prior to his death, he had been awarded the DSO (with 2 bars), the DFC and the Czech War Cross.

John Alan Broadley 1921-1944

John Alan Broadley was born in 1921 at Leyburn, Yorkshire to Thomas, and Irene Broadley. 'Bill' Broadley was educated at Richmond School and enlisted in the RAF in 1939 with the Service Number 47690. Broadley began training as a Sergeant Observer. He joined No. 9 Squadron in May 1941 and became Pickard's regular navigator, flying against such targets as Cologne and Dusseldorf. He also flew with Pickard during 'Operation Biting' and was later posted to No. 161 (Special Duties) Squadron. He was posted to No. 487 Squadron RNZAF and finally to No. 21 Squadron. Whilst serving with this unit, he again flew with Group Captain Pickard.

He had been awarded the DSO, DFC and DFM at the time of his death. Today, he lies buried in Plot 3 Row A Grave 11 in the Saint Pierre Cemetery in Amiens.

Pickard VC?

At one point the wooden cross marking Pickard's grave was marked VC DSO DFC Bar. It would also appear that he was put forward for the award of the VC by Lord Londonderry. The award was under consideration, but Basil Embry refused to support it. He claimed that the raid was a normal precision attack and as such did not warrant such a high award. The official reason for the refusal was that Pickard had already been decorated in line with other officers with similar achievements and that press reports had exaggerated the importance of the raid - the same reports that Embry had a major part in creating.*

Wilhelm Mayer, 1917-1945

Mayer was born on 5th December 1917 at Fürth in Bayern. He joined the Luftwaffe in 1941 and, after completing his basic flying training, was posted to JG 26 on 1st August 1941. His first operational mission took place on 12th February 1942, when he participated in Operation Donnerkeil (the aerial protection of the Scharnhorst and the Gneisenau battle cruisers as they made their Channel dash from Brest). On 18th February 1944, Mayer shot down Pickard and Broadley's Mosquito near Saint-Gratien. On 16th April 1944, Mayer was awarded the Deutsches Cross in Gold for fifteen victories. On 19th November 1944, Mayer recorded his final victories: two Spitfires shot down near Kirchhellen. These two Spitfires gave Mayer a total score of 27 victories. In addition to these, Mayer also claimed a further twelve unconfirmed victories.

---

* *Alex Hamilton; interview with Embry quoted in After the Battle magazine No.28*

On 4th January 1945, a small formation of Fw190 D-9 fighters took off from Nordhorn. Whilst still forming up they were bounced by No.442 Squadron Spitfires. The combat was vicious and dramatic; one of the RAF's victories that day was Mayer himself. His FW 190 D-9 (Blue 16) crashed at Lohnerbruch. On 12th March 1945, he was posthumously awarded the Ritterkreuz.

Wilhelm Mayer, 2nd from left, with fellow pilots of 6/JG26 in the summer of 1942 before the staffel was redesignated 7/JG26 in October 1943.

THE LOSS OF MOSQUITO VI MM404 SB-T
464 SQUADRON OF McRITCHIE AND SAMPSON

Flying westwards on their return, the Mosquitos of McRitchie and McPhee were joined by two Typhoons from 174 Squadron flown by Pilot Officers Burton and Markby. At 12.10 hours they passed over Avesnes-Chaussoy. Construction of a V-1 site there had begun and clusters of light anti-aircraft batteries (mostly 20mm but some 37mm guns) were positioned around the area. Three kilometers further south-west, small batteries were dotted here and there, particularly around Fresneville. These anti-aircraft batteries were positioned behind a small patch of scrubland and had been alerted by previous air activity in the district. As soon as the two Mosquitos skimmed over the trees, the batteries opened fire.

The Mosquitos could not avoid the fire as they were flying so low. McRitchie managed a short burst at one of the guns, but could take no evasive action as a series of shells slammed into his Mosquito. The fuselage had ragged holes blasted through it. In a split second more shells followed, smashing into the cockpit and one engine. McRitchie was peppered with small pieces of shell and jagged Perspex splinters. A shell fragment punched into his right arm and other hit his right thigh. He was also left with several minor head wounds. One of these wounds, just above McRitchie's right eye, started to bleed profusely and obscured his vision. McRitchie shouted for help from his navigator, Flight Lieutenant 'Sammy' Sampson, but there was no answer.

Covered in blood and with the wind shrieking through the shattered Perspex panels, McRitchie turned to look at his navigator. Sampson was also covered in blood and was slumped forward in his seat. He was dead.

A recently discovered and previously unpublished photo of MM404, the Mosquito in which McRitchie and Sampson were shot down on 18th February 1944. Tom Willis Collection.

In spite of the shock and the pain, McRitchie managed to carry on flying with his left hand, virtually 'hedge-hopping'. Out of danger from the gun battery, he was not convinced that he could make it back to England in this state. The controls of the aircraft were sluggish and a long smoke stream was coming from the damaged engine and trailing behind. McRitchie managed to fly on for another eight or nine kilometres. Then, half paralysed, he could hold on no longer and closed the throttles. The Mosquito hit the frozen ground on its belly at a speed of about 150mph. Eventually it came to a halt, its twisted propeller blades having dug into the ground. Fortunately, there was no fire.

The Mosquito landed in the district of Villeroy, some twenty kilometers to the south-west of Oisemont. All was quiet after the Mosquito had come down, apart from the ticking as the engines cooled down. Inside the cockpit there was no movement. The area had many anti-aircraft batteries and searchlight emplacements and the crash had not gone unnoticed. Several German soldiers headed towards the downed aeroplane.

Squadron Leader McRitchie was removed from the cockpit, barely conscious. Incredibly, he managed to stand and take a few steps, but the soldiers shouted at him to stay still. He did so and immediately collapsed to the ground, where he was left for some time.* Finally, the soldiers took him to a local hospital where he stayed for two days. He was then transferred to the St-Victor hospice in Amiens, just 500 metres away from the prison, indeed, a wing of this very hospital had been damaged in the raid. A total of 26 wounds were found on his body, mainly on his right-hand side.

He was treated on the same ward as a group of USAAF airmen. One of these men was 2/Lt Edward Shevlin, a bombardier from a Liberator that had been shot down close to Doullens after dropping arms and equipment for the Resistance. Shevlin had received emergency first aid from Dr Jean Ducellier, the author's father, but was too seriously injured to be treated by Dr Ducellier and so was admitted to the hospice on 2nd March 1944. After the war, Shevlin said that he remembered McRitchie being in the hospital as a patient.

The right-hand side of the cockpit, where Flight Lieutenant Sampson was seated, had taken the full force of most of the blasts and shell splinters. Sampson's body was extracted from the cockpit and placed temporarily in a small building located at the intersection of the D180 and the road leading directly to the village of Villeroy. The building has since been demolished.

Due to the rural nature of the area, few eyewitnesses remember the incident. However, Henri Morgand, who lived in the village of Villeroy, remembers returning from work on the afternoon of 18th February. He was cycling down the road when he spotted the Mosquito lying in a flat field in line with the Oisemont road.

It is also recorded that he was shot at by Germans after climbing out and fell to the ground where he lay semi-conscious for 20 minutes.

McRitchie's Mosquito was speedily removed from the site of the crash and the history of the event quickly faded into obscurity. In all the numerous publications concerning the Amiens Raid, not one has given the precise crash details of McRitchie's Mosquito.

A local newspaper, *Le Progrès de la Somme*, published a small article on Tuesday 22nd February 1944 announcing the crash. It contained incorrect information and no mention of the casualty names.

English Plane Shot Down

An English plane has been shot down on the territory of the community of Villeroy. The pilot* was killed. Another crew member who was wounded was taken into hospital by German soldiers.

McRitchie outside the prison in 1994

Despite Sampson's tragic death, this incident does not attract as much attention as the crash of Pickard and Broadley's Mosquito. This is for two reasons. First, the recovery and collection of Pickard and Broadley's bodies by the villagers at Saint-Gratien was an exceptional incident and witnessed by many people. Normally the German forces or authorities strictly forbade interference with Allied crashes.

Secondly, the attention paid to Pickard by the British authorities after the Liberation far exceeded that of any other Allied aircrew, many of whom died in similar circumstances. During the compilation of the official raid history published on 28th October 1944, Basil Embry wanted it to be known that Pickard actually flew over the crash site of McRitchie's Mosquito to investigate. This detail was pure fiction of course.

*The dead man was Sampson, not the pilot, and the wounded man was McRitchie.

Flight Lieutenant McPhee had been flying with McRitchie; to one side and behind, and he was in this position when the guns opened fire. Also not far away were the Typhoons of Pilot Officers Burton and Markby. Even though none of the pilots saw the crash of McRitchie's Mosquito, they certainly saw the guns open fire.

The following reports were submitted by these pilots.

First account:

> A/C 'T/464' (Sqn Ldr McRitchie) was seen to bomb the target. He was also seen to attack a presumed gun site at Fresneville. The a/c dropped behind 'V/464' (Flt Lt McPhee) and was not seen again. Fighters reported seeing the a/c under control with one engine on fire.

Second account:

> 2 a/c have not yet returned, 1 of these a/c attacked a gun position near Fresneville (M 79 60) and dropped to starboard.

Third account:

> One Mosquito after attacking target was seen at Fresneville (M 79 60) At 12h10 at 50 feet leading his formation. It attacked a gun position and shortly afterwards dropped to starboard. It was not seen again.

From these accounts compiled on the afternoon of 18th February, it can be seen that the RAF may have estimated where McRitchie had crashed. The position stated as M 79 60 on the charts at the time corresponds perfectly to Fresneville village.

The pilots reported that McRitchie attacked the gun battery. However, the reality is slightly different. McRitchie was surprised by the gunfire and, having no time to avoid it, simply returned fire. There is no evidence to suggest that he deliberately went to attack these guns, although he later claimed that he was looking for potential targets at the time. McRitchie later spoke to Group Captain Mark Lax and their conversation confirmed that he was surprised by the gunfire:

I was hit about 30 miles from the target, pretty near the coast. I was flying at 50-100 feet looking for military vehicles to shoot up. I suddenly saw some guns on the slope of a hill, directly in front, blinking at me as they fired. There was not the time to avoid them, there being about three beside each other. I fired at the middle gun and believe I silenced it, but there was no way of avoiding the others.

McRitchie returned to Amiens for the 50th anniversary of the raid in 1994 and reconfirmed these details.

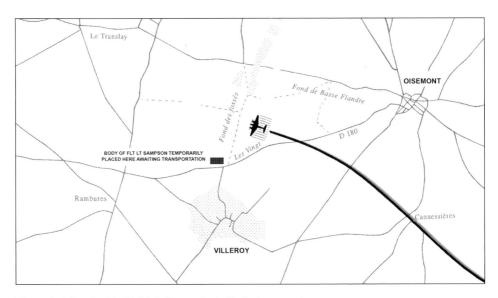

The path taken by McRitchie's Mosquito in its last moments.

Richard Webb Sampson, 1905-1944

Flight Lieutenant Sampson, son of Percy Wallace Sampson and Jeannine Palmer Sampson, had been born on 21nd December 1905 in Dannevirkee in New Zealand. He lived in Waipukurau, Hawks Bay, and embarked on the ship 'Tamarca' at Wellington in 1940. Sampson arrived in England on 3rd November 1940, where he stated he had been born in 1908 so that he appeared young enough to enlist for aircrew.* Sampson's brother, Henry W. Sampson, was killed in 1942 whilst flying with 149 Squadron. Sampson himself carried out a total of 74 operations; 64 of these as a gunner in 151 Squadron Defiants. He then became a navigator for the same squadron and flew a further four missions before being transferred to 464 Squadron. Sampson was killed at the age of 38 and is buried at Poix-de-Picardie cemetery, where he still rests today in Row D, Grave number 31.

*Livry-Level had also done the same thing to get into the RAF.

ATTACK ON FLYING OFFICER RENAUD'S TYPHOON IB
JR133 174 SQUADRON

Shortly before Pickard's Mosquito was shot down, a FW190 had broken out of the cloud cover. Its pilot spotted Typhoons some distance away and decided to pursue them. Closing the distance, the FW190 pilot fired a short burst at the Typhoon flown by a Canadian pilot, Flying Officer Renaud.

It would seem that the German pilot made such good use of the cloud cover that the attack went unnoticed by the other pilots. Renaud's fellow pilots assumed that he was shot down by light anti aircraft fire - no one saw the FW190 shoot him down. Even Flight Lieutenant Mallet, flying just in front of Renaud, was not aware of a problem until Renaud informed him over the radio that he was making a forced landing. Mallet later went on to report:

```
F/O Renaud was hit by Flak over the target and reported that he was
going to force land.
```

(174 Sqn ORB. NA Ref. AIR 27/1109)

Renaud was flying Typhoon JR133 which rolled off the production line shortly after this example, JR128 seen in the colours of 183 Squadron

Renaud did not spot his attacker. The attack was quick and lethal; there was no time to react. Seconds after the FW190's muzzles began to flash, Renaud was aware of a series of large bangs. Cannon shells slammed into Renaud's Typhoon and it began to stream smoke. With his aircraft severely damaged, Renaud radioed his colleagues to inform them that he would have to make a forced landing. His radio then went silent. The crippled Typhoon flew over Poulainville, skimming the rooftops and just managing to avoid a small group of houses. Skilfully, Renaud managed to put the five-ton aircraft gently down, just missing some tall trees, and stopped just a few metres from the Amiens-Doullens road. The huge propeller blades bent and twisted as the Typhoon skidded along the snow-covered ground, leaving a black trail of oil over the disturbed soil. As it finally came to rest, the snow melted and steam hissed out from beneath the overheated engine.

The aircraft did not catch fire, unlike another Typhoon 1b that had crashed nearby at Beauval on 19th August 1943 whilst trying to make an emergency landing; its pilot died in the blaze.

Two Polish workers saw Renaud's aircraft make its emergency landing. They ran over and saw that the pilot was wounded and was having difficulties moving, he was struggling but still seated in his aircraft. At that moment, a group of German soldiers arrived and ordered the two men to leave the scene. The soldiers then assisted Renaud from the cockpit. Once on the ground it was apparent that Renaud could not walk due to a knee injury, so the soldiers used their rifles and a coat to form a makeshift stretcher. Renaud was taken to 'Chez Paulette', a nearby café, before being taken to hospital.

Hilaire Resve also witnessed the crash of Renaud's Typhoon. Resve was eleven at the time and had just left school. Seeing the crash, he ran over with all the natural inquisitiveness of a young boy. The German soldiers were occupied carrying the injured pilot across the field, so Resve was able to clamber up on the wing and have a good look inside the cockpit. He noticed blood and wondered whether the pilot was injured by a bullet or from the impact when he crash-landed.

Later that afternoon the divisional clerk of Amiens made a telephone call to the Prefecture of the district. The time of this call was 17.30 hours:

Towards 12.20 hours during an aerial combat, an English fighter JR133 XP was shot down near Poulainville. The machine fell in the fields close to the small hamlet of Le Ramponneau and did not cause any damage. The pilot named 'Rennie' is wounded. He was transported by the Germans to the new hospital at Amiens.

Messages addressed to the Prefecture were often very 'approximate' about the date and time that incidents had actually taken place and some messages erred by a day or more. In this instance, we know that Renaud's Typhoon came down at 12.05 hours and not 12.20 hours as stated in the message. Furthermore, whilst the squadron code and serial number of Renaud's Typhoon are correct (XP) and (JR133), the name of the pilot was incorrectly given as 'Rennie'.

Another point of interest is that the Germans in this area usually sent wounded crew to one of their own military hospitals, usually Luftwaffe Hospital 8/XI located in St-Victor Hospice in Amiens. However, the message states that Renaud was taken to a new hospital in Amiens. This was probably because the wounds that Renaud had suffered did not require a great deal of medical attention, although the fact that the St-Victor hospital at Amiens had just been damaged by a 500lb bomb may also have influenced the decision.

So who was the pilot of the FW190 that shot down Renaud's Typhoon? Oberleutnant Waldemar Radener subsequently claimed that he had shot down a 'kill' at 12.05 hours - undoubtedly Renaud's Typhoon.

LOSS OF FLIGHT SERGEANT BROWN'S TYPHOON IB JP793 174 SQUADRON

Henry Brown was a 23 year-old from Derby and was accompanied by Flying Officer Vatcher as they returned over the Channel. At 12.34 hours when some 20 miles from Beachy Head, Brown climbed into some very thick cloud and then disappear from sight. Neither he nor his Typhoon were ever found. He is remembered on the Runnymede Memorial for missing aircrew on panel 216.

```
F/O. Vatcher and F/Sgt. Brown escorted a couple [of Mosquitos] to mid-
Channel, the latter last being seen climbing into a thick snow cloud 20
miles S of Beachy Head.
```

(174 Sqn ORB. NA Ref. AIR 27/1109)

It is possible that Brown's control surfaces had iced up, or that he ran out of fuel. Vatcher landed at Westhampnett just after 12.45 and waited in vain for Brown to appear.

OTHER FIGHTER ATTACKS

All research undertaken indicates that ten to twelve FW190s from 7/JG 26 took part at various points in the activity against aircraft of the Amiens raid. The lack of sightings is partly attributable to the skillful tactics of the pilots. However, it is also probable that many of the fighters used the clouds as cover and did not come out from this cover because they expected that more British fighters would be flying as top cover for the Mosquitos. This high cover had originally been planned, but failed to materialise. The Luftwaffe pilots who actually came below the cloud layer were few in number. Their method was to descend rapidly and always to attack the rear aircraft of any formation they came across.

The evidence points to at least four attacks;

1) Feldwebel Mayer claimed a Mosquito shot down north-east of Amiens at 12.05 hours (Group Captain Pickard's).
2) Oberleutnant Radener claimed a Typhoon shot down at at 12.05 hours (Flying Officer Renaud's).
3) An unknown pilot (possibly Oberleutnant Radener) attacked a Mosquito over 92 rue Louis Thuillier, Amiens, at 12.07 hours.
4) Feldwebel Mayer claimed a Mosquito 'probably' shot down to the north of Amiens at 12.15 hours.

Monitoring the Luftwaffe VHF radio messages, the British 'Y' Service recorded these messages:

```
12.05 hrs.
German a/c reported 4 Typhoons and Mosquitos over Amiens.*
12.07 hrs.
a) One German a/c reported 2 victories.
b) German aircraft report Mosquitos and Typhoons still over Amiens.
```

11 Group ORB. NA Ref. AIR25/208

There was a combat in the area of Amiens involving a Mosquito and an FW190 that probably relates to the claim at 12.07 hours. Several cannon shells smashed through a window at 92 rue Louis Thuillier, exploded in the kitchen and injured Mme. Jeannot, wife of the Divisional Police Commissioner, in her right arm. The fighter responsible must have

* *It should be noted that the term 'Amiens' included not only Amiens but also the surrounding area.*

been flying and firing westwards, and at very low altitude as the position of the kitchen was typically 'Amienoise' - facing east. Claude Leleu, who was living in rue Vaquette at the time, also witnessed a Mosquito being pursued at this time over Amiens. Looking at the flight plans of the Mosquitos it is likely that the target was Flight Lieutenant McPhee's plane. McPhee's aircraft was flying in last position and was therefore particularly vulnerable to attack. However, it has not been possible to locate any reports that confirm an attack upon McPhee's aircraft. Of the Typhoon pilots only Flying Officer Markby (Red 4 with No. 174 Squadron) saw any enemy aerial activity; he spotted two FW190s as he joined the Mosquitos south of Amiens but was unable to engage because they climbed into cloud at 1,000 feet.

It is logical to assume that the two FW190s Markby saw had just made a failed attack on McPhee's Mosquito.

Feldwebel Mayer also submitted a claim for a 'probable', in addition to Pickard's Mosquito. The FW190s of 7/JG 26 were still north-east of Amiens and first located four Mosquitos at around 12.11 hours. Mayer kept his eye on the four aircraft flying west. He turned, coming up behind a Mosquito, and opened fire 12.15 hours - a radio message to that effect was picked up by the 'Y' Service. Mayer was perilously low and had to climb quickly and violently to avoid crashing, thus losing sight of his target. Seeing the Mosquito dive away after the engagement, Mayer could easily be forgiven for believing that he had just shot down a second Mosquito. However, he was convinced that it would be foolhardy to circuit the area and check for a crash because of the number of Allied aircraft in the area. He therefore climbed to regain the cover of the clouds. Mayer and his staffel dropped out the clouds several times in the hope of finding more aircraft, but at 12.26 hours they were recalled to base.

There is no record of a Mosquito crew reporting Mayer's attack, perhaps the crews simply didn't consider the incident worth recording.

One of the third wave Mosquitos landed at RAF Ford in Sussex with damage Category 'AC', requiring repair work of at least 36 hours or more. Was this the plane that had been attacked by Mayer? Had some of Mayer's shells actually hit their target? In 1945 Squadron Leader Livry-Level, who had flown in the third wave, told local man George Cagnard that he had been attacked by an FW190 on the way home. Livry-Level told Cagnard that he had dived towards Molliens-au-Bois and then suddenly spotted overhead power lines. He was not able to climb to avoid them so flew right under the cables. This seems to confirm Mayer's 'probable' claim in the northern area of Amiens.

Further facts seemingly reinforce Livry-Level's account. In 1944, there were two 90Kv power lines stretching from Mazingarbe towards Arras. These two power lines still exist and pass between Molliens-au-Bois and Saint-Gratien. However, whilst the aircraft of No.21 Squadron passed to the north of Amiens, they had no reason to go as far north as Molliens-au-Bois.

AIR SEA RESCUE

THE SEARCH OVER THE CHANNEL FOR THE MISSING AIRCRAFT

Between 12.30-13.05 hours four fighters from No.247 Squadron launched an Air Sea Rescue search:

Typhoon lb JP910	P/O N. R. Bennett
Typhoon lb JP482	W/O A .E. Diggins
Typhoon lb JP785	Sgt S .R. Ryen
Typhoon lb JP246	Flt Sgt G. M. Campbell

These pilots initially patrolled the area of Selsey Bill and then received orders to carry out a search in the Beachy Head area. They were looking for Flight Sergeant Brown's Typhoon that Vatcher had reported missing off Beachy Head. However, due to extremely poor weather conditions the search was soon called off, even though Brown had not been located.

Information exchanged between Hunsdon and Ford airfields revealed that neither Pickard nor McRitchie's Mosquitos had returned. There was no information whatsoever about Pickard's disappearance, but McRitchie's plane had been seen going down over France by Markby and Burton of No. 174 Squadron. It was considered entirely possible that an aircraft had made it to the coast and then crashed into the Channel.

Another Air Sea Rescue mission was organized, this time the task fell to No.613 Squadron based at RAF Lasham. No. 613 Squadron was equipped with Mosquito Mk VIs and often participated in missions against V-1 sites in Northern France. It had a good record and was considered to have the best chance of finding a missing crew if they had come down in the sea.

At 15.45 hours six Mosquitos were prepared for the search mission at Lasham. They had been tasked to cover the Channel route all the way to Tocqueville in France:

Mosquito VI LR374 Sqn Ldr Newman, pilot, and navigator Flt Lt Trevers.

Mosquito VI LR370 Flt Lt Smith, pilot, and navigator Flg Off Hepworth.

Mosquito VI LR358 Flt Lt Gardener, pilot, and navigator P/O Thomas.

Mosquito VI LR355 Flt Lt Bodington, pilot, and navigator Flt Sgt Wicks.

Mosquito VI LR351 Flt Lt Cobley, pilot, and navigator Flg Off Williams.

Mosquito VI LR364 Flg Off Middlemas, pilot, and navigator Flt Sgt Whincup.

Originally these crews had been ordered to participate in operation 'Ramrod 565'- an attack on a V-1 site at Bonnetot to have taken place at 12.00 hours that day. Confirmation of the mission had been received at 10.44 hours and the time of the attack had been put back to 14.00 hours. However, at 12.52 hours, the teleprinters confirmed that this mission was to be cancelled due to severe weather conditions. The Mosquitos were therefore available to take part in the search.

The Noball operation laid on for mid-day was cancelled after briefing owing to weather being unsuitable for fighter cover to take off. 6 A/C took off on an air sea rescue sweep at 15.45h to look for Gp Capt Pickard whom it was thought might have come down in the sea off Tocqueville, but nothing was found. 2 aircraft flown by Flt Lt Bodington and Flg Off Middlemas landed at Dunsfold owing to snow.

613 Sqn ORB. NA Ref AIR27/2117.

APPENDIX 2

THE BOMBING IN DETAIL

During the post-raid debriefing, the aircrews submitted reports about their actions. These survive as Appendix A of Squadron Leader Houghton's report.

3 Mosquitos of 487 Squadron attacked the eastern wall at 1203 hours, just clearing the wall on a heading 250 degrees dropping 6 x.500 MC TD 11 Secs and 6 x 500 SAP 11/'3'. The leader's bombs were seen to hit the wall 5 feet from the ground, whilst other bursts were seen adjacent to west wall, and overshoot in fields to the north.

Two Aircraft of 487 Squadron attacked the northern wall at 1203 hours just clearing the wall on a heading of 150 degrees with 2 x 500 MC TD 11 secs, 2 x 500 SAP 11 secs and 4 x 500 GP 11 Secs. These attacks were directed at places later reported breached, by reconnaissance aircraft. One bomb seen to hit the large building, and the north side of the eastern building was also reported hit.

Two Mosquitos of 464 Squadron bombed the eastern wall at 1206 hours from 50 feet on a heading of 150 degrees and 250 degrees with 4 x 500 SAP and 4 x 500 GP 11 sec. This wall appeared unbreached before attack. Results unobserved.

Two Mosquitos of 464 Squadron bombed the main building at 1206 hours from 100 ft heading 150 degrees and 250 degrees with 4 x 500 SAP and 4 x 500 GP 11 sec. The north wall appeared already damaged. One aircraft was seen to bomb and has not returned (see missing).

One Mosquito MK IV of F.P.U. circled the target three times between 1203 and 1210 from 400 to 500 feet using a cine camera but carrying no bombs. He reported a large breach in the eastern centre of the north wall and a hole through the wall to the east of the breach, a hole in the northern side of the eastern wing of the main building, a breach in the northern end of the western wall and considerable damage to extension building at west of main building. As well as damage to western end of main building. A number of men were seen in the courtyard near the separate building, which appeared to be a work-shop, and 3 men running into fields from large breach in northern wall.

Photographic reconnaissance two days after the raid

By 11.45 hours on Sunday 20th February 1944, work teams had begun clearing the prison and the nearby route d'Albert of debris. As they were doing this, four aircraft appeared overhead at low altitude. The roundels were clearly visible and a scene of general panic ensued. Flying over the prison, the planes swung round to begin another approach.

Eyewitnesses below watched the aircraft and later reported what they had seen to journalists from several local newspapers. As a result the *Journal d'Amiens* published a report on 22nd February that stated:

'On Sunday at about midday, 48 hours after the tragic raid, four British planes of the fighter type flew twice at extremely low altitude over the debris of the prison of Amiens.'

In fact, the planes were Mustangs from No.400 'City of Toronto' Squadron RCAF. Each was equipped with a camera positioned just behind the pilot. The people here had seen solitary reconnaissance aircraft before, but this was the first time a formation of four had been seen (the Allies usually sent single aircraft, normally at high altitude). On occasion they had been seen at low level particularly if they were assessing a site of particular interest, such as those associated with V-1s. It does seem unusual for four planes to be involved, particularly with a nearby Luftwaffe airfield and the presence of light anti-aircraft units.

The four Mustangs were:

Flt Lt A. S. Collins Mustang I	AP202	-N
Flg Off E. Garry Mustang I	AP222	-E
Flg Off A. A. McKiggan Mustang I	AM158	-L
Flg Off W. H. Godfrey Mustang I	AM176	-A

At 11.06 hours on the morning of Sunday 20th February, the four Mustangs took off to undertake the low level reconnaissance mission to Amiens Prison. The mission was officially classified as a 'Noball'*. However, it was really a 'Duty Noball' as it had a very specific target to photograph. At 11.40 hours the planes arrived in the area of St-Pierre, the visibility was quite good and all the fields were covered in snow as far as the eye could see. The planes made their first pass over the prison, banking to one side so that their cameras could get the best angle. Completing a second flyover, the Mustangs then headed off towards the west, passing over the rooftops at extremely low level. As they approached Abbeville they saw a train, a very tempting target. Despite being engaged on a reconnaissance mission these aircraft were armed in the same manner as their regular counterparts and had orders to investigate any targets of opportunity as well as photographing the prison (the sortie also seems to have the features of a 'Rhubarb'** type operation).

Flying Officer Garry was the first to dive towards the target, opening fire. The bullets sent up great spurts of frozen soil and snow, then the target was covered in a sparkling shimmer of explosive strikes that danced along the train. Further bullets overshot and smashed into the granite stone ballast, scattering it everywhere. This took place in a split second and Garry did not even have time to see if there were any dramatic results from his attack. The squadron records note:

> Good visibility in France, cloud cover of 10/10th at 1000 feet or less. Whole area covered in snow…Train damaged by Flg Off E. Garry with bullet strikes seen, three miles to the North of Abbeville.

The aircraft then encountered sporadic 20mm anti-aircraft fire, which they were able to avoid. Approximately 5 kilometres south-east of Cayeux, the planes attacked an artillery battery but discovered that the area was covered in small light AA units. Soon they were boxed in by concentrated areas of Flak.

This localised anti-aircraft fire found its target. A small explosive shell crashed into the camera housing of Flight Lieutenant Collins' Mustang. Some fuselage panelling was detached, rivets were ripped from their positions and the camera was blown out. The next

* An operation connected to V weapon sites.

** A fighter sweep to find and attack targets of opportunity.

A Mustang performing a low-level pass similar to the type carried out over Amiens.

'casualty' amongst the four aircraft was Flying Officer McKiggan's plane, which was caught in a hail of 20mm Flak. All McKiggan could do was to descend to a lower altitude and the wingtips of his Mustang smashed through some treetops as he sped past. He returned to base successfully, minus a few inches from one wing tip. The time was 12.38 hours:

Gun position SE Cayeux attacked, intense light flak encountered over area six miles SW Abbeville also area 4 miles SW Cayeux. 'Camera kit' in Flt Lt A.S. Collins aircraft blown away by flak. Flg Off A.A. Mc Kiggan in attempting to take evasive action hit tree tops but returned safely with damaged wing tips.

The films that were developed from the cameras of this reconnaissance mission resulted in some superbly clear images.

On one remarkable photograph, taken at a very low altitude one can clearly see:

1 - The western end of the north wall of the east wing has been destroyed.
2 - The gable at the east of the north wing is also destroyed.
3 - Severe bomb damage to the roof of the western wing.
4 - Damage at the junction of the western and northern wings.
5 - The small buildings attached to the western end of the prison building are completely destroyed.
6 - A large breach is evident in the northern enclosure wall.
7 - A hole to the east of this large breach in the northern wall.
8 - A large breach in the western wall in its northern part.
9 - 4 impacts grouped together in the field.
10 - 2 impacts in the fields near the large breach in the western wall.

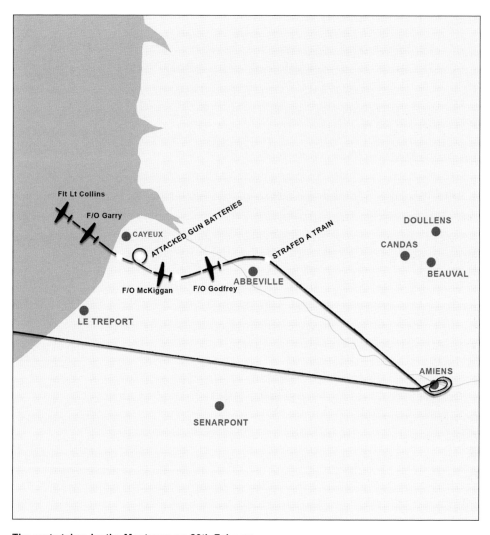

The route taken by the Mustangs on 20th February.

Photographic reconnaissance five weeks after the raid

Another reconnaissance flight took place over the prison on Thursday 23rd March 1944, five weeks after the raid. Once again, the mission was carried out by No.400 Squadron, although they used Spitfire XIs instead of Mustangs on this occasion. They were briefed to carry out seven photographic operations over France, including Amiens Prison.

```
23-03-1944. Weather clear sunny day. Local flying carried out in Spit
and Mosquito. 7 op jobs carried out involving photographing of special
targets and airfield in N France.
```

The other six operations were:

- The aerodromes of Vitry, Cambrai-Epinoy, Cambrai-Niergnies and Achiet
- The aerodromes of Laon and Creil
- The area to the south-east of Caen
- The area of Caen and Le Havre
- The area of Le Havre
- Various V-1 sites

At 13.59 hours on 23rd March, Flight Lieutenant J. A. Morton, flying Spitfire XI PA894, took off from Odiham. The flight took place at high altitude until the target was sighted, followed by a rapid descent. By 14.45 hours the aircraft had descended to a very low altitude as it passed over Amiens Prison. Several good exposures were taken and the Spitfire returned to base at 15.30 hours.

```
400 Squadron - Spit PA894.Flt Lt J.A. Morton. Take off 1359h return
15.30h. Success. On course as planned and Fix taken. No E/A. No
flak. No shipping. Weather: Channel 5/10 At 20,000 feet visibility
20 miles.
```

The results obtained from this operation were excellent. Many details were seen in the photographs, including:

- A breach in the southern wall of the enclosure to the west of the large entry door.
- A large breach in the northern end of the west enclosure wall.
- Two breaches in the north enclosure wall.
- The destruction of the south wing of the prison, in particular of its south-eastern half.
- An enormous hole in the roof at the junction of the west and north wings of the main prison building.
- Damage to the north wing.
- Damage to the workshop in the south-eastern courtyard.
- The destruction of the annex at the east end of the main building.
- Destruction of the annex at the west end of the prison.
- Destruction of the annex at the end of the north wing of the prison.
- Multiple impacts in the prison south-eastern courtyard.
- Several impacts outside the prison complex: one on a building to the west of the west enclosure wall, one in the fields to the north of the west wall and one in the fields to the north of the north wall.

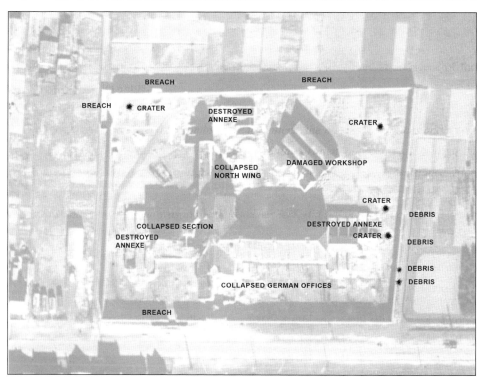

The destruction of the eastern frontage of the southern wing is also very clear in this photograph, as is the enormous hole in the roof. It is also apparent that all four wings of the prison received at least one hit. Four breaches had been knocked into the enclosure wall (one in the southern wall, one in the western wall and two in the northern wall).

British investigation of the effects of the raid, 8th September 1944

When Squadron Leader Houghton arrived in Amiens on Friday 8th September 1944, he had four main areas of investigation.

(1) To give a report on the victims and the damage caused by the raid.

(2) To evaluate the opinions of the local population.

(3) To determine which prisoners belonging to the Resistance actually escaped.

(4) To investigate the circumstances surrounding the death of Group Captain Pickard .

> On Friday, 8th September, 1944, I visited the Prefecture de la Somme in AMIENS and examined the files relating to the attack on the prison and extracted copies of correspondence attached at Appendix B.

Houghton subsequently took back to England copies of the four reports completed by the Chief of Police and the Prefect:

1) The report completed by the Chief of Police of the RG on 19th February 1944.

2) The report from Prefect Baube made to the Vichy Government on 21st February 1944.

3) The report from Chief of Police Jeannot concerning the prisoners, made on 23rd February 1944.

4) The report from Prefect Baube presented to the Secretary General in Paris on 24th February 1944.

A report was also compiled on the number of people killed and wounded, based on the accounts of eyewitnesses. Three witnesses made significant contributions to this report:

1) M Henry Delaunay.

2) M Louis Magiras, Head Warden, Amiens Prison.

3) M Henri de Bailliencourt, a haulage contractor who lived near to the prison at the time of the raid.

From the figures given in various sections of Appendix B and the estimate by the Head Warden, the final figures for persons involved were;

At the time of the attack the number of prisoners detained was:

Criminal or political prisoners arrested by the French authorities:	520
Political prisoners arrested by the Germans:	180
Total:	700

After the attack:

Still detained

Criminal or political prisoners arrested by French	192
Political prisoners arrested by Germans	74

Killed/Injured

Killed (of whom very few were political prisoners)	102
Wounded and in hospital	74

Escaped

Political prisoners arrested by the French	29
Political prisoners arrested by Germans	50
Prisoners convicted for various offences	172

Total	700

Houghton did not submit a precise report about the bomb damage. Instead, he used a copy of a general plan of the prison, upon which he indicated where the various categories of prisoner were detained and the areas either totally demolished or suffering slight damage. It is to this section of the report that the British authorities would refer when writing the official history of the raid published on 28th October 1944.

In addition to this plan, the investigator reported on some other very interesting details:

Other facts are that some 7 or 8 bombs did not explode and that some 17 bombs bounced outside the prison, and it was seen that 30 houses were destroyed or damaged, though only one person was killed. A wing of a nearby hospital had also been hit and this hospital was occupied by Germans. None of the prison staff were injured nor were there any Germans in the prison.

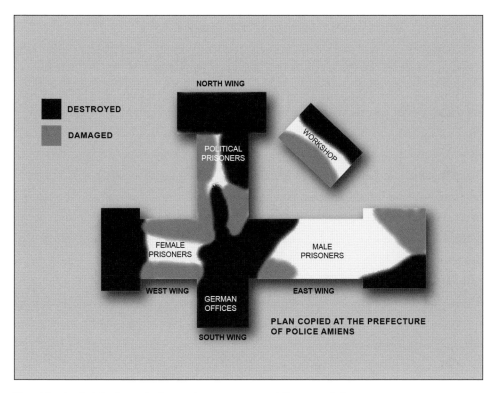

Houghton's sketch showed where prisoners were and the area of damage.

It is accurate that only one person was killed outside the prison (Mme Letien in No 17 rue Voltaire). However, it is not correct to claim that 'none of the prison staff were injured nor were there any Germans in the prison'. Several warders were injured and at least one killed. Likewise, several German soldiers died. Houghton based his statement on a lack of evidence; he had not been able to find any references to Germans killed in the reports from the Prefecture, but this was not unusual as the occupying authorities generally did not reveal the numbers of soldiers killed.

When it came to public opinion, Houghton recorded:

```
From all sources it was clear that the population of AMIENS had
wondered why the attack had been carried out, more particularly since
the section of the prison occupied by Political prisoners was the
most seriously damaged, but that within a few days, when it became
known that Monsieur VIVANT had escaped, together with so many other
Political prisoners, the attack was generally applauded.
```

Just before the file was finally closed, Flight Lieutenant Kenneth G Hesketh, the representative of the RAAF War Museum visited Amiens on 4th July 1946 to carry out a final investigation. He returned from Amiens with five photographs of the prison, in particular two exposures taken inside the prison two days after the bombing. These photographs show the damage and blasted doors, as well as the breach of the northern and western walls. In addition to the photographs, Flight Lieutenant Hesketh submitted a translation based official souces in Amiens:

```
Amiens, 5th July, 1946.


Summary of the account of the air bombardment on 18th February
1944.


On the 18th February, 1944, at mid-day, seven or eight British
aircraft flying low over the Saint Pierre quarter dropped approximately
50 bombs which fell on the prisoners' quarters of the Amiens prison,
causing numerous casualties and severe material damage.


Victims
Up till this date, 26th February 1944, 93 victims are accounted for
as follows:-
85 bodies have been recovered from the ruins.
8 wounded have been detained in Amiens Hospital.


Only one person was killed outside the prison - in the Rue
Voltaire.
88 people were wounded inside the prison and four outside.
Attached are casualty lists:*
Among the wounded were:
a) Two Guardians of the Peace on duty at the prison at time of the
attack.
b) Three prison warders.
```

These Lists were not considered worthy of preservation for historical purposes and have been omitted. (Hesketh's note).

Material damage:

The prisoners' quarters were partly destroyed, however, the right Wing which suffered the least can easily be repaired; it will take 100 to 120 prisoners. A section of the Hospice Saint Victor, occupied by the Germans (Luftwaffe Hospital) was demolished. Specifically 43 houses have been more or less damaged and elsewhere there has been light damage. Several of the bombs fell in the gardens of the route d'Albert and one in front of the Etévé garage, at the corner of the boulevard de Beauvillé and the route d'Albert, smashing a former toll post and an anti-tank defence.

All the political detainees escaped from the prison into the city and countryside. Patrols were organized by various police services who were able to apprehend 264 escapees - 208 from the French Section and 56 from the German Section. Those from the French Section on recapture were placed under guard in a disused factory in the rue de Faubourg de Hen; those from the German Section in the Citadelle.

On the day of the attack the effective total of prisoners was 712 of whom 190 were in the German Section. Of these:

(i) 264 of the political prisoners have been recaptured

(ii) 93 were found dead

(iii) 86 are in hospital

(iv) 30 are at liberty

(v) About 20 prisoners were wounded and have reported that they are receiving care at home.

(vi) 25 prisoners due for release in a few days assisted in the work of restitution and have been authorised to stay in the city.

This makes an approximate total of 518 prisoners recaptured, leaving presumably 194 at liberty.

THE FINAL ASSESSMENT OF THE BOMBING
THE TYPES OF BOMBS DROPPED ON AMIENS PRISON

All the bombs used for the attack on Amiens Prison were 500lb (225Kg) with a detonator set to delay the explosion for 11 seconds. This allowed the low-flying aircraft time to leave the area safely.

Two types of bombs were used for this attack:
-   The traditional high explosive 500lb MC bomb (Medium Capacity)
-   The S.A.P. type (Semi Armour Piercing)

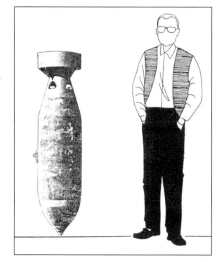

For supply reasons, a number of MC bombs were replaced with American GP (General Purpose) bombs. These American bombs had no notable differences in blast or function from their British counterparts; the only difference was the shape of the main body and the fin section. The detonators in the American bombs had also been adjusted to give the same 11 second delay.

There were two types of American GP 500lb bomb:

The AN-M 43 Bomb
Length: 150.26 cm
Diameter: 36.02 cm
Weight: 508 pounds or 230.12 kg

The explosive characteristics of these bombs varied slightly according to the type and the date of manufacture.

The S.A.P. 'Semi Armour Piercing' 500lb bombs of American origin also varied slightly according to the different models.

The AN-M 58 Bomb
Length: 146.81 cm
Diameter: 29.97cm
Weight: 501 pounds 227.40 kg
Main body of the bomb: 119.88 cm length

The number of bombs used during the attack on Amiens Prison

According to the original orders, it was envisaged that the eighteen Mosquitos would carry four 500lb bombs each, two in the bomb bay and one under each wing.

A total of seventy-two 500lb bombs were due to be released on the prison, if all of the planes attacked. In the event, the third wave did not attack and only ten Mosquitos released forty bombs over the prison. This gives the following figures:

First wave: No.487 Squadron
First section: six MC T.D. 500lb bombs and six SAP 500lb bombs
Second section: four MC T.D. 500lb bombs and four SAP 500lb bombs

Second wave: No.464 Squadron
First section: six GP 500lb bombs and six SAP 500lb bombs
Second section: four GP 500lb bombs and four SAP 500lb bombs.

Not all of these bombs fell on the prison and not all of them exploded. In the reports of the Prefecture examined and collected on 4th July 1946, it was ascertained that:
-   17 bombs fell outside the enclosure wall of the prison.
-   23 bombs fell inside the enclosure wall of the prison.
-   7 (or possibly 8) of these bombs did not explode. It is possible that the airspeed of several attacking aircraft was too high (they had been briefed to limit their speed to 240 knots) resulting in rupturing the outer casings and damage to delicate fuse mechanisms.

The position of the bomb impact points as seen after the raid

Thanks to the excellent low altitude photography carried out on 23 March 1944 and various other reports, the majority of the impact points of the bombs can be determined.

Seventeen bombs can be identified as exploding inside the the prison enclosure walls:

Southern wall

- One bomb created a large breach in the southern wall, just to the west of the large entry door. (1 - Smith)

Eastern wall

- Three bombs smashed through the eastern wall at its southern end and finally exploded near the eastern annex. (2 - Iredale) (3 - Sugden) (4 - Sugden)

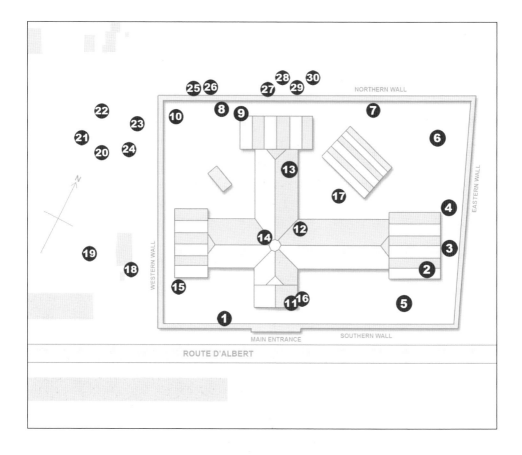

- One bomb passed above the south part of the eastern wall, making a crater to the south of the east wing. (5 - Iredale)
- Another bomb passed over the wall in the northern section and exploded in the courtyard. (6 - Monaghan)

Northern wall

- One bomb perforated the northern wall in the eastern section and exploded, creating a large breach in this wall. (7 - Darral)
- Another bomb smashed through the north wall in its western section and exploded in the courtyard, creating another breach in the wall. (8 - McRitchie)
- One bomb perforated the north wall at approximately three metres high to the east of the previous breach, exploding in the courtyard but not destroying the wall. (9 - McRitchie)

Western wall

- This wall was breached in its northern section by a single bomb that exploded in the courtyard, destroying a section of the wall. (10 - McPhee)

The main prison building

- One impact on the south wing on its eastern frontage. (11 - Smith)

- One impact at the junction of the east and north wings. (12 - Darral)

- One impact on the eastern side of the north wing. (13 - Monaghan)

- One impact on the roof of the prison at the junction of the west and north wings. (14 - McPhee)

**The famous first breach made by Smith in the front (south) wall to the left of the main entrance on the route d'Albert.
(No 1 on the map)**

In the courtyard:

- One impact to the south of the annex on the west end of the principal building. (15 - Sparks) It must be pointed out that this building was also severely damaged by the blast from the bomb that fell through the roof and exploded inside the prison.
- One impact to the east of the south wing of the prison. (16 - Sparks)
- One impact between the workshop and the northern frontage of the east wing (17 - Darral)

Six unexploded bombs were found in the prison courtyard. It is possible that three were located as follows:

- One was likely to be in the corner of the courtyard between the east and north walls.
- Another was likely to be at the foot of the east wall in its southern section. This conclusion is reinforced by the fact that a white area, corresponding to the rubble that fell outside the wall, can been seen on photographs. There was also an area of disturbed ground inside the courtyard, but no breach. This was where a bomb had punched through the brickwork.
- Another impact point was near the junction of the north and west walls, the small size of this area indicates an unexploded bomb that was dug out and removed.

IMPACT POINTS LOCATED OUTSIDE THE ENCLOSURE WALLS

Smith's Two missing Bombs

One of the bombs released during this raid exploded in an anti-tank ditch that had been excavated to the north of the boulevard de Beauvillé, actually on the other side of the route d'Albert, opposite the Étévé garage. Today, this site is where the boulevard de Roubaix begins; this did not exist in 1944. Another bomb thumped down and careered along the route d'Albert, leaving long streaks of grazed tarmac until it came to a stop just outside No.212 route d'Albert, a charcuterie. Henri Lamarche remembered the incident vividly. At the time, he was twelve years old and had just returned from the St-Pierre School from where his mother had collected him. There on the pavement lay a battered 500lb bomb. Both he and many other residents considered it to be a miracle that it did not explode. It would appear that part of the fuse mechanism had been damaged upon impact.

By plotting the locations of the bomb in the ditch and the unexploded bomb in route d'Albert, it seems likely that both originated from Wing Commander Smith's aircraft.

Near the walls:

- One bomb dropped by Sparks exploded on a building parallel to the western wall of the enclosure at its south end, not far from route d'Albert. (18)

- One bomb, possibly also one dropped by Sparks, exploded to the west of this building, in gardens to the north of route d'Albert. (19)

- Five bombs exploded in gardens near the northern section of the west wall, four were dropped by Jennings and one by McPhee. (20) (21) (22) (23) (24)

- Two of McRitchie's bombs exploded in gardens to the western end of the north wall. (25) (26)

- Four bombs exploded in gardens east of bomb No.8's breach in the north wall and did not cause any damage to the wall. It would appear that all four bombs were dropped by Fowler. (27) (28) (29) (30)

SUMMARY OF THE BOMBING PATTERN OF THE FORTY BOMBS DROPPED

23 bombs fell inside the enclosure walls:

- 17 exploded.
- 4 hit the main prison building.
- 4 created breaches in the enclosure wall.
- 6 bombs did not explode.

17 bombs fell outside the prison enclosure walls:

- 13 fell in the immediate proximity of the enclosure walls and four 250 to 700 metres from the centre of the prison.

16 of the 17 bombs exploded.

What had not been appreciated by the planners of this raid was the structure of the wall and the ground conditions. When the enclosure wall had been constructed, the outer course of brickwork was poorly cemented and was considerably 'weaker' than anticipated; this explains why a large number of bombs went straight through. The hard-frozen ground also caused many bombs to skip and skid, often careering for considerable distances over the ground before exploding.

Damage Outside the Prison

- 3 demolished houses in rue Voltaire (Nos 15, 17 and 19).
- 43 houses in rue Voltaire and route d'Albert damaged to varying degrees.
- A wing of the Saint-Victor old peoples' home destroyed.

A: The south wing where the German offices were. *P. Joly Collection.*

B: The breach at the north-west corner.

A: The north wing seen through the breach towards the eastern end of the north wall. *P. Joly Collection.*

B: The north wing. On the left is the workshop and to the right the single story annex. *P. Joly Collection.*

A: The north wing seen from inside the east wing.

B: The north wing showing the extent of damage and collapsed floors.

Both P. Joly Collection.

Opposite page: The junction of the north and east wings from where the photo at the top of this page was taken. *P. Joly Collection.*

A: The junction of the north and west wing.
P. Joly Collection.

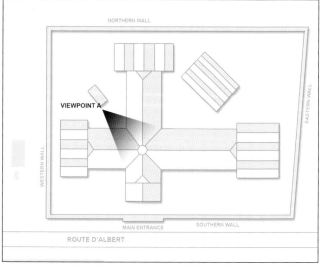

THE VICTIMS

Final assessment of the victims

It is impossible to specify, with absolute certainty, the number of people killed and wounded in the raid as figures vary from one report to another. The calculation has been further compounded by censorship and missing records. Approximately 700 prisoners were in the prison: 180 in the German area and 520 in the French area.

On 5th July 1946 Hesketh, the Australian investigator at Amiens, estimated that:
- 85 bodies were extracted from the ruins.
- 8 of the wounded later died, giving a total of 93 deceased.
- 92 wounded: 88 inside and 4 outside. (The majority were hospitalized but others received care at home).

However, 'Le Journal d'Amiens' announced the death of the 96th victim on 2nd March 1944. Furthermore, the report compiled on 8th September 1944 by Squadron Leader Houghton, gave a total of 102 people killed. Perhaps the bodies of the German soldiers who had been killed in the prison are included in these figures?

The explosion of the bomb in rue Voltaire

At 12.03 hours an air raid siren sounded in rue Voltaire, a small road some 200 metres to the west of the prison. It startled Mme Letien, who was visiting Mme Desmedt at No.14 whilst Mme Letien's husband Etienne was at work. Both ladies were terrified as the crash of large bombs began to resound across the district. Mme Letien initially decided to stay at No.14, but then decided to go back to her own home during the lull in the bombing after the first wave. Running across the street, Mme Letien unlocked her door and had just opened it when the aircraft of the second wave commenced their attack. She went straight in, not stopping to lock the door, and headed to a small staircase leading to the cellar. A massive explosion shook the entire district and thick dust hung over a large area of the street. The whole house had collapsed on top of Mme Letien, crushing the poor unfortunate lady to death.

Rue Voltaire was a scene of devastation. The blast of the 500lb bomb had smashed and splintered front doors, shattered windows and scattered debris all over the place. The bomb that had caused such devastation had shot over the roof of No.16 and smashed into the front of No.17, where it exploded. In 1943, the Breton family had been living at No.15 and the

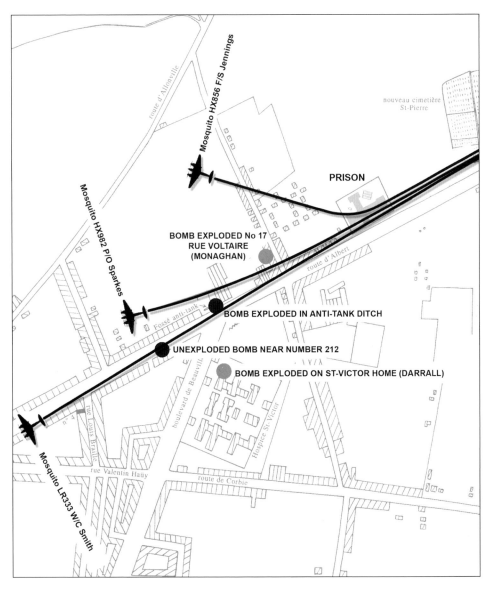

Lefebvre family at No.19. However, both houses appear to have been unoccupied at the time of the raid and, fortunately, no bodies were found in the rubble.

The Boulanger family lived at No.18 and had decided to stay indoors during the raid. Marcel Lamarche and his family lived at No.16, just opposite Mme Letien's house. At the time of the raid, Marcel Lamrache was actually in prison, but his wife Charlotte was at home. Her sister, Suzanne Thierry, had only just left the house to go to work whilst the two children, Pierre and Henri, were safely at school. Despite some damage to the houses, nobody in either No.18 or No.16 was hurt.

Once the alarm had ceased, Charlotte Lamarche, who was covered in choking brick dust, ran out of the house towards the St-Pierre school to be with her children. The alarm that had sounded just a little after midday had made the schoolteacher and pupils head for the shelters in the playground. A few minutes after the sirens ceased, both Henri and Pierre were surprised to see their mother running towards them. Henri Lamarch recalls:

In 1944, we lived at No.16 rue Voltaire. From the window facing our courtyard we could clearly see the prison about 200 metres away, separated from us only by some gardens.

On the morning of February 18th, my brother and I were at the St-Pierre school for boys near the route d'Albert. Today it is known as rue Leon Dupontreué, about 900 metres from our house. The morning was nearly finished and our teacher M Gauduin was just on the verge of dismissing us, when the sirens started. Quickly, everyone went to the shelters located in the playground of the school.

We had hardly descended the steps when we heard the roar of planes passing very low. It seemed they were just above our heads. We all tumbled over and lay in a tangled heap. Just after the noise of the planes came the deafening crash of huge explosions. We had no doubt that the bombs had fallen very close to us; some children began to cry. The teachers reassured us, just as more planes were heard and yet more explosions. Eventually, all that could be heard was the siren. One of the teachers left the shelter to look around. He returned and said that it seemed the bombs had fallen at the top of the route d'Albert, near the prison. This was not good news and made my brother and I very anxious as our mother was in the house in that area. A few minutes passed

17 rue Voltaire, where Mme Letien was killed. - now re-built.

after the sirens stopped and then the all clear sounded. We left the shelter and went to the canteen. Many mothers arrived, all looking desperately for their children. Everyone seemed to have been thrown into a panic. Suddenly, our mother arrived. She was unrecognisable, a dust-covered figure with her hair all over the place. Short of breath, she announced that the prison had just been bombed, and that Mme Letien's house had been totally destroyed. As we all walked back, she explained that it was miraculous that she had escaped injury.

At the time of the explosion, she was leaning against a wall separating the dining room from the kitchen. She saw the door pass by her as it was blasted from its hinges, parts of furniture also flew past. Then there was an enormous cloud of dust that several people thought was a fire. She said her only thought was to come and get us and that she had left the house 'open to the winds'.

The return journey home was incredible. Escaped prisoners ran past, some in tattered clothing. There were all sorts of things lying in the road, bits of furniture, glass, knives, spoons, all lying in the dust.

The route d'Albert was packed with vehicles heading up to the prison, the ambulances and other vehicles headed back down the road once they were full of wounded for the hospital. It seemed to be true carnage everywhere. In front of No.212 lay a large bomb which had not exploded. It rested against the front door. Arriving at the start of rue Voltaire we saw that the house of Mme Letien was just a pile of bricks and beams which almost entirely blocked the street. We had to climb a massive pile of shattered bricks to get to our front door.

The two houses either side of No.17 were wrecked and completely blown open, we could see their floors and furniture just hanging there. A team of Civil Defence was already active in the street, clearing debris, looking for trapped survivors or injured persons. Amongst the rescuers we saw a priest; it was Pourcher the Abbot of our parish. Just then someone found a leg in the bricks and rubbish, it was obvious the person was dead so the priest left to attend the prison.

Poor Mme Letien had been subjected to the full blast of the bomb. The bomb had passed close to the roof of our house. It smashed through the front of the house opposite and exploded in the cellar staircase. Later, when all the rubble was removed, its impact point could be seen clearly.

Our house had its door hanging off and many windows broken. Inside, it was total disorder: everything was destroyed, a mix of broken chairs, souvenirs, mementoes and bricks. There was even a bed blown out into the street covered in bricks and glass. Our roof only suffered a little damage.

My brother and I took advantage of the chaotic scene to quietly slip away and go to look at the prison. As we approached, we could see huge holes in the walls and piles of tumbled down bricks. Some people were trying to rescue some unfortunate person from beneath a huge pile of building debris. It was a terrible sight. Casualties were being taken to a nearby house where they were sorting the dead from the dying and those just wounded. A row of stretchers could be seen from the beginning of rue Voltaire, they were lined up in front of the Herbet restaurant. It was a sight I will never forget. Back at our house, my mother, an aunt and two uncles tried to cover the shattered windows and doorways so that we could remain in the house for the night. During the night, the prison was illuminated by large lights as the rescue work continued.

St-Victor Hospice

One of the last bombs to fall exploded on a building situated in the north-west of the St-Victor hospice. Part of the hospice had previously been transformed into Hospital 8/X1 for the Luftwaffe, however, it is impossible to determine if there were any German casualties caused by the bomb that hit the hospice. *Le Journal d'Amiens* stated that two people had been killed or injured at St-Victor, but it is not clear whether they were civilians or Germans.

Estimate of the German victims

It is extremely difficult to make an assessment of the German victims of the raid. The British official history published on 28th October 1944 indicates:

……the Germans themselves suffered considerable casualties…

Damage to the St-Victor Hospice - taken while snow still lay on the ground. P. Joly Collection.

Reports published by the newspapers of Amiens, such as *Le Progrès de la Somme*, gave no information about any victims apart from the two injured people at St-Victor hospice. The Germans would have censored these reports due to the sensitive nature of the information and it is probable that the German authorities were trying to hide a larger figure, whilst appearing to be accurate and honest. Several witnesses reported seeing a German soldier crushed to death near the German offices in the southern wing of the prison.

How many Germans were actually in the prison at the time of the raid? The documents prepared by 'Henri' (Maurice Genest) in September 1943 stated that the day shift comprised six soldiers, whilst four soldiers were on duty at night. However, George Platel stated he was in the presence of five Germans (three soldiers and two civilians) in a prison office immediately before the raid. It is entirely possible that 'Henri' did not encounter all of the soldiers in 1943 and that his figures might be inaccurate. At the time of the raid it is estimated that there were probably around ten Germans on duty at the prison.

Since no official details are available on German deaths or injuries resulting from this raid, one useful source of information is the burial register of the large German cemetery at Bourdon. This cemetery was the final resting place for all Germans killed in the districts of Pas-de-Calais and the Somme from 1940 to 1945; some 21,379 men. The burial registers record 17 German soldiers who died on 18th February 1944. *(See opposite page.)*

No bombing other than of Amiens Prison took place in northern France on 18th February, and no aerial operations had taken place over the area on 16th or 17th February. It is possible that some of the dead soldiers had been wounded days, or weeks, before they died and so were not casualties of the Amiens raid. It is equally possible that some of the Germans wounded in the Amiens raid may have died days, or weeks, after the attack. On average, it seems that there were two or three German deaths every day throughout the whole area during this period; given these figures, it therefore seems reasonable to conclude that around 15 German soldiers were killed as an overall result of the prison raid.

These soldiers were not all in the prison at the time of the raid; some casualties may have been caused when Pilot Officer Fowler attacked an army lorry between Flixecourt and Amiens. Some may also have been killed by the bomb that hit a wing of the St-Victor hospice. Casualties may even have been sustained when Squadron Leader McRitchie returned the fire of the anti-aircraft units.

Looking at the facts, it seems probable that the number of Germans killed in the prison did not exceed ten, possibly less if one takes into account the deaths in the truck, the anti-aircraft unit and the St-Victor incidents. The war-time British claim that 50 Germans were killed is clearly incorrect.

RECORDED GERMAN FATALITIES ON 18TH FEBRUARY 1944 IN THE AMIENS AREA

Claesges Karl Heinz	Grenadier	04-11-1925 + 18-02-1944	Aged 19
Nieper Paul		11-04 –1918 + 18-02-1944	Aged 26
Stahl Willy	Gefreiter	16-07-1922 + 18-02-1944	Aged 22
Puster Friedrich	Gefreiter	06-09-1907 + 18-02-1944	Aged 37
Griesche Adolf	Gefreiter	10-01-1900 +_18-02-1944	Aged 44
Rosel Otto	Gefreiter	04-09-1904 + 18-02-1944	Aged 40*
Heese Karl	Obergefreiter	16-01-1921 +18-02-1944	Aged 23
Wallerus Johann	Obergefreiter	21-06-1906 + 18-02-1944	Aged 28
Unger Rudolf	Obergefreiter	27-01-1911 + 18-02-1944	Aged 33
Kreul Heinz	Unteroffizier	28-10-1920 + 18-02-1944	Aged 24
Rachfat Karl	Unteroffizier	20-01-1919 + 18-02-1944	Aged 25
Kohler Werner	Feldwebel	01-05-1920 + 18-02-1944	Aged 24
Sawatzki Kurt	Feldwebel	13-04-1919 + 18-02-1944	Aged 25
Schwarzenholtzer Eugen	Feldwebel	15-04-1896 + 18-02-1944	Aged 48 **
Fast Henry	Flieger	21-06-1901 + 18-02-1944	Aged 43
Gerjets Georg	Oberbootsmannmaat	27-12-1896 + 18-02-1944	Aged 48
Lotz Karl	Frontarbeiter	26-10-1903 + 18-02-1944	Aged 41

* *Interestingly, it is known that there was a guard at Amiens called Otto.*

** *Schwarzenholtzer was definitely killed in Amiens Prison as he was recorded as working in the German offices.*

THE GERMAN REACTION AND REPRISALS

In the initial aftermath of the raid the Germans were as bewildered as the local population about why a civilian prison had been bombed. They focused their attention on the situation within the prison and set about trying to locate as many of those who had escaped as possible, assisted by the Gendarmes and the Milice.

Extensive searches were undertaken at railway stations and through local woodlands. In addition, due to the high visibility of escapees against the snow-covered fields, aircraft from Luftwaffe bases were called in to scour the area. Reinforcements using armoured cars and motorcycles converged on the area and assisted the searchers, often far beyond Amiens. A number of prisoners were re-arrested very quickly; some of these were later shot for having taken advantage of the raid to escape, but this cannot be classified as a 'reprisal'.

After several weeks the Gendarmes began to lose interest in searching for escapees; they adopted the attitude that the petty criminals had never been sentenced to be bombed and so deserved to escape during the raid. Several prisoners, such as Dr Tempez, who stayed behind to help the wounded, were later executed. In such cases the Germans were carrying out sentences which had been passed by the courts prior to the raid.

Announcements were made making threats against the families of escapees but reprisals directly attributable to the raid itself appear to have been non-existent. This may have been because there was no evidence that the local civilian population was connected with the raid. The local Gestapo did interrogate several known Resistance prisoners in an attempt to establish a link between the prison and a request for the raid, but nothing was ever established.

The main aim of the escapees was to get as far away as possible in the quickest time, or alternatively to lie low locally for as long as it took things to quieten down. Some escapees, such as Raymond Vivant, disguised themselves and, with the help of the Resistance in supplying documentation etc, eventually went elsewhere by train to relatives or friends. The authorities had hardly any idea who had escaped or who had been killed. Widespread random checks took place on houses, garden sheds and even entire streets. Massive financial incentives were offered for information leading to the re-arrest of escapees. The Gestapo at the time seemed more concerned with the potential information lost in the raid and identifying bodies, looking for any important prisoners who had been killed, simply because they were thoroughly annoyed that they had been denied the possibility of 'interviewing' them in relation to their suspected or actual Resistance activities. A few people were arrested for having assisted escapees, but generally there were no reprisals.

APPENDIX 3

PRESERVED DOCUMENTS

Drawing up your chair to the table in the reading room of The National Archives, the key document for the famous Amiens Prison Raid lays before you. A foolscap manila folder from the Air Historical Branch of the Air Ministry with its hand written title; No. 2 Group, Attack on Amiens Prison 18th Feb. 1944. Below the title are two small, square, green stickers, one saying 'Closed until 1977' is crossed out, the other says 'Closed until 1972'. This is the path many an historian has taken before you, for within this folder's covers are the key documents relating to one of the most famous RAF missions of WW2.

The flimsy pages, torn and frayed on their edges by many a hand, are held in place by a plastic treasury tag and a short length of blue string. All pages within the file are post-raid, mostly from September and October 1944 when the 'official' story of the raid was being prepared for the press.

A less well known file is AIR37/806 - 2 Group Targets. This file contains papers from 11th February to 2nd March 1944 and is concerned with the operational details of the attack.

Documents contained in AIR37/15 and AIR37/806

Extracts from many of the documents contained in these file have been quoted in part. These are transcripts of the full documents so that the extracts may be seen in their proper context.

HEADQUARTERS, ALLIED EXPEDITIONARY AIR FORCE
KESTREL GROVE, HIVE ROAD
STANMORE, MIDDX

11 FEBRUARY 1944,

REF: AEAFI/MS.13110

SUBJECT: Special Operation

TO: Air Marshal Commanding, Second Tactical Air Force.

1.   Attached is a copy of Air Ministry letter 55/44/D of I (R) dated 10 February, 1944, which requests that a certain important target in France be attacked before the 16th of February.

2. The Air Commander in Chief has accepted this commitment and desires that the mission be given to your Air Force for accomplishment. He believes the operation deserves our best efforts and intends that you employ any combination of your forces required to ensure its success.

3. Arrangements have been made for a representative from Air Ministry Director of Intelligence (Research) to visit your headquarters at Uxbridge at 1100 hours on Saturday, the 12th of February, to give you all information necessary to brief the crews of the unit or units that you may assign to the task.

For the Air Commander in Chief
Allied Expeditionary Air Force

A. C. Strickland
Brigadier General
D/S.A.S.O.

NA Ref. AIR37/806

This is the earliest document to be found (numbered 8a), dated 11th February 1944; a memo from Brigadier General A C Strickland of the Headquarters, Allied Expeditionary Air Force, to the Air Marshal Commanding, Second Tactical Air Force (Air Marshal Sir Arthur Coningham, KCB, DSO, MC, DFC, AFC).

It refers to an attached letter, Air Ministry letter 55/44/D of I (R), dated 10th February, 1944, but sadly, the letter (presumably once 8b) is nowhere to be found.

Note of action

Ref enc 8A - a meeting was held at T.A.F. at which S.A.S.O. 2 Gp, G/C
Jameson 11 Gp, G/C Palmer DD of I (R), W/C Pleasance and others were
present. The general plan agreed was that R/P Typhoons should breach
the walls and Mosquitos following up should shake up the prison.
Details of the plan were to be worked out by 2 & 11 Gps. The attack
could not take place before Feb 16th as the prisoners could not be
informed before that date. The Air C in C wants to know details of
the prison and results of the attack.

13 Feb 44   H Pleasance W/C Ops 1(b)

NA Ref. AIR37/806

This hand-written minute describes the conclusions of the meeting at Uxbridge on 12th February. Clearly the 'cover story' is already in place at a very high level since reference is made to informing 'the prisoners' of the attack. The original letter states,

a certain important target in France be attacked before the 16th of February.

Yet this minutes states

The attack could not take place before Feb 16th

There is an important difference here, for if the attack was indeed designed to influence Rommel during his visit to the area, the attack could not be allowed to take place too early. To prevent questions from 2 Group as to why the 'prisoners' could not be helped earlier, the remark about informing them of the attack has been made.

11 Group,

2 Group

2 T.A.F. Main.

From: Air Ministry, D.D.I.2.

Ref: DDIS/70/44.

Date: 14th February, 1944.

PRISON BUILDINGS - AMIENS AREA.

With reference to the meeting which took place in No.2 T.A.F. Main Headquarters on Saturday, 12th February between representatives of the addressees and D.D.I.2., herewith an interpretation report by Medmenham on the building concerned.

Some additional information has been included referring to nearby groups of buildings.

A/V/M. Embry. D.S.O., A.F.C. has taken a personal copy of the interpretation report.

Palmer

Group Captain.

NA Ref. AIR37/806

(Above); the covering letter (numbered 9a) and (right) the Photographic Reconnaissance Unit interpretation report (numbered 9b) from RAF Medmenham of photos taken of the prison. This was the report that the raid was largely based upon.

MOST SECRET

14.2.44.

INTERPRETATION REPORT Z 59 (R)

This report gives certain specified details of the buildings marked A, B and C on the attached photographs (Nos 3141–3142 of Sortie E/798).

Building A

Cross-shaped building (prison).

i) The height of the surrounding wall is 22 feet.

ii) It is difficult to make any accurate measurement of the thickness of this wall. The wall does not appear to be unusually thick for its height and as may be expected is thicker at the base than at the top. It can be stated, however, that the wall does not exceed 4 feet in thickness and is probably considerably less than this.

iii) Dimensions of area enclosed by the wall are as follows:

North side	425 feet.
South side	410 feet.
(adjoining main road)	
East side	325 feet.
West side	315 feet.

iv) The height of the main building to the eaves is approximately 48 feet and to the ridge 62 feet. There are therefore four or five storeys but the exact number cannot be ascertained from the photographs.

v) No machine-gun posts visible are in the immediate neighbourhood of the building but these could of course be concealed.

Buildings B

This appears to be a small housing estate consisting of a number of semi-detached two storey dwellings with gabled roofs. The layout is regular, each house having a small garden. There is no photographic evidence to suggest that the buildings are used otherwise than as private houses.

Building C

The buildings are marked on the town plan as 'HOSPICE ST VICTOR' and their layout and design would correspond to that of an institute for the poor and aged. The grounds are surrounded by an 11 feet wall but there is no photographic evidence of military occupation. Outside the grounds about 80 yards to the north there is a trench near the road junction.

MOST SECRET   DISTRIBUTION

R.A.F. STATION,   A.D.I. (Ph)   4
MEDMENHAM   File   1
                                             5

The instructions for the raid AO 241 - NA Ref. AIR37/806

```
B/CAST + EMERGENCY + FORM 'B'                B  71 11 M/B2/3A   FEB 44
HNO   T   140 A/F
UGI       T        11 GROUP


V GPB GPB 5:18        ''O''         FORM 'B'


FROM 2 GROUP 180940 A
TO 140 WING/AIRFIELD
INFO 11 GROUP, HQ TAF MAIN, HQ ADGB,               HQ AEAF.
SECRET QQX BT


AO 241 18TH FEB
```

INFORMATION. MOSQUITOS OF 140 AIRFIELD ARE TO ATTACK THE PRISON AT AMIENS IN AN ATTEMPT TO ASSIST 120 PRISONERS TO ESCAPE. THESE PRISONERS ARE FRENCH PATRIOTS CONDEMNED TO DEATH FOR ASSISTING THE ALLIES. THIS AIR ATTACK IS ONLY PART OF THE PLAN AS OTHER ASSISTANCE WILL BE AT HAND AT THE TIME.

DATE AND TIME.   18TH FEBRUARY 1944.
                    ZERO: 12.00 HOURS.

ROUTE. BASE – LITTLEHAMPTON – VIA APPROPRIATE LATTICE TO TOCQUEVILLE – SENARPONT – BOURDON – ONE MILE SOUTH DOULLENS – BOUZINCOURT – 2 MILES WEST SOUTH WEST ALBERT – TARGET – TURN RIGHT – ST. SAVEUR –SENARPONT – TOCQUEVILLE – HASTINGS – BASE.

BOMB LOAD: 2 X 500 LB. M.C. MKIV FUSED T.D.
                    11 SECS.
                    2 X 500LB S.A.P. FUSED T.D.
                    11 SECS.

METHOD OF ATTACK. ALL AIRCRAFT TO ATTACK AT LOW LEVEL.

1ST. ATTACK. SIX MOSQUITOS AS DETAILED BY O.C. 140
                    AIRFIELD.
INTENTION. TO BREAK THE OUTER WALL IN AT LEAST TWO PLACES.
METHOD. LEADING THREE AIRCRAFT TO ATTACK EASTERN WALL USING MAIN ROAD AS LEAD IN. SECOND SECTION OF THREE AIRCRAFT WHEN TEN MILES FROM TARGET WILL BREAK AWAY TO RIGHT AT SUFFICIENT HEIGHT TO ALLOW THEM TO WATCH LEADING THREE AIRCRAFT AND THEN ATTACK NORTHERN WALL ON A NORTH-SOUTH RUN, IMMEDIATELY FOLLOWING THE EXPLOSION OF THE BOMBS OF LEADING SECTION.
TIMING. ATTACK TO BE AT ZERO HOURS.

2ND. ATTACK. SIX MOSQUITOS AS DETAILED BY O.C. 140
                    AIRFIELD.
INTENTION. TO BOMB THE MAIN PRISON BUILDING.

METHOD. LEADING THREE AIRCRAFT TO ATTACK SOUTH EASTERN END OF MAIN BUILDING AND SECOND SECTION OF THREE AIRCRAFT TO ATTACK THE NORTH WESTERN END OF BUILDING. ATTACKS TO BE CARRIED OUT IN SIMILAR MANNER TO 1ST. ATTACK ABOVE.
TIMING: ATTACK TO BE MADE AT ZERO HOURS PLUS 3 MINS.

3RD. ATTACK. SIX MOSQUITOS AS DETAILED BY O.C. 140 AIRFIELD.

INTENTION. THIS FORCE IS A RESERVE, AND WILL APPROACH THE TARGET AS IN THE TWO PREVIOUS ATTACKS, ONE SECTION FROM THE EAST AND ONE FROM THE NORTH, BUT WILL BOMB ONLY IF IT IS SEEN THAT ONE OF THE PREVIOUS ATTACKS HAS FAILED.
TIMING. ATTACK TO BE MADE AT ZERO PLUS 13 MINS.

FIGHTER SUPPORT. EACH FORMATION OF SIX MOSQUITOS WILL HAVE ONE SQUADRON OF TYPHOONS AS CLOSE ESCORT. FIGHTERS WILL RENDEZOUS WITH MOSQUITOS AS FOLLOWS.

      1ST. ATTACK. 1 MILE EAST LITTLEHAMPTON AT
                  ZERO MINUS 45 MINS.
      2ND. ATTACK. 1 MILE WEST P X LITTLEHAMPTON
                  AT ZERO MINUS 42 MINS.
      3RD. ATTACK. LITTLEHAMPTON ZERO MINUS 32 MINS

SIGNALS.   1ST ATTACK. BOMBER CALLSIGN: DYPEG.
                    GROUND CONTROL CALLSIGN: AILSOME
                    ON 2 GROUP GUARD 1.
                    BOMBER LEADER MAY CALL ESCORT
                    DIRECT IN EMERGENCY ON 11 GROUP
                    GUARD 1.
                    FIGHTER CALLSIGN: GARLIC.
            2ND ATTACK. BOMBER CALLSIGN: CANON.
                    GROUND CONTROL CALLSIGN:
                    BELLFIELD ON 2 GROUP GUARD 1.
                    BOMBER LEADER MAY CALL ESCORT
                    DIRECT IN EMERGENCY ON 11 GROUP GUARD 1.
                    FIGHTER CALL SIGN: CAJOLE.
            3RD ATTACK. BOMBER CALLSIGN: BUCKSHOT.
                    GROUND CONTROL CALLSIGN: GREENSHIP
                    ON 2 GROUP GUARD 1.
                    BOMBER LEADER MAY CALL ESCORT DIRECT
                    IN EMERGENCY ON 11 GROUP GUARD 1.
                    FIGHTER CALLSIGN: DUNLOP.

GENERAL.   EMERGENCY HOMING TO FRISTON ON 2 GROUP GUARD.
              A.V.XXXX A.S.R. ON 2 GROUP GUARD.
              SPECIAL V.H.F. CODEWORD: RENOVATE.

NOTES (1) FOLLOWING EACH ATTACK SECTIONS OF THREE AIRCRAFT OF EACH FORMATION ARE TO ENDEAVOUR TO REGAIN CLOSE COMPANY AS SOON AS POSSIBLE.

B.T   180940 A

           Stills from the Cine film of attack at Amiens
                     18th February show.

A. 1 Breach in E. wall
B. 2 breaches in N. wall
C. Large breach at junction of W. and N. walls.

MAIN BUILDING.
Junction of N. and E. Wings on N. side is badly damaged.
Northern end of N. wing badly damaged.
Remainder of building obscured by smoke.

To: W/Cmdr. Pleasance.

G/Cpt. Palmer D.D.I.

NA Ref. AIR37/806

                                              A.E.A.F.
                                             XXXXXXXXX
                                           KESTREL GROVE
                                          XXXXXXXXXXXXXX
                                               HIVE ROAD,
MOST SECRET

TIM/S.7.   2nd March, 1944

Dear…….

        I herewith send a copy of the letter concerning the operation
against the Prison at Amiens.

2. I have sent a copy to Basil direct.

                        Yours

              (Signed) Trafford Leigh Mallory

Air Marshal Sir Arthur Coningham
        K.C.B., D.S.O., M.C., D.F.C., A.F.C.,

Headquarters, 2nd Tactical Air Force, (Main)
Uxbridge,
Middlesex.

NA Ref. AIR37/806

This is the covering memo dated 2nd March 1944 from Headquarters, Allied Expeditionary Air Force to Coningham (HQ 2 TAF) for a letter concerning the operation. A copy of the letter was sent to Basil Embry but, again, there is no letter.

By 8th September, Atcherley's man, Squadron Leader Edwin Houghton had arrived in liberated Amiens to make his investigation. From interviewing the key figures, including the Head Warden of the prison and the Chief of the FFI in Amiens, the facts were quickly established.

NA Ref. AIR37/15

```
REPORT ON THE ATTACK ON PRISON AT AMIENS BY 10 MOSQUITOS OF 140
                    WING - 18th FEBRUARY, 1944.
-------------------------------------------------------------------

Attached at Appendix A is a 2 Group Summary of the Operation and a
message, dated 23rd February, 1944, received through Intelligence
sources, giving the success of the attack.

                    -------------------

        On Friday, 8th September, 1944, I visited the Prefecture de la
Somme in AMIENS and examined the files relating to the attack on the
prison and extracted copies of correspondence attached at Appendix B.

        I interviewed the following Frenchmen:-
1. Henry Delaunay
2. Monsieur Magiras Louis, Head Warden, Amiens Prison.
3. Monsieur Henri de Bailliencort, Haulage Contractor - who lived
close to the prison.

        At Appendix C is a translation of the letter dated 21st
February, 1944, in Appendix B.

        From the figures given in various parts of Appendix B and an
estimate by the Head Warden, the following are the final figures for
the number killed and the number that escaped as a result of the
attack:-

        DETAINED AT THE TIME OF THE ATTACK.

        Criminal or Political prisoners arrested by the
        French Authorities                              ...... 520
        Political prisoners arrested by the Germans     ...... 180
                                        Total  ......  700
```

AFTER THE ATTACK:
```
     Still detained- (a) Criminal or Political
                         prisoners arrested by the
                         French                          ...... .192
                     (b) Political prisoners
                         arrested by the Germans  ....... 74
Killed (of whom a very few were political prisoners) ....... 102

Wounded and in Hospital                             ....... 74

Escaped- (a) Criminal or Political prisoners arrested by
             the French (A list is given at         ....... 29
             Appendix B .They were charged with
             being members of Secret Societies,
             Communists and terrorists)
         (b) Political prisoners arrested by
             the Germans                             ....... 50
         (c) Usual criminal prisoners               ....... 179
         TOTAL ESCAPED - 258
                                   Total                     700
```

It was not possible to discover from this source the reason for the detention of the Political prisoners arrested by the Germans because in all the records the reason was stated to be unknown nor were the French ever told when the Germans intended to execute the Political prisoners. One point was clear - that the most important prisoner to escape was a Monsieur VIVANT, the Sous Prefect of ABBEVILLE, who was arrested by the Gestapo on 14 February, 1944. 4 days before the attack or at about the same time that we were asked to carry out the attack. Monsieur VIVANT is now in the Ministry of the Interior, Place Beauvau, Paris, in General de Gaulle's government. (Without having seen Monsieur VIVANT, I think it probable that we were asked to carry out the attack by the French in London, mainly to effect his escape. Monsieur VIVANT was a key member of the Resistance at ABBEVILLE and probably had in his possession important secrets of the Resistance organization).

From all sources it was clear that the population of AMIENS had wondered why the attack had been carried out, more particularly since the section of the prison occupied by Political prisoners was the most seriously damaged, but that within a few days, when it became known that Monsieur VIVANT had escaped, together with so many other Political prisoners, the attack was generally applauded. Other facts are that some 7 or 8 bombs did not explode and that some 17 bombs bounced outside the prison, and it was seen that 30 houses were destroyed or damaged, though only 1 person was killed. A wing of a nearby Hospital had also been hit and this Hospital was occupied by Germans. None of the prison staff were injured nor were there any Germans in the prison.

Saturday, 9th September, 1944.

I went out to the North of AMIENS to the places where 2 of our aircraft were reported to have been shot down, to establish identities and to find out the cause. A single-engined fighter was hit by flak over AMIENS and crashed, whilst flying low at POULAINVILLE, 4 miles North of AMIENS. The number of the machine was D.R.133 - X.P., and the pilot, by the name of RENNIE, was wounded in the knee and taken into the new hospital at AMIENS by the Germans.

After the bombing of the prison was completed, 1 Mosquito flew E.N.E. towards QUERRIEU (2062) and BEHENCOURT (2266). It is possible that the machine was already slightly damaged, although still under control, from small arms fire emanating from the German hospital near the prison. A farmer, Monsieur DOURFAUT, at MONTIGNY (2166) saw a single-engined enemy aircraft on the tail of the Mosquito and saw the Mosquito's tail shot away, whereupon the Mosquito spun in, the tail falling at 178662 and the engines and forepart at 175663. Empty cartridges which had fallen from the enemy fighter were recovered by a farmer at 198645.

The son of the Mayor at ST. GRATIEN, Monsieur GAGNARD-PINKET went out to see the crash and found both occupants burnt up. On one body he found a motor licence with the name JOHN ALLEN BROADLEY (Group Captain PICKARD'S Navigator) and the body had the back of the head broken open. The other body was too burnt up to be recognisable, but there was a shoulder strap with 4 stripes. He took away the effects which he has since handed over to a Major of the R.A.M.C., acting on behalf of Wing-Commander Wilson. Two hours later a party of Germans arrived who sent them away. They went out next morning and found the bodies still there with no guard and so brought them back into the village and had coffins made. Later that day the Germans returned with Oak coffins and admonished the French for interfering. The Mayor's son marked the German coffin containing the remains of BROADLEY with 4 scratches. The Germans took the coffins and buried them in the cemetery at ST. PIERRE, just East of Amiens Prison (120595). A Friend of the Mayor watched the internment and the graves are in the British part of the Cemetery, marked with crosses on the sketch at Appendix D. It would be necessary to examine the scratches on the coffins to establish which grave is which. The graves are well cared for.

On Sunday morning, 10th September, 1944, I visited Doctor MACHOIRE, No. 6, Place St.Michel, AMIENS, Chief of the F.F.I. in AMIENS, who had until then been visiting Paris to see General LE CLERC. I wanted to establish with him who the request for the attack had come from and how many people were due to be executed and the successes of the attack. He said that the request had not come from him but that the F.F.I. worked in water-tight compartments for security reasons and it was probable that the request had come from within the prison through our agents, but that he would get in touch with Monsieur VIVANT and other members of the Resistance Movement who had escaped from the prison and establish the facts for us. I said that someone would call on him in a fortnight's time when he would have the facts ready.

E. HOUGHTON, S/Ldr.

Houghton was unable to establish why the 'political prisoners' had been detained because all records stated 'unknown'. He notes that the probable reason for the attack was the detention of Monsieur VIVANT, the Sous Prefect of ABBEVILLE.

Whilst this might seem a plausible explanation, Vivant's arrest came three days *after* Brigadier General Strickland's request to make the attack – a fact of which Houghton would have been unaware.

Houghton then goes on to establish in great detail the circumstances of the loss of Pickard's Mosquito and Renaud's Typhoon. On his final day Houghton visited Doctor Machoire, Chief of the Amiens FFI. in an attempt to establish who the request for the attack had come from, how many people were due to be executed and the success of the attack. He was unsuccessful in this, but Marchoire offered to get in touch with Monsieur Vivant, who had escaped and was then in General de Gaulle's Government in Paris, to establish the facts.

Houghton's Report - Appendix A

```
3 Mosquitos of 487 Squadron attacked the eastern wall at 1203 hours,
just clearing the wall on a heading 250 degrees dropping 6 x.500 MC
TD 11 Secs and 6 x 500 SAP 11/'3'. The leaders bombs were seen to
hit the wall 5 feet from the ground, whilst other bursts were seen
adjacent to west wall, and overshoot in fields to the north.
     Two Aircraft of 487 Squadron attacked the northern wall at
1203 hours just clearing the wall on a heading of 150 degrees with
2 x 500 MC TD 11 secs, 2 x 500 SAP 11 secs and 4 x 500 GP 11 Secs.
These attacks were directed at places later reported breached, by
reconnaissance aircraft. One bomb seen to hit the large building, and
the north side of the eastern building was also reported hit.
     Two Mosquitos of 464 Squadron bombed the eastern wall at 1206
hours from 50 feet on a heading of 150 degrees and 250 degrees with 4
x 500 SAP and 4 x 500 GP 11 sec. This wall appeared unbreached before
attack. Results unobserved.
     Two Mosquitos of 464 Squadron bombed the main building at 1206
hours from 100 ft heading 150 degrees and 250 degrees with 4 x 500
SAP and 4 x 500 GP 11 sec. The north wall appeared already damaged.
One aircraft was seen to bomb and has not returned (see missing).
     One Mosquito MK IV of F.P.U. circled the target three times
between 1203 and 1210 from 400 to 500 feet using a cine camera but
carrying no bombs. He reported a large breach in the eastern centre of
the north wall and a hole through the wall to the east of the breach,
a hole in the northern side of the eastern wing of the main building,
a breach in the northern end of the western wall and considerable
damage to the extension building at west of main building.  As well
as damage to western end of main building. A number of men were
seen in the courtyard near the separate building, which appeared to
```

be a work-shops, and 3 men running into fields from large breach in northern wall.

Four aircraft of 21 Squadron received V.H.F. messages from "F", 464 Squadron, and F.P.U. aircraft when between two and four miles from the target, instructing them not to bomb. Target was seen covered with smoke: they brought bombs back.

Missing: One aircraft, last seen circling target and heard giving V.H.F. message instructing not to bomb, has not returned to base. One Mosquito, after attacking target was seen at FRENEUVILLE (M.7960) at 1210 hours 50 feet leading his formation. It attacked a gun position, and shortly afterwards dropped to starboard, it was not seen again.

(Since reported by I.R.C. [International Red Cross] S/L MacRitchie P.o.W. and F/L Sampson buried at Poix).

Message, dated 23rd February, 1944.

"I thank you in the name of comrades for bombardment of prison. The delay fixed for the attack was too short; we were not able to save all. Thanks to admirable precision of attack the first bombs blew in nearly all the doors, and 150 prisoners escaped with the help of civilian population. 12 of these prisoners were to be shot on the 19th. Bombing was too violent; 37 prisoners were killed, some of them by German machine-guns. 50 Germans also killed. To sum up it was a success. No plane down over Amiens, but we are having pilots looked for."

NA Ref. AIR37/15

Appendix A of Houghton's report is a 2 Group report on the operation and, typed on the same page, is the text of a message dated 23rd February received 'through Intelligence sources'.

Houghton had done a thorough job, and his superiors were in possession of most of the salient facts; not all of which were palatable. This 'message of thanks' obtained, not by Houghton, but 'through Intelligence sources' actually originates from 'C' General Sir Stewart Menzies, head of MI6.

Houghton's Report Appendix B1 contains this message from the Prefect of Police in French. This translation appears as Appendix C of the report.

From The Prefect of Police of the Somme.   **21st February 1944.**

I have the honour to confirm to you my telephone call of Friday 18th February, informing you that on 18th February, a little after mid-day, some Anglo-American Aircraft, flying low, attacked the northern part of the town of AMIENS with a certain number of explosive bombs.

The objective seems to have been the prison which was entirely destroyed.

About 30 houses close to the prison have also suffered considerable damage. Two unfurnished ones have been particularly damaged and in one house a person has been killed. In another part a wing of the hospital at ST VICTOR which was used as a hospital by the occupation troops had been partly damaged.

Two of the attacking aircraft have been shot down as a result of aerial combat.

The prison held about 840 civil or political prisoners and 180 prisoners locked up by order of the Germans, and of this population more than 50 worked outside on various tasks.

At the time of writing 77 corpses have been recovered from the wreckage and 78 people are in hospital of whom many are seriously wounded, but all these victims were prisoners, the prison staff did not suffer.

At the same time these figures are only provisional, the searching of wreckage which is being actively pursued is not yet complete.

Among the important persons who had been arrested by the Germans and who have escaped during the bombardment is M. Cruel, Chief of the Prefecture detained since 11th November 1943.

Among other things I want to inform you of the disappearance of M.VIVANT, Sous-Prefect D'ABBEVILLE, arrested by the Gestapo and imprisoned at AMIENS on the 14th February 1944. After investigations by the German authorities M.VIVANT had been seen safe and sound a few moments after the bombing.

Immediately after the news of this aerial attack, help was organised and the various services of the A.R.P. were employed to dig out the victims and to sort out enormous masses of material. Also the police authorities and Gendarmes have carried out active investigations day and night in order to find the many people who profited by this bombing in order to escape.

At the actual time of the bombing there were 192 prisoners locked up by the French authorities, 54 prisoners by the German authorities, and about 20 women also arrested by the Germans, who have been reinterned.

The count of escaped prisoners isn't yet exactly known because of the impossibility of identifying several corpses and because of the number of victims who are still in the wreckage.

I want to emphasise considerable difficulties arising out of the imprisonment of civil and political prisoners after the destruction of the only prison in the town of AMIENS. Prisoners are at this moment provisionally locked up under the surveillance of urban police in an ancient building which gives no guarantee against the risk of escape.

[The remainder of the letter was not translated in Appendix C, but has been here for the sake of completeness.]

The German authorities were approached with the view to reassigning to this use several buildings currently occupied by them, such as the citadelle or the barracks, but they did not succeed, and I fear that they will be refused.

Undoubtedly, the condemned will be forwarded to other establishments by the order of the director of the penitentiary district of Poissy. However, the prisoners cannot leave Amiens, where they are at the moment. The absence of a prison would present a serious inconvenience.

Under these conditions, and in agreement with the director of the penitentiary district of Poissy, I envisage the installation, not far from the destroyed prison, of barracks surrounded by barbed wire, intended to be used as a provisional prison. Monitoring of this camp, whose construction will take time, will not be difficult to carry out and will require, undoubtedly, recourse to the police force of the city, whose manpower is already insufficient in the current districts.

The Prefect

Signed

PS. At the time I address this communication to you, I have just been advised that the German police force continues its search to discover a building suitable to contain the French and German prisoners.

Houghton's Report Appendix B2
(Translation)

Information provided by M. Jeannot
Divisional Commissioner

Situation of the prisoners at the prison on 23 February 1944.
(15 hours)

Before the Bombing
        French area   448 men
        French area   72 women
                             520

    German area   180 men and women

                  total 700

After the Bombing

        Recaptured   182
        52, rue de la republic   26 women
        German area at Dury   8 women
        Citadelle   48 men
        At the hospital   74 casualties
        At the disposal of chief
              warden   20
        Killed   88
                                  446 persons.

Which gives a population of 700 people.

    254 absent.

Houghton's Report Appendix B3
Translation

Amiens, 18 February 1944.

Telephone Message
Divisional Commissioner:

Today at 12.20 hours during an aerial combat, an English fighter aircraft marked J.R. 133 X.P. crashed at Poulsinville.

The aircraft fell in a field, at the hamlet of Le Ramponneau, next to Poulsinville and caused no damage.

The pilot Rennie is injured. He was taken by the Germans to the new hospital in Amiens.

Houghton's Report Appendix B3
Translation

Amiens, 18 February 1944
17.30 hours

Today, 18 February 1944, at 12.20 hours during an aerial combat, an English aircraft crashed at St Gratien. The aircraft fell in a field, near a wood.

The two occupants were burnt and have been taken from the wreckage by the inhabitants of the village.

A guard has been provided by German soldiers.

THE LIST OF KNOWN ESCAPED POLITICAL PRISONERS

ESCAPED POLITICAL PRISONERS (Men) — Translation (FRENCH AREA)

Name	Status	Place and Date of birth	Home Town	Release date	Reason for arrest
ROUXEL Auguste	Sentenced	Fion le Grand 22/1/99	Creil	6/7/43	Contravening regulations against secret societies
HENONMONT Maurice	ditto	Margny 23/3/10	Margny	6/7/43	ditto
VYBERT Jean	ditto	Lop 29/3/12	Nogent-sur-Oise	6/7/43	ditto
LONGA Jean	ditto	Croix-la-Foret 12/9/87		6/7/43	ditto
WARGNIER Marceau	ditto	Mons-en-Chaussee 13/5/43 [sic]	Montataire	16/7/43	ditto
THUILLIER Maurice	ditto	Amiens 15/2/03	Amiens	16/7/43	ditto
DEVILLERS Georges	ditto	Toutencourt 1/8/08	Aveluy	13/2/44	Communist Propaganda
LEQUEAU Pierre	ditto	Penhars 23/7/98	Pont-Ste-Maxence	7/8/43	ditto
MOTELET Serge	ditto	Pont-l'Eveque 25/2/24	Noyon	16/7/43	ditto
DELCOURT Roland	ditto	Creil 12/4/03	Moyenneville	6/8/43	ditto
MICHEL Marcel	ditto	Montataire 16/2/01	Nogent (Oise)	1/8/43	ditto
DUTRIEUX Julien	ditto	Creil 18/1/15	Creil	11/8/43	ditto
PORET Nestor	ditto	Betigny 6/8/87	Chauny	11/11/43	ditto
OXTAVE Andre	ditto	Paris 11/8/10	Tourcoing	3/2/43	ditto
RAT Leon	Accused	Clairy 28/11/20	Clairy	3/2/43	Association with Terrorists
MALERIEUX Emile	Accused	St Quentin 4/5/85	Peronne	Accused	ditto
PRIERTLEY Andre	Accused	Flamicourt 30/12/21	Sormon	Accused	ditto
GRISENTELLE Alexandre	Accused	St Michel 4/7/88	Peronne	Accused	Secret Association
BOCQUET Gratien	Accused	Mamet 25/6/13	Roisel	Accused	Terrorist Activities
FRANCQ Jean	Accused	Helmincourt 25/12/33 [sic]	Helmincourt	Accused	ditto

Name	Status	Place and Date of birth	Home Town	Release date	Reason for arrest
HEC Gilbert	Sentenced	Noyon 8/7/29	Noyon	Accused	ditto
DUMONTOIS Rene	ditto	Hussigny 20/2/28	Noyon	Accused	ditto
BEAUSSEAU Louis	Accused	Laigneville	Breuil	Accused	Violence against law enforcers
CARON Jean	Sentenced	Meru 24/11/22	Meru	29/9/48	
STOPIN Etienne	ditto	Cavigny 14/12/19	Mouy	29/9/53	ditto
MICHEL Yves	Accused	Amiens 16/6/26	Vitry s/Seine	Accused	Terrorist Activities

WOMEN

DUJARDIN Gisele	Sentenced	Abbeville 18/6/21	Amiens	3/11/43	Communist Propaganda
MEULLEMESTRE Andree	Sentenced	Clermont 25/9/14	St Pol	15/4/43	ditto
GUILLEMONT Eliane	Accused	Corbie 3/11/17	Peronne	Accused	Terrorist Activities

The next document in the file is a letter from Air Commodore H A Jones, Directorate of Public Relations, to Air Vice-Marshal Basil Embry dated 13th October. It refers to the press embargo that had been imposed on the raid, that had now been rescinded, and offers a 'story' which, the author of the letter assures, had been approved by Basil Embry and Coningham 'some months ago'.

```
                    Directorate of Public Relations
                              Air Ministry
                                   King Charles Street
                                        Whitehall S.W.1.
                              13th October, 1944.

Dear Basil,

        You will recall that some time ago it was proposed that a story
should be issued of the attack on Amiens Prison on 18th February, 1944.
        At the request of high authority, however, we withheld
publication and it was not until a few days ago that we were informed
that there would now be no objection to the release of our narrative
to the press. Meanwhile, we have been pressed by newspapers and other
sources which had become aware of the exploit to obtain removal of
the embargo on the story, and this pressure has again been resumed.
        We feel we must put out some official account of the operation
as soon as possible, as the prison is no longer in occupied territory
and stories of the attack are likely to be picked up at any moment
by the war correspondents who are in France.
        I understand that Atcherly recently visited the gaol and
collected further evidence. I should be most grateful, therefore,
if you would kindly let me know if the attached story, which was
approved several months ago by Air Marshal Coningham and yourself -
and has just been approved by high authority here, subject to certain
amendments incorporated in the attached - is an accurate version of
this gallant operation. You will, I know, appreciate how important
it is that our story should not be contradicted in any particulars
by new information made available.
        I also understand that Atcherly found the grave of Group
Captain Pickard and it would be very good of you if you would please
give me a short description of it and say where it is situated, so
that I may include the information in our bulletin.
        Also attached is an account of the attack by an R.A.F. cameraman
who flew with the force which carried out the operation. Will you
please state whether you approve it for publication? (It has not yet
been sub-edited).
        As Admiral Thomson, the Chief Censor at the Ministry of
Information, is urging me to release the story for publication in
the Sunday papers of 22nd October, I should be most grateful if you
would be good enough to let me have a reply as early as possible

                    Yours Sincerely

                    H A Jones
```

NA Ref. AIR37/15

There follows this account of the raid sent by Air Commodore Jones, Directorate of Public Relations.

THE GAOL BREAKERS

"Mosquitos are to attack the prison at Amiens in an attempt to assist 120 prisoners to escape.

"These prisoners are French patriots condemned to death for assisting the Allies.

"This air attack is only part of the plan as other assistance will be on hand at the time."

This was the briefing at an Allied Expeditionary Air Force intelligence room. It was the prelude to one of the most spectacular R.A.F. operations of the war and it is not until now that the full account of the exploit may be revealed.

Frenchmen were lying in the gaol awaiting death for their brave efforts in the Allied cause. Some had been condemned for assisting Allied airmen to escape after they had been brought down in France. It was clear that nothing less than a successful operation by the R.A.F. to break down the prison walls 20 feet high and 4 feet wide - even at the risk of killing some of the patriots they wished to rescue - would afford these men any reasonable chance of escape.

The R.A.F. undertook this exacting task, accepted the risk of killing people who in any event were to be put to death by the enemy, and eventually learned that as a result of their attack on the prison 150 prisoners escaped. Thirty seven prisoners were killed by the bombing and by machine-guns of the German guards when the break in the walls was made. Fifty German soldiers were also killed by the bombing.

To carry out the action three Mosquito day bomber squadrons of the R.A.F. 2nd Tactical Air Force were selected - one Australian, one New Zealand and one home squadron. Several Mosquitos were hit by flak but their pilots brought them home.

Group Captain P.C.Pickard D.S.O., D.F.C., this time flying in Mosquito "F for Freddie", commanded the operation - from which he never returned - but did not fly in the leading position. The New

Zealand section was led by Wing Commander I.S. Smith D.F.C. and Bar, of New Zealand; the Australian section by Wing Commander R.W. Iredale, D.F.C, of Australia; and the home squadrons section by Wing Commander I.G.F. Dale.

The plan of attack had been carefully pre-arranged. the day, the hour and the minute had been fixed under utmost secrecy. If the Germans had any suspicion that a rescue bid was to be made, the prisoners would have suffered instant death.

The detailed plans, as issued to the crews, were as follows:-

"Method of attack - all aircraft are to attack at low level. The first attack, six Mosquitos, as detailed.

"Intention - to break the outer wall in at least two places.

"Method - leading three aircraft to attack eastern wall, using main road as lead in. Second section of three aircraft, when ten miles from target, will break away to right at sufficient height to allow them to watch the leading three aircraft and then attack the north wall, immediately following the explosion of the bombs of the leading section.

"Second attack - six Mosquitos.

"Intention - to bomb the main prison building.

"Third attack - six Mosquitos.

"This force is a reserve and will bomb only if it is seen that one of the previous attacks has failed.

"Fighter support - each formation of Mosquitos will have one squadron of Typhoons as close escort".

The attack was carried out as planned on 18 February, 1944, although a snow storm early in the morning of the day it was made had temporarily threatened to jeopardise the whole operation. The two leading sections struck first the wall, breaching it in two places, and then the prison building. The third section were not required to attack.

At well over three hundred miles an hour, Wing Commander Smoth's leading section flew straight down the Albert Road leading to Amiens and saw the dark building of the prison surrounded by high walls, clearly outlined in snow-covered fields. They released their bombs and just cleared the prison wall. Several bombs hit the wall about five feet from the ground and when the Australian section swept in, Wing Commander Iredale found the prison yard full of smoke.

"The results", he said, "were rather difficult to see owing to the smoke and dust which were billowing about, for not only had holes been made in two of the walls but a large part of the main building had been hit".

A pilot with a close view of the attack was Flight lieutenant A.T. Wickham, A.F.C. of Tetbury, Glos., who made three runs across the target taking pictures and a film record.

"in one wall", he said, "there was a big hole and a great breach in the other. Three men were running out through the largest hole. Inside the prison yard I could see about thirty people, all dressed in brown dungarees, racing for freedom through holes in the wall".

"Everything went as it was planned", said Wing Commander Smith, who led the first section in. "It was a foul morning, with snow storms and a low cloud base. We met to consider the plan. Everybody wanted to go on the operation. My boys put up a wizard performance.

"There were many niceties about the operation, for in fact there were two jobs to be done. First, we had to blow the walls down to let the prisoners out of the yard; and, second, we had to blow the ends off the building to kill the guards - who should have been eating at that time - and thus open up the prison building itself, so that the prisoners could escape. It was a cruciform building with the guard-houses at the ends of the long arm, surrounded by the 20-foot wall.

"The timing of these two tasks had to be in seconds. For safety we flew in somewhat loose formation until we came near the run in and then everybody tightened up wing-tip to wing-tip and we just cleared the wall and no more, after letting our bombs go".

A Canadian, Flight Lieutenant John L. McCaul, D.F.C., 28-year-old Navigator, of Toronto, said: "As we had to put our bombs in the right places we navigators were much too busy to have time to look around. I only had one glimpse as we swept round to turn for home of the figures from the gaol stumbling across the adjacent fields."

Flying over the prison at four to five hundred feet during the attack was a Mosquito of the R.A.F. Film Unit. Its pilot reported: "The attacks made a large breach in the eastern and northern walls and there was a hole in the northern side of the eastern wing of the building. Considerable damage was done to the extension building west of the main building.

"I saw a number of men in the courtyard", he said, "near the separate building which appeared to be workshops. I saw three men in the fields from the northern walls".

Flight Lieutenant B.D. Hanafin, son of Colonel P.J. Hanafin, Raigmore, Inverness-shire, was leading the second section of the three Mosquitos in Wing Commander Smith's first section of six. (Each section of six Mosquitos were divided into two sub-sections of three each). On the way to the target an engine seized up and Flight Lieutenant Hanafin feathered the airscrew. Gradually he dropped behind and although he tried to unfeather the airscrew the engine became dangerously hot and he had to drop out of the operation. The leader, Wing Commander Smith, ordered the other two aircraft to carry on. On his way home on one engine Flight Lieutenant Hanafin flew through intense flak and received a bullet or pieces of shrapnel in the shoulder which for some time paralysed one side of his body. So he came home "On one engine, one leg and one arm" and made a landing at a south of England base.

The remaining aircraft of F/Lt. Hanafin's sub-section following their leader in on the attack; did not entirely escape. A large hole was blown in the wing of the aircraft of P/O M Sparks*, of Auckland, New Zealand. It measured two feet by two feet six inches and caused the handling of the aircraft to be very difficult. the pilot had full rudder trim on but it was still hard to hold the aircraft level. He flew back to England, however, and landed, coming in fast on the approach to make a successful "pancake".

The daring and dash with which the pilots carried out this attack was equalled by the skill and efficiency with which the navigators did their part of the work. They spent many hours over maps and charts before the operation and thoroughly studied the courses and tracks.

Sparks was actually in the lead section of three

Wing Commander Smith, the leader, said he had never seen better flying or navigation in his life. "It was like a Hendon display", he declared. "We flew at the lowest possible height, so that we could place our bombs exactly at the base of the walls. But even so, my bombs went through the first wall, across the yard and into the wall at the other end. Even if we'd wanted to stop and look, the plan made that impossible. We came straight out and made for home".

Lee Howard (navigator and cameraman in the Film Production Unit Mosquito) wrote a personal account of the raid that found its way to the Directorate of Public Relations and was sent to Embry by H A Jones for his approval. From an historian's point of view it is invaluable, but Atcherly and Embry did not approve. This is his full account.

We all stared at the big box as we came into the briefing room. It lay on the table at the front of the room, before the map on which our route was marked. It was about five feet square and six inches deep. Clearly a model of the target; it couldn't be anything else.

I was particularly intrigued by the thing. Unlike most of those present, I had been given preliminary details of the raid the evening before, because there are certain additional preparations the film cameraman had to make which take time.

Most of the other members of air crew were quite used to my knowing what was happening long before they did, and several of them asked me what the raid was all about.

Normally I would have answered their questions; but this time, when I had seen Group Captain Pickard the evening before, he had done nothing other than indicate the nature of the attack in the most general terms.

He had told me where it was; he had told me the route by which we were getting there; and he had told me I would like the raid. "It's going to make a grand story for you", he said. "You should get some damned good pictures; I think you'll find it's very photogenic".

"A big factory of some kind?" I hazarded.

"Well - something like that, in general," he replied. "You'll understand the need for absolute secrecy when you hear all about it at the briefing."

And with that I had had to be content.

The mystification of the air crews was increased somewhat by the very elaborate precautions to maintain the secrecy of which Group Captain Pickard had spoken. There were Service police guarding the briefing room; the one by the door had a list of the names of those entitled to enter, and even when one was inside the target model was still hidden from view.

In addition, it was snowing heavily outside - certainly very poor flying weather - and we were all fairly convinced that any normal trip would have been cancelled from the weather point of view alone. This one must have been different, with a vengeance.

I had already fitted my two fixed cine cameras into the Mosquito and had stowed away my two hand-held cameras in the nose, ready for use. My hands were numb with the cold, and I warmed them by the stove while we waited for the briefing to start.

Finally Group Captain Pickard came in, followed shortly afterwards by the Air Vice-Marshal commanding our Group, who stood at the back of the room and listened.

"Your target today", said the G.C. "is a very special one from every point of view. There has been no little debate as to whether this attack should be carried out, and your A.O.C. more or less had to ask for a vote of confidence in his men and his aircraft before we were given the chance of having a crack at it. It could only be successfully carried out by low-level Mosquitos; and we've got to make a big success of it to justify his faith in us, and prove further, if proof is necessary, just how accurately we can put our bombs down.

"The story is this: in the prison at Amiens are one hundred and twenty* French patriots who have been condemned to be shot by the Nazis for assisting the Allies. Some have been condemned for assisting Allied airmen to escape after being brought down in France. Their end is a matter of a day or two. Only a successful operation by the R.A.F. to break down their prison walls can save them, and we're going to have a crack at it to-day. We're going to bust that prison open."

*Changed in pencil on the draft to 'many'.

"If we make a good job of it and give the lads inside a chance to get out, the French underground people will be standing by to take over from there.

"There are eighteen of you detailed for this trip. In addition, the Film Unit's special aircraft is coming along to see what sort of job you make of it.

"The first six of you are going to breach the walls. Now, these walls have got to be broken down if the men inside are to get out successfully. This will mean some real low-level flying; you've got to be right down on the deck. The walls are only about twenty-five feet high, and if we're not damned careful our bombs are going to bounce right over them and land inside the prison and blow everybody to smithereens.

"We have told the men inside of the risk, through the underground movement, and they're fully aware of the possibility.

"We've got to cut that risk down to the minimum. You've go to be below the height of the wall when you let them go; down to ten feet, if possible. There are no obstructions in the way on your run up, so you should be able to make it.

"We have a model of the prison, which you are all going to study in detail shortly. You will notice that the prison itself is in the form of a cross, and that at its east and west ends are small triple buildings which, according to our information, are the quarters of the Nazi prison guards.

"The second six aircraft are going to prang those quarters. I don't suppose all the Nazis will be inside at once, but we're sure to get some of them and it'll add to the general confusion and give the prisoners a better chance.

"The film aircraft will follow this second formation and will orbit the target, filming the results of the raid."

The Group Captain looked at my pilot. "We're dropping 11 second delay bombs, Tony", he said. "You will have to lose a minute or so near the target to give them a chance to go off before you run over the prison. Then you can make your runs as the cameraman wants and as you consider expedient".

Tony nodded.

The Group Captain continued: "The first six aircraft are on target at exactly midday. The second six will attack three minutes later.

"Now, the last six will arrive 10 minutes after this second attack. Their job will depend entirely on the success or failure of the first two sections. If the job has been well done, they will pass north of Amiens and set course for home, bringing their bombs back with them."

The Wing Commander who was leading the last six aircraft stood up. "Who is to decide whether the attack is a success or not, sir"? he asked.

Group Captain Pickard considered. "I shall be flying towards the end of the first twelve", he said. "When I've dropped my bombs I shall pull off to one side and circle, probably just to the north of the prison. I can watch the attack from there; and I'll tell you by radio. We'll use the signals 'red' and 'green', repeated three times; so that if you hear me say 'red, red, red' you'll know you're being warned off and will go home without bombing. If I say 'green, green, green' it's clear for you to go in and bomb."

"As an additional precaution, the film aircraft will have just as good a view as myself of the whole show - perhaps even a little better - so it can act as cover. If you don't hear me give the signal and hear the answering acknowledgment, Tony, you can give the 'red' or 'green' yourself before the third six come in to bomb."

Eventually the briefing was nearly over. We had studied the route again and again; we had studied the model of the prison until we knew it better than our own homes; the navigators, of which I was one, had checked and counter-checked their work. Hot tea was brought around; and, as we rested a moment from the high-speed work and concentration of the last three hours, the G.C. had a final word to say.

"It's still snowing, and the visibility is not so good; but we can get off the deck all right. I've just had a final word with Group on the phone and they've given us the O.K. to go. This is one raid where a cancellation is unthinkable; if the slightest hint of what we are going to try to do were to leak out, every one of those men would be shot instantly. So - let's get going and make a good job of it".

I just had time to check over my cameras, and then we were taxying for the take-off. A moment or two after the second six had gone we, too, belted down the runway in a shower of fine snow. Airborne, we climbed to 300 feet and set course. The aircraft ahead were invisible; the ground below us could be seen only vaguely through the swirling snow.

We were about three minutes late at the coast, where we were to pick up our escort of Typhoons. This was the first time I had experienced the joys of a fighter escort; normally Mosquitos operate alone, being well able to take care of themselves, but this target was very near to an enemy-occupied fighter airfield and the boys needed a free hand to ensure their doing a good job of work, so the powers above had provided us with two Typhoons each to chase away inquisitive Huns.

In addition, we were to be given further fighter cover of two squadrons of Typhoons which would be around and about the target when we got there. Being a few minutes late with our rendezvous with the Tiffies I thought perhaps we might miss them. As we tore over the coast - we were going pretty fast, in an endeavour to catch up with the second six - both Tony and I saw aircraft ahead, and as we gained on them we were able to identify them as Mosquitos and Typhoons.

We were still belting along when, as if from nowhere - I made a mental note of it, to remind me how easy it is to be "jumped" by fighters if one doesn't keep a good look out - a couple of the Typhoon boys were sitting, one each on our wingtips.

This is as good a place as any to record our immense admiration of those boys; fighter escort was a novelty to me and I couldn't quite see why we, in Mosquitos, had one; but long before the trip was over I had become an enthusiastic advocate of fighters in general and our two Tiffies in particular. They stuck to us like glue; I'm sure if we'd gone down a railway tunnel they would have come right with us.

It must be remembered that our aircraft behaved differently from all the others. The others attacked and went home; ours stayed at the target and made three runs without dropping any bombs at all. Our two Tiffies couldn't have had the faintest idea what we were supposed to be doing, since no-one had told them we were a film aircraft; but they watched faithfully whatever we did, and when we moved from the scene, along they came again.

As we crossed the Channel the weather changed, and nearing the French coast it was quite sunny. We climbed to cross the coast, and as we went over France lay spread before us, carpeted in white. It altered the appearance of the ground quite a lot but this didn't seem to trouble the leading navigators, who found their way unerringly to turning point after turning point, finally bringing us right on to the main Albert-Amiens road, which led straight to the target and provided an unmistakable guide.

As we charged down the road we saw the leading aircraft's bombs exploding,though we were too far off to make out much detail. Tony did a broad sweep to starboard to lose a little time and when we came up to the target we did a couple of fairly tight circuits to the north of it to allow the remainder of the bombs to explode. I went down into the nose to do the filming, and as I peered out of the side I saw the Group Captain's aircraft orbiting near us.

I believe this is the last time he was positively seen by anyone on the trip; he did not return from the operation.

I had just time to note the G.C.'s aircraft, and to think I'd never seen so many Typhoons apparently playing at figure-skating over the target, when Tony's voice warned me "Here we go". I switched on the fixed cameras and started operating the one in my hand, too.

The target was a remarkable sight. There was a strong east wind blowing and smoke was streaming in thick clouds across the western end of the prison; but the hole in the wall, a beautiful round hole - ideal for getting out of prisons - stared us straight in the face. We could both see tiny figures running like mad in all directions; then we were over and racing round in a tight turn.

"Going round again", said Tony; and round again we went.

Again I stared, more at the hole in the wall than anything; it fascinated me. We were so tightly banked in this turn that I could scarcely move; but it was obvious that things were happening very quickly down below, and that the band of patriots who had to escape were standing not upon the order of their going.

"Like another"? asked Tony; so we made our third and final run. It was as we did this that I realised how one could tell Nazis from prisoners; on our every run the Germans threw themselves flat on their faces, but the prisoners went on running like hell. They knew whose side we were on.

As we flew away from the prison Tony switched on the radio and gave the "red, red, red" signal that sent the last formation home with their bombs.

The author of this article, Flying Officer Lee Howard, is a member of the operational section of the R.A.F. Film Production Unit - a flying cameraman and navigator who works in Mosquito aircraft.

Members of the operational section of the Unit, who fly both by day and by night in almost every type of British light, medium and heavy bomber, are the men who take all the pictures of the R.A.F. raids seen in newsreels through the world.

This is the story of one of those raids - a special low-level attack by Mosquitos of the Second Tactical Air Force.

The request from Public Relations must have rattled the corridors of power rapidly, for Air Commodore Atcherley was having nothing of this and responded by return. In his long letter, Atcherley made some interesting remarks, (highlighted on the next page in bold);

A.O.C.

    I opened the attached D.O. letter and enclosures from D.P.R.
- in your absence. It may assist you, in view of D.P.R's remarks in
his 3rd paragraph, if you can refer to some considered critisisms of
the two accounts of the operation which he has forwarded.

2.   Obviously the D.P.R. intends the story to be splashed across
the British newspapers. **We know that the French are a bit out of
sympathy with the purpose of the operation, and it is reasonable
to assume that if uninformed and misleading criticisms (verbally
or Press) from France are to be anticipated, we shall have to make
certain of the intelligence 'facts' in the D.P.R.'s official account.**
I suggest we can make the facts incontestable if Shallard visits
Tubby Grant at once, and obtains from him the revised Monk Street
opinion — if it is revised. We need their estimate of the number of
prisoners held prior to the attack including the number who were
due to be executed. We also need the figures of casualties (killed
and wounded) and the number of successful escapes resulting from
the attack. You will note that these important details figure in the
accounts of the operation forwarded. Firstly therefore, will you
permit the suggested visit?

3.   The next point is that the accounts which have been forwarded
are frightful blurbs, contain an amount of useless padding and a
lamentable dearth of the interesting and obtainable facts. It would
be wise to ensure that the tone of the article which will be issued
under official auspices leaves nothing to be desired as regards our
treatment of our own share in a very gallant operation. I hate the
personal references and all the other clap trap in which the original
authors have as usual wallowed. I think Pick deserves a proper
write-up, to which I am sure you would like to attend personally.
The only individuals who should be mentioned by name are I suggest
the Leader, and the Leaders of the sub-formations. The latter in
my opinion should be mentioned simply in the manner in which the
Admiralty recite names of Sea Captains when reporting action at sea.
You will not want the A.M.C-in-C., or any of our business rivals to
have opportunity to poke fun at us, or feel sore because of apparent
attempts to give ourselves a build-up. Anyway, the operation more
than merits proper treatment. Pick deserves a decent obituary, with
some reference to gallant record and inspiring leadership.

4.   **On this last point Int and I surmise that he broke away
from the escort and main formation in order to investigate closely
McRitchie and Sammy's crash. He must have been well aware that in
doing so he was taking a chance on enemy fighters. While pre-occupied
watching the ground in the search of survivors of the first crash, he
was probably bounced by the two 190's which the local French testified
to having seen pursuing him (then travelling northwards) and which
finished him by blowing his tail off. We have, as you know, got the
empty shell cases in our possession, picked up by the same French**

family who later removed Pick's and Broadley's bodies, and followed up the Huns internment arrangements until they were able to locate, mark, and photograph the graves. If any line-shooting is permissible in the official story, then I think this not unreasonable surmise might be allowed a place. It would be typical of Pick to leave the formation to follow one of his own lame ducks, and I feel reasonably sure in fact this is how he met his end. It will do no harm, and probably a lot of good, to let that be recorded. I believe Iredale and Shallard could collaborate to write a much better account of the operation than the one enclosed, and I strongly recommend you to let them do it. Perhaps you will write the portion relating to Pick yourself.

5.   I feel also that the account would be incomplete without at any rate the following photographs (all already in existence or possible to obtain):

i) The model of the prison used for briefing.

ii) Stills from the film taken of the actual attack.

iii) Close-ups of the actual damage and breaches effected on the prison buildings and it's walls, taken from the ground now. (The prison is still unrepaired). As the account gives at some length the detailed nature of the orders issued to the various elements of the attack, it would surely be of the utmost interest to accompany the accounts with actual photographs of the structural results. After all, they were tricky tasks and it will be of the greatest value to O.R.S. and Operations Staffs in the future if we exploit this unique opportunity.

iv) The photograph of Pickard's and Broadley's graves – the photos of his crash and of the removal of the bodies, should obviously be treated as private property of Mrs. Pickard.

D.F.W. ATCHERLEY
Air Commodore,

14th October, 1944   S. A. S. O.

NA Ref. AIR37/15

Basil Embry replied to Jones on 17th October offering the version of the story proposed by Atcherley. He ended his covering letter;

"I note on reading your letter through that you accuse me of approving the draft several months ago – a very fast ball!"

Clearly, Embry had no intention of authorising its use.

```
                                     SECRET
                            Royal Air Force,
                                  Mongswell Park,
                                       Wallingford,
                                            Berks.

2G/RES/DO.                      17th October, 1944

Dear

      Many thanks for your letter of the 13th October, 1944, enclosing
the story on the Amiens Prison operation.

      To tell you the truth, I did not care for the story as written
very much, because it rather goes against the grain in this Group to
mention names of individual members of aircrews and we have always
aimed at maintaining our 'peace' standards !!!

      However, we felt it was wrong to be entirely destructive, and
so we have attempted a new draft. I have no doubt you will criticise
our draft from the Press angle, just as much as we criticised
your's!!! Any how, I hope it will meet the case.

      I note on reading your letter through that you accuse me of
approving the draft several months ago - a very fast ball !

                            Yours

                            Basil
```

NA Ref. AIR37/15

On 21st October Air Commodore H A Jones sent Basil Embry another version of the story to be released to the press. His final paragraph reads;

"I'm sorry about my statement that you had approved the draft some months ago. I was informed that you, or your deputy on your behalf, had in fact done so. It is a grand story, one of the best that has come out of the war, and I want to get it as right as possible."

Directorate of Public Relations

Air Ministry

King Charles Street

Whitehall S.W.1.

13th October, 1944.

Dear Basil,

Many thanks for your letter of 17th October which I have discussed with Peck.

I understand your views and have arranged for the main part of your account to be used in the proposed Air Ministry bulletin.

I know you will appreciate, however, that we must take account of the "Press angle", as you say, though I hope that our final effort will not displease you.

You mentioned the reference to individual members of aircrews. Some of the references in the draft I sent you will be deleted as you wish in the revised story, but I feel bound to retain mention of Dominion personnel.

We also propose to let the B.B.C. broadcast from discs made at the time by W/Cdr. Iredale, and by F/Lt. Wickham, who was in the photographic aircraft.

It will not now be possible to publish the story in the Sunday papers tomorrow, but it may be released in time for the following Sunday.

I'm sorry about my statement that you had approved the draft some months ago. I was informed that you, or your deputy on your behalf, had in fact done so. It is a grand story, one of the best that has come out of the war, and I want to get it as right as possible.

Yours

H A Jones

NA Ref. AIR37/15

After two further drafts, the story was released to the press for publication on 29th October, 1944. The final version has little relation to the 'truth' even as established for Atcherley and Embry by Squadron Leader Houghton in September.

NOT FOR PUBLICATION, BROADCAST IN OVERSEAS BULLETINS OR USE ON CLUB TAPES BEFORE 2330 B.S.T. ON OCTOBER 28 (I.E. FOR SUNDAY PAPERS). NOT TO BE BROADCAST IN THE MIDNIGHT NEWS OF OCTOBER 28/29. OVERSEAS MESSAGES SHOULD BE PREFACED WITH THIS EMBARGO.

Air Ministry News Service   Air Ministry Bulletin No. 16106

ATTACK ON THE AMIENS PRISON
AN EPIC R.A.F. OPERATION.

"Mosquitos are to attack the prison at Amiens in an attempt to assist more than 100 prisoners to escape.

"These prisoners are French patriots condemned to death for assisting the Allies."

This was the briefing one day of air crews at an Allied Expeditionary Air Force intelligence room, and it was the prelude to an epic operation by the Royal Air Force. For security reasons it has not been possible until now to give a full account of the exploit.

Frenchmen were lying in the jail awaiting death for their brave efforts in the Allied cause. Some of them had been condemned for assisting Allied airmen to escape after they had been brought down in France. It was clear that nothing less than a successful operation by the R.A.F. to break down the prison walls - even at the risk of killing some of the patriots they wished to rescue – would afford these men any reasonable prospect of escape.

The R.A.F. undertook this exacting task, accepted the risk of killing people who, in any event, were to be put to death by the enemy, and eventually learned that as a result of their attack on the jail, many prisoners escaped and considerable casualties were caused among the German guards.

The prison was a cruciform building in a courtyard, surrounded by a 20 feet high wall, some 3 feet thick. The yard was fenced internally to segregate the prisoners while they were at exercise. Accuracy in attack was regarded as essential, for whereas on the one hand the walls and buildings required to be breached, on the other, in order to reduce casualties to a minimum, it was important that the least possible force should be used.

The jail was guarded by German troops living in a special wing, the location of which was exactly known. The attack had to be sufficiently discriminating to ensure that decisive force was used against this part of the building. The timing factor, too, was important, for the escaping men were to receive valuable assistance by patriots from outside if these patriots could be warned of the exact time of attack.

The task, therefore, called for secret and detailed planning, and a model of the prison and its surroundings was made from photographs and other information already in the Air Ministry's possession. Thus, in planning and briefing every aspect was studied.

To carry out this exceptional operation, the task was entrusted to a Mosquito wing of the R.A.F. Second Tactical Air Force comprising British, Australian and New Zealand squadrons, and including R.C.A.F. airmen, commanded by Group Captain P.C.Pickard D.S.O. and Two Bars, D.F.C., one of the most outstanding and experienced bomber pilots in the R.A.F.

It was decided to allocate two fighter squadrons for escort duties, from a fighter group that played a memorable part in the Battle Britain.

The task added to the many difficult and diverse operations which the Mosquitos of the Second Tactical Air Force have performed - operations which have included the destruction of the single-building German Headquarters of Civil Administration in the centre of the Hague, numerous enemy army barracks, or chateaux converted for occupation by German troops in France, German army headquarters in the field, electric power stations and other targets which demanded the most exacting precision attacks.

Of all these operations, however, the Mosquito air crews counted as the most intricate the action against the Amiens prison on 18th February, 1944. On the morning of that day the aircrews rose before dawn for their very careful briefing, to find the airfield covered with snow and low cloud, and with little prospect of clearance.

Once the plan was outlined, the crews, the most experienced from each squadron, were determined to press home their attack in spite of the adverse weather. It was obvious that the prison walls must be broken in at least two places to enable any escape whatever to be made. At the same time, both ends of the main building had to be hit to release the prisoners from to their confinement. Accordingly, the first wave of six aircraft was detailed to breach the wall, on its north-east and north-west perimeter. The second wave of six aircraft was to divide and open up both ends of the jail, and to destroy the German guards' quarters. A third wave was available should any part of the plan miscarry.

To obtain the accuracy required, it was necessary to bomb from "deck level" and each wave had to be so timed that the results were achieved in their right sequence and to avoid casualties by collision over such a small target.

A Mosquito was allotted to the operation to make film and photograph records of the attack.

It was an hour before midday when the squadrons left their snow covered airfield to rendezvous with their fighter escort on the south coast of England. From there the formation flew at sea level to the French coast, swept round the north of Amiens and approached their objective along the straight Amiens-Albert road on which the prison is located. The second wave, on approaching the target, saw that the first wave had been successful.

Through the dust and smoke of the bombing the corners of the jail were seen, enabling an accurate attack to be made. This, too, was so successful that Group Captain Pickard, circling the target, was able to send the third wave home without any necessity for its attack. The photographic Mosquito, making three runs over the objective, saw the breaches in the wall, the ends of the building broken, prisoners running out through the breaches, Germans lying on the ground, and on the last run, some patriots disappearing across the snow on the field outside the prison.

The operation was not completed without loss, however, for two Mosquitos, one of which carried Group Captain Pickard and his navigator, Flight-Lieutenant J.A.Broadley, D.S.O., D.F.C., D.F.M. of Richmond, Yorkshire, were shot down by enemy fighters, as also were two of the fighter escort. Saddened as they were by this loss of their leader and other colleagues, the aircrews who took part in the operation felt that the sacrifices had not been in vain when it became known that a high percentage of patriots had escaped. Although, as was unavoidable, some of the patriots were killed by German machine-guns as well as by bombs, it is known that the Germans themselves suffered casualties from the attack.

Since the successful liberation of France and subsequent relief of Amiens by the Allies, it has been possible to collect certain details, particularly of our losses, which had hitherto been unobtainable. All that was originally known of Group Captain Pickard's fate was that his aircraft was last seen circling over the prison slightly above the height at which the three waves of Mosquitos were attacking.

His purpose was to decide whether or not sufficient force and accuracy had been achieved by the first two waves and to order the reserve wave to attack or withdraw, accordingly. It was for this reason that he had detached himself from the main formations to a position which, though it was dangerous, he could best see and direct the operations.

It now seems certain that when he had ordered the last wave to withdraw without dropping its bombs, he saw one of his Mosquitos brought down by the fierce light flak put up by the German defences. Determined to investigate the crash, to discover the fate of the crew, he was himself "bounced" by a pair of F.W.190's sent up to intercept our aircraft. Caught thus pre-occupied, and detached from the friendly fighter escort, which by then was covering the withdrawal of the main formations, he fell a victim to the enemy fighters.

He was shot down a few miles from Amiens and his body, with that his navigator, was subsequently recovered by friendly villagers, who had seen the whole action. The Germans forced the villagers to hand over the bodies but were unable to prevent them attending the burial in the cemetery alongside the prison.

As soon as his comrades reached Amiens after the invasion, seeking news of the aircrews' fate, the villagers presented them with photographs of the graves and a few personal belongings which they had secreted from the Germans for the months before the invasion in order that his identity and that of his navigator might be established. Tragic though Group Captain Pickard's loss is, there is consolation in the knowledge that it occurred while he was leading probably the most successful operation of his gallant and brilliant career. The attack on Amiens prison will remain one of the most memorable achievements of the Royal Air Force.

The final documents relate to the visit made to Amiens by Flight Lieutenant K.G. Hesketh, the RAAF War Museum Representative. He compiled this account from official sources in Amiens and collected five photographs from the French Police. They were taken two days after the attack by an official French Police photographer, with the approval of the German military authorities.

The first of Hesketh's photos showing the breach in the west wall

Amiens, 5th July, 1946.

Summary of the account of the air bombardment on 18th February 1944.

On the 18th February, 1944, at mid-day, seven or eight British aircraft flying low over the Saint Pierre quarter dropped approximately 50 bombs which fell on the prisoners' quarters of the Amiens prison, causing numerous casualties and severe material damage.

Victims
Up till this date, 26th February 1944, 93 victims are accounted for as follows:-
85 bodies have been recovered from the ruins.
8 wounded have been detained in Amiens Hospital.
Only one person was killed outside the prison - in the Rue Voltaire.
88 people were wounded inside the prison and four outside. Attached are casualty lists:18
Among the wounded were:
a) Two Guardians of the Peace on duty at the prison at time of the attack.
b) Three prison warders.

Material damage:
The prisoners' quarters were partly destroyed, however, the right Wing which suffered the least can easily be repaired; it will take 100 to 120 prisoners. A section of the Hospice Saint Victor, occupied by the Germans (Luftwaffe Hospital) was demolished. Specifically 43 houses have been more or less damaged and elsewhere there has been light damage. Several of the bombs fell in the gardens of the route d'Albert and one in front of the Etévé garage, at the corner of the boulevard de Beauvillé and the route d'Albert, smashing a former toll post and an anti-tank defence.
All the political detainees escaped from the prison into the city and countryside. Patrols were organized by various police services who were able to apprehend 264 escapees - 208 from the French Section and 56 from the German Section. Those from the French Section on recapture were placed under guard in a disused factory in the rue de Faubourg de Hen; those from the German Section in the Citadelle.

On the day of the attack the effective total of prisoners was 712 of whom 190 were in the German Section. Of these:

(i) 264 of the political prisoners have been recaptured
(ii) 93 were found dead
(iii) 86 are in hospital
(iv) 30 are at liberty
(v) About 20 prisoners were wounded and have reported that they are receiving care at home.
(vi) 25 prisoners due for release in a few days assisted in the work of restitution and have been authorised to stay in the city.

This makes an approximate total of 518 prisoners recaptured, leaving presumably 194 at liberty.

The second and third of Hesketh's photos showing
internal doors in various states of disrepair.

The fourth of Hesketh's photos showing the chaotic scene in the centre of the prison.

The fifth of Hesketh's photos showing the breach in the front (south) wall with the rubble removed and a temporary wooden fence put in place.

APPENDIX 4

INVASION PLANS AND MISINFORMATION

THE BRITISH VIEW OF THE FRENCH RESISTANCE IN 1944

```
TOP SECRET
J.I.C. () 159 (0)
19TH April, 1944
```

                    WAR CABINET
            JOINT INTELLIGENCE SUB-COMMITTEE

                  FRENCH RESISTANCE
        Report by the Joint Intelligence Sub-Committee

        We circulate, for the consideration of the Chiefs of Staff,
the annexed Report, which has been prepared in consultation with
S.H.A.E.F. and S.O.E.

                  FRENCH RESISTANCE

OBJECT
1. To consider the effects of the resistance in France:-
        (a) at the present time
        (b) when we re-enter Western Europe.

RESISTANCE MOVEMENTS
2. The main movements are:-
                Armée Secrète
                Escapees to the Maquis
                Francs Tireurs et Partisans
                Group de l'Armée (Giraudist)
                British Officered Circuits.

At appendix 'A' are the brief notes on the characteristics and
political affiliation of the above movements.

3. In addition to these movements there are:-

(a) Polish Group. This consists mostly of miners in the Lille area.
They are under the Polish Government in London and liaison is
maintained through S.O.E. Their strength is unknown. They have been
found unreliable by R.A.F. escapers.

(b) Other minor Resistance Movements. These are in course of affiliation
with the Armée Secrète or are being integrated in some other way.

FACTORS
4. General.
The following factors affect both the present level of activity and
D. Day potentialities.

(a) Arms and Strength. Up to the end of March some 80,000 weapons
had been distributed to the French Resistance. (See Map at Appendix
'C'). The figures given are less known losses but a deduction of 20%
must be allowed for further unknown losses and deterioration. On the
other side, there have been further recent deliveries of about 20,000
weapons, and there are also the stocks of French arms already in
the hands of the Resisters. Taking these figures and estimates into
account it is considered that there are now in France about 100,000
men provided with arms and ammunition. The total numerical strength
of the resistance movement is much greater but cannot be considered
of military value without arms.

(b) Organisation. There exists an organisation to co-ordinate the
activity of all important groups. The control of the Armée Secrète is
shown in the chart at Appendix 'B' which also shows the liaison and
supply links with S.O.E. and the Bureau de Renseignements et d'Action
- Londres (B.R.A.L.). All the groups have links between each other
and there is also a link with the resistance movements in Belgium.
      The organisation is not claimed to be complete but it has been
built up from its beginning about a year ago.
      The standard of efficiency varies widely from bad to excellent
in individual groups.
      There is a tendency, especially in the Armée Secrète, to
create a large central directing organisation in France with various
committees and a staff on semi-military lines. This has obvious
dangers from a security point of view as penetration by the enemy at
the centre might result in his getting information which would bring
disaster to the groups in the field. This danger is fully appreciated
by the B.R.A.L. and S.O.E. who maintain direct contact at Regional
and Departmental levels for this reason.

(c) Unity of Purpose. Political differences exist. In central
organisations, committees, etc. there are squabbles, jealousies
and jockeying for position especially concerning matters of post
liberation appointments and policy. Among the groups in the field
there is greater unity now than earlier. An example is the acceptance
by the various groups in certain districts of leaders (Ohefs de
Groupement) who are Giraudists.
      The Communists are undoubtedly hoping and working for power
after liberation. So far as present resistance goes, they are putting
the elimination of the Germans first and they are undoubtedly very
efficient in their work. Their fighting organisation, the Francs Tireurs
et Partisans (F.T.P.) consists of a large proportion of men who are
not Communists at all but have joined the F.T.P. because of its
vigour and efficiency in the cause of liberation. Many F.T.P. groups
have promised to co-ordinate their activities within the framework
of National French Resistance on and after D. Day.

(d) Counter measures by Vichy. These are increasing and are directed by a ruthless man, Darnand, of whose personal courage and drive there can be no doubt. There is no evidence that this is as yet seriously hampering development either of actual operations or organisation.

(e) Counter measures by Germans. It is quite clear that the Germans have participated with Vichy forces in operations against the escapees to the Maquis in Haute Savoie. There is also evidence that Darnand's decision to co-operate in every way with the Germans has been received with dismay by the French police, resulting in protests and resignations.

EFFECTS

5. Present effects of Resistance.

Present day activity has resulted in putting out of action several of the highest priority targets from the list agreed by Bomber Command and M.E.W. as contributing to the German war effort. It is true that the effects of current sabotage are often felt by the French civil population. For example, railway sabotage causes dislocation of civil traffic over which immediate German needs have priority, nevertheless the putting out of action, within 3½ months, of 730 locomotives (even though repairable) out of a total of the French Railways of 10,000 has added to the overall strain on the German railway system. Relatively few Germans have been killed by Resisters, a fact for which the certainty of reprisals against hostages is doubtless largely responsible.

The conclusion is, therefore, that the effect of present day activities upon the German war effort is appreciable although it cannot be stated that the German military machine is thereby seriously impaired.

FRENCH RESISTANCE
COMPOSITION AND CHARACTERISTICS

1.   'Resistance' is represented by five main movements, the first of which, the Armée Secrète, is far the greatest numerically and is itself formed from a number of component groups.

The five movements are:-
Armée Secrète
Maquis
Francs Tireurs et Partisans
Group de L`Armee (Giraudist)
British officered circuits.

2. ARMEE SECRETE
The governing body of the Armée Secrète in France is the 'Conseil de la Resistance' in Paris, under the guidance of the Bureau de Renseignements et d`Action - Londres   (B.R.A.L.) acting on orders from the French Committee in Algiers. The Conseil de la Resistance consists of delegates from Resistance movements plus representatives

of French political parties and trade unions. Formed out of the Conseil de la Resistance are two Executive Committees, one each for the Northern and Southern regions - geographically the former occupied and unoccupied zones.

Attached to the Executive Committees are Commissions each containing technical advisers with representatives of each Resistance Movement. The North and South Zones are in turn split up each into six Regions under control of a Chef de Region General and the last step down in the vertical hierarchy is to the Chef de Departement, controlling resistance within the department.

For their part the B.R.A.L. maintain contact and control through their own representatives, the chief of whom have independent communications by W/T assistants. These representatives are Officers Delegues Militaires. The S.O.E. (and American S.O.) effectively controls the B.R.A.L. policy for developing the Armée Secrète since S.O.E. provides and operates the W/T communications between Resistance in France - London and Algiers. They also provide the aircraft supplying and maintaining French Resistance.

The Resistance Groups are:
       a) CEUX de la LIBERATION.   Northern Zone.
       Good solid type - middle class - non political.

       b) CEUX de la RESISTANCE.   Northern Zone.
       Bourgeoisie and Reserve Officer class - largely non political.

       c) LIBERATION NORD.   Northern Zone.
       Socialist organization - mainly political.

       d) FRONT NATIONAL.   Northern Zone.
       Communist Political. Control the F.T.P. (see para 4 below)

       e) LIBERATION SUD.   Southern Zone.
       Socialist organization - mainly political.

       f) COMBAT.   Southern zone.
       Non-political - Middle class.

       g) FRANCS TIREURS.   Southern zone.
       Radical and Republican - Not to be confused with Communist
                        'Francs Tireurs et Partisans'.

3. MAQUIS.
This word has become so popular and acquired such a romantic flavour that there is a danger that the para-military importance of this movement may be exaggerated.

The Maquis was originally formed of youths avoiding deportation to Germany. It is being organized on a tripartite basis (France-Anglo-American) and the material is considered first class. In areas where they are organised they operate through their Chief Maquis Officer attached to the Chef de Region General representing the Conseil de la Resistance. In the Haute-Savoie / Jura and Isere areas, we have Inter-Allied Missions in direct W/T communication with London, and similar Missions are designed for other Maquis areas.

4. FRANCS TIREURS ET PARTISANS (F.T.P.)
This is the Communist controlled para-military section of the political movement styled Front National. The Front National sits on the Conseil de la Resistance but keeps the F.T.P. outside the Armée Secrète although accepting the S.O.E. directives for D. Day action.

5. GROUP de L'ARMEE (Giraudist).
This is largely drawn from the old demobilised Vichy Army. It has a high proportion of trained officers.

6. BRITISH OFFICERED CIRCUITS.
In addition to the Conseil de la Resistance groups, S.O.E. operates some 40 independent sabotage circuits in France, each circuit being British officered and having direct W/T communication with S.O.E. in London. Their control, security and organisation are most efficient and they contribute a large proportion of the current sabotage now taking place. In the last 4 months 44 British and American Officers have proceeded to France on missions, principally to double-bank existing groups or to split larger groups into two or more independent water-tight circuits.*

(NA Ref CAB121/311)

* From January 1944 'The Sussex Plan' dropped 51 teams each consisting of an officer and a W/T operator into France. Commander Kenneth Cohen (MI6 / SIS), Colonel Francis Pickens Miller (OSS) and Gilbert Renault 'Colonel Rémy' (BCRA / BRAL) were the controlling officers.

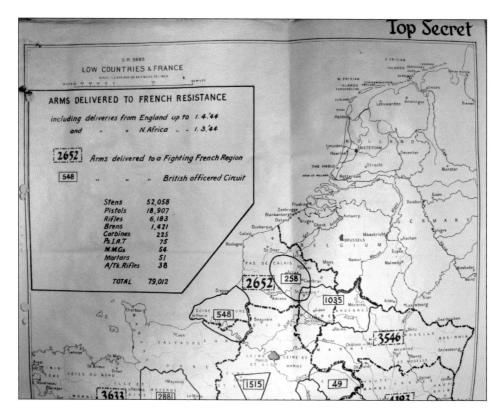

The map referred to in the document showing the number of arms dropped into France.

The Allies had precise plans for the use of these Resistance organizations.

'Resistance must be handled so that, at all times, it will give the greatest possible assistance to Overlord in all stages. Resistance is a strategic weapon. It is only very rarely that it can be used tactically.'

MESPOT / FORTITUDE CHANGES IN NAME

The plan to mislead the German defending forces about the coming invasion of Europe has its origins in 'Appendix Y' to Operation Overlord, which was approved on 20th November 1943. After the agreement on Allied strategy at the December 1943 'Big Three' conference in Tehran an overall deception plan for Europe, Africa and the Middle East was written and called 'Plan Bodyguard'.

In January 1944 'Appendix Y' was used as the basis for 'Plan Mespot', which was specifically concerned with the cover and deception schemes for north-west Europe - the D-Day landings at Normandy. 'Mespot' was developed during January before being submitted to the Chief of Staff on 30th January. 'Mespot' was approved, but a request was made that the code-name be changed to something 'more suitable'.

```
SUPREME HEADQUARTERS
ALLIED EXPEDITIONARY FORCES
G-3 DIVISION

SHAEF / 17213 / Ops                          10 February 1944

Subject:    New code word for 'MESPOT'
To AC of S, G-3.
Reference your note and attached correspondence, here is a more
suitable list from which to choose a new code word for 'MESPOT'

                        'BULLDOG'
                        'AXEHEAD'
                        'TEMPEST'
                        'SWORDHILT'
                        'FORTITUDE'
                        'LIGNITE'

                                  J.V.B. Jervis-Read
                                  Lt-Colonel GS
                        Deputy Chief Ops B sub-section


                  Copy to:
                        Chief Plans & Ops Section.
                        Chief, SD Section
                        File. S.H.A.E.F. / 18216 / Ops.
```

NA Ref WO219/2204A

On the original document *'FORTITUDE'* was ticked and 'Mespot' became Plan Fortitude.

It is not recorded as to why the Chief of Staff and Churchill were insistent upon changing the name of the operation, but there are three theories:

1/ It may indicate that a change was made to the content of the plan – perhaps the deletion of references to Amiens Prison. The issuing of Mespot (10th February) and the rapid change in name to Fortitude (18th February) arouses curiosity, as does the extreme lengths that were taken to ensure the total destruction of all files relating to Mespot.

2/ Mespot was British soldiers' slang for Mesopotamia (Iraq) – a notably unsuccessful WW1 campaign in which 92,000 British Indian Army soldiers were lost.*

3/ Mespot was also British soldiers' slang for a prostitute, or 'female genitalia'.

As a former British Army officer, Churchill would have been well aware of the use of 'Mespot' and doubtless considered it unsuitable for such a crucial military operation!

In 1920 Churchill was Secretary for Air and War in Lloyd George's government. The British had 14,000 regular army troops and over 80,000 Indian soldiers stationed in Mesopotamia at a cost of between £14 million and £18 million per year. Churchill wanted to use the new 'air power' to save money and asked Hugh Trenchard, the Chief of the newly created Royal Air Force Air Staff, if he thought the RAF could help matters in Mesopotamia.

Churchill was willing to use any means necessary to achieve his goal, including poison gas bombing. He actually argued that gas was more 'humane' than conventional bombing. Churchill wrote to Trenchard, 'I think you should certainly proceed with the experimental work on gas bombs, especially mustard gas, which would inflict punishment on recalcitrant natives without inflicting grave injury on them.'

Once deployed in Iraq the RAF proceeded to bomb civilians and tribal insurgents alike. Arthur Harris, who as head of Bomber Command laid waste to many German cities in WW2, took part in the bombing of civilians as a wing commander. He wrote, 'The Arab and Kurd now know what real bombing means in casualties and damage. Within forty-five minutes a full-size village can be practically wiped out and a third of its inhabitants killed or injured.'

So successful was the RAF bombing that, in March 1922, it was given control over security in Mesopotamia. For the next decade the RAF continued to bomb anyone that defied British rule.

```
                    SUPREME HEADQUARTERS
                ALLIED EXPEDITIONARY FORCE
                       G-3 Division
SHAEF / 18216 / Ops.                    18 February 1944


Subject:   Plan 'FORTITUDE'
To: AC of S, G-3
```

DISCUSSION

1 - The British Chiefs of staff approved Plan 'MESPOT' now called Plan 'FORTITUDE'.

"BIGOT"

```
                    SUPREME HEADQUARTERS
                ALLIED EXPEDITIONARY FORCE
                       G-3 Division
SHAEF / 18216 / Ops.                    23rd February 1944


Subject:   Plan 'FORTITUDE'
To: A.C. of S, G-3
```

Plan 'FORTITUDE' formerly called 'MESPOT', the cover and deception plan in support of 'NEPTUNE*' is forwarded for information. This plan supersedes APPENDIX 'Y' to C.O.S.S.A.C. (43) 28 dated 20th November, 1943.
Directions giving effect to the plan will be issued separately.

```
                              H. R. Bull
                         Major-General.US Army
                            To: A.C. of S, G-3
```

NA Ref WO219/2204A

*NEPTUNE: The more precise codeword for the Normandy landings. OVERLORD was a more general term for operations in Western Europe, including Normandy.

SUPREME HEADQUARTERS
ALLIED EXPEDITIONARY FORCE

To Air Chief Marshal Sir Trafford L. Leigh-Mallory K.C.B. D.S.O.
Air Commander in Chief, Allied Expeditionary Air Force.

Reference S.H.A.E.F. (44) 13 dated 23 February 1944 and C.O.S.S.A.C.
(44) 4 dated 7 January 44 Para 26.

 GENERAL.
1) The object of plan FORTITUDE is to induce the enemy to make faulty
disposition in N.W. Europe before and after the NEPTUNE assault.

PRESENT SITUATION.
2 - Certain measures giving effect to plan 'FORTITUDE' have already
been initiated by the Supreme Commander. These measures which are
listed at appendix A are subject to adjustment as a result of
detailed planning.

EXECUTION OF OPERATION.
3 - The Supreme Commander is to coordinate and control the execution
of the plan as a whole and is to be responsible for the following
arrangements:
a) the implementation of the plan by special means.
b) political warfare and propaganda.
c) the occupation and Scandinavian operation (SHAEF (44) 13 para 16-
22-9

4 - The Allied Naval Commander, Expeditionary Force, the Commander-
in-Chief of 21 Army Group, and the Air Commander in Chief A.E.A.F.
will be responsible to the Supreme Commander for directing towards
the Pas-de-Calais the threat created by the forces under their
control and for concealing the state of readiness of these forces so
as to indicate 'NEPTUNE' D plus 45 as the real target date.

5 - They will also be responsible for making preparation to continue
the threat against the Pas-de-Calais after Neptune, D Day.

6) They will adhere to the broad design of plan FORTITUDE, allotments
of wireless deception units and major equipment.

7) The allotment of the wireless deception units and of the major
equipment likely to be available is at appendix 5.

```
SUPREME HEADQUARTERS
ALLIED EXPEDITIONARY FORCE
G-3 Division
S.H.A.E.F. 18216 / Ops.


Subject Plan FORTITUDE.
Ref. S.H.A.E.F. / 18216 / Ops dated 23 February 1944
Appendix A to SHAEF (44) 13 dated 23 February 44   1/ A/ B/ C/ D
therewith should not have been attached to that paper and should be
destroyed.

The attached destruction certificate should be completed and returned
to this HQ as soon as possible.
```

Thus Appendix A the old appendix (SHAEF/18216 / Ops of 17th January 1944) was attached in error to this new plan for Fortitude on 23rd February 1944.

SHAEF realized the error and requested that the three Commanders-in-Chief of the Allied Task force must return a completed destruction certificate to HQ. However, this message was highly confidential and was 'protected' by the stamp 'BIGOT' indicating that only the addressee should open such marked mail items. Clearly the inclusion of Appendix A was 'rather awkward' and the level of attention paid to its absolute destruction is noteworthy.

COVER PLAN FOR ALLIED INVASION

```
                                    "BIGOT"
                                    US - SECRET
                                    BRITISH - MOST SECRET
30th January, 1944
PLAN 'MESPOT'
INTRODUCTION
```

1. With the object of inducing the enemy to make faulty strategic dispositions in relation to operations by the United Nations against GERMANY in 1944, Plan 'BODYGUARD' outlines the following cover and deceptive policy in the EUROPEAN Theatre.

2. The enemy should be induced to believe:-
    a. That forces are being held in readiness in the UNITED KINGDOM for a return to Western EUROPE at any time in the event of a serious GERMAN weakening or withdrawal.
    b. That an operation would be carried out in conjunction with RUSSIA in the spring with the immediate object of opening a supply route through Northern NORWAY to SWEDEN, thereafter enlisting the active co-operation of SWEDEN for the establishment of air bases in Southern SWEDEN to cover an assault on DENMARK from the UNITED KINGDOM in the summer.
c. That a large scale cross-Channel operation with a minimum force of fifty divisions and with craft and shipping for twelve divisions would be carried out in late summer.

3. Plan 'BODYGUARD' also indicated that a tactical cover plan designed to deceive the enemy as to the timing, direction and weight of 'NEPTUNE' should be executed when the imminence of cross-Channel operations indicated that invasion was likely to take place before late summer.

4. Within the framework of 'BODYGUARD', Plan 'MESPOT' outlines the cover and deception policy for North-West EUROPE, based on the following assumptions:-
    a. That the target date for 'NEPTUNE' will be 1st June, 1944.
    b. That NO real operations, other than 'RANKIN'*, will be carried out in NORWAY before D day 'NEPTUNE'.
    c. That Operation 'ANVIL'** will be a threat capable of being carried out against relatively light opposition.

---

*RANKIN: A group of plans to exploit any sudden German weakness or surrender that would force immediate Allied action prior to NEPTUNE such as a shift of forces to the Russian Front..

OBJECT

5. To induce the enemy to make faulty dispositions in North-West EUROPE before and after the 'NEPTUNE' assault, thus:-
    a. Reducing the rate and weight of reinforcement of the target area.
    b. Inducing him to expend his available effort on fortifications in areas other than the target area.
    c. Lowering his vigilance in FRANCE during the build-up and mounting of the 'NEPTUNE' forces in the UNITED KINGDOM.
    d. Retaining forces in areas as far removed as possible from the target area before and after the 'NEPTUNE' assault.

CONSIDERATIONS

AREAS

6. Plan 'BODYGUARD' indicates SCANDINAVIA as the most suitable area against which to maintain a long-term threat, Northern NORWAY being an intermediate objective leading to the establishment of air bases in Southern SWEDEN. SWEDEN would be unlikely to concede her Southern airfields to the Allies with GERMANY still in occupation of Southern NORWAY. An assault in DENMARK demands the prior occupation of the STAVANGER - OSLO area, therefore the target for a deception operation should be extended to include this area.

7. As 'NEPTUNE' preparations proceed, the significance of the threat against NORWAY will tend to decrease and for the sake of plausibility should not be over emphasised. At this stage the character and location of the 'NEPTUNE' forces will become increasingly evident to the enemy and a cover area, as far removed as possible from the real assault area, should be threatened. The PAS DE CALAIS best fulfils the conditions of plausibility.

TIMING

8. Climatic conditions do not normally allow operations in Southern NORWAY before 1st April, and in Northern NORWAY before 1st May. As it would take at least three months to occupy Southern NORWAY and to establish air bases in Southern SWEDEN, the enemy would expect us to assault NORWAY as early as possible if DENMARK were to be invaded in the same year. Furthermore, to contain GERMAN forces in SCANDINAVIA, a threat should be fully developed about one month before the target date of 'NEPTUNE'. It would further assist 'NEPTUNE' to continue the threat for as long as possible after D day 'NEPTUNE'.

** ANVIL: The American landings in the south of France beginning 15th August 1944.

9. The SCANDINAVIAN threat should therefore be fully developed by 'NEPTUNE' D minus 50 and maintained.

10. It would be plausible for the enemy to believe that the hazards of a cross-Channel operation demand the maximum assistance from all other fronts and in particular from the RUSSIAN front. As the enemy might well be led to believe that large enough forces cannot be assembled in the UNITED KINGDOM in time to take advantage of the RUSSIAN winter offensive, the cross-Channel operation should be timed to take advantage of the summer offensive. Climatic conditions on the Southern RUSSIAN front allow this offensive to start early in May and be extended to the whole front by the end of May. The enemy should be led to believe that we intend to allow the offensive to develop for six weeks until about 'NEPTUNE' D plus 45, before launching large-scale cross-Channel operations.

11. By 'NEPTUNE' D minus 30, the movement and administrative preparations and the concentration of air forces will be nearly complete, and the concentration of craft and shipping will be between 70 and 80 per cent complete for 'NEPTUNE'. Those preparations, and the type and location of the forces will begin to threaten the 'NEPTUNE' area only, unless preparations for the concentration of similar forces are made in EAST and South-East ENGLAND. In order, however, to minimise our state of preparedness as a whole, the long-term preparations in the EAST and South-East should indicate a later target date.

12. If before 'NEPTUNE' D day, however, it becomes evident that the enemy does NOT believe in the later target date, preparations in the EAST and South-East should be accelerated and the threat to the PAS DE CALAIS be fully developed.

STRENGTH OF FORCES

13. A total of about fifty-eight divisions would be required for the deceptive operations: that is, two to Northern NORWAY, six to Southern NORWAY and fifty to the cross-Channel operation.

14. At the present rate of build-up in the UNITED KINGDOM there would only be about fifty-three divisions, with craft and shipping for twelve available for operations by 'NEPTUNE' D plus 45. We should, therefore, induce the enemy to believe that the deficiency of about five divisions will be made up from the USA during the operation. At the same time, in order to emphasise the later target date, we should minimise the state of preparedness of the 'NEPTUNE' forces by misleading the enemy about their state of training, organisation, equipment and their location.

STORY 'A'
From now until the 'NEPTUNE' assault

15. The enemy should be induced to believe that the Allies will carry out the following operations in North-West EUROPE in 1944.

OCCUPATION OPERATIONS
16. From 1st February, 1944, balanced forces are being held in readiness to occupy any part of North-West EUROPE in the event of GERMAN withdrawal or collapse.

SOUTHERN NORWAY
17. With a target date of 'NEPTUNE' D minus 30 an operation will be mounted from the MERSEY and HUMBER and the ports to the NORTH to invade Southern NORWAY. The assault will be made in the STAVANGER area by one infantry division and one regimental combat team supported by parachute troops and commandos, followed up by one infantry division.

18. The force will be built up to a total of six divisions within three months, a proportion of this force being mountain trained. An advance to OSLO will be made along the coast by a series of mutually supporting land and amphibious operations, involving the use of landing craft sufficient to lift one brigade group.

19. Allied naval forces will escort the convoys and support the assault and subsequent amphibious operations. The assault will be supported by carrier-borne aircraft. Long range fighters will be flown in from the UNITED KINGDOM as soon as airfields are captured.

NORTHERN NORWAY
20. With a target date of 'NEPTUNE' D minus 30, an operation will be mounted by US, BRITISH and RUSSIAN forces against Northern NORWAY to open road and railway communications with SWEDEN. The operation will be supported by ANGLO-AMERICAN naval forces including aircraft carriers.

DENMARK
21. As soon as the Allies are firmly established in Southern NORWAY with allied air forces operating from there and Southern SWEDEN, an assault will be launched on DENMARK.

22. On or about 'NEPTUNE' D minus 30, the enemy should be led to believe that the forces for both SCANDINAVIAN operations are mounted and are held in readiness to be launched at short notice.

PAS DE CALAIS
23. With a target date of 'NEPTUNE' D plus 45, a cross-Channel operation will be carried out by a total force of twelve divisions. The assault will be made in the PAS DE CALAIS area by seven divisions, two EAST and five SOUTH of CAP GRIS NEZ. The follow-up and immediate build-up will be a further five divisions. The force will be built up to the total of fifty divisions at the rate of about three divisions per day.

MAP OF THE ALLIED DECEPTION PLAN FOR THE INVASION OF NORTH-WEST EUROPE IN THE MONTHS BEFORE D-DAY

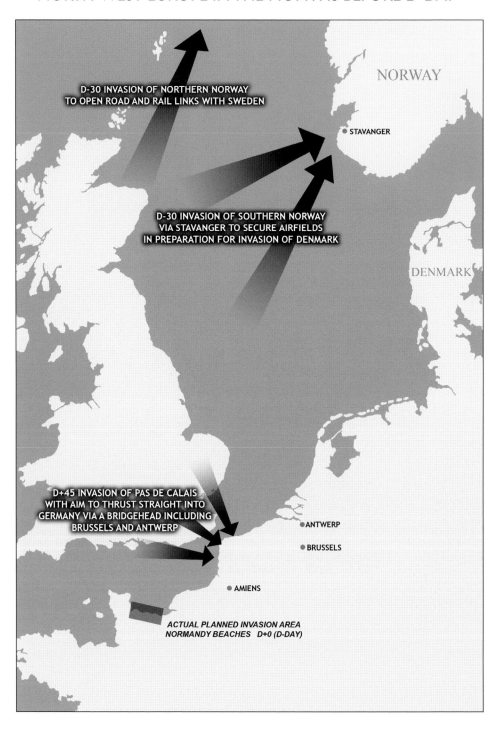

MAP OF THE ALLIED DECEPTION PLAN FOR THE INVASION OF NORTH-WEST EUROPE IN THE WEEKS AFTER D-DAY

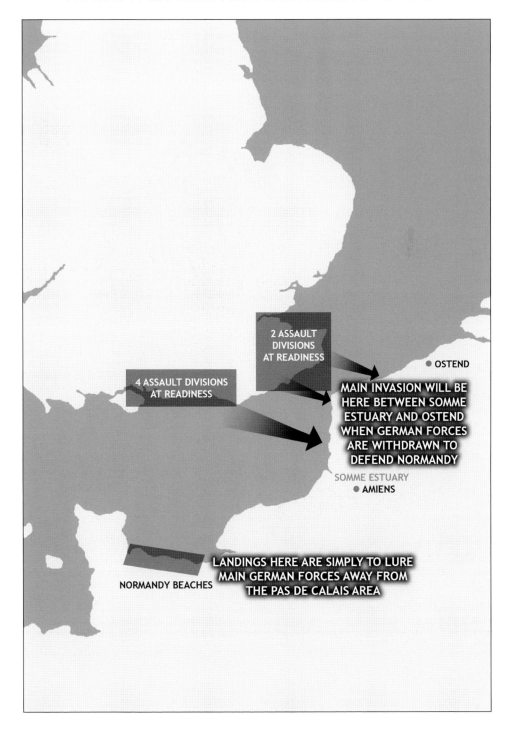

24. The first phase of the operations will be the establishment of a bridgehead which must include the major port of ANTWERP and the communication centre of BRUSSELS. From this bridgehead large-scale operations will be conducted against the RUHR with the final object of occupying GERMANY.

25. The operation will be mounted as follows:-
Two assault and one follow-up divisions from the WASH to DEAL.
Five assault divisions from the SOUTH coast.
Two follow-up divisions from the BRISTOL CHANNEL.
One build-up division from the HUMBER and TYNE.
One build-up division from the MERSEY and CLYDE.

SOUTH OF FRANCE
26. With a target date 'NEPTUNE' D plus 45, an amphibious operation will be launched from bases in the MEDITERRANEAN, against the area TOULON - MARSEILLES, with the primary object of introducing FRENCH forces into FRANCE.

CHANGE OF TARGET DATE
27. If at any time before 'NEPTUNE' D day it is discovered that the enemy does not believe in the later cover date, the threats to the PAS DE CALAIS and SOUTH of FRANCE will be rapidly developed.

STORY 'B'

From 'NEPTUNE' D day

28. After D day of 'NEPTUNE' and for as long as possible, the enemy should be induced to believe that subsequent operations will be carried out as given below.

PAS DE CALAIS (Maintenance of the threat)

29. The operation in the 'NEPTUNE' area is designed to draw GERMAN reserves away from the PAS DE CALAIS and BELGIUM. Craft and shipping for at least two assault divisions are assembled in the THAMES Estuary and South-East coast ports; four more assault divisions are held in readiness in the PORTSMOUTH area and will be mounted in craft and shipping from 'NEPTUNE'. When the GERMAN reserves have been committed to the 'NEPTUNE' area, the main allied attack will be made between the SOMME and OSTEND with those six divisions in the assault.

SOUTH OF FRANCE
30. The assault on the SOUTH coast of FRANCE will be made any time after 'NEPTUNE' D day.

The success of the first phase relied on the ability of the Allies to convince the Germans of three key points:

1) The Allies would not attempt an invasion in the north-west of France before an operation had been carried out against Norway as the Allies did not have sufficient forces to undertake two operations at the same time. This relied on convincing the Germans that there was a threat to Scandinavia.

2) The Allies would not invade the coast of France before six weeks into the Russian Summer Offensive (mid July) because they were hoping that the Atlantic Wall defences would be reduced due to pressure from the Eastern Front.

3) That the preparations for an invasion were far from complete.

However, three principal difficulties were quickly drawn to the attention of the Allied command:

1) It was not likely that the Germans would believe in the Scandinavian threat. An Allied attack on Scandinavia would require the intervention of the Russian forces and the Germans knew that the British would not want to see the Russians creating an opening towards the west through the Baltic and on to Norway.

2) The Germans believed that an invasion could not occur until the beginning of the Russian Summer Offensive. The simple fact of making Allied plans known to them would not make the invasion credible.

3) It was admitted by all the staff involved that preparations for invasion could not be hidden after February 1944.

More serious still was the realisation that, if the Germans saw the real preparations taking place in the south-west of England, they would naturally deduce that the most likely place for an invasion would be Normandy.

So, the Tactical Cover Plan had to be implemented at this time to make the Germans think the invasion date was later, thereby stopping them from transferring reinforcements to Normandy.

> 'Although the Controlling Officer gained the approval of the Russians for BODYGUARD so far as this theatre was concerned, there was no co-operation.
> We did in fact use the argument fairly hard, through 'Special Means', that the Russian Offensive would precede the continental assault, thereby rendering the maximum assistance to the more hazardous operation.'

NA Ref WO219/2204A

The problem with the plan was making it appear 'credible', and this is where the raid played its part. As a tool of 'Special Means' it gave immediate credibility to all the rumours and information that had been passed skilfully onwards, eventually, to the Germans. 'Special Means' information was already in the Germans' possession, the raid gave this credibility, thereafter the Germans were even more receptive to further mis-information. Although an early example of the first measures of Operation Fortitude, the raid was not the first measure. The operation was, in itself, embedded in a series of slowly leaked messages, all paving the way for the next step.

February 18th 1944 was the climax of this particular part of the deception plan. The bombing of Amiens Prison was a key part of a giant jigsaw, each piece carefully offered up to the enemy to build up a believable and credible claim that the Pas-de-Calais was imminently under threat from Allied invasion.

However, as soon as the raid had been carried out, it was made to seem that Churchill and others had an abrupt change of direction. Anouncements from the Prime Minister and other government / military officials made drastic efforts to imply that the Allies were experiencing unforeseen difficulties, seemingly they had not considered all the problems that could arise from the planning of such a complex operation as an invasion. Continuing speeches and statements further implied all such problems would be resolved by the Spring.

CONTROL OF THE PRESS

As of 4th January 1944 censorship was imposed on the content of all official, public and other speeches, both in England and in the USA. Lieutenant General Morgan, Chief of Staff of the Allied Supreme Command, drew the attention of the British War Cabinet to the harmful effects which certain inopportune statements by officials could have on the strategies being applied to the enemy:

COS (44)

                    4 January 1944

War Cabinet
Chiefs of Staff Committee

Cross Channel Operation

Thirty-Eighth report by the Chief of Staff to Supreme Allied Commander

 1 - Strategic Deception plan.

 I desire to draw attention to the adverse effect on the Strategic
Deception Plan of much of the present trend in public pronouncements
by persons in official positions, relative to the imminence of an
invasion of the continent, based in the U.K.
As you are aware an essential element of the deception plan is that
the enemy may be led to believe that this invasion cannot take place
until an appreciably later date than the target date. Steps are being
taken to that end.
It is felt that the reiteration of such public statements does tend
to invalidate the effect of the approved Deception Plan and I suggest
that careful consideration be given to bring this matter to the
attention of the British and American authorities concerned.

F.E. Morgan, Lieutenant General
Chief of staff to the supreme Commander

Office of the War Cabinet
       SW1 4 January 1944
       + COS (43) 779 (O) (Revise) -

COS (44) 3rd meeting (O)   5 January
1944
5- Cross Channel operation-
COS (44) 7 (O)

                                       Thirty-eighth report

COSSAC.

The committee considered the thirty-eighth report by the Chief of Staff to the Supreme Commander. Sir Alan Brooke (Chief of the Imperial General Staff) said that he was in full agreement with the remarks relating to the necessity to control public announcements regarding the imminent operations. He suggested that this question might be raised when the general question of security for operation OVERLORD was submitted to the War Cabinet and the Minister of Information.

Measures were taken on January 4th to resolve the issues raised by COSSAC. Indeed the official speeches and declarations now formed part of the arsenal for the plan of deception and intrigue. It was essential that politicians did not say anything that may have had a detrimental effect upon the plans for Overlord. From now on both COSSAC and the Prime Minister were involved in discreetly processing and passing on information to the Germans through their own speeches and press releases.

Thus all official speeches were prepared and adapted according to directives from SHAEF and the London Controlling Section in order to support the plan of deception.

THE GERMAN REACTION TO OPERATION FORTITUDE
HOW DID THE BOMBING OF AMIENS PRISON HELP FORTITUDE SOUTH?

Consequently the enemy can but wonder, since it is clearly and irrefutably established that the prison was the target of the aviators, which secret organisation dictated this order?

(Le Progrès de la Somme 20 and 21 February 1944)

The success of the Allies in arousing German curiosity is evident here, taken from a regional daily newspaper under German control. The Allies had succeeded, they had got the Germans thinking about *secret organisations* - the bombing of Amiens prison had suceeded in its aim.

The answers that the Germans were seeking would be supplied by the Allies using 'Special Means' rumours and misinformation, presented and delivered at the appropriate time, via carefully prepared messages. The information would always appear plausible; achieved through a concoction of true and false elements. The truthful sections could be verified and were facts that the Germans were already aware of; the fictional element could not be disproven. The key was to convince the enemy that he had obtained this information by virtue of his own, skilful, effort. To bomb a civilian prison containing more than 700 people, making obvious breaches in the walls, could only induce the Germans to think that the Allies wanted to release, or even eliminate, certain prisoners. Logically, the only reason for this would be that one or more prisoners had access to top-level information, information that the Allies did not want to fall into the hands of the Germans.

Obligingly, it would seem that both the occupying authorities and the French thought in this manner. In the beginning, the German authorities thought that the purpose of the operation must have been to release key Resistance operators to assist the Allies and that an invasion was imminent, probably on the Picardy coast.

It was not long before the German authorities established that the 'Resistance Release Theory' was without firm foundation. However, the lack of evidence did not stop the Germans from examining all the possibilities. They wondered who could have been in the prison; perhaps a key member of the French Resistance or an Allied agent? The Germans believed there was something curious going on, or that one of the prisoners knew something of great importance. After all, surely no one would bomb a civilian prison without good reason?

Captured German files and post-war interrogation of officers revealed that the German High Command was convinced that preparations for landings were well advanced by February 1944, and did not believe the Bodyguard claims that it would come in late Summer. The German belief was that the invasion would come in the Pas-de-Calais - head-on - without any deception and that the Allied forces were 50% greater than they actually were. General Blumentritt believed that the Allies would charge straight into Germany, thus cutting off forces in France. The purpose of a landing in Normandy was therefore to lure his troops south so that they would fall into the trap and be cut off - exactly the aim of Fortitude.

If one believes Admiral Friedrich Ruge, a Naval specialist attached to Army Group B, then it would appear that right up until the actual Normandy landings German opinion was always divided as to where an invasion would take place. Hitler believed an invasion could take place just about anywhere with a large port area, which he considered essential for an invasion. Hitler had written on 3rd November 1943,

'I can no longer be responsible for further weakening in the West in favour of other theatres. I have, therefore decided to strengthen its defences, especially in the place from where we shall begin the long-range fight against England [the V weapons north of the Seine]. For there the enemy must and will attack, and - unless anything deceives - the decisive landing blow will be struck.'

An intercepted and de-coded conversation between Hitler and the Japanese Ambassador on 28th May 1944 gave the Allies the general opinion that Hitler's impressions of the impending invasion largely corresponded to those that the Allies wished the Germans to adopt. Hitler even spoke of bridgeheads being established in Normandy. The OKW,

Germany's High Command, still viewed the Pas-de-Calais as the best opportunity for invasion by an Allied offensive that had as its aims the ultimate conquest of Germany. Field Marshal von Rundstedt thought the best opportunities for the Allies lay on both sides of the Somme Estuary. The German Navy considered that Rundstedt's view was implausible and that the Allies may have tried along the beaches at Antwerp, or perhaps the bay of the Seine that was protected from the strong westerly winds by the Cotentin peninsula.

After a period of consideration Rommel decided that Rundstedt's theory, of a landing near the Somme, was the most practical. His logic was that the Allies were systematically destroying the transport routes inland from Normandy, and that they were heavily mine-laying in the Pas-de-Calais so both these areas would be unsuitable. Rommel did, however, also consider that one or more diversion may take place.

What is certain is that right up until 6th June 1944 the Germans had no real idea where the invasion would be attempted.

As for the date of 15th July, that had been heavily suggested as the date for an invasion, one can never truly determine just how far, if at all, the Germans believed this. It would seem, if anything, that most Germans expected the invasion to be sooner. Certain officers within the OKW did accept that, until 15th July had passed, this date would likely see an invasion of the Pas-de-Calais area. This is obviously a measure of the success of Operation Fortitude.

Rommel, however, as soon as 6th June had passed, only considered the possibility of another invasion landing in the Pas-de-Calais for a very short period. Strategically though, the OKW still considered this to be a very viable threat and refused to move any of the forces stationed there towards Normandy. It is possible to find hints of this indecisiveness in German strategy from *Le Progrès de la Somme* newspaper that, on 1st June 1944, reported:

'The invasion of the European continent will take place this summer,' writes The New York Times.

Whilst in Berlin on June 6th 1944 - D-Day itself - it was announced:

'The efforts of General Eisenhower will also extend to the coastal areas located between the Somme Estuary and the Seine.'

This was the area which the OKW considered to be the most likely invasion zone at that time, much more so than the zone between Boulogne and Calais.

Le Progrès de la Somme, Thursday June 8, 1944

AN EXTENSION OF THE OPERATIONS

One believes, as does Berlin, that the efforts of General Eisenhower will also extend to the coastal area located between the Somme Estuary and the Seine. One does not expect however, that an immediate attack on the coast between Boulogne and Calais, which is closest to England, will take place. Today, June 8th 1944, it is evident in the Somme region that there are provisions to keep roads clear of traffic as the fear of an imminent invasion in this area is great.

Le Progrès de la Somme, Thursday June 8, 1944

OPINION

By order of the MilitarBefehlshaber in France the travelling of any civilian vehicles is prohibited in this area. Exempt from this restriction are all vehicles of the German army or those conducting vital work, providing that the latter are registered and carry special authorisation.

Any civilian vehicles infringing this decree will be requisitioned immediately. Their owners and drivers will be placed before a German court charged with an act of sabotage.

This restriction will not be applicable to the civil vehicles rented by the German army if these vehicles are driven or accompanied by German soldiers.

Der Felkommandant

Le Progrès de la Somme, Thursday June 9 1944

FAILURE OF A LANDING IN THE PAS-DE-CALAIS

Last night the German coastal batteries of Pas-de-Calais ruined an attempt by the Allies to get a foothold in this area.

Under fire from the coastal batteries the Allied formation which tried to approach was surrounded by smoke and retreated.

Le Progrès de la Somme, June 16 1944

THE REICH SENDS RESERVES INTO THE AREAS THREATENED BY INVASION

It is not only towards the coasts of Normandy that the German reserves are being sent. The commander of the soldiers of the Reich has also sent important forces towards other coastal sectors of France threatened by invasion.

This fact was particularly underlined today by Field Marshal von Rundstedt. This proves that the German staff are taking countermeasures according to a plan determined with precision to begin the decisive battles against the armies of Montgomery.

Le Progrès de la Somme, June 17 1944

THE WEHRMACHT COULD LIQUIDATE THE ANGLO-AMERICAN BRIDGE-HEAD…

… IF OTHER LANDINGS ARE NOT MADE

Berlin,

'If we knew', declared a senior military official in Berlin, 'that in the eight or fifteen days to come, no other bridge-head was to be created by the Anglo-American armies, we would be able to liquidate their existing Normandy bridge-head'.

We could easily do this if no other areas were attacked by the Allies… Eisenhower is perhaps wishing to create a bridge-head at Caen—Sainte-Mere-Eglise only to encourage the German command to commit all its forces there and yet they could make landings elsewhere with even stronger forces. Where and when will the second invasion landing be made?

Le Progrès de la Somme, June 22 1944

WHEN AND WHERE WILL THE SECOND LANDING TAKE PLACE?

Berlin June 19,

The question of knowing when and where the second Anglo-American attempt at an invasion landing will take place is always the current topic of conversation. Perhaps in the North? One would think that the setting in motion of the new German weapons against England would encourage the enemy to direct his next action against the defences behind which, according to him, are the bases of these new weapons. Or perhaps in the south of France?

For the next ten days of June the newspaper ran articles about the intensity of fighting in the Normandy area, but on 1st July the considerations regarding another invasion in the Pas-de-Calais area had still not totally disappeared.

Le Progrès de la Somme, July 1 1944

THE NEXT PLACE FOR AN ALLIED LANDING

Berlin,

Speaking about the effects of the V-1 weapon on England the 'National Zeitung' writes, 'The only possibility remaining with the enemy is the finding and destroying of launch sites for this new weapon. So far the Allied airforces have been unable to achieve this, even with the dropping of, as they claim, 40,000 tons of bombs on the areas where they believe these sites to be located. The enemy must therefore use his ground forces and may even wish to actually capture some of the launch sites. Obviously we must wait and see what direction reinforcements landing in Normandy will take. But it is almost without doubt the V-1 will dictate their primary objectives.'

On Saturday 8th July 1944 *'Le Progrès de la Somme'* informed its readers of a change within the ranks of the German General Staff:

FIELD MARSHAL VON KLUGE WILL REPLACE MARSHAL VON RUNDSTEDT AS COMMANDER IN CHIEF OF THE WESTERN GERMAN ARMIES
General Headquarters of the Führer.

Field Marshal von Rundstedt, whose health has left much to be desired for some time has been replaced as Commander-in-Chief of the West by Field Marshal von Kluge. The Führer has sent a personal message to Field Marshal von Rundstedt thanking him for his prominent services under such difficult circumstances and expressing recognition for them.

Le Progrès de la Somme, July 17 1944
Berlin,

Field Marshal von Kluge, who has been named Commander-in-Chief of the German Forces in the West, has just carried out a tour of inspection on the coast of the Channel. He initially visited the sector located between the mouth of the Somme and Dunkirk, where he obtained such decisive successes in 1940. He saw that buildings which his previous offensives had left intact had now been destroyed by the Allied air offensive.

Whilst the inspection progressed he was given reports by the three officers in charge of the sectors. After his visit he expressed his complete satisfaction at the state of the fortifications and the defensive positions associated with them.

On Tuesday July 18th readers were informed that:

THE GERMAN COMMANDER FIELD MARSHAL VON KLUGE DECLARES THAT ANY ALLIED ATTEMPT AT AN INVASION WILL RAPIDLY COME TO AN END
We expect a new attack.

In this combat situation it is a question whether it will or won't happen, the German military command will bring any invasion attempt rapidly to an end, but we await the enemy. Every hour we expect a new attack.

On 19th July the question of a new invasion landing still arose:

WILL THERE BE ANOTHER INVASION LANDING?
Berlin,
The question of knowing if a new Allied invasion landing is imminent for the west, was answered by a qualified military personality:
'Even if we had precise signs of this we would not confirm it. The possibility of an invasion landing always remains. However the engagement of the Allied troops in Normandy is already important, if one believes that some 80 of Eisenhower's divisions will be tied up there.'

The Allied planners of 'Fortitude' had predicted the following response from elements of the XV Army after the landings had taken place:

Unit	Location	Expected in Normandy
1st SS Panzer Division	Turnhout	D-Day+3 to 7
2nd Panzer Division	Amiens	D-Day+3 to 7
116th Panzer Division	Pontoise	D-Day+1
84th Infantry Division		D-Day+3 to 7
85th Infantry Division		D-Day+3 to 7
331st Infantry Division		D-Day+3 to 7

However, by 13th June only the 2nd Panzer Division had moved to Normandy. The 1st SS and 116th Panzer Divisions moved *towards* the Pas-de-Calais on 10th June! On 15th June the OKW were still waiting for the phantom FUSAG to attack across the Straits of Dover and reported, *'To sum up, despite the absence of any concrete information about the enemy's actual intentions, it can only be said that there is no serious evidence against the early deployment of the American Army Group and our own measures must therefore take this possibility into account.'*

The number of infantry divisions in the Pas-de-Calais *increased* from nineteen on D-Day to twenty-two by 22nd July.

On the 7th June 1944 the XV Army, stationed in the area of Pas-de-Calais, should have been sent as a reinforcement for the forces already present in Normandy. However, the

---

* *Lagebericht West dated 15th June 1944. Quoted by Hesketh in Fortitude.*

Commander-in-Chief of the Wehrmacht prohibited any movements in this direction by the Commander of Army Group B. The refusal to move these troops was due to Hitler and the Commander-in-Chief expecting a second invasion landing.

General Speidel himself wrote: 'This suspicion of a second landing was to play a major part during the first six weeks of the invasion'. Had the Tactical Cover Plan been a success? Overall it had been, although the stubbornness of Hitler and the chiefs of the OKW extended its effect far above anything the Allies could have hoped for.

According to General Speidel and Admiral Ruge, Rommel had concluded quite quickly that a second invasion landing was unlikely, based on high level information that claimed there were only between thirty and fifty divisions in the eastern part of Britain. Rommel was obliged to take account of the apparent concentration of Allied forces in the south-east of England and believed that if a second invasion were nevertheless to take place, it would be made between the Somme and the Seine.

From 15th June Rommel no longer believed the threat of a second invasion because the Allies were now so firmly established in Normandy. General Speidel confirmed that it was not until the middle of July that the Commander-in-Chief of the Wehrmacht accepted the move of just part of the XV Army towards Normandy. The actions of the German High Command may seem, at first, surprising; although perhaps not if one considers that Operation Fortitude had achieved its objective in full.

The German reluctance to move forces away from the Pas-de-Calais was the very essence of Mespot / Fortitude South and the men who planned the deception must have congratulated themselves on their success. However, they may not have known that they had an unlikely ally at Hitler's side! Leutnant Colonel Alexis Baron von Roenne was trusted by Hitler himself to interpret the intelligence being presented to him. Von Roenne had correctly predicted the British and French reaction to the invasion of Poland in 1939 and had been correct on many key matters since. Hitler trusted him implicitly. However, from 1943 onwards, Roenne deliberately started to pass false information about Allied strength, disposition and invasion plans. Why this was so has not been explained, but he was a committed opponent of Nazism and perhaps hoped to bring a swift end to the regime and a war that he now believed was already lost. Von Roenne 'interpreted' Bodyguard and Fortitude for Hitler and deliberately passed every 'fact' directly to Hitler even though he knew them to be false! On 11th October 1944 Hitler had him put to death, hanging from a meat hook by his throat. He had been plotting to overthrow Hitler and was a friend of Von Stauffenberg - leader of the plot to assassinate Hitler.

HOW THE INVASION WAS ANTICIPATED IN EUROPE

This sample of newspaper reports gives an insight into how German occupied Europe saw the coming invasion. 'Le Progrès de la Somme', under German control, reported:

Le Progrès de la Somme, Friday January 21, 1944.
'THE INVASION WILL TAKE PLACE BEFORE MARCH 15'
ANNOUNCES CHURCHILL
Stockholm, January 19.
'Before the middle of March, the world will be witness to one of the largest military gatherings that has ever taken place.'
This statement was made by Churchill, when he left the House of Commons, in answer to a deputy who asked him when the invasion would start.

Le Progrès de la Somme Saturday January 22, 1944.
THE DIFFICULTIES OF AN INVASION ARE LARGE
... CONSIDERS THE REUTERS AGENCY
London,
The Reuters agency underlines the difficulties of an invasion of Europe. It tries to show the equality and perhaps the numerical and matériel superiority of the German forces which currently defend France, Belgium, Holland, Denmark and Norway.
The invasion in Sicily was only one small operation, whilst the tonnage of supplies necessary for an invasion amounts to millions. It is necessary to take account that the Anglo-American naval reserves have been weakened by the attacks carried out by submarines. The problem does not only consist of bringing troops onto the coasts of Europe, but also all the essential matériel.

Whilst there was no doubt that there were difficulties facing the invasion, it is noteworthy that all countries facing the Channel or the North Sea are quoted in relation to the invasion threat.

Le Progrès de la Somme, Tuesday January 25, 1944.
At the moment the Allies seem to be planning several offensives at the same time as a prelude to their great attempt at invading Europe, in order to put the German command in uncertainty and therefore to oblige it to disperse its forces on several fronts.

Once again, on February 2nd, just before a by-election, Winston Churchill reiterated that an invasion was imminent.

Le Progrès de la Somme, Friday February 4, 1944.

'GREAT BATTLES ARE IMMINENT' ANNOUNCES Mr. CHURCHILL

London, February 2.

In a letter addressed to the governmental candidate for a by-election, Churchill declared that the tasks that his government must assume had never been more difficult than now.

Many battles have already been fought which were sometimes favourable to us, sometimes unfavourable. More importantly battles which will cause common suffering to all the English are now imminent.

Le Progrès de la Somme, Saturday February 5, 1944.

'THE ENEMY CANNOT SURPRISE US' DECLARES THE BERLIN PRESS

Berlin, February 3.

During the tour of inspection carried out by General Jodl on the coasts fronting the English Channel and the North Sea, the Berlin press announces, under the title 'the enemy cannot surprise us' an article by Dr. Stoober, a war correspondent who writes:

'We know that opposite us lies an army of invasion, equipped with the most modern equipment and ready to attack the continent'.

'Its chiefs envisage an attack on various points of the European western coast, there is little other option'.

Moreover, in the eyes of the German Command, the Eastern Front remains a defensive front, it is certain that the staff of the Wehrmacht does not want to engage the troops that it holds in reserve for a new campaign in Russia. It intends to keep these forces for the battle which is to come in the West and its plan will contain the Bolsheviks until a decisive result is obtained in the West.

It is in this context that it is necessary to consider the military situation which, in the next days, will have its centre of gravity moved to the point where the Anglo-American forces will start the great offensive that has been heralded so much.

Le Progrès de la Somme, Tuesday February 8, 1944.

DO THE SOVIETS INTEND TO INVADE NORWAY?

Oslo, February 5.

What makes the Soviets wish to launch a seaborne invasion of Norway? Asks this paper, while referring to the official German statement which reports the latest submarine attack against a convoy travelling towards Murmansk; the convoy included invasion-type landing craft. This fact caused a great feeling of wariness and concern in Norway, because it is obvious that these craft could only have been used against Norway. On this subject, the German newspaper 'Aftenposten' draws attention to some articles from the Swedish press which concern Soviet espionage and propaganda in Sweden.

The newspaper of 12th February, contained a leading article by G - S Savigny, that assured readers simply that the question on the agenda was the imminence of an Allied invasion, and also considered the difficulties that would be experienced.

Le Progrès de la Somme, February 12, 1944.

INVASION

Will the great invasion operation come on the coasts of France or the Netherlands?

Does this Anglo-American operation threaten Spain?

Questions are always arising.

In any case one realizes the difficulties which an attempt on a scale much larger than Italy would present.

In Sicily, success was easy because of the lack of defences and very little resistance presented by the Italians. In Salerno, the attackers only had one German division to face.

Finally at Nettuno the absence of fortifications and air superiority gave great advantages to the Anglo-American troops.

In spite of that, they were not able to advance for nineteen days, while the armies coming from the south gained ground painfully as it was defended step by step.

One can easily consider just what even more powerful forces would be necessary to attack the defended front of the Atlantic which is not only strongly reinforced, but occupied by the best German troops under the command of Field Marshal Rommel.

These troops have orders to hold the sea front. The work carried out to the rear does not indicate lines of retreat, but are defences against possible parachutists or air attacks.

One can thus realize that the battle of the West, if it broke out, would be vastly different from that in Italy.

G-S Savigny

On 16th February, Field Marshal Von Rundstedt, Commander-in-Chief of the German troops on the western front, declared that he was aware that the Allies had finished their preparations for invasion.

Le Progrès de la Somme, Wednesday February 16, 1944.
'THE ENEMY HAS FINISHED HIS PREPARATIONS FOR OFFENSIVE,
BUT WE ARE READY... ' DECLARES MARSHAL VON RUNDSTEDT
Field Marshal von Rundstedt, Commander-in-Chief of the German troops on the western front has just announced to Mr. Georg Schroeder, Chief of the agency Transocéan, the following declaration;

We know that the enemy has finished his preparations for the offensive, but we are ready.

He will encounter a coastal front on a completely different scale to those of which he has attacked up to now.

THE DEFENCES OF THE ATLANTIC

The defences of the Atlantic with its steel and concrete fortresses has profited from all the experience gained in the previous engagements near the Maginot Line. The Maginot Line consisted of concrete structures deprived of any notable length or depth; on the other hand these principles have governed the installation of very different coastal defences. They are reinforced structures which are more effective and are also bomb proof. They are built to a design that cannot be simply advanced over by an enemy. Behind them is a complex system of support structures over the surounding countryside. The ground is mined, blocked and covered with obstacles and anti-tank defences, items that were ignored by the builders of the Maginot Line.

THE COAST WILL BE HELD TO THE LAST MAN.

Along the beaches, barriers will prevent the landing craft and ships from unloading, and then the minefields will pose another threat.

Measures which, of course, must remain secret, have been taken for a long time to protect against such landings. There is no possibility of surprising or avoiding these defences. The deeply spread out coast and its fortifications must be held to the last man. Under these conditions the enemy formations which may have managed to unload will be scattered by the well armed fortifications.

RESERVES

Huge reserves to the rear which consist mainly of tanks and motorized divisions are grouped so as to be able to launch all out counter-attacks at very short notice. We Germans have the advantage of solid fortifications. We will lead the fight by using these fortifications and we also have other means which I will indicate in greater detail at a later time for obvious reasons.

On February 18th 1944, the date of the raid, the lead writer for the paper assured its readers that invasion was imminent.

Le Progrès de la Somme, Friday 18 February 1944
PREPARATIONS FOR ENGAGEMENT

A few days ago we exposed the difficulties that the Anglo-American forces would encounter if they tried to attack the French Channel coast. The obstructions and defences accumulated here by the German High Command constitute a formidable line of defence. One only has to read the statements made by Field Marshal Von Rundstedt to understand just how formidable these defences are. In particular the parallel he draws with these defences and those of the Maginot Line. A parallel that shows it is impossible for the Allies to go around the new German defences. A mass of weaponry has been accumulated in these areas to assist in defending against the Allies if they set foot on French soil (if they do they will suffer huge losses). It is quite true what the Field Marshal said, 'The enemy has finished its preparations, but we are ready.' The Field Marshal waits for the invasion knowing he can count on the determination of his troops.. G-S Savigny

Churchill began his 'propaganda' on 17th January, attempting to persuade the Germans that an invasion was imminent; before 15th March, although not a hint was included as to where this was to take place. Despite the various deceptions employed, creating pressure on the coastline from Norway to Spain, Churchill implied that the Pas-de-Calais was a very likely area. The threat there could never be ignored by the German High Command (OKW).

Churchill reiterated this almost daily, whilst the OKW and German controlled press responded by declaring, not only that they knew, but that they were more than ready for the invasion when it came. Local administrative authorities in Northern France and Pas-de-Calais / Somme areas began to make preparations to evacuate all non-essential people from coastal areas, a huge task in itself. The pressure was certainly building up!

Of course no particular place for the invasion had been or could be announced by the Allies, but German focus was heavily centred on the Pas-de-Calais.

Then on 18th February 1944 the RAF raid on the prison at Amiens took place. To the locals as well as the occupying Germans, it seemed the invasion was imminent in this area.

The following day, 19th February, nothing was reported in *Le Progrès de la Somme* newspaper. However, the Swiss press continued theorising as to the difficulties the Allies were going to experience in the forthcoming invasion. This article concluded that it appeared this nervousness on the part of the Allies was not favourable in executing such a complicated military manoeuvre.

Le Progrès de la Somme, Saturday 19 February 1944.
NERVOUSNESS

The Swedish newspaper 'Folkets Dagblad' published an article on the psychological preparation of England for the invasion on the continent.

The coolness with which Germany faces this war of nerves shows that the armies of the Reich are very well prepared to face this invasion.

Back in England, every effort has been made to establish what the German response and strength facing this invasion will be. These efforts continue and all accounts from London indicate that the planning has been meticulous and will be completed with clockwork precision.

However, already one hears the whispers and rumours which indicate all will not run quite so smoothly as the Germans fully intend to upset this precision planning.

This is reinforced by the sheer energy and combat experience of the Germans who will defend themselves with vigour and never miss the opportunity for clever initiatives and ideas. It has also to be declared that Germany will launch some very violent counter attacks upon England.

All this is undoubtedly reasonable and it would be wise for the English to be very well prepared and to accept that all will not run quite as smoothly as they anticipate.

By 20th February 1944, opinion was widespread in Northern France that invasion was really imminent. Evacuation programmes for non-essential persons were featured in *Le Progrès de la Somme* newspaper on this day and also on 21st February.

Le Progrès de la Somme, 20 and 21 February 1944.
EVACUATION OF REGIONS ADJACENT TO THE NORTH SEA COAST
Lille, February 20.

The evacuation of certain localities close to the North Sea coast is currently in hand.

This operation is carried out under the best conditions possible and with order and great organisation.

M. Darrouy, Deputy Prefect North, went to Dunkirk to personally take care of the execution of the evacuation orders.

The 'Secours National', the French Red Cross, and teams from the Commission of Youth are all assisting.

The evacuated persons are taken by train towards the L'Aube or Cote-d'Or regions, except for those who may already have found refuge with family and friends in other areas. The 'Secours National' are ensuring food supplies to all those in transit'.

Le Progrès de la Somme, 26 February 1944.

SOMME. THE OPINION OF THE COASTAL POPULATION

The Prefect of the Somme reinforced the orders from Feldkommandantur 580 of Amiens, and stated that all non-essential persons should leave the coastal areas.

This advice was particularly addressed to children less than 14 years of age (who should be accompanied by their mothers) pregnant women and persons aged 65 years and over along with any invalids. People who are necessary to the economic and administrative sectors (i.e. public service employees, factory workers, craftsmen, farmers, farm labourers, etc.) will remain. Upon leaving, all persons should register their new addresses with the Mayor of their district, who will then supply them with a voluntary evacuation card.

In the area that was considered to be under threat, everyone was surprised when, on 20th and 21st February, *Le Progrès de la Somme* announced that Churchill was to be replaced as Prime Minister by Field Marshal Smuts.

This false rumour put out by the German-run press was a ploy to cause confusion and bewilderment, in all probability it caused amusement amongst the Allies, but Stalin's interpretation may have been more serious. He may have believed he had not been privy to such a governmental change, and considered that with a fundamental change in government it might not be possible for the British to launch an invasion. Churchill and Stalin did not agree on many things. This rumour confirms that the Germans were aware of this and were attempting to capitalize on the doubts and suspicions between the leaders.

Le Progrès de la Somme, 20 and 21 February 1944.

FIELD MARSHAL SMUTS TO REPLACE MR CHURCHILL

New York, February 19.

A correspondent in Washington writing for the 'Wall Street Journal' has just published an article in which is stated:

'From the confidential dispatches recently received here, one has caused an incredible sensation, in relation to the forthcoming upheaval of the British Cabinet. Namely the position of the Prime Minister, Mr Churchill, who shall be replaced by Field Marshal Smuts in three weeks. One cannot obviously at this moment deny or authenticate such a rumour.

It is also alleged that Field Marshal Smuts would be far more diplomatic in his approach to the Russians. However, here in Washington very little credence is given to this rumour.

On 23rd February *Le Progrès de la Somme* informed its readers that Field Marshal Rommel had been on an inspection of the defensive fortifications along the Normandy coast. This report was made some eight days after Rommel had inspected these defences on 14th and 15th of February.

Le Progrès de la Somme, February 23, 1944.
MARSHAL ROMMEL INSPECTS THE NORMANDY DEFENCES
The agency D.N.B. has announced that Marshal Rommel recently inspected the defensive installations along the Normandy coast.
He paid particular attention to the details of the coastal defences all the way down to the smallest sectors. As a result he is convinced of the complete effectiveness these will have.

On 24th February 1944, *La Progrès de la Somme* continued to expose the intricacies of propaganda. Indeed it was stated that the Prime Minister now had serious differences of opinion with Stalin. Therefore the possibility of any effective co-operation between the Allies and the Russians in an invasion of northern Scandinavia seemed very unlikely to the Germans.

Le Progrès de la Somme, February 24, 1944
'I HAVE NEVER GIVEN A GUARANTEE THAT 1944 WOULD SEE THE END OF THE WAR' DECLARES MR. CHURCHILL IN A SPEECH TO THE COMMONS
London, February 22.
Speaking to the Commons, Mr. Churchill declared,
'The Anglo-American air raids on Germany must be currently regarded as the principal fact of our offensive. During spring and summer next the scale of these attacks on Germany will be increased...'
IN CONNECTION WITH THE 'DIFFERENCES IN OPINION'
Mr. Churchill then raised the subject of the talks in Cairo, Tehran and Moscow:
There would be very few differences in opinion between the three great powers, he underlined, if their representatives could meet once a month.
I hope that it will be possible to hold similar conferences throughout the war.
The question was put as to whether the good relations with Moscow emphasized in Tehran were considered stable and lasting.

Churchill replied, 'I am able to reassure Parliament on this most important point'. None of the positive developments delivered in Moscow and Tehran have been lost. I have personally raised with Stalin the question of the future of Poland. Stalin and myself agree on the need for compensating Poland at the expense of Germany, in the north and the west…'

Le Progrès de la Somme, February 25, 1944

THE INVASION - IT WILL TAKE PLACE AT EASTER

The Reuters agency announced that Mr. E.D. Howe, Minister for Munitions, made it clear to the Canadian Commons that the invasion of the European continent by the Anglo-American troops would take place in the next few months.

For three months, it declared, the Canadian Government has received from Great Britain very urgent cables requiring the immediate delivery of ships necessary for the operation.

On Thursday 24th February 1944, Dr. Goebbels published an article in Berlin that informed his readers once again about the problems that the Allies were having and would have with an invasion. This article was later published in *La Progrès de la Somme* on February 26th.

Le Progrès de la Somme, Saturday February 26, 1944

AN ARTICLE FROM DR. GOEBBELS CONCERNING THE SECOND FRONT

Berlin, February 24.

In a weekly article for the review 'Das Reich' Dr. Goebbels mentioned the possibility of an Anglo-American invasion in the west, and the risks of conducting such an operation. It suggests that as the date becomes nearer for the Allies their concerns are ever increasing.

THE STEPS TO BE TAKEN

It has become necessary for Churchill and Roosevelt to take these steps. Initially they had thought that the war would progress in a different manner. This being that the Wehrmacht and the Red Army would be heavily engaged in the East. Such an action would literally leave Europe open for them. However this illusion has since disappeared. In this war the victorious will be those that seize the opportunities and not those who delay.

Le Progrès de la Somme continued to report on the alleged and known problems that would face the Allies.

Le Progrès de la Somme, February 27, 1944.

SPEECH OF MR CHURCHILL

It should be noticed that Mr. Churchill does not present to Parliament the difficulties which face the Allies. He is no longer of the opinion that the great military operation can be undertaken before March 15th.

It is true that he denied making the prophecy that this would be a rapid conclusion to the war. Today we foresee the contrary; there will still be a long conflict ahead, as the invasion is no longer imminent. Churchill's declarations seem to be reflected in the speeches of the Canadian Prime Minister too. However, it could be that these assertions are an attempt to hide the true intentions of the Allies hoping to slacken German vigilance.

G-S Savigny

G-S Savigny, the lead-writer for *Le Progrès de la Somme*, followed the evolution of the situation very well. For him, obviously, at the end of February 1944 the Allies were not near to launching an invasion on the north-west coastal areas of France. He also poignantly added that this could, however, be an Allied deception.

Le Progrès de la Somme, Saturday February 29, 1944.

TOWARDS THE SEA

We have exposed the ends to which the Bolsheviks in the north of Europe are working towards, and how they hoped that the capitulation of Finland would enable them to reach the Norwegian territories leading to the Atlantic Ocean.

This race for the sea has been the constant objective of Russia. This empire which covers an immense number of territories, almost two thirds of the World's land surface, has always had a desire to have access to any ocean possible. It has always been the opposition of other maritime powers that have denied this. This had been tried by Peter the Great in attempting to open a port, but the gulf of Finland only gave him access to an enclosed sea. Everywhere else Russia ran up against England. This superb maritime power was regarded as the most serious threat to any Russian expansionist proposal. The same problem was encountered in Iran.

There too Russia sought access to the ocean and found it once again came to face British opposition. But today, by a strange rôle reversal, the United Kingdom — too weak to prevent it, watches as Russia continues towards the sea.

APPENDIX 5

GENERAL OUTLINE OF THE STRUCTURE AND ORGANISATION
OF THE RAF IN 1944

At this stage of the war, the Americans had two huge air forces in the Northern European theatre, comprising the 8th and the 9th Air Forces. The RAF comprised Bomber Command, Fighter Command and Coastal Command; there was also Training Command and a whole host of other auxiliary units. Combined they were a vastly effective force against Germany and her allies.

Each RAF 'Command' was further divided into 'Groups'

Bomber Command Groups: 1, 2, 3, 4, 5, 6, 8, 91, 92, 93, 100

Fighter Command Groups: 10, 11, 12, 13, 83, 84, 85

It was a complex organization that was modified continually throughout the war. An example of this is the combined operations under the AEAF (Allied Expeditionary Air Force) formed at the end of 1943. This was a true Anglo-American force that included bombers and fighters from the American 9th as well as several groups from the RAF. These were collectively grouped under two large organizations: 'ADGB' or 'Air Defence of Great Britain' which included several Groups such as:

No 10 Group Fighters

No 11 Group Fighters

No 12 Group Fighters

No 13 Group Fighters

The other organization was the 'Second Tactical Air Force' which included Groups such as:

83 Group Fighters

84 Group mainly Fighter / Bombers

85 Group a strategic fighter reserve.

2 Group light and medium Bombers

   2 Wings of medium bombers 'Boston' IIIAs and the B-25 'Mitchell' II

   2 Wings of light bombers: de Havilland 'Mosquito'

No. 38 Group was a more loosely knit group primarily concerned with transport and communications.

2 Group was under the control of the 'Second Tactical Air Force' . Each Group was divided into Wings. At the outset of the war each wing belonged in theory to an individual aerodrome. However, by 1943, with the conflict evolving as it did, this rigidity of organisation was relaxed. From 1943 the Wings and Groups would regularly move from airfield to airfield.

At the time of the mission on 18th February 1944, 2 Group comprised four wings:

No 137 Wing based at Hartford Bridge

No 138 Wing based at Lasham

No 139 Wing based at Dunsfold

No 140 Wing based at Hunsdon

The structure of each wing generally comprised three squadrons:

No 137 Wing

88 Squadron	Boston IIIA
342 Squadron	Boston IIIA (Free French Air Forces)
226 Squadron	B-25 Mitchell II

No 138 Wing

107 Squadron	Mosquito VI
305 Squadron	Mosquito VI (Polish)
613 Squadron	Mosquito VI

No 139 Wing

98 Squadron	B-25 Mitchell II
180 Squadron	B-25 Mitchell II
320 Squadron	B-25 Mitchell II (Dutch)

140 Wing

21 Squadron	Mosquito VI (R.A.F.)
464 Squadron	Mosquito VI (R.A.A.F.)*
487 Squadron	Mosquito VI (R.N.Z.A.F.)*

Although fully integrated within the RAF, the New Zealand and Australian Squadrons, as with many other Commonwealth squadrons, proudly retained their individual identities.

Within 140 Wing, each squadron was identifiable by a two-letter code on each aircraft

21 Squadron	YH
464 Squadron	SB
487 Squadron	EG

In addition to these markings, each aircraft had an individual identification letter painted on the fuselage on the opposite side of the roundel. The serial number of each aircraft appeared on the fuselage just before the tail section. Each squadron was composed of two Flights, namely A and B Flights.

On 18th February 1944, 2 Group was under the control of Air Vice-Marshal Basil Embry. The Group Headquarters was at Mongewell Park in Berkshire to the west of London. It was from here that the order to proceed was issued, the decision so eagerly awaited by 140 Wing personnel some fifty miles away at Hunsdon.

Hunsdon

Hunsdon is a small village about twenty miles north of London where work had started on laying out an airfield just before the war. On 31st December 1943 Hunsdon's staff and the local villagers had witnessed with awe and thrill the arrival of three squadrons of de Havilland Mosquito Mark VIs belonging to No 140 Wing, from No's 21, 464 and 487 Squadrons.

No. 21 Squadron (RAF)

Formed on 23 July, 1915, No. 21 Squadron took part in numerous aerial operations in France during World War 1. Like many squadrons, it was finally disbanded after the conflict in October 1919, only to be reformed in 1935 as a bomber squadron. Initially it was equipped with the Blenheim IV, then the Lockheed Ventura; it received its first Mosquito VI in September 1943. When these Mosquitos were delivered in December 1943, the squadron was based at Sculthorpe, Norfolk, and then moved to Hunsdon in Hertfordshire. It remained there until April 1944, when it transferred to Gravesend.

No. 464 Squadron (RAAF)

Formed on 1st September 1942, at Feltwell in Norfolk, and initially equipped with the Lockheed Ventura. In July 1943 this Squadron, as with all those belonging to the group, was withdrawn from Bomber Command to be placed under the control of the Second Tactical Air Force.

No. 487 Squadron (RNZAF)

Formed in 1942 it too, like No. 464 Squadron, was initially equipped with the Lockheed Ventura. On 1st June 1943 it was detached from Bomber Command to be included in the new Second Tactical Air Force. By August 1943 it was equipped with the new Mosquito VI and arrived at Hunsdon.

Groundcrew load a 500lb bomb under the port wing of SB-V MM403 a 464 Squadron Mosquito flown by Flt Lt McPhee on the Amiens Raid. Of interest to modellers is the removal of the exhaust shrouds and the low camouflage demarcation line on the rear fuselage confirming that this and indeed other aircraft on the raid carried the day fighter scheme of Dark Green and Ocean Grey uppersurfaces over Medium Sea Grey undersurfaces.

REFERENCES AND BIBLIOGRAPHY

The National Archive:

AIR25/195 - 11 Group ORB

AIR25/208 - 11 Group ORB Appendix

AIR26/204 - 140 Airfield ORB

AIR27/34 - 3 Sqn ORB

AIR27/264 - 21 Sqn ORB

AIR27/1109 - 174 Sqn ORB

AIR27/1170 - 198 Sqn ORB

AIR27/1171 - 198 Sqn ORB Appendix

AIR27/1482 - 245 Sqn ORB

AIR27/1924 - 464 Sqn ORB

AIR27/1935 - 487 Sqn ORB

AIR27/2117 - 613 Sqn ORB

AIR29/481 - Film Production Unit ORB

AIR37/15 - No. 2 Group: Attack on Amiens prison, France, 18 Feb 1944

AIR37/23 - 2 Group ORB

AIR37/45 - 2 TAF Photographs of targets

AIR37/806 - 2nd Tactical Air Force: No 2 Group: targets

CAB121/311 Report on Resistance. Cabinet Office: Special Secret Information Centre: Files B/Special Operations

WO219/2204A Mespot / Fortitude. War Office: Supreme Headquarters Allied Expeditionary Force: Military Headquarters Papers, Second World War G 3 Division, Operations B. Plan Fortitude. Plan Mespot: comments by British Chiefs of Staff

Books

4 longues années d'occupation 1940-1944, Andre Coilliot.

Armes secretes et ouvrages mystérieux de Cherbourg à Dunkerque, M. N. Cuich.

Avec les soldats de Rommel, Rémy Vernoy

Aviateurs dans l'aventure, Jean Hallade.

Compagnons de l'honneur, Rémy. Édition France Empire

Constructions spéciales, Roland Hautefeuille.

Et l'Angleterre sera détruite, Rémy. Éditions France Empire

Et les murailles tombèrent, 18 février 1944, Jack Fîshman, Robert Laffont.

Fortitude, Larry Hakes, Robert Laffont.

Fortitude, Roger Hesketh, St Ermin's Press

Great successes of espionage, Janusz Piekalkiewicz. Beech.

Histoire de la Résistance, Henri Nogueres, Robert Laffont.

Hommes et Combats en Picardie 1939/1945, Jacques Béal, Hammer editions.

Invasion 1944, Hans Speidel, Editions Berger-Levrault.

Jéricho - Fortitude. Les sables de l'oubli, Michel Talon, Martel éditions.

Le Focke Wulf 190, J Bernard Frappé and J.Y. Lorant.

L'étrange histoire des armes sécretes allemandes, Victor Debuchy.

L'opération Jericho, Rémy, Famot editions.

L'opération Jericho, Rémy, Presses Pocket 1963.

L'opération Neptune, Commander Kennet Edwards RN 1947.

La Résistance dans le Ternois, Réne Guittard.

La somme dans la guerre 1939-1945, Jacques Béal, Editions Horvath-Hammers.

Les Années 40, Hatchette

Les bombardiers attaquent, Sir Arthur Harris, Librarie Plon

Les martyrs de la Résistance dans l'Amiénois, Jacques Lejosne.

Les operations en Europe du corps expeéditionnaire allié, General Dwight D. Eisenhower.

Les paves de l'enfer, Dominique Ponchardier, Editions J'ai Lu

Libération du Nord et du Pas-de-Calais, Etienne Dejonghe and Daniel Laurent, Hatchet.

Normandie 44, François Bédarida, Albin Michel.

Operation Mincemeat, Ben Macintyre, Bloomsbury

Rommel face au débarquement 44, Amiral Friedrich Ruge, Presse de la Cité

The Gestapo Hunters, Lax and Kane-Maguire, Banner Books

ACKNOWLEDGEMENTS

I would like to thank all the people, both individuals and those in official capacities, who enabled me to gather and collate the documentation required to make this work possible.

Numerous organizations have assisted in the supply of detailed information; particular credit must go to a number of international organisations.

In Britain: to The National Archives (PRO), Kew; Mrs. Sheila Walton of the University of Keele; and the Imperial War Museum. In Germany: to the German military archive in Freiburg. In France: to the departmental records of the Somme and Pas-de-Calais; the President for the General Council of the Somme; and the Historical Service of the National Gendarmerie, Maisons-Alfort.

In addition, thanks must go to M. Patrick Joly of Amiens for the use of his photographic archives (mainly from the collection of André Claudel).

Furthermore, mention must be made of the numerous people who offered help and assistance in gathering information and conducting additional research in what was a particularly complex episode in the local history of Amiens.

Particularly prominent is the detailed research and investigation involving eyewitnesses and associated documentation undertaken by Pierre Ben. Thanks also to Dr Guy Troché, Dr Claude Archambault, George Facquier, Jacques Lejosne, Claude Leleu, Daniel Leroy, Paul Bulot, Michel Olen, Gilbert Descamps, Henri Morgand, Pierre Cagé, Edgard Durand and his wife, Jacques Bruaux, Gisele and Gabriel Souhait, Hilaire Resve, Serge Chatelain, Henri Lamarche, Pierre Maille, Leslie Atkinson, Albert Bosman, Colonel Leon Bourdon, Serge Blandin, Jean Van Laere, Francis Moitié, George Platel, Seymour B. Feldman, (American fighter pilot and RAF volunteer) Group Captain Marc Lax, Anne McRitchie, Michel Collet, Director of Publication of the Courrier Picard, Henri Couturier, and Jacques Béai. Thank you to you all, and also to those not mentioned who have helped so much with the research.

Once again, thank you to my wife Jackie, both for her assistance and patience. Thank you also to my two children, Karine and Jean-Pascal who, like their mother, have been both patient and interested in my research.

Permission for the reproduction of photographs granted from the following organizations: Defense Intelligence Agency, The Pentagon; Imperial War Museum; The National Archives (PRO) Kew; Ministry of Defence, University of Keele. Documentation from UK sources is reproduced with the permission and control of Her Majesty's Stationery Office.

Additional thanks must go to:

M. Michel Collet, Director of Publication of the Courrier Picard, who gave his authorization to reproduce the photographs and texts previously published in the Courrier Picard. M. Jacques Béal who kindly gave permission to reproduce the photographs of Field Marshal Rommel's visit to Picardy and in particular to Amiens, photographs previously published in his books *Hommes et combats en Picardie* and *La Somme dans la Guerre 39/45* Martelle editions.

INDEX

People

Places

Military Units

Resistance Organisations

Operations

Miscellaneous